THE FORGOTTEN ATHLETES OF THE AMERICAN FORCES FAR EAST

A Resource and Record of U.S. Military Service Sports from Mid-1950s Korea and Japan

....THE ARMY ALL-STARS CONQUER THE AIR FORCE 21-6 IN RICE BOWL

Photo: 1956 Rice Bowl, Tokyo, AFFE/8A (Rear) Information Office, "Two Years of Progress," 1957.

"It was the best game I ever saw. Every player did exactly what he was supposed to do. I'll always remember this game." –
General I. D. White, United States Army

ISBN: 979-8218715090

"A good athlete is a good soldier" - Maj. Gen.
F.C. Holbrook, Commanding General, United
States Army, 1955.

ACKNOWLEDGEMENTS

Thank you to all the very knowledgeable and helpful people who made this project possible!

Thank you to the archivists at National Archives II in College Park, Maryland. I spent many days at their facility poring through old documents and photos. The expert archivists were very patient in helping me navigate the immense and complex system.

Thank you to the librarians at the Hoover Library in Jefferson County, Alabama, who helpfully assisted me in tracking down old and obscure materials for my research. The Hoover library is a premier library when it comes to quality of service and availability of resources. I spent a lot of time there!

Thank you to Dottie from the Birmingham, Alabama, Inter-Library Loan Department for helping me with my numerous requests to obtain far-away obscure books and materials. Your kind patience and readiness to help was a blessing.

Thank you to Paul W. Bryant Museum curator and photo archivist, Brad Green, at the great University of Alabama, Tuscaloosa, for his helpful generosity and sharing of some superb archival documentation pertaining to 1950s Alabama baseball and football with Far East connections. Roll Tide!

Thank you to Dustin Perry from Camp Zama Public Affairs Office in Kanagawa Prefecture, Japan, who graciously answered my numerous questions concerning possible Camp Zama historical documentation from the post-Armistice period.

Thank you to Christopher Malpass from Inter-Library Loan and Document Services at UNC Wilmington, North Carolina, who graciously provided scanned copies of many pages of the rare 1954

Armed Forces Sports Almanac pertaining to football and basketball Service Sports.

Thank you to my family for putting up with my frequent research trips and time squirreled away in my writing area. I couldn't have accomplished this without their unwavering support and feedback.

Thank you to Raelene Mack with Assist Graphics for the awesome book cover design.

Thank you to U.S. Military veterans who answered the call on our behalf. Thank you for your service!

CONTENTS

SERVICE SPORTS
BACKGROUND/OVERVIEW

There is an enormous amount of written material pertaining to the Korean War years, but relatively little has been written about the post-Armistice period, specifically regarding the U.S. Military Service Sports/Recreation programs from the mid-1950s in the Far East. This book attempts to fill that gap.

The United States Military established American control in Korea, south of the 38th parallel, on 7 September 1945 (1), and U.S. Military bases exist in Korea and Japan to this day.

My father, Jerry G. Kingrey, played football for AFFE/8A 7th Division "Bayonets" in 1955 (Far East active-duty service dates 1 August 1954 to 1 June 1956). His saved materials, including photos, game programs, and other documentation from his time in Korea are what prompted my interest in writing about this subject.

This is primarily the story of American Forces Far East (a.k.a. Far East Command, or FEC) full-contact American-style football in post-Armistice Korea; however, basketball, baseball, and mention of other major (and some minor) recreation sports are included due to the robust nature of those leagues as well as the availability of associated information.

Note: The AFFE abbreviation is alternately referred to in archival documentation as "Armed Forces Far East," "American Forces Far East," or "Army Forces Far East." 8A is an abbreviation for Eighth Army. In this book, I use AFFE collectively to refer to the broader American Forces Far East, with the intent of including all major branches, such as Far East Air Forces (FEAF), etc.

The AFFE sports leagues were known collectively as "Service Sports," or "The Sports Program," under the larger umbrella of "Special Services," and were played primarily in Korea and Japan.

The leagues were comprised of active-duty military members (there were leagues for all major branches – Army, Navy, Air Force, Marines), and there were intra-branch and inter-branch competitions during the applicable season; there were also All-Star and All-Service championships following the regular season of the particular sport.

That said, archived information found by the author was mostly dominated by Army and Air Force sports activity - less so for Navy and Marines.

It's important to distinguish the Service Sports teams from the well-known Military Service Academy teams (Army, Navy, etc.), which compete in the NCAA and are not known to have had a direct association with the Service Sports programs run by Commands at the company, post, regimental, and division levels.

The Service Sports level of play was often very high and was in some cases at a semi-professional level, or at least a semi-major collegiate level. Team rosters frequently included future and past college sports stars, and it was not uncommon to have future and past professional athletes on team rosters.

For example, Cecil (Pete) Silas, a 6'6" Service Sports basketball player out of Fort McClellan, Alabama, who played college basketball at Georgia Tech on a full scholarship and had won a Pan-American Championship with the U.S. basketball team in 1955, later played professionally with the Phillips 66ers basketball team.

Once out of the service, Mr. Silas was not done with his high-achieving ways - he eventually worked his way into the position of Chairman and CEO of the giant Phillips Petroleum company.

2

Did you know that renowned football coach Paul "Bear" Bryant from Texas A&M at the time, and later with the powerful Alabama Crimson Tide, had traveled to the Far East to conduct coaching clinics along with other coaching greats of the day?

Did you know that Service Sports star Kenneth Murray Jr. had been an NBA player, held the all-time St. Bonaventure scoring record, and was a basketball All-American in 1950? Mr. Murray was a player/coach at Fort Dix, and had also spent time as a player/coach at Camp Drake in Japan, where he led his team to become Central Japan Champions and finalists in the Far East Championship tournament.

These are but a few examples of the quality and level of play and coaching that existed in Far East Service Sports in the mid-1950s. In fact, Baltimore Orioles baseball scout Freddy Hofmann told *Army Times* newspaper on 22 January 1955 that "People in this country have no idea of the recreational program in our Army and Air Force overseas" (2).

Far East coaching clinic visits by powerful, well-known Continental United States (CONUS) coaches speaks to the high quality of Far East Service Sports player and coaching personnel:

> The men who instruct at the clinics come to the Far East as volunteers on invitational orders shared by the Department of Defense, and are prominent men in coaching and officiating ranks of colleges and professional teams in the United States. These men do not receive any salary and in many cases give up lucrative positions in the States by making the trip to the Far East (3).

The 23 November 1953 Stars and Stripes reported that American football scouts were present for the "Thanksgiving Classic" between the Camp Tokyo Bulldogs and the FEAF Base Tornadoes, showing that Far East sports had been on mainstream radar. Maybe overseas Service

3

Sports teams from the mid-1950's and beyond have been a well-kept secret?

QUALITY SERVICE SPORTS THRIVED IN THE MID-1950s

Review of archived *Stars and Stripes* newspaper editions from the mid-1950s shows that not only football thrived in the Far East Service Sports program, but so did other sports, such as baseball, tennis, track and field, and basketball.

AFFE leagues mimicked major-college-level sports in many ways, including by organization, talent, rosters, coaching, and by the noted skills clinics given by visiting CONUS major-college coaches, etc. And it was not unusual for Far East championship and All-Star football games played in Japan to sometimes attract tens of thousands of fans.

In 1954, for example, the U.S. basketball team, which included Service Sports players, in preparing for the Pan-American Games, was scheduled to play preliminary games on the "same card with pro and college teams" (4). Other records suggest there were instances when bigger Service Sports teams were listed in the same published statistical tables alongside NCAA college football teams.

Though CONUS Service Sports football for the most part is not generally within the scope of this book, it too was very robust: The 31 July 1954 *Army Times* reported that Fort Belvoir, Virginia, football games had attracted 5000–9000 fans per home game in 1953 (5). These sports leagues, particularly those of football and to a lesser extent, basketball and baseball, were significant and are worthy of historical scrutiny.

The weight of the evidence suggests that Service Sports "took off" in the mid-1950s, which was a time of relative innocence and perhaps archaic standards. For example, Service Sports personnel trying out for the 1956 Olympic Baseball Team were required to have "high moral character" and to have "conduct and character beyond reproach," as certified by their Commanding Officer. The humble requirement to show up for tryouts with "baseball shoes and glove in their possession" speaks of a different time.

PURPOSE OF BOOK, SOURCES, METHODOLOGY

This book will provide a general history of why these men and women were in Korea and Japan in the first place. It will discuss structure and organization to the extent that available records allow, will look at living conditions on posts/bases, will review games which were regularly reported on by *Stars and Stripes* and *Army Times* newspapers, will discuss the political and military milieu under which these leagues flourished, and will discuss and review biographical information from select Service Sports stars and notable athletes.

While it's compelling to learn about well-known athletes who had competed in relative obscurity in their chosen sport overseas, we mustn't forget the "unknown" players who worked just as hard and whose presence made the whole thing work; their efforts are worthy of review.

Though the focus of this book is primarily on Service Sports teams and tournaments based in Korea, Japan, and to a lesser extent Okinawa, when it comes to discussion of All-Army or All-Service tournaments, backgrounds of players and other unique situations, there will be some overlap with the robust CONUS (stateside) Service Sports system, which may enter discussions to a varying degree.

Information included in this book was gleaned from archived *Stars and Stripes* newspapers; *Army Times* newspaper archives; original source material from the United States National Archives II in College Park, Maryland; library books; personal materials; U.S. Library of Congress;

news articles from the internet; military archives; universities; personal site visits in Japan; and other miscellaneous sources.

The *Pacific Stars and Stripes* newspaper from the 1950s says that it was edited, published, and printed in Tokyo, Japan, and was also printed in Seoul, Korea, seven days a week by the Troop Information and Education Section, Army Forces Far East. The Officer in Charge at the time was Maj. Joseph F. Morgan.

There were circulation offices at Camp Crawford, Chiba, Chitose, Epa Jima, Fukuoka, Gotemba, Itazuke, Iwakuni, Kokura, Nugata, Okinawa, Osaka, Ota, Otsu, Sapporo, Sasebo, Sendai, Shiroi, Tokyo, Yokohama, Yokosuka, Zama, and Hachino.

A large amount of information was obtained through military memos, which will be found generally arranged chronologically in the main section: "Football Games and Other Sports/Recreational Activity." In other sections/chapters, military memos are introduced to support narrative discussion.

It is plausible that Military Service Sports memos have never before been married to news articles from mainstream publications to create a cohesive picture of the Service Sports environment, particularly in the Far East.

NOTES ON PUNCTUATION, GRAMMAR, AND READABILITY

Note: When reproducing correspondence in typed form, I tried to maintain the punctuation as it appeared in the original correspondence, correct or incorrect. Obvious original errors I tried to note with "sic". You may notice what appear to be some punctuation inconsistencies, however, there were minor style inconsistencies in original documents, i.e. sometimes the rank "Lt" would end with a period and other times not.

Where possible, when reproducing memos or texts for purposes of this history, I attempted to break up long blocks of text into more easily digestible paragraphs while still maintaining the original format as much as possible.

Also, original/primary documents were scanned by the author, and the quality of the physical scan varied depending on the quality of the original document. The vast majority were legible, but there were times when one or two characters/letters were undecipherable. In those cases, I either used my best judgment, or I entered a notation describing illegibility from the original source.

HISTORY – POLITICAL/MILITARY

Source material for this chapter/section includes physical documents from National Archives II in College Park, Maryland; it is plausible that contents of some of these rare documents have not been publicly published or widely distributed to date.

Service Sports did not take place in a vacuum. Korea was fresh off a brutal and bloody war, and societal wounds had not yet had time to heal in the mid-1950s. It's important to first understand the state of Korean society and political environment at the time.

Korea is a land of ancient culture and customs; a gentle people - slow to anger - but once aroused by injustice, capable of fierce and single-minded opposition. The physical setting was generally mountainous terrain, which was not yet fully tamed with paved highways and modern conveniences in the mid-1950s.

The weather was and is inhospitable; sweltering in the summer, and unbearably cold in the winter. Simply existing in Korea tested foreign troops like few had been tested before, but the post-Armistice hardships were perhaps offset a great deal by warm-hearted Korean civilians who seemed to welcome and appreciate the American military presence.

First, a brief relevant military/political background.

The Korean Armistice Agreement was signed 27 July 1953. Though fighting ended, the Armistice Agreement did not require withdrawal of foreign troops from Korea (1), and despite the end of active combat, there is to this day no peace agreement between North and South Korea; the two countries remain divided by the approximately 2.5 mile wide demilitarized zone (DMZ) at the 38th parallel.

In his book, *A History of Korea*, Jinwung Kim says, "The Korean Peninsula was in total ruin, with its cities, towns, and villages ravaged by battle" (1). Kim described economic inflationary conditions as well as heavy-handed government control under Korean president Syngman Rhee (1948–1960).

There was also frequent hostility toward United States forces emanating from North Korea, which came in the form of harsh verbal attacks and military provocations.

An 18 August 1955 letter (6) from Harlan C. Parks, Major General, United States Air Force (United Nations Command Side Military Armistice Commission) to Major General Jung Kook Rok, Korean People's Army, found in the National Archives II communications archival records, pointedly addressed a 17 August 1955 incident in which a United States single-engine training aircraft was fired upon by the Korean People's Army while in the Demilitarized Zone:

> On 17 August 1955, at about 1530 hours our time, 1500 hours your time, a single engine training aircraft of our side, while on a routine training mission, was fired upon by personnel of your side ... This unprovoked hostile act was clearly witnessed by United Nations Command ground observers who saw your side open fire while the defenseless plane was over the Demilitarized Zone, and subjected to continuous murderous and devastating ground fire until the aircraft crashed into the territory under the military control of your side.
>
> This aircraft carried no armament whatsoever, and was performing routine training flight when it inadvertently intruded over the Demilitarized Zone ... your trigger happy gunman, without warning or without waiting to ascertain if the aircraft would positively intrude your territory, opened fire without provocation while the plane was still over the Demilitarized Zone.

9

The Military Demarcation Line is difficult at best to positively identify from the air. *That inadvertent intrusions by both sides would inevitably occur was recognized and provided for in the drafting of the Armistice Agreement* (italics added).

Since the signing of the Armistice, planes of your side have intruded over the Demarcation Line into the territory of our side on 53 different occasions ... In all of these cases our side gave your aircraft pilots the benefit of the doubt that their intrusion was inadvertent and in not a single instance was either AA ground fire or air-to-air fire directed against them.

This unbroken record of compliance with the spirit of the Armistice Agreement and humane attitude by our side is in sharp contrast to the long list of inhumane atrocities perpetrated by your side, of which the incident of August 17th is but the latest ... Several times in recent months it has been necessary for me to protest the wanton murders and acts of inhumanity committed by your side.

And now, despite the often repeated protestations of peaceful intentions and goodwill expressed by you and other leaders of your side, I must again protest most strongly this latest violation by the KPA/CPV ... of the Armistice Agreement and of the rules of conduct observed by all civilized nations, demand that the pilot and passenger of this aircraft be returned immediately to United Nations Command control and that the personnel responsible for this provocative act be punished in accordance with paragraph 13 e (sic) of the Armistice Agreement.

On December 7, 1955, Hengkun Lee, General, ROK Army, wrote to General Lyman L. Kemnitzer, Commander-in-Chief, Far East Command & UN Command (7), regarding another incident:

My Dear General,

As you know, a serious situation has developed that calls for resoluteness and unhesitating forthrightness of action. I refer to the invasion of Korea territorial waters by armed Chinese Communist vessels and the abduction of four ROK Coast Guardsmen at 0405 hours on 25 December 1955.

We hope the release of the four Koreans may be accomplished peaceably … but perhaps in the ultimate of even greater importance, is the necessity of guaranteeing the security of our coastal defenses to prevent a repetition of the invasion of our waters. It is obvious that the naval patrol forces are presently inadequate in numbers and facilities to prevent infiltration of enemy vessels … the urgency of the situation is great and our Joint Chiefs of Staff is agreed that if the United Nations Command fails us at this time we must meet the situation ourselves.

Other nations may restrain themselves in liberating unjustly held personnel, for one reason or another, but the Republic of Korea sees the situation clearly and is committed to whatever action becomes necessary to effect their liberation.

These intense communications illustrate the at-times precarious peace, and were a reminder that although the war had stopped, it was not officially over.

UNITED STATES' ROLE IN THE FAR EAST, AND KOREAN PRESIDENT RHEE

The United States understood its role in the Far East as well as its assumed responsibilities; a "Chief of Staff Weekly Conference" memo found in National Archive II archival records (8) said, in part:

(1) J-2 continues to keep a careful surveillance on those political and military leaders who are in position to control the destiny of the ROK. (2) All commanders and their Staffs to continue the Commander in Chief's policy of exhibiting an open and frank approach to all our ROK officials; at the same time, very firm attitude on all matters for which the US is wholly or partially responsible. (Conference attendees: Gen Magruder, Gen Rogers, Gen Lacey, Gen Gaither, Gen Craig, Adm Smith, Adm Temple, Col Gosorn, Col Benson, Lt Col Foster).

On 15 August 1955, Korean president Syngman Rhee spoke on the tenth anniversary of the liberation of Korea regarding peace and communist aggression (9). President Rhee referred to President Eisenhower as a "very good friend," and said that Eisenhower had encouraged a "peace of forbearance" between conflicting parties. Rhee related that Korea had "suffered from war more than any other country in modern times," and added that "we are still struggling with the terrible effects which it has had upon our economy and in our daily lives."

Rhee, however, did not believe in a "status quo peace," rather that the "freedom of the captive peoples" must be restored. Rhee's ultimate goal was the liberation of the North Korean people.

In an interesting side note, Rhee had not wanted to sign the Armistice agreement, preferring instead to reunite the peninsula by force (10). A harbored bitterness was evident in his writings.

A 27 January 1954 (11) General Staff News Summary discussed Korean president Syngman Rhee's opinion on how the Allies could have achieved certain victory with use of the Atomic Bomb:

President Syngman Rhee clashed yesterday with former UN Commander Gen. Mark W Clark over conduct of the Korean war and said use of the atomic bomb would have meant an Allied victory.

12

Rhee, commenting on an article written for *Colliers* magazine by Clark, agreed with the four-star former commander that the Korean War could have been shortened if the UN "Had got tough faster. But signing of the truce nullifies the sacrifices made by brave boys from all over the world."

Rhee said he took exception to Clark's reference to former Eighth Army Commander Gen. James A. Van Fleet, claiming that Clark spoke "disparagingly" of Van Fleet in the article. "I do not wish to judge which of these two generals is right on the question of whether or not we could have pushed up to the Yalu River at that time, but I do wish to testify that practically all our armed forces were waiting for the order to march north."

Rhee said there were opportune moments for a victory drive northward, "but perhaps Gen. Clark did not know it, as he was stationed in Japan instead of having in Korea the headquarters of the commanding officer of the UN forces fighting in Korea."

Interestingly, Rhee is not the only public figure to have considered nuclear detonation to gain advantage and victory in Korea. *Army Times* reviewed a book on 23 October 1954 titled *MacArthur 1941-1951*, written by Maj. Gen. Charles A. Willoughby and John Chamberlain (12).

Mr. Montgomery said the book "… reveals unpublished military facts and judgments. It reveals, for example, that MacArthur proposed a novel atomic attack in conjunction with a double-envelopment operation up both coasts of North Korea, to clear the Chinese Communists out of North Korea early in 1951."

Though MacArthur may have considered use of atomic force in Korea, he had opposed dropping the atomic bomb on Hiroshima, as "he thought Japan was ready to surrender," according to Gen. Willoughby. Mr.

Fairfax, however, felt the book was "marred by omissions and generalities."

Despite the good fortune that the war did not go nuclear, the fallout from fighting reverberated well past Armistice.

The volume of writing on immediate post-Armistice Korea (mid to late 1950s) pales in comparison to the amount of writing about the war-years, as previously noted, but Kim provides context for this discrepancy on page 420:

> In the United States, immediately after fighting ceased, the Korean War was soon forgotten. That it has been called the "forgotten war" may be attributed to the fact that the United States neither won nor lost. Because it was unpopular among the general population, book publishers and movie makers, unlike their response to World War 2 or the Vietnam War, were reluctant to exploit the Korean War either for educating or entertaining the public. From the early 1980s, however, historians, especially revisionists, began to rediscover and write about the Korean War.

> Also, a North Korea-initiated provocation example: "A stark reminder that the Korean War remains unfinished was the unprovoked North Korean artillery attack on South Korean territory (Yonp'yong-do) near the Northern Limitation Line on 23 November 2010."

In his book, *Korea's Place in the Sun*, author Bruce Cumings said that America wanted to cut back on money going to people like Rhee and the "immense outflows to defend them," though Cumings also said the U.S. Army wanted to maintain "huge" armies, "... to contain communism" - themes that generally continue in one form or another to the present day (13).

EFFECT OF THE WAR ON THE KOREAN PEOPLE

The war resulted in deep psychological implications for the people of Korea who endured violence, were separated from their families, and suffered generational damage, as depicted by author Hoenik Kwon of the University of Cambridge, in his publication, *After the Korean War* (14).

Mr. Kwon said, "… the relational suffering refers to the ways in which the violence of the Korean War induced brutal and enduring effects into the milieu of communal and family relations (gwangye)". Family relationships were separated north from south and in general by the disruption and communication barriers created by war.

The fallout is heartbreaking, as told in Kim's writing: "A house in the city's old quarter is distinct from the neighboring houses. The owner of this house has refused to renovate it for the past six decades, defying the general trend in his hillside neighborhood for fear that his elder siblings might not be able to find their way back home. All of his brothers and sisters left northward during the war and have not yet fulfilled their promise of a prompt return to their then eleven-year-old youngest sibling." Broken family units hit hard for a people accustomed to strong bonds of family and community.

Kim says the Korean War experience was "a profoundly injurious experience not merely for the combatants but also for many more people who had no professional role in the three-year-long conflict … Kim points out that the civilian sufferings of the Korean War are not well known to the outside world, or for that matter, even the Koreans themselves."

Kim continued: "These two phenomena - family separation and collective liability - induced acute existential and moral crises in family

15

and kin groups, who struggled in the post war years with the desire to reunite, on the one hand, and, on the other, the fear of being deemed guilty by association."

Kim reported that people suspected of sympathizing with communism or socialism had sometimes been arrested or even killed by South Korean combat police and military police.

United States military forces operated in this environment of disruption and societal injury.

U.S. MILITARY PRESENCE IN KOREA AND JAPAN

United States military presence in South Korea and Japan continues to this day, though its structure has been changed and modified over time according to the *Eighth Army Blue Book* (15). For example:

> During the Korean War, Eighth Army served as both a field army and a theatre army and throughout the preponderance of the Cold War, it remained primarily a theater army. On 20 November 1954, it was merged with U.S. Army Forces Far East (AFFE) as the major Army command in the region.
>
> On 1 July 1957, AFFE was discontinued and United States Forces Korea was officially activated; thus, 8th Army was consolidated with USFK and the United Nations Command with headquarters in Seoul.

U.S. Troops had been stationed in Japan pursuant to the United States-Japanese Security Treaty of 8 September 1951 with the ostensible mission of containing communism (16); "The treaty allowed the United States to station troops in Japan, and made the Japanese islands into an important facet of America's global containment structure."

In his *Short History of Japan* (17), author W. G. Beasley asserted that post-war American strategic interests remained unresolved, given that "Cold War conflict was still a real possibility." The United States and Japan's security pact "extend(ed) to Japan a promise of nuclear protection in return for lease of American bases in the Japanese islands. Arrangements were included for legal jurisdiction over American servicemen there …"

The 12 September 1953 *Stars and Stripes* reported that U.N. Allies were to keep troops in Korea, "until the country is unified and peace is certain" (Ed. note – troops are still in Korea). The article said that five of the seven countries in the Commission on Korean Rehabilitation had troops in Korea.

Also pointed out was that Australia, Netherlands, Philippines, Thailand and Turkey had troops in Korea, and that Chile and Pakistan did not (18).

Historical records show examples of U.S. military location and mission changes in the Far East - The 17 July 1954 *Army Times* (19) reported on redeployment of some U.S. Armed Forces in an article titled, "1st Cav. Move Opens Army Redeployment in Far East." The article said that "The famed 1st Cav. Div. will soon turn over the defense of Hokkaido, northernmost of the Japanese Islands, to Japan's new army - the first in a series of moves to redeploy American forces in the Far East."

The Pentagon believed changeover would occur in the fall and the division would then be based on Honshu, Japan's main island. "U.S. Radar and antiaircraft units would remain on Hikkaido (sic) until the Japanese can take over these functions themselves … *the basic idea … has always been to remove American troops the moment natives are able to fend for themselves* (Author's italics*)*."

The article said the 1st Cavalry had moved to Hokkaido in January 1953 and that the change would, "contribute to the flexibility of U.S. and UN forces …"

Who was in charge of the United States Eighth Army in the Far East after the war? The *Eighth Army Blue Book* says Eighth Army Commanders during the immediate post-Armistice period were: Gen. Maxwell D. Taylor, February 1953 – April 1955; Gen. Isaac D. White, July 1955 – July 1957; Gen. George H. Decker, July 1957 – June 1959. Gen. Carter B. Magruder was Eighth Army Commander from July 1959 – July 1961.

More troops staying in place, other troops moving:

The 13 February 1954 *Army Times* reported, "'Bayonet' to Stay in Korea" (20):

> The Army will have nine divisions overseas under this plan. Five of them will be in Europe, three in the Far East and one in Hawaii. The 1st Cav. Div. and the 24th Div. would remain in Japan (the 24th would be renumbered), and the 7th Div. would remain in Korea.

> The Army would see strength reduction of 300,000 over the ensuing 16 1/2 months, and "The Army will also be cut in size from the planned 1,164,000 at the end of fiscal 1955 to between 950,000 and 1,000,000 men by the end of fiscal 1956."

The 4 December 1954 *Army Times* (21) discussed the movement of 24th Division to Japan from Korea. The move had involved "between 15 and 16 thousand duffel bags," and was the approximate scope of moving "Compton, Calif., Calumet City, Ill., or Salisbury, Md. to a new location over a thousand miles away."

Moving the "Victory" division involved fifteen thousand unit members, three regiments, and 800,000 board feet of lumber to make necessary boxes (the lumber was salvaged "from everywhere") for three million pounds of equipment. There was an actual "box and crate" engineer assigned to ensure proper box construction using the minimum amount of nails necessary. Weapons and sensitive signal equipment had to be protected against "rust and weather."

Furthermore, the move could only be done with "hard work and organization," to which an Eighth Army advisory team assisted.

Interestingly, during this operation, troop morale remained high due to the expectation of "good duty" in Japan.

Even with the benefit of high morale, personal issues, as is frequently the case, were on the minds of Army personnel:

The 28 August 1954 *Army Times* includes a letter from SFC William F. Musgrave pertaining to "Korean Tour." The letter-writer was interested in "various plans put into effect and currently in the fire to induce more qualified men to reenlist." He wasn't sure about the direction of Army policy, and noted that "The new reenlistment bonus bill and restoration of fringe benefits have given a big boost to the reenlistment program."

PFC Musgrave asked rhetorically, "While Air Force policy says 12 months is maximum time for family separations, the current Marine policy says 14 months is enough for Korea – why then does the Army try to sell a married man 16 months in Korea?" An 18-to-20-month separation from his family would be considered by a soldier as a "drawback." He said, however, men could be away from their families for up to 20 months in total.

And finally, "When I read that the Army plans concurrent travel in '55 to Europe and then look at this situation in Korea they don't add up to equality. Europe and Korea are definitely different theaters and I'm of the opinion that if the tour in Korea were shortened to compare with other services, reenlistments would certainly increase."

Personal concerns unsurprisingly included financial worries:

The *Army Times* reported on 25 September 1954 concerning Army relief to AFFE soldiers and their dependents:

TOKYO. – Army Forces Far East has disbursed almost $200,000 in loans and grants in the past year to approximately 1200 AFFE soldiers and their dependents through the Army Emergency Relief program.

The loans and grants ranged from amounts as low as $10 to as much as $1500, and covered such emergencies as hospital, medical, funeral and travel expenses, loss of pay, nonreceipt of allowances, rental payments and other emergencies listed as confidential.

The U.S. Army admirably utilized soldier's skills, abilities, and resources to help Korea:

Army Times of 12 November 1955 reported that Army Engineers had been assisting Korea in rebuilding their infrastructure with labor assistance from Republic of Korea Army personnel on larger Armed Forces Aid to Korea (AFAK) projects (22):

"Give a U.S. Army engineer a hammer, saw, bag of cement, and some old packing cases (and the ubiquitous bulldozer, of course!), a bit of ground and things happen," said the editorial in a Korean daily newspaper here.

The specific subject at hand was the part the Army Corps of Engineers has played in the construction phase of the Armed Forces Aid to Korea program.

Of the $20 million allocated for 2163 projects in the Armed Forces Aid to Korea program, a total of $13-million, $600,000 has been expanded for 1908 projects by June 30, the end of fiscal 1955.

Most of the AFAK program has been undertaken in the section of Korea lying south of Seoul and extending to Pusan on the Peninsula's southernmost tip. This area is the responsibility of the Korean Communications Zone, and projects, sponsored by individual army units or commands, are administered by the Corps of Engineers.

Dangerous duty:

While helping the Korean population and carrying on with their normal duties, Americans on South Korea Army bases post-Armistice were not out of danger, despite cessation of formal hostilities. There were incursions and firefights which continued sporadically into the mid-1950s and beyond.

Whether they kept this in the back of their minds or not as they went about their sometimes-mundane duties is not known with certainty, but how could it not have been the case? The war was not technically over and remains unresolved to the present day despite ceasefire having been declared.

The prospect of re-engagement was not an impossibility. Yet even in this challenging environment, organized sports thrived. These young men and women, willing participants in a mid-century conflict on the other side of the world, *heroes*, would not be dissuaded from testing their mettle in competitive sport.

Not all news out of Korea was negative.

The 29 January 1954 General Staff News Summary (23) reported:

> (A) Japanese guard at a US Air Force base was reported in good condition today after three American airmen gave him blood transfusions for two days. The three servicemen, all air police, offered the blood after guard Ginjiro Kobayashi was reported dying after a stomach operation. The three air police knew the Japanese guard from their post duty …

The newspaper Yomiuri quoted Mrs. Kobayashi at her husband's bedside as telling the three Americans, "The blood of love saved my husband."

There were challenges for civilians to access Korean territory.

Following is a letter in the National Archives II records, from Mr. William P. Hirsch to the Visa Department of Korean Mission, dated 28 December 1954, which sheds light on the challenges facing a civilian attempting to enter the Republic of Korea (ROK) at the time. Note: ROK is the official term for South Korea, but South Koreans often refer to South Korea as simply "Korea" (and North Korea as "North Korea"). The letter is a response to having been denied entry into ROK (24), and it reads as follows:

> TO: Korean Mission, 1-5 Pakeya Cho, Ababu, Ninato-Ku, Tokyo Attn: Visa Department
>
> Dear Sirs:
>
> About 10 days ago I was advised by the international travel section of the United Nations Command that my application for entry into the Republic of Korea had been approved by both the United Nations Command and the Korean Mission.
>
> I, therefore, would appreciate your considering this letter as a request for reconsideration and favorable approval of my application to enter your country and, in seeking this, wish to cite the following facts:
>
> (1)   I deem myself a loyal and trustworthy American citizen and my presence in Korea will not, in any way, prove detrimental to the government of the Republic of Korea.

(2)   My business in Korea will be solely with the Army and Air Force Post Exchange Service, who have granted the right to establish a concession in the Post Exchange in Seoul, servicing US and UN personnel only.

(3)   I will be there to establish the concession, making all necessary arrangements with the Exchange Officer, hire and train local Korean Nationals, and, in some small measure, assist the Korean economy.

(4)   While in your country I shall have the logistics support of the RCA distributors, the KORCAB Corporation, Post Office Box 5, Kwang-Wha-Moon, Seoul. (See their letter of December 13, 1954).

I should like to point out that upon the advice of the initial approval, I made necessary arrangements for my family in Japan, sold my car, and have employed a Korean National to assist me in my work in Seoul. All of these actions on my part have resulted in monetary expenditures and promises and with the revoking of the entry permit I have been placed in a most embarrassing situation.

My past history has proved an honorable discharge from the United States Army in 1946 as an officer. At present, I am the First Vice Commander of the Tokyo Post Number 1 of the American Legion and I'm very active in local community charitable and civic activities.

In the event that character references are deemed necessary by the Mission, I am very happy to refer you to any or all of the following individuals:

> Hon Carlos Rodriguez-Jimenez, Minister of Venezuela
>
> Col William Ryder, Military Attache of the US Embassy, Tokyo
>
> John J. McSweeney, Manager, Chase National Bank, Tokyo
>
> Howard Spaub, Secretary-General of the Priparipe Mission, Tokyo
>
> William E. Short, Security Officer, Northwest Airlines, Tokyo
>
> Col Harrison Markley, Civil Affairs, I Corps, Korea

In view of the above, I respectfully request approval of my application to enter the Republic of Korea.

CONTEMPORANEOUS GENERAL STAFF NEWS SUMMARIES

Archived General Staff News Summaries provide interesting glimpses into events of the day; some perhaps not publicly or at least widely reported:

A 19 January 1955 General Staff News Summary discussed an unsuccessful assassination attempt of Gen. Maxwell D. Taylor (25):

> Military authorities undertook extraordinary precautions today for the safety of Gen. Maxwell D. Taylor, AFFE/8th Army

Commander, following an unsuccessful assassination attempt Tuesday at ROK Army headquarters in Taegu.

Gen. Taylor escaped unharmed after a Korean Army major, identified as Kim Ki Ok, leaped through a window at ROK Hq. and pointed an automatic pistol at Gen. Taylor before being subdued by guards. After the incident US military police supplied the general with special burp-gun and carbine armed guards. Gen. Taylor flew to Seoul late yesterday after the incident and was there today.

Those with him at the time of the attempted killing said the General was unruffled and calm throughout. INS included an unconfirmed report that the ROK major threatened Gen. Taylor in order to back up his personal demand that US forces support South Korea in a military attack into North Korea to unify the country by force.

A 16 February 1955 General Staff News Summary reported on general conditions in Korea at the time (26):

3 Koreans were killed, two others were critically injured and four were reported missing following a gasoline explosion yesterday afternoon in Seoul along with the 8th Army's fuel pipeline.

Two American soldiers received minor injuries, an 8th Army spokesman said. Their names were withheld. Cause of the explosion has not yet been determined, ... a fire ... (which) broke out following the blast was brought under control in about 25 minutes, the spokesman said.

A 15 June 1956 HQ AFFE/8A (Rear) Daily News Summary (27) said,

The Defense Department said today evidence has accumulated for more than two years that could be used as a basis for formally renouncing the Korean Armistice agreement of 1953.

The evidence, they said, is that the Communists have flagrantly violated the Armistice ban on introduction of new weapons into North Korea, while the weapons of U.S. Forces in South Korea have grown increasingly obsolete because of this clause. A spokesman said no immediate steps toward renunciation of the agreement are contemplated.

Army memos and "Circulars" provided additional information regarding troops and the living environment:

A 30 March 1955 Circular (28) addressed community relations by "fostering better relations between the civilian population and military personnel of their commands to achieve ultimate elimination or minimization of problems detrimental to the best interests of the United States."

(Community relations) ... provide(s) a friendly medium for liaison, discussion, and consultation by: exchanging information of mutual interest; advising appropriate civilian officials, community leaders, and United States forces commanders on matters affecting the community and the United States forces; creating an understanding by local citizens of certain United States forces decisions, directives, and regulations; studying local problems affecting the community and/or United States forces; evaluating, at the request of either party, the possible effects of contemplated actions by the civilian populace or the United States forces.

A 7 June 1955 document from National Archives II, written by James B. Quill, Brigadier General, General Staff, discussed steps taken to dissuade Korean civilian trespassing "in the vicinity of the main battle positions for troop occupancy and for troop training," noting that an increasing number of civilians had settled in the area. There was "good arable land," but it was located within artillery range "firing points." There were occasional "errant rounds," and civilians occupying adjacent areas did so at their own risk (29)

It is within this milieu that the AFFE full contact football conference and Service Sports recreation programs existed and thrived. It was a time of dynamic change and trial and error in the administration of the changing Korean political and social landscape. Fortunately, enough relics of that era survive to help tell the story of this amazing time in overseas Service Sports.

HISTORY PERTAINING TO AFFE SPORTS

A 2011 study entitled *A History of Recreation in the Military*, on behalf of the Department of Defense (DoD) Legacy Resource Management Program (30), discussed military recreational facilities in a chronological context (*"Approved for Public Release; distribution is unlimited"*).

The study was primarily focused on CONUS sites, but it provided an interesting history of the development of military sports/recreation:

> Sports were ... encouraged to be played during the troops' free time ... The military recognized the importance of having organized recreation and created the Moral (sic) Division that later became the Special Services ... The core recreation programs were developed between 1946 and 1955 and ran by a combination of active military and civilians ... also soon after (WWII), the Inter-Service Sports Council was established in October of 1947, so that service-wide championships in various sports could be held with the Army, Navy, and Air Force on an equal basis (Figure 37).

> Recreation was beginning to see a change after World War II ... College football was changing some at this time as well. Many of the players were older than the typical college student. Large numbers of them had played in the service and were now attending college as a benefit of the GI Bill. This increased the demand for players and the excitement of recruiting across the country. Bowl games in 1954 brought in over $2.5 million in gate receipts alone (Author: This is plausibly a reference only to CONUS NCAA football bowls. The amount would be approximately $30,000,000 in 2025 dollars).

Clearly the mid-1950s were a time of exceptional Service Sports competition in CONUS and the Far East, in particular. As the assembled documentation will show, many of the players were mature enough to have previously played their sport professionally, or at least in college. The war interrupted professional sports careers and participation with college teams. An unknown number of athletes had completed combat service in the Korean War and were battle-tested and tough. Many returned to CONUS after their service and proceeded to excel at the highest levels of their sport.

The Service Sports program was prescient in recognizing service member needs, and was diligent in providing an exceptional level of ongoing competition opportunities.

The DoD study continued with commentary on various facilities, including "Field Houses/Gymnasiums":

> Recreation centers and gymnasiums held a variety of activities for military personnel. Typically a large gymnasium could be converted for many uses. It was primarily a basketball court, but nets could be installed for badminton or volleyball.

Figure 37. Fort Jackson Field and track meet awards, 20 June 1953 (NARA 111-SC Box 250 424337).

Following is a sample photo from the DoD study of a field house at Fort Knox from 1957.

Figure 138. Fort Knox Gammon Field House basketball floor, 7 Feb 1957 (NARA 111-SC 491774).

Baseball was another popular sport on military installations.

> Baseball fields were fairly easy to create and therefore popped up at military installations throughout the United States and abroad … Baseball brought together many people who may not have associated with each other previously.

Football, however, was the granddaddy of all the Service Sports, attracting the largest crowds as well as top military brass who were often accommodated with prime seating and services during games. The DoD study continued:

> During the 1940s military (Service Sports) football teams played college teams. Randolph Field appeared in the Cotton Bowl and was actually ranked number one in October 1944. Great Lakes Naval Training Station beat Notre Dame at Soldier Field in Chicago … During World War II there were several mock "bowl" games. The teams involved were usually Navy and Army All-Star teams and festivals at the bowls mirrored those back home on New Year's Day. Some of the bowls held were the Arab Bowl, Poi Bowl in Hawaii, and the Lily Bowl in Bermuda.

Figure 234. Great Lakes baseball grandstand, 25 Apr 1938 (NARA 71-CA Box 146).

Figure 217. Football season on a US ship somewhere in the Pacific, 14 Dec 1943 (NARA 80-G Box 504 204987).

Figure 223. Football in North Africa, 1 Jan 1943 (NARA 111-SC Box 699 332713).

Figure 225. Football in Iran, 31 Dec 1944 (NARA 111-SC Box 699 332722).

Figure 242. Fort Benning Doughboy Stadium, 6 Sep 1939 (NARA 342-FH Box 1059 3B-17283).

Figure 287. Fort Jackson All-Army Field and Track Meet ceremonies at Patton Stadium, 12 Jun 1953 (NARA 111-SC Box 255 430773).

The DoD study described football stadiums of the past:

> Football stadiums were typically much larger than baseball stadiums, and therefore were not as numerous. Football stadiums often were combined with a running track to incorporate more than one activity … unlike baseball stadiums, football stadiums did not have covered seating areas.

The DoD report came to the conclusion that recreational complexes "are necessary for the physical and mental health of their service members," and that they were an "integral" part of the homeland mission of the DoD. Recreation assisted service members in combatting stress and boredom while promoting efficiency and morale, though the installations were "rarely (considered) directly mission supporting."

The authors made a distinction between service installation recreational resources and the programs of military academies, in that at academies such as the US Military Academy at West Point, US Air Force Academy, and the US Naval Academy, recreation was integral to the curriculum.

Though the DoD study's focus was facilities as they pertain to the National Historic Preservation Act of 1966, the authors capably provided a window into the history of the Service Sports programs and facilities.

NEWS ARTICLES/MILITARY MEMOS PERTAINING TO FACILITIES

Post-Armistice military posts were often populated with multiple sporting and recreational facilities. The 27 February 1954 *Army Times* reported on "Big Post Loaded with Gyms, Libraries" (31): "Forty-eight libraries – 22 theaters - 16 hobby craft shops. There are hundreds of American cities that cannot boast of such recreational facilities and very few American military installations have numerous places for off-duty enjoyment, and yet all of these – and many more – are to be found within the Camp Tokyo area."

Tokyo-area recreation programs were administered by Camp Tokyo Special Services. 110,000 people per month visited the 48 libraries. There were 22 theaters, visited by 180,000 per month. And, "when it comes to athletic-minded people, Camp Tokyo Special Services offers one large sports arena, 6 gymnasiums, 44 bowling lanes, 28 tennis courts, and 14 swimming pools. Intra-service competition is directed in baseball, golf, tennis, bowling, basketball, football, boxing, and wrestling. In addition, athletic events featuring varsity teams from the major Camp Tokyo installations are attended by large numbers of enthusiastic spectators."

18 November 1954 correspondence from Lt Col Leo Kleiman to various AFFE Commanding Generals of the Eighth Army, Korean Communications Zone, XVI Corps, Ryukyus Command, Central Command, Southwestern Command, and Camp Zama, discussed Welfare and Recreational Construction.

The correspondence said that "Major commands are submitting a large number of requests for nonappropriated (sic) funds for welfare and recreational construction and improvement projects." Lt Col Kleiman referred to the 30 August 1954 Budget Conference and the fiscal year 1955 Supplementary Budget regarding "information desired and deemed necessary."

Factors to be considered were: Permanency of installation where facility is to be constructed, close coordination with other commands where current planning indicates a change in area responsibility or transfer of troops, availability of utilities and ability of post engineer to provide maintenance and repairs, availability of personnel to operate facilities, reasonable time allowed for approval of funds, preparation of detailed plans, reviews by the engineer, letting of contracts and construction.

Not all Service Sports facilities involved contact sports. A 12 October 1955 memo from National Archives II says that Philip G. Whele, Brigadier General, U.S. Army Commanding, submitted a "Request for bowling alleys," as "I desire to move forward with this very worthwhile project" (32).

In summary, Service Sports existed pre-Korean War, but the weight of evidence suggests a rapid expansion of Service Sports offerings and competition in the Far East post-Armistice. Service Sports in the mid-1950's was robust and popular with both participants and fans alike. It's apparent that sporting activity was highly encouraged by Command Staff, both as a way to relieve stress, but also as a way to foster competitive, war-fighting spirit. It was a remarkable time in the Far East.

7ᵀᴴ INFANTRY DIVISION "BAYONETS" HISTORY

Photo: 1950s Camp Casey, Korea,
https://www.qsl.net/w/wd4ngb//army/cory7.jpg

Roving Historian (33) summarized the Bayonets' substantial commitment and sacrifice in the Korean War:

> The Korean War Armistice was signed on July 27, 1953. During the Korean War, the Bayonets were in combat for a total of 850 days. They suffered 15,126 casualties, including 3,905 killed in action and 10,858 wounded. The 7th Infantry Division remained on the DMZ, its headquarters at Camp Casey, South Korea until 1971. On April 2, 1971, the Division was deactivated at Fort Lewis, Washington.

It is with the uncompromising Bayonets Division that our story begins.

37

A guidebook/history for personnel about to serve in Korea, published by Headquarters 7th Infantry Division, Office of the Commanding General, H. G. Moore, Major General, July 1970, provides background and information about the 7th Infantry Division (34).

Major General Moore said the 7th Division motto was, "Hold your Bayonets High," and that this motto had been earned by "their valiant actions and the blood they shed."

Major General Moore elaborated, "What will 13 months in the 'Land of the Morning Calm' mean to you? It can be a chance to sharpen military skills with the unit which guards 'Freedom's Frontier.' Training must always keep troops at a high state of readiness, ready to meet any aggression that might attempt to cross that frontier."

Photo:1950s Camp Casey, Korea, https://www.qsl.net/wd4ngb/casey%2054-7.jpg

The guidebook gave a detailed history of 7th Division military engagements, from the Battle of Leyte in the Philippines, to Korea, where they had accepted surrender of Japanese troops and where they later liberated Seoul, and fought in the bloody Pork Chop Hill combat action.

The 7th Division's heroics in Korea, including "many hand-to-hand battles," led to the 7th Division becoming known as the "Bayonet" Division.

The guidebook continued by noting the Division "has over 1000 days of combat and 15 campaign streamers. The tenacity of its fighting record is reflected in suffering over 26,000 combat casualties and the 7th Infantry Division's 15 Medal of Honor winners reflect the valor of its soldiers."

The 7th Division was officially moved to Japan in December 1948, however, "the nerve center of the 7th Infantry Division" remained Camp Casey, Korea. The 7th, among other units, had been housed at Camp Casey, which was dedicated in 1952 to Major Hugh B. Casey, "who died there in a plane crash in 1951."

The scene was set: "The Republic of Korea, stretching from the Demilitarized Zone (DMZ) on the north to Pusan on the South, contains about 30 million people packed into an area about the size of New York state." The heaviest rains occur June to August and temperatures range from "below 0 in the winter to slightly over 100 in the summer."

Korea was described as a land which was "somewhat confusing," as "you see an International Airport capable of handling the largest jets, but just outside are thatched huts with dirt floors, dusty roads, and poverty … the paved road leading to the 7th Division area was more or less a dirt trail five years ago" (Author note: keeping in mind this description was from 1970).

The Special Services program was highlighted, calling it "one of the most comprehensive and extensive recreational programs in Korea. It is the effort and intent of their program to promote the highest degree of mental and physical well-being and morale of 7th Division personnel."

The 7th Division Bayonet new-soldier guide said that "Korea is the only command in the Army where division level sports competition is permitted (34) ... brigade and company level sports are likewise emphasized." The high quality of 7th Division sports was recognized: "Bayonet teams consistently win the majority of Eighth U.S. Army championships."

Sports facilities included gymnasiums, softball fields, bowling alleys, tennis courts, handball courts, baseball diamonds, a swimming pool, and a golf course. The home field of Bayonets football was Camp Casey's Schoonover Bowl football field.

Camp Casey occupies 3500 acres in Dongducheon, South Korea, and is still an active U.S. Military base at time of this writing.

MY DAD, JERRY G. KINGREY, 7TH DIVISION "BAYONETS" FOOTBALL

Jerry was born on 23 July 1935, in Worthington, Minnesota, and he passed away on 2 August 2012. He grew up in poverty and with challenging circumstances, losing his father much too early. But like many small-town boys in those days, he relied on his athleticism and sports to stay busy and out of trouble.

Jerry excelled in contact sports such as basketball and football. He was big and strong - 6'4" and about 200 pounds throughout his adult life. He was primarily left-handed, but was also quite ambidextrous, which was a significant asset in the sports he favored.

Jerry entered into service with the Minnesota National Guard in the early 1950s, and was honorably discharged 31 March 1961 as an E-6, Sgt. First Class, USAR. His active-duty Korean Service, per his DD-214, lists service with HQ & HQ CO, 31st Inf Regt., from 20 June 1955 to 23 June 1956, whereupon he reverted to the National Guard Minn MIL DIST.

Jerry's time in Korea, of course, was post-Armistice. Despite ongoing sporadic hostilities, it is not known if he saw or participated in any fighting actions. He made it to Korea in time to participate in the 1955 Service Sports fall football season, playing for the AFFE/8A "7th Division Bayonets" football team based out of Camp Casey.

This particular AFFE league included 7th Division, ASCOM City, Seoul Military Post (SMP), 24th Division, and I Corps. The games ran from 24 September to 24 November (see game program photos below).

There is no indication Jerry played football in Korea other than for the 1955 season. He likely participated in basketball competitions, but no formal support for that was found.

41

Jerry was very active in his own and his children's sports as well as in coaching, but he was cut down too early by Multiple Sclerosis in his later years. He died at age 77.

Jerry didn't discuss his Army life, or even Service Sports, for reasons unknown, though I believe that was not uncommon with his generation. I wish I had "picked his brain" about it while he was living, but I was late to the party. Dad – thank you for your service.

Photo: Jerry receiving an award, year unknown. Jerry G. Kingrey personal collection, © All rights reserved.

Photo: Jerry (#6) fighting for a rebound, North Dakota State University basketball; year and photographer unknown (post-military service; late 50s). Jerry G. Kingrey personal collection, © All rights reserved.

Cornerback Jerry G. Kingrey intercepts pass, Korea, 1955. Jerry G.
Kingrey personal collection, © All rights reserved.

Photo: Jerry Kingrey, Korea. Jerry G. Kingrey personal collection, © All
rights reserved.

AFFE/EIGHTH ARMY
FOOTBALL CONFERENCE
7TH DIVISION "BAYONETS"

VS
ASCOM CITY "RAMS"
16 OCTOBER 1955

AFFE/8A FOOTBALL SCHEDULE

DATE	VISITORS	HOME TEAM
24 September	24TH DIVISION	ASCOM CITY
25	7TH DIVISION	SMP
1 October	7TH DIVISION	24TH DIVISION
2	I CORPS	ASCOM CITY
8	I CORPS	7TH DIVISION
9	SMP	24TH DIVISION
15	SMP	I CORPS
16	ASCOM CITY	7TH DIVISION
22	SMP	ASCOM CITY
23	24TH DIVISION	I CORPS
29	ASCOM CITY	24TH DIVISION
30	SMP	7TH DIVISION
5 November	24TH DIVISION	7TH DIVISION
6	ASCOM CITY	I CORPS
12	7TH DIVISION	I CORPS
13	24TH DIVISION	SMP
19	I CORPS	SMP
20	7TH DIVISION	ASCOM CITY
24	ASCOM CITY	SMP
24	I CORPS	24TH DIVISION

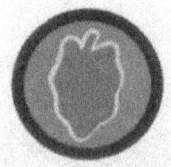

46

ASCOM CITY RAMS

NO	NAME	POS	HT	WT	HOME TOWN
20	Robert Boring	QB	6'	185	Kansas City, Kan.
21	Francis Newman	HB	5'9"	170	New Orleans, La.
22	Duward Brooks	HB	6'1"	180	Witchita Falls, Tex.
24	Elmer Manatowa	HB	5'7"	155	Cushing, Okla.
25	Bobby Redmond	HB	5'9"	176	Little Rock, Ark.
26	Henry Johnson	HB	5'6"	160	Washington, D.C.
27	Charley Conger	HB	5'9"	165	Custer, S.Dak.
28	Alex Litman	HB	6'1"	194	San Angelo, Tex.
30	Raymond Miska	G	6'	190	Wharton, Texas
31	Carl Lizona	C	5'11"	185	Gulfport, Miss.
32	Edward Bastien	FB	5'10"	210	
33	Robert Byley	FB	5'10"	200	Chicago, Ill.
34	George Garrett	G	6'2"	200	Brawley, Calif.
35	Jim Magner	G	5'10"	190	Bethesda, Md.
37	C J Steiner	C	5'7"	195	Downers Grove, Ill.
39	Robert C Opp	C	5'10"	195	Akron, Ohio
40	John W Conlin	E	6'1"	193	Ann Arbor, Mich.
41	Jack Rutherford	E	6'4"	195	Dallas, Texas
42	Willie Zackery	E	6'1"	196	Atlanta, Ga.
43	Paul Fortenberry	E	6'2"	185	Big Spring, Texas
44	Jim Conley	G	5'11"	210	Berkley, Calif.
45	James C Graves	E	6'	175	Ontario, Calif.
46	Bernard Conway	G	5'10"	180	Mancelona, Mich.
47	Thomas Lamb	G	5'11"	210	
48	John Hoffman	E	6'	175	Alexandria, Va.
49	Richard Nelson	E	5'11"	195	
51	Arthur Prchlik	T	6'2"	200	Cleveland, Ohio
52	Roger Hardacre	T	6'	205	Anderson, Ind.
54	Everett Wilson	T	6'	190	Coatesville, Pa.

ASCOM CITY RAMS

NO	NAME	POS	HT	WT	HOME TOWN
55	Claude P Sandlin	C.	5'11"	212	Honolulu, Hawaii
56	Jack Erickson	T	6'1"	220	Thief River, Minn.
57	James Blackburn	T	6'2"	205	Cushing, Okla.
58	Christopher Wilson	E	6'2"	205	
59	Harry Kalale	T	5'11"	205	Honolulu, Hawaii
29	Robert Biggerstaff	QB	5'9"	160	Asheville, N.C.

Major Berry F Powell   Officer-in-Charge
Lester L McIntyre   Manager
MSgt Thomas W Hopkins   Line Coach
Al Glover   Trainer

OFFICIALS.

Referee   DeGiovonni
Umpire   Hershey
Head Linesman   Downs
Field Judge   Starkey

MUSIC:

BY THE 7TH INFANTRY DIVISION BAND

48

7TH DIVISION BAYONETS

NO	NAME	POS	HT	WT	HOME TOWN
10	Bill Lugar	QB	5'11"	175	Pittsburg, Pa.
11	David Kempker	QB	6'1"	180	Holland, Mich.
12	Connie R Browning	QB	5'10"	175	Radford, Va.
20	John G Allison	FB	5'9"	190	Brentwood, Calif.
21	George W Wright	LH	6'	175	Washington, D.C.
22	Glen Petty	LH	5'9"	177	Green Bay, Wis.
23	Willie C Leffall	LH	5'10"	175	Fresno, Calif.
30	Charlie Morris	RH	5'8"	180	Thomson, Ga.
31	Phillip O Bamford	F	5'10"	187	Merthuen, Mass.
32	William Mixon	FB	5'11"	185	Birmingham, Ala.
33	Homer O Young	FB	6'	200	Alliance, Ohio
40	Dean Rice	RH	6'1"	200	Norman, Okla.
41	Bobby L Williams	RH	5'6"	165	Richmond, Calif.
42	John E Martin	RH	5'8"	161	Cincinnati, Ohio
50	George C Boyer	C	6'2"	215	Jacksonville, Fla.
51	David L Lane	C	6'1"	200	Phenix City, Ala.
52	Harold E Nutt	C	6'2"	210	Marshall, Texas
60	Paul E White	C	5'10"	195	Hayesville, N.C.
61	George S Thomas	RG	6'	200	Atlanta, Ga.
62	Peter Good	LG	5'8"	200	South Orange, N.J.
63	Robert H Schaeffer	LG	5'10"	200	Chicago, Ill.
64	Walter Smyth	RG	5'11"	176	Rallins, Wyo.
65	Donald P Rodriquez	LG	6'	190	Ventura, Calif.
66	James Miller	RG	5'9"	195	Madisonville, Ky.
67	Angelo A Diorio	LG	5'9"	205	Chicago, Ill.
68	Armando Scogna	RG	5'11"	205	El Segundo, Calif.
70	John Lezdey	RT	6'1"	230	Pittsburg, Pa.
71	Joseph D Hergest	LT	5'10"	200	Ekath, La.
72	Roosevelt Lee	RT	5'11"	205	Sarasota, Fla.

49

7TH DIVISION BAYONETS

NO	NAME	POS	HT	WT	HOME TOWN
73	Willis A Johnson	RT	6'	205	Canton, Ga.
74	Max N Kitzelman	RT	6'3"	230	Omaha, Neb.
75	Ben Boykin	RE	5'11"	230	Brooksville, Miss.
80	Preston J Ingram	LE	6'	205	Oklahoma City, Okla.
82	John Sevanich	RE	6'1"	195	McKee Rocks, Pa.
83	Michele A LaSorsa	LE	6'	190	Providence, R.I.
84	Peter Kayavas	C	6'	195	Woburn, Mass.
85	Vernon Shultz	RT	6'	200	Britton, S.D.
86	Jerry Kingrey	RE	6'4"	205	Worthington, Minn.
87	Robert L Knight	LE	6'4"	215	Stoneham, Mass.
	Walter J Stohr	RG	5'8"	200	Pittsburgh, Pa.

LT. George Morris
Lt James Ritz   Head Coach
Lt James Hahn   Backfield Coach
Lt Lloyd Hill   Line Coach
PFC Meyers Pait   Manager
Pvt Earl Ramsden   Asst Manager

George C Boyer   Team Captain
James Miller   Team Co Captain

DECLASSIFIED PHOTOS FROM 7TH MP CO., 7th INFANTRY DIVISION, & CAMP OTSU (NATIONAL ARCHIVES II)

```
DOD STILL MEDIA DEPOSITORY
BLDG. 168, N.D.W.
WASHINGTON, D.C.  20374-1681

SDAN: C 11110              DATE: 24 Feb 1956
SAVRIN:
SERVICE ID: 18(1)-2233-3/AFFE-56-2674-C
PHOTOGRAPHER: Pvt. Letven

Korea....Capt. Norton M. Tripp, CO, 7th MP Co., 7th
U.S. Infantry Division, inspects vehicles of the MP
roving patrol before they go on duty.  Left to right
are:  SP3 Jonnie Bass, SP3 Edward F. Hochecker, Cpl.
Albert Geyer, Capt. Tripp, SP3 Henry Roten, Cpl.
Donald Loxinske and SP3 Paul F. Bailey.



OFFICIAL U.S. ARMY PHOTO              (RELEASED)
```

```
DOD STILL MEDIA DEPOSITORY
BLDG. 168, N.D.W.
WASHINGTON, D.C.  20374-1681

SDAN: C 11109              DATE: 24 Feb 1956
SAVRIN:
SERVICE ID: 18(1)-2233-2/AFFE-56-2672-C
PHOTOGRAPHER: Pvt. Letven

Korea....Capt. Norton M. Tripp (left foreground), CO,
7th MP Co., 7th U.S. Infantry Division, inspects the
weapon of SP3 Johnnie Bass at guard mount at company
headquarters.
```

```
OFFICIAL U.S. ARMY PHOTO                    (RELEASED)
```

DOD STILL MEDIA DEPOSITORY
BLDG. 168, N.D.W.
WASHINGTON, D.C. 20374-1681

SDAN: C 11100   DATE: 1956
SAVRIN:
SERVICE ID: 3(1)-2284-11/AFFE-56-2641-C
PHOTOGRAPHER: SFC. Weimer

Camp Otsu, Japan....SFC. Yukio Sano, (second from
right), Japanese Security Guard, and Miss Fumiko Ueno
(right), Security Guard Section, check the passes of
Miss Akiko Tsuchida (left) and Miss Kazuko Yaoamoto,
both Japanese employees at the camp.

OFFICIAL U.S. ARMY PHOTO   (RELEASED)

FOUNDATION – FAR EAST SPORTS PROGRAM

During my research at the National Archives in College Park, Maryland, I came across a document written by Lt. Col. Leo Kleiman, AGC, Asst AG, dated 5 October 1954, which, although not written at the inception of the Sports Programs, appears to be as close to a foundational document for the Far East Army program that I've seen, keeping in mind that not all documents and records were saved or archived. The available evidence is piecemeal, at best.

I will attempt to paraphrase it here:

Subject: United States Army Forces, Far East, Sports Program

5 October 1954

Purpose: This directive establishes a United States Army Forces, Far East, sports program designed to promote comprehensive sports activities at all levels of command, through an integrated system of geographical area conferences under which participation and administration are centralized, and provides for progression into higher level competitions in certain selected sports.

Objectives: The objectives of the United States Army Forces, Far East, sports program are to aid in the mental, physical, and moral development of Army personnel in the United States Army Forces, Far East, and stimulate a high degree of esprit-de-corps by: Encouraging maximum participation in wholesome recreative sports during free time hours on a voluntary basis; expanding the opportunity for individuals to engage in sports of their own choice; improving sports skills and techniques through the media of qualified coaching and officiating;

providing incentives for continually increasing competitive and spectator interests; fostering international goodwill and understanding by maintaining close relationships with indigenous communities in sports activities of mutual interest; and, where practicable, competing with and against civilian teams.

Sports conference areas: For purposes of sports administration and competition, the following geographical areas of the United States Army Forces, Far East, are subdivided into sports conferences as indicated:

Japan: The Commanding Generals, XVI Corps, Central and Southwest Commands are authorized to designate sports conference areas, within respective command boundaries, which will best serve the mission and functions of each command. However, titles of sports conferences, so established, will conform to those shown below.

Commanders concerned will advise this headquarters, at the earliest practicable date, as to the geographic limits of each conference and any changes which may occur from time to time. Any changes in the composition of conference areas or the establishment of sports leagues which overlap into other command areas must have the approval of this headquarters.

XVI Corps: Hokkaido Sports Conference and Northern Honshu Sports Conference.

Central Command: Tokyo area Sports Conference and Yokohama area Sports Conference.

Southwestern Command: Southern Honshu Sports Conference and Kyushu Sports Conference.

Ryukyus Command: Commanding General, Ryukyus Command, is authorized to establish such conference areas for Army personnel in the Ryukyus Command as are considered best adaptable to the policies and procedures contained herein. The Commanding General, United States Army Forces, Far East, will be kept advised as to any changes in conference organizational structure.

Korea: Insofar as practicable, the Commanding Generals, Korean Communications Zone and Eighth Army, are authorized to establish conference areas and/or designate tactical organizational sectors as conference areas, whichever most suitably conforms to the participation capabilities and admission limitations of respective commands. Any pattern established, however, will be in keeping with the general provisions of this directive.

The Commanding Generals, Korean Communications Zone and Eighth Army, will notify the Commanding General, United States Army Forces, Far East, of any changes in respective conference organizational structures.

Composition: Each conference will be composed of all United States Army Forces units and/or organizations located within conference boundaries. Commanding generals of the areas indicated in paragraphs … above, may invite individuals, units, and/or organizations of another service to participate in team and individual sports competitions at installation and conference levels but not at major command levels where teams are competing for the right to represent the command in United States Army Forces, Far East championship events, leading to All-Army competitions except as indicated … above. No sports tournaments which will conflict with the established United

States Army Forces, Far East, sports program as currently in operation will be conducted by units or commands.

Definitions: <u>Intra-Installation Programs</u> Are defined as the sports programs conducted at each post, camp, and station in which no inter-installation competitions are scheduled. <u>Intra-Conference Programs</u> will be those sports competitions between posts, camps, and stations and/or separate units and organizations within each conference area. These competitions will be designed so as to determine conference championships in each sport. <u>Inter-Conference Programs</u> will be those competitions between sports conferences and each geographic area covered ... above, to determine a major command championship for entry in AFFE championship events. <u>United States Army Forces, Far East Championship Events</u> will be those tournaments and meets scheduled by this headquarters for the purpose of ascertaining champions in certain selected sports.

Responsibility: In order to provide continuity and maintain normal command channels, the following responsibilities are announced: Headquarters, United States Army Forces, Far East, will exercise command supervision over all phases of the United States Army Forces, Far East, sports program (and will) supervise and govern a United States Army Forces, Far East, Sports Council, subdivided into committees, as shown below, which will serve as advisory groups on related functions. The Sports Committee will be composed of one representative from each addressee command. This committee will advise concerning all sports covered by this directive.

Major Subordinate Commands - Commanders of the following major subordinate commands will be responsible for supervision of sports conferences: <u>XVI Corps</u> – Hokkaido

Sports Conference and Northern Honshu Sports Conference. Central Command – Tokyo Area Sports Conference, and Yokohama Area Sports Conference. Southwestern Command – Southern Honshu Sports Conference and Kyushu Sports Conference. Eighth Army, Korean Communications Zone and Ryukyus Command – Such sports conferences as may be established in accordance with ... (the) above.

Each commanding general concerned will assign a competent commissioned officer or a qualified civilian sports director, whichever is considered most appropriate, to serve as Conference Director of each sports conference covered by this directive.

In Korea, those assignments may be on an additional duty basis or as a full time duty performed by personnel assigned to Eighth Army and/or Korean Communications Zone, as determined by the respective Commanding General.

Conference Directors will be responsible to the Commanding General concerned for the administration and conduct of conference activities, including the organization and operation of leagues and tournaments and the assignment of officials thereto; promotion of and assisting of intra-installation sports programs; organizing and conducting conference officiating and coaching clinics; coordinating arrangements with WAC Detachment sports representative for WAC sports activities; coordinating arrangement for sports competitions with indigenous teams and civilian communities within conference boundaries; and related conference duties.

Commanding Generals will establish a Sports Council for each sports conference which will be representative of units, organizations, and installations within conference areas. These councils will serve as the commander's advisory groups on all matters pertaining to respective conferences, including joint Japanese-American recreational activities. Meetings will be held as frequently as considered necessary, but not less often than once every six months.

Conference directors will function as chairman and recorders or these positions may be filled by majority vote of council members. Minutes will be kept and submitted to respective major command commanders for approval within ten days following each meeting. Upon approval one copy of the minutes will be forwarded to this headquarters, Attention: Special Services Officer.

Councils will be empowered to settle all disputes and protests connected with the intra-conference competitions, suspend, for limited periods of time, players, coaches, or officials for unsportsmanlike acts; proposed rules and regulations, within over-all policies, covering activities of each conference; assure strict compliance with the provisions ... below; and will individually promote and encourage maximum sports activities and participation within their own units, organizations, and installations.

Operations. Commanding Generals concerned will organize each sports conference in order to best accomplish the following:

Intra-Installation Programs. Assure the operation of competitive sports programs at each post, camp, station, and in separate units and organizations, with a view toward every military person's actively engaging in sports of his own choosing. Such activities will be comprehensive in scope and designed to progress into conference championships.

Intra-Conference Programs. Insofar as practicable, operate inter-post, camp, and station leagues in major sports, to include but not limited to football, basketball, baseball and boxing, with emphasis being placed on maximum spectator interest and player participation; conduct tournaments and meets in as many other sports, such as tennis, track and field, swimming, golf, etc. as practicable; coordinate free-time recreational sports with on-duty physical training programs to accomplish complete cooperation in the development of physical fitness and to generate interest in improving sports skills; conduct a Women's Army Corps sports program for those sports that WAC personnel may most desirably compete in; provide suitable awards for all competitions so as to encourage maximum participation at all levels; conduct training programs and clinics to continually improve conference coaching and officiating; promote close relationships with local indigenous communities in the furtherance of recreational activities of joint interest.

General Policies and Procedures, Amateurism. Amateurs may compete with and against professionals in all sports except boxing without loss of amateur standing, providing such competition is in connection with the United States Army Forces, Far East, sports program. Military teams may compete against civilian professional teams without jeopardizing the amateur standing of competitors, when the contest is staged by a military unit or organization. Any member of the Armed Forces who engages in professional games or contests as an individual or as a member of a team other than a service team, shall thereby render himself ineligible to compete as an amateur. Prior to permitting them to compete in sports events which are for amateurs only, such as those officially sanctioned by the United States Amateur Athletic Union and the United States

Olympics Committee, commanders concerned will ascertain the amateur status of each participant. The number of officers on teams competing in United States Army Forces, Far East, championship events will not exceed 50% of the total team strength on the playing field or court at any one time. Unit identity and/or distinctive team names should be preserved at all levels of competition in order to sustain organizational esprit-de-corps. Teams comprised of personnel from two or more units will carry the unit designation of the organization with the predominant number of participants.

Maximum levels of competition. Teams entered in inter-conference basketball, baseball, football, and soccer competitions will be from regiment, regimental combat teams and/or units with an aggregate strength not exceeding 5000 men. Flag-football, softball, and volleyball teams will be from companies, batteries, or comparable sized units. The grouping of smaller units which have an aggregate strength not exceeding 250 men is authorized. Companies and batteries with the strength exceeding 250 men will field two teams. Competition levels for all other team sports will be determined by the Sports Council for each conference. In individual type sports, the most outstanding athletes will be selected, on an individual basis, as team members at all levels of competition.

Eligibility. Personnel will not be transferred, placed on TDY, or otherwise attached to units for the purpose of strengthening sports teams. When a team representing its parent unit or organization is entered and the progressive levels of tournament play to determine the United States Army Forces, Far East championship team, the personnel of that team will not be augmented or reinforced at any level of play.

If a member of a team is transferred, sustains an injury or for military reasons is unable to continue play, the parent unit or organization may substitute a member of that unit or organization to fill the vacancy. The individual substituted must have been a member of that unit or organization prior to the entry of its team in the progressive tournament play for the United States Army Forces, Far East Championship. It shall be the responsibility of each Sports Council to establish the dates for submission of rosters for appropriate leagues and tournaments in the lower levels of progressive play.

An officer authorized by each major commander will certify that his team has not been strengthened through personnel transfers or reinforced by the selection of outstanding individuals from the parent organization as indicated ... This certificate will be submitted to reach the host command headquarters, Attention: Special Services Officer at least 72 hours in advance of the opening date of the United States Army Forces, Far East tournaments. An information copy of this certificate will be forwarded to this headquarters.

Pay of Officials. Payment of commissioned officers who are warrant officers acting as officials at sports events will be in accordance with paragraph 6c (3) Army Regulations 210-50, 4 November 1953, "Payment from non-appropriated funds two commissioned officers or a warrant officers for services rendered is not authorized, except for personal expenses when voluntarily officiating at sports events or in the conduct of educational, religious or entertainment activities."

Personal expenses may include maintenance of required uniform, necessary travel, subsistence and lodging incident to participation in such activities. Home team installations will be responsible for compensation of all officials who officiate at contest played at such installations. Maximum rates of pay shown in the ... table may be exceeded when necessary for AFFE–level tournament competitions.

Supply and equipment. Commanders concerned will be responsible for providing supplies and equipment for teams and/or individuals from their commands who compete in inter-conference and United States Army Forces, Far East, championship events. As protection against eye cuts and ear and head injuries, a light weight (sic) head guard will be warm by each participant in boxing matches conducted by any post, camp, and station or separate organization of the united (sic) States Army Forces, Far East. These head guards will provide a layer of protective material, at least one-half inch in thickness, covering the ears, eye ridge, temples, and back of head.

Trophies and Awards. No cash prizes will be awarded any contestant in any sports event. United States Savings Bonds and similar instruments are considered to be cash prizes. Trophies, medals or awards, (other than cash), may be awarded in connection with sports events within the following maximum costs:

> Intra-Installation or Regimental Events. Individual awards $7.50; team awards $15.00.

Intra-Conference or Major Command Events. Individual awards $10.00; team awards $20.00.

Sport	Authorized Level of Compensation	Maximum Rate Per Game	Maximum No of Officials Recommended
Badminton	Tournaments only	$5.00 per day	1 Referee
Baseball	Battalion	$10.00 per game	2 Umpires per game
	Regimental or Intra-Conference	$20.00 per game	3 Umpires per game
Basketball	Company or Battalion	$6.00 per game	2 Officials
	Regimental or Intra-Conference	$20.00 per game	2 Officials
Bowling	Tournaments only	$5.00 per day	2 Foul judges each
Boxing	Regimental or Intra-Conference	$10.00 per day $5.00 per day	1 Referee 3 Judges each
Football(11 Man)	Regimental or Intra-Conference	$80.00 per game	4 Officials
Flag-Football	Company League play	$9.00 per game	3 Officials
Horseshoes	Tournament only	$5.00 per day	1 Referee
Handball	Tournament only	$5.00 per day	1 Referee
Hand Grenade Throw	Tournament only	$5.00 per day	1 Official
Softball	Company	$6.00	2 Umpires
Swimming	Meet only	$7.50 per day each	1 Starter 1 Clerk
Track & Field	Meet only	$7.50 per day each	1 Starter & Clerk

9

AFFE Championship Events. Individual awards $25.00; team awards $75.00.

Rules. Rules of the following organizations will govern conduct of all sports contests conducted as part of the United States Army Forces, Far East, sports program [Author note: There is a list of which organization's rules are used for each sport; the main sports featured in this book (football, basketball) adhered to National Collegiate Athletic Association (NCAA) rules.

Boxing and Track and Field adhered to National Amateur Athletic Union (now AAU) rules].

Commanders will insure (sic) compliance with provisions of Letter, AGAC-C (M) 220.3 (18 May 54) C-1, Department of the Army, 24 May 1954, subject: "Assignment and Utilization of athletes, Entertainers, and other Nationally known Personnel," and Letter AG 200.3 (22 Dec 52), GA this headquarters, 22 December 1952, Subject: "Assignment of Personnel." "Known name athletes" will not receive preferential treatment because of their athletic ability nor will outstanding athletes be retained at processing centers or replacement depots.

Publicity. It is desired that continuing publicity be given to the United States Army Forces, Far East, sports program through every possible source and that each activity be widely publicized in order for every individual to be completely aware of events being staged and to assure full and active spectator interest.

There appears a brief history of "Special Services" Bowl Games in the 20 December 1953 Torii Bowl program (Air Force vs Navy), prepared by Lt. Col. E. E. Allen, HQ. 3 rd. MARDIV; LCDR Arthur B Lyons, COMNAVFE; Mr. L. Hoeck, HQ AFFE; and Mr. John Scially, HQ. FEAF, as follows:

At home in the United States during this season of traditional "bowl" games with all the attendant color and atmosphere surrounding them are being played in various sections of the country. Football classics such as the Rose Bowl of Pasadena, California; the Cotton Bowl of Dallas, Texas; Miami's Orange Bowl; and the Sugar Bowl of New Orleans, Louisiana; bring together some of the finest teams in the land in contests which will determine to a large degree the relative merits of football as it is played in different sections of the United States.

"Bowl" Games in overseas theaters were first inaugurated on New Year's Day of 1946, in keeping with an important part of the mission of Special Services, which is to make recreation away from home as near as homelike as possible wherever American troops are stationed. Far East annual bowl affairs presently consist of Japan's Torii Bowl and Rice Bowl, Guam's Sweat Bowl, Okinawa's Rock Bowl, and Philippine's Bamboo Bowl.

The Bowl classic in Japan was originally set up as a service game between All-Star teams of Korea and Japan. In 1948 the game was made an inter-service affair between the Air Force All-Stars and the Army All-Stars from units in Japan.

In previous Rice Bowl contests, Japan's 1946 team defeated Korea 6-0, while Korea upset Japan 19-13 in 1947 and repeated in 1948 by a score of 18-13, 1949 saw the Army All-Stars defeating the Air Force All-Stars by a 13-7 score with the Air Force coming back to defeat the Army 18-14 the following year. Last year Navy defeated Air Foace (sic) in the First Annual Torii Bowl 20-13 and Army defeated Navy in the Rice Bowl 25-6.

In order to determine a Japan Inter-Service Football Champion, it is necessary this year to add another Bowl game so that all four (4) branches of service: Air Force, Navy, Army and Marines may participate. Earlier this year representatives of all four branches of service met and the result of the draw produced the Air Force playing Navy in the Second Annual Torii Bowl in Tokyo, and the Army playing the Marines in the First Annual Sukiyaki Bowl in Kyoto, Japan on the same day. The winner of the Torii Bowl will play in the winner of the Sukiyaki Bowl in the Sixth Annual Rice Bowl – the winner to be declared the 1953 Inter-Service Champions.

This Torii Bowl game-program summary is integral for purposes of understanding the overall history, structure, and bowl game legacy of the AFFE Special Services football program. There is very little published or searchable information about the various bowl games, but I suspect there are game programs or other memorabilia out there, possibly stored in someone's home – please contact the author if you have something you would be willing to contribute to a future edition (affe8a@gmail.com).

Somewhat surprisingly, I have been unable to find any AFFE bowl game video footage or further photos of actual bowl game action. I would appreciate hearing from someone if you have something that documents one or more of the bowl games from the mid-1950s.

FOOTBALL GAMES AND OTHER SPORTS/RECREATIONAL ACTIVITY

"There is little recompense for Army athletes except the admiration of one's comrades-in-arms" - Maj. Gen. F.C. Holbrook, Commanding General, United States Army, 1955.

This section describes sports events and activity pertaining to the AFFE Service Sports program. Entries were taken from military memos, contemporary newspaper sports articles, and archival documentation.

This section is intended not to be a narrative as much as it is a record and history through chronological documentation, though there is some accompanying commentary. I also expanded athletic reports by researching and providing background information on some of the athletes, particularly those whose pre- and post- service accomplishments were notable.

You will notice some apparent gaps in time and information. This is not oversight, but simply a product of incomplete archival records. In actuality a very small percentage of records were kept and archived over many decades (National Archives II, Maryland, claims only 3% or less of all records were kept/archived), and those that *were* kept were often housed in scattered locations, databases, and facilities. What you will see in this section has been pieced together from many different sources.

While it remains an open question as to whether AFFE major Service Sports such as football and basketball were on par with their CONUS counterparts, I offer as evidence the contents of this book, which clearly outlines the generally high-level competition within AFFE.

The level of excellence was not only a product of the individual talent of AFFE athletes, but it was also a product of the highest level of instruction by way of guest-coaching and referee clinics conducted on a

69

regular basis. These clinics featured top American college coaches and referees.

There was a reason 30,000-plus fans turned out to see championship football played in amazing venues like Meiji Stadium and Korakuen Stadium (which preceded the Tokyo Dome at its current site).

It should be kept in mind that the 1954 AFFE Service Sports seasons took place not long after Korean fighting had formally ceased, making it reasonable to expect some ramp-up in quality and overall performance level over time. I believe the mid-1950s were the pinnacle of old-school Service Sports in the Far East.

The extent of Service Sports in the Far East from 1946 to Korean War Armistice is less clear, though *Pacific Stars and Stripes* reported a fair amount of stateside military sporting news during that time. Keep in mind that a large Far East base like Camp Casey in Korea, which was heavily involved in mid-1950s Service Sports, was not established until 1952.

1930s MILITARY FOOTBALL; A PRECURSOR TO "MODERN" SERVICE SPORTS

Despite the apparent scarcity of older historical information for overseas Service Sports, specifically football, the 13 June 1986 *Los Angeles Times* reported on domestic United States Military Service League football, which included heroes from the 1930s to the 1950s, such as Tex Guentert, Albert Jantz, Bill Asimos, Robert (Bull) Trometter, and A.C. Raimondi. The article interestingly noted that "None made a name for himself in professional sports, but all had a tremendous impact on the people of San Diego" (35).

Mr. Dolan said that "Military sporting events were considered the 'in' place to be in San Diego." He further said that military sports had declined during the Vietnam War and never fully recovered; the emphasis was changed from varsity sports to intramural competition.

Among the best military football teams in San Diego was Battle Force of the Navy, Mr. Dolan wrote. From 1931 to 1933, Battle Force amassed a record of sixteen wins and three losses. The player-coach was Tom Hamilton, an All-American halfback from the Naval Academy, said Mr. Dolan.

In 1931, this team defeated Army All-Stars 17-0; its first win against the Stars since 1926 (35). They repeated the win in 1932 with a score of 32-0. Both games had been played in front of 70,000 fans at Memorial Stadium in Berkeley, California. Mr. Hamilton said they "took the best players from submarines, battleships, cruisers, and so forth." Battle Force also beat the Marines handily in 1931, 1932 and 1933 in front of capacity crowds at Balboa Stadium.

Mr. Hamilton said he never had equal manpower to the Battle Force teams when he coached at the Naval Academy and Pitt (35). The Marines, however, later beat Santa Clara which had recently appeared in the Sugar Bowl, and the San Diego State Aztecs.

Mr. Dolan quoted Bull Trometter, who played for the Marines from 1935 to 1940, as saying "There were about 26,000 or 27,000 Marines in the service then. We had two teams; San Diego on the West Coast and Quantico on the East coast … you're talking about … 80 people total on the two teams."

Stan Winters, Special Services Director at the Naval Training Center from 1945 to 1980, told Mr. Dolan that "During the war years, all of the name athletes were in some branch of the service. The sports tapered off after World War II, but there was still good competition. Then came the Korea thing in the 1950s, and people were pressed back into the service."

Marine coach Scotty Harris said military athletes "Lived a pretty good life. A lot of them worked in Special Services ... we used to practice until 5 or 6 at night. We expected them to put out, too."

Mr. Hamilton said that "Tex (Guentert) would have been an All-American if he had gone to college. He was a great ballplayer." The Marines also had a very good player in Volney (Skeets) Quinlan, who eventually played for the Los Angeles Rams.

The Marine team was disbanded in 1964 and was never reorganized.

1953

The 17 June 1953 edition of the *Stars and Stripes* provided some insight into what was to come with an "Announcement" stating that,

> All former football officials, coaches, and players interested in officiating football games this year are requested to contact Mr. John P. Scially, executive secretary of the Japan Athletic Officials Association ... The first meeting is planned in early July. FEAF (Far East Air Force) and AFFE football official clinics will be conducted the weeks of August 10-14 and August 17-21 respectively (36).

The *Stars and Stripes* reported on 16 February 1953 that "American soldiers in Korea have the highest morality of any group of people in the world," according to Rt. Rev. Austin Pardue, Episcopal bishop of Pittsburgh (37). He said, "If the American people at home gave proportionally, there wouldn't be any poverty or want." He added, "They have reached a spirit of humility, true humility in helping each other stay alive."

This commentary favorably speaks to the quality of individuals who would participate in Service Sports post-Armistice, as illustrated below:

Stars and Stripes reported on 13 March 1953 the astonishing story of Dick Kempthorn. Former Michigan football star and Service Sports player, 2d Lt. Dick Kempthorn, freed a fellow pilot from a burning airplane with his bare hands (38).

1st Lt. Henry Rock's P51 Mustang was taxiing slowly on the runway, "zigzagging from side to side so he could see ahead," when he was hit by another plane which had landed behind him, not noticing Rock's plane.

The second P51 hit Rock from behind, and "drove right up on top" of Rock's plane, while the propeller "chewed through the tail and fuselage of Rock's plane and came to a rest with the propeller and propeller hub directly over Rock's cockpit."

Fire broke out due to a broken fuel line and Rock's exit from his plane was blocked.

Kempthorn "sprinted 200 yards to the crash scene" and jumped on the plane. He "tore at the windshield canopy of thick, bulletproof glass" and pulled it loose, but Rock's path to safety was still blocked by a gunsight, until Kempthorn broke the one-eighth inch thick metal with his bare hands.

Rock said, "I was absolutely trapped. I didn't think there was any way possible to get out. Fire was coming up through the cockpit … It would ordinarily take a good sledgehammer blow to dislodge that gunsight." Kempthorn cut the straps holding Rock in place and pulled him to safety, after which the plane exploded.

Mr. Kempthorn's obituary is a fountain of information. He died on 8 February 2019 at the age of 92 (39). In the Detroit News article, Mr. Paul said that "Richard 'Dick' Kempthorn made his mark on the field for the Michigan Wolverines as member of the 1947 and 1948 national champions, and as the team's Most Valuable Player during the 1949 campaign."

Mr. Paul said that in 1966 Mr. Kempthorn had spoken with 17-year-old (and later famous NFL star) Dan Dierdorf, wherein they discussed the University of Michigan. Mr. Dierdorf eventually chose Michigan and became an All-American, a College Football Hall-of-Famer, and a pro football Hall-of-Famer. Mr. Dierdorf and Mr. Kempthorn maintained their friendship for more than 50 years.

Mr. Dierdorf had an interesting observation about Mr. Kempthorn, in which he said,

> "Michigan is a school where they do everything right … Dick is one of those guys where the world is very black and white … he never varied from that straight and narrow path, where there was a right way to do things … that's just the way he is." Mr. Kempthorn had begun his career at Miami as a fullback and linebacker before he joined the Marines, with whom he saw combat on the USS Wild Hunter in the invasion of the Philippines during World War II (39).

Post-war, Mr. Kempthorn played only one football game in 1947 before becoming a starter in 1948. After the 1949 season, however, he didn't pursue professional football, though Mr. Dierdorf believes he could have. He was drafted in the 1948 NFL draft in the 14th round, and in the All-American Conference in the second round, but he ultimately decided not to pursue this path, having instead chosen to work for the family car dealership businesses.

Kempthorn later enlisted in the Air Force and served three years in Korea, where he flew more than 100 missions, and, according to his obituary, he "once rescued a fellow pilot from a burning jet in Japan and eventually would receive the Distinguished Flying Cross" (39). His Michigan teammates signed a football and sent it to Korea. Mr. Dierdorf said that Mr. Kempthorn, "… led a life worth remembering at everything he accomplished."

Stars and Stripes reported on football coaching clinics in the 25 July 1953 edition: "Grid Coaches End Clinic in Far East" (40), noting "The seeds of the Army's 1953 football season in the Far East weigh over 14,000 pounds, as 68 economy sized soldiers graduated from the AFFE football clinic at Camp Yokohama's Fryar Gym." They would now begin building teams in the home units.

The coaches were from units and football conferences in Ryu-kyus, Korea, Hokkaido, Northern Honshu, and Yokohama areas, "and were topped by 240-pounder, PFC Charles McDonald, Athens, O., from the mountaineers of Eta Jima. He was a tackle for Ohio University, Athens, O., in 1948, '49 and '50."

60% of the graduating coaches had college football experience, and "nearly all of them boast playing experience." Ray Elliot from the University of Illinois, Rusty Russell from Southern Methodist, and Len Casanova from the University of Oregon gave the coaches a five-day course on organizing and running their future grid "elevens."

Also on 25 July 1953, *Stars and Stripes* reported on a new headquarters for AFFE at Camp Zama, which would be a facility for 3000 men at a cost of $5,000,000. The new facility consolidated supporting units, which had been "scattered throughout Yokohama" (41).

The facility would accommodate "the tremendous expansion of personnel at Zama during the next few months," and "most post recreational facilities will be doubled in capacity."

The headquarters was modeled after the Pentagon, and was built of reinforced concrete. It was to be "a hub of recreational facilities for the surrounding area," and would include a 9-hole golf course, a 12-lane bowling alley, visiting VIP quarters, a fieldhouse in which "three basketball games may be played simultaneously," as well as a new airstrip. The service club would be converted to a recreation center for civilian employees on the post.

The 12 September 1953 *Stars and Stripes* reported that the 27th (Wolfhound) Infantry regiment provided "an enlarged peacetime morale-building program for frontline troops" by expanding the athletic and recreation schedule; "the new program calls for maximum participation in a variety of sports to attain higher troop morale." There would be company-level competition, and "Each battalion will have a number of volleyball and basketball courts, boxing rings, and athletic fields for general sport activities" (42).

In keeping with the above entry concerning facilities, the 16 September 1953 *Stars and Stripes* told us that "Warriors at 23d Infantry Regiment are busily engaged in constructing a huge sports arena for use on their unit day" (43). The arena was to be located in the center of the regimental area, and would include softball and football fields, volleyball courts, a track, and horseshoe lanes.

More facilities news: On 8 October 1953, *Stars and Stripes* reported that 2d "Spearheader" Battalion of the 38th Infantry Regiment had opened new athletic facilities, including two football fields; "a vigorous program of inter-company athletics has been set up" (44).

The U.S. military was not alone in promoting healthy recreation. The 11 October 1953 *Stars and Stripes* said that the British 1st Commonwealth Division had set up "an extensive athletic and recreational program" to include three types of football: soccer, rugby, and Australian Rules football. Australian Rules was "regarded by some as the roughest form of football" (45) - there is no protective equipment.

Another aspect of the program was PT (physical training) leader's courses, which served the purpose of "hardening the men and showing them ways of educating fellow soldiers in the proper physical training methods." Lastly, the article discussed "language difficulty" with the French-Canadian leaders who spoke only French, though their arm and hand gestures were "surprisingly well understood."

The 6 November 1953 edition of the *Stars and Stripes* reported that Marines from Camp Fisher would meet Army at Camp Gifu in a Southern Honshu Conference football game (46).

11 November 1953 *Stars and Stripes* included an article on the Special Services, noting that "The athletics program of Special Services is probably the most extensive" (47). It said the program, which began in 1943, "has become an established and vital part of Army life ... In an overseas theater such as the Far East Command, Special Services activities do much to combat the morale-destroying effects of boredom, loneliness and homesickness ..." In Japan, Korea, and Okinawa there were 54 service clubs "which have an average total monthly attendance of 1.5 million."

Sports occupied a major portion of the serviceman's recreation time. There were 18 sports activities, from "skiing to swimming ... several hundred teams represented units from company to command level in sports such as basketball, baseball, football, softball, and volleyball." It was noted that "leading personalities in the field" gave instructional clinics, including Len Casanova ... Tippy Dyer, Ray Oosting, and Bruce Drake."

The 19 November 1953 edition of the *Stars and Stripes* told readers that 1st Lt. Gerald L. Roberts spent three hours on Saturdays giving a sports clinic for Korean boys ages 5-13 at the 57th Battalion's McDonald Field (48). He taught boys fundamentals of softball and football. There were about 50 "enthusiastic participants."

The 23 November 1953 *Stars and Stripes* reported that Thanksgiving activities in the Tokyo area would include a football game between the Camp Tokyo Bulldogs and the FEAF Base Tornadoes (49), noting that

"Americans and Japanese alike are expected to be on hand in large numbers to witness the two powerful service teams battle it out for American and Japanese scouts in Japan and Okinawa." This would be the fifth anniversary of the Thanksgiving Classic which began in 1948.

The Tornadoes had finished second in the Northern District of the Air Force Conference (7-2), and the Bulldogs were Central Command Army champions (6-1). The article said that the Bulldogs had a slim weight advantage at a 204 lb. average on the line, with the Tornadoes having a 184 lb. average on the line.

Bulldog halfbacks included Johnny Kaston, who had played at Boston University for four years, and Charles Cravey, who played with the University of Washington. Tornado halfbacks included Art Paul, "a veteran of four years with service football," and Don Hildreth, who had been a player at Oregon State. Hildreth was also listed as the 1952 All-Air Force high hurdles champion.

Coaches included Lt. Don Martin for the Bulldogs and Larry Rouble for the Tornadoes.

"Tickets for Japanese are on sale for 50 yen." In U.S. ducats, the price was $1.00 for adults and 50 cents for students. There was music scheduled for halftime as well as Queen representation.

24 November 1953 *Stars and Stripes* announced that in an effort to increase morale, the 3rd Division would build "four large recreation centers located to serve the maximum number of men with the most recreation and entertainment possible" (50). The 24 November edition also announced that Shirley Peterson and S/Sgt. Martha Williams would reign as co-Queens at the fifth annual Camp Tokyo-FEAF Base Thanksgiving Day football game at Meiji Stadium for the benefit of the Far East Boy and Girl Scout Fund.

According to the 25 November 1953 *Stars and Stripes*, 15 buses would carry grid spectators to Meiji Stadium for the Thanksgiving Day football game from the Grant Heights commissary, the Washington Heights Commissary, the Dai Iti Hotel, the Osaka Hotel, the NYK Bus Terminal, the Jefferson Heights Administration Office, the Finance building, and the Palace Heights Administration Office. The buses would be marked "football special."

This edition also discussed a friendly dispute among football fans as to in which part of the United States the best football is played. It was said that "Southerner" players sometimes go to teams in the north, and vice versa. The article said that because the Big Ten dominated the Rose Bowl series against Pacific Coast Conference, that the Midwest "is tops."

The November 24th edition also had an interesting discussion of the evolution of the football itself, "descended from the Rugby ball used in the 1800s" (51). The shape of the ball had "evolved considerably in the 84 years the game has been in existence."

Football originally started with a rugby-type ball, which lasted approximately 40 years. When the forward pass was introduced to the game in the early 1900's, the ball was refined to a more streamlined shape to accommodate spiral passing, described as a "prolate spheroid." In the 1930s, the shape of the ball settled into the standard modern-type football.

The 28 November 1953 *Stars and Stripes* reported that a "large holiday crowd" witnessed Nagoya "trample" Itami 19-7 to clinch the Southern Conference Air Force championship in Nagoya's Mizuho Stadium (from photo caption).

Camp Tokyo Bulldogs beat the FEAF Base Tornadoes 28-0 (*Stars and Stripes* photo caption) "at Meiji" in the 5th Annual Turkey Day Classic. Noted in the photo caption are FEAF end Grady Merriman and FEAF tackle Ernest Fitzgibbons, as well as Frank Miyaki, Bob Kruckenberg, and Chuck Ilianokalea of FEAF. Shown also was Jim Gregorson of Camp Tokyo (52).

The 29 November paper further reported Rice Bowl results from HQ Chunchon Area Command, Korea. The Thanksgiving Day football "Rice Bowl" game ended with a 55th Transportation Truck Battalion 26-0 victory over the 69th Transportation Truck Battalion (53).

Mentioned were the outstanding performances of Richard Davies, Algusta Yarbary, Herschel Garrett, George Keely, Raymond Winkler, and Larry Tankersley of the 55th.

Thanksgiving Day had more football action, including a tilt between the 45th Division Thunderbirds and the 67th Ordnance team. The Thunderbirds had come "roaring back," sparked by the "brilliant passing of halfback Glen Braunschwig, former University of Wisconsin football player."

Another former Wisconsin player, "Frosty" Parrish, contributed to a first half score for the Thunderbirds. The first half of the game was said to have been a "hard fought defensive battle," and the final score was 19-0, Thunderbirds.

In yet another game summary for that busy Thanksgiving Day, we learn that "Middies win Korea Army-Navy Game." This contest took place in Pusan, where the "Navy Detachment powered its way to a 26-20 football victory." The game was "billed as the Korean version of the Army-Navy game."

Photo: Paloma Mizuho Stadium, pre-renovation, 15.08.2016 © 円
周率3パーセント (CC BY-SA 4.0)

)

Photo: Paloma Mizuho Stadium, year unknown, pre-renovation -
Wikimedia Commons

Former All-American TCU halfback, Gil Bartosh, "smashed through Army's defense for all four of the Sailor's touchdowns and passed to Red Rehwalt for two conversions." Nearly 5000 fans had been in the stands at the Korean Base Section's Hialeah Compound Field.

The players had been attached to fleet activities in the Pusan area, and were part of an Army All-Star "aggregation" (54). Notable players were Bartosh and Rehwaldt of the Navy, and Dave Hart and Ben Coot from the Army.

Gil Bartosh had been known as the "Granger Ghost" for his days playing football for Granger High School in Granger, Texas, in the 1940s. His obituary provides extensive details on his life and football career (55).

Mr. Bartosh lived from 21 May 1930 to 4 June 2016. He was a football star at Granger High School, and later excelled at TCU, leading the league in rushing in 1950, and earning All-Southwest Conference honors.

In 1951, he "helped lift the Frogs to a SWC title and a trip to the Cotton Bowl."

> (Mr. Bartosh) served as a U.S. Naval officer during the Korean conflict and played service football for the U.S. Navy's Yokosuka Seahawks. One of Gil's most prized possessions was the Army-Navy game ball he was awarded in Pusan, Korea, in 1953. In 1954, Gil's team capped a perfect season by going 11-0, outscoring opponents by a combined total of 391-41. The team was crowned Central Command Conference Champions. Gil was named to the Central Command all-star team and was the top vote getter for the offensive backfield.
>
> (*Author note: This is one of the rare former AFFE player obituaries which contains detailed information about their Service Sports playing days overseas.*)

Mr. Bartosh played one year professionally in the CFL, and then turned his attention to coaching, where he attained further success, including WAC Co-Coach of the Year and entry into the Texas High School Hall of Fame and the Texas Coaches Association Hall of Honor.

Thank you for your service, and rest in peace, Mr. Bartosh.

The 4 December 1953 *Stars and Stripes* said that buses were being made available for the 6 December AFFE semifinal football game between the Camp Tokyo Bulldogs and the 187th Airborne Rakkasans at Camp Drake Field, and "187th Drills for Crucial Tokyo Tilt" (56). Note: "Rakkasan", roughly meaning "umbrella man" in Japanese, had been derived "from the shape of the parachute canopy" (57).

The game "should be one of the best of the season," as the Rakkasans had been undefeated and secured victories with "overwhelming scores." As noted, the *Rakkasans had posted an incredible 391 points against opponents throughout the season*. Working hard were halfbacks Harold G. Call and E. Surma, who were Rakkasans' leading scorers.

This same edition further reported that FEAMCOM placed five players on the Air Force Japan All-Northern Conference football team, including quarterback Rock Campbell; "The Marauders, who won eight and lost three during the regular season, were voted all of the slots on the right side of the line by coaches and sports writers around the league."

Conference champion Misawa added two linemen, Roy Hinna and Bob Heard, also earned Japan All-Northern Conference honors. Former college players included Bud Turrentine with Johnson, Fred Britton with Ohio and Trinity, Roy Hina with Western Kentucky, Luke Welch with Baylor (two-time All-Southwest), Del Flanagan with Georgia Tech, and Sam Petrovich with Marquette. Rock Campbell and Frank Miyaki had been with Washington State.

An interesting side note in this same edition said that the famous Roger Bannister would not be able to compete at indoor meets in the U.S. due to his hospital work as a medical student. Who knew that the world's first sub-4:00 miler would also find success in the medical field? It's interesting to consider that our football heroes had been playing contemporaneously with one of the world's most well-known running stars.

The 4 December 1953 edition also tells us that halfback Staten Webster "won top honors in the Hokkaido Sports Conference scoring parade this season by tallying eight touchdowns for the fourth place Camp Crawford Special Troops." Fullback Ralph Patrick of the fifth place Chitose Special Troops came in second with seven touchdowns - incredible performances by both.

5 December 1953 *Stars and Stripes* reported that the 187th Rakkasans had been favored over the Bulldogs in the semifinal of the Army section of the AFFE football tournament (58). The 187th RCT Rakkasans had averaged 65 points in six games. Camp Tokyo Bulldogs' 8-1 record included a loss to "the powerful Yokosuka Navy, with halfback John Kaston."

The Rakkasans featured Howard Call, who scored an impressive eleven touchdowns for the year. The winner of the match would travel to Sendai "for a crack at the winner of the XVI Corps playoff," with a shot to be crowned Japan's All-Army Champion. Following that game the "Army champ will meet the Navy titlist for the right to meet the winner of the Marines-Air Force game in the Rice Bowl on Jan. 1."

The 7 December 1953 *Stars and Stripes* reported, "Camp Tokyo Gridsters Crush Rakkasans 35-0" (59). The paper said, "Some 3000 fans looked on in amazement yesterday as an underdog Camp Tokyo football team romped to an easy 35-0 upset victory over the highly touted 187th RCT Rakkasans at Drake Field." The Bulldogs set the pace with an 88-

yard drive following the opening kickoff for a score by halfback John Kaston.

The victory gave Camp Tokyo a place in the Japan All-Army Championship the following Sunday at Sendai (noted elsewhere in the same edition to be the largest city in Northen Honshu at the time, with 400,000 persons) against XVI Corps. The article said that the Rakkasans, though favorites, had never been close in the blowout match.

Halfback Charles Gravey and quarterback Al Caruso contributed to the win with scoring plays. The Bulldog's other quarterback/defensive player, George Pickett, intercepted a pass and then later "tossed a 12-yarder to Dusty Rhodes in the end zone." The story wryly ends with plaudits for Rakkasan players, stating "quarterback Ed Maher and end Joe Portash were the standouts for the *overrated airborne crew* (Ed. – italics added)."

The 8 December 1953 edition (60) also reported victory for the Ashiya Mustangs over the Clark Air Force Base All-Stars in the Philippine's Bamboo Bowl, 44-6.

The Atsugi Flyers warmed up for their semi-final All-Service football championship battle with Nagoya (the Air Force representative) on December 20 at Meiji Stadium; the winner would play the winner of the Army-Marine game in the Rice Bowl on 1 January.

The 10 December 1953 *Stars and Stripes* announced, "KBS Champs Get Awards" (61). The Hialeah Warriors, Korean Section champions, received the KBS football trophy at a sports banquet in the mess hall on the Hialeah compound. "Co-captains Jim Hock, Chicago, Ill. and Cpl. Bob Lovely, Boston, Mass., received the trophy for the team." The award was presented by First Lt. Anthony Cerrilli, from Aliquippa, Pa.

The Warriors had won ten straight games during the season. They were awarded a trophy for being compound champions; "Tokens of appreciation and trophies were also awarded to the team physician and assistants."

Bob Lovely's obituary (62) says that his life's passion was football, and that he had been a member of the University of Tampa's Hall of Fame (1964 induction), and he played in the NFL with the Chicago Cardinals. "He served in the Army and was a veteran of the Korean War." He was born in South Groveland, Massachusetts, and died on 7 August 2017. He was preceded in death by his wife, Jean, and is survived by many who loved him. RIP, hero.

Stars and Stripes reported 18 December 1953 that Camp Tokyo Bulldogs were winners of the 1953 AFFE Football Championship in Tokyo, and that they would be traveling to Kyoto to participate in the Sukiyaki Bowl against the Camp Fisher Marines. The Bulldogs would be staying at Camp Otsu (63).

At the same time, *Stars and Stripes* reported on a Touch Football Championship game from Pusan, South Korea, in which the 98th Quartermaster Battalion beat the 8043rd AU 7-0. The first quarter score came on a pass from Fred Eichenberg to George Quinn. The Army unit had not been scored against until this game.

Page 11 of the 18 December edition included photos of "two top backfield men," Ted Rodrique of Lynn, Massachusetts (Air Force), and Shaun Coughlin of Rochester, NY (Navy). The picture caption said, "Service Stars Ready for Bowl Games." The caption also confirmed the Camp Tokyo Bulldogs would meet the Camp Fisher Marines in the Rice Bowl on New Year's Day.

1954

The 2 January 1954 *Army Times* edition (64) included on page 25 an article discussing Rycom All-Star football team versus 29th RCT

"Once again the 29th RCT dominated Rycom football. The 29th won the league championship by whipping the 97th AAA 25-0 in the final game of the year and also placed six men on the first All-Rycom team as well as four more on the second team."

League coaches selected the following 1953 All-Rycom Teams:

> **First Team**: Ends – John Simas (Service Command) and Lou Vendova (29th RCT), Tackles – Al Sensley (97th AAA) and Harry Steuber (29th RCT), Guards – Bill Schutice* (Port Command) and Dan Wiseman (29th RCT, Halfbacks – John Flemming and Howard Porsey (both 29th RCT), Fullback – Jim McGill (Port Command).

> **Second Team**: Ends – John Busby (29th RCT) and Ken Darrow (Salisbury Sound), Tackles – Ken Ely (29th RCT) and Carl Frudley (97th AAA) and Russ Hayward (29th RCT), Center – Jim Arwood (29th RCT), Quarterback – H. C. Bloss (Salisbury Sound), Halfbacks – Hal Jackson (97th AAA and Fred Nissel (Port Command), Fullback – George Van Zant (Service Command).

> *"Shutice" might be "Shultice", as it appears elsewhere.

The 2 January 1954 edition of the *Stars and Stripes* reported: "Marines Defeat AF in Tokyo Rice Bowl" (65). The article appeared on the front page. Camp Fisher beat Nagoya's Air Force Comets 13-10 at Meiji Stadium. *It is also noted the paper reported the service league score with the American NCAA college football Bowl scores, as if there were no difference.*

The detailed Rice Bowl story appears on page 15, "Marines Top AF in Rice Bowl 19-13." The story is accompanied by a picture of Camp Fisher's Leon Carson breaking through the Comets' defenses. The picture caption said the game was the "seventh renewal of the annual grid classic." The article said, "Camp Fisher's power-laden marines yesterday annexed the Far East interservice football championship as they outclassed Nagoya AFB 19-13 in Meiji Stadium."

The stadium crowd was estimated by *United Press* to be 15,000; however, the PEAF PIO's crowd estimate was 37,000.

It was reported there had been a 13-13 deadlock in the final period when "Horace Rankin broke through the weakened Nagoya line for a touchdown," which led to the win. Nagoya had no prior defeats for the season.

The article highlighted plays by Ted Rodrique and D. Hurdel and Jim Yakota of the Airmen, as well as the play of Leon Carson. It was noted that the "shifty Marines were almost breaking through the line at will." The game review stated, "Nagoya, a good team in their league, just didn't have the power or class to spark a last-quarter rally and their passes were intercepted by Marine stalwarts three times in the last stanza." The game was witnessed by FEAF Commander General O.P. Weyland and Maj. Gen. Robert H. Pepper, Commandant of the 3rd Marine Div.

The 2 January edition also reported that "Ord Blasts Navy 67-12" in Phoenix, Arizona, showing that service football was alive and well stateside.

The *Army Times* newspaper of 9 January 1954 (66) had a small entry regarding "Ivy League Star," further supporting the quality of athletes in the Far East:

> Lt. Charles DeVoe, who captained Princeton to the Ivy League basketball title in 1951-52, is now a player-coach in the 45th Divarty League.

The 23 January 1954 *Army Times* (67) provided a chart showing dates and location of various sports' Eighth Army Sports Championships and

All Far East Championships, from volleyball to basketball to badminton. Selected sports are shown below:

Eighth Army Sports Championships

Sport	Level	Rules	Squad	Dates	Host
Volleyball	Company	USVA	10	June 8-10	IX Corps
Track, Field	Individual	NAAU	18	June 12-14	Seoul
Baseball	Regiment	NBL	18	Aug. 23-29	I Corps
Basketball	Regiment	NCAA	12	Feb. 22-25 ('55)	Seoul
Boxing	Individual	NAAU	13*	Mar. 19-21 ('55)	IX Corps

*To include one entry in each of ten weight classes, plus coach manager, and officer-in-charge.

All Far East Championships

Sport	Dates	Host	Location
Basketball	March 10-15	Okinawa	Surkiran Arena
Boxing	March 31-April 4	Central Com.	Camp Yokohama
Track and Field	June 25-26	XVI Corps	Schimmelpfennig
Baseball	September 7-12	Central Com.	Camp Tokyo

Of historical interest, a 28 January 1954 General Staff News Summary (68) discussed an AAU invitation to Russian athletes:

> U.S. Amateur Athletic Union (AAU) extended an invitation to Russia to send a team of athletes to compete in the U.S. for the first time in history. AAU Secretary-Treasurer Dan Ferris wrote directly to Moscow, informing the AAU counterpart — the All-Union Section of Light Athletics — that "We would be glad to have you come anytime," up to and including the last outdoor meet of the season, scheduled for May 28 in New York. Ferris said the original invitation covered only the indoor track season, which ends March 27th at Chicago.

The 6 February 1954 *Army Times* discussed "Community Centers Being Built In Korea" (69). The structures were to be "part of an Eighth Army-wide program to provide better leisure-time facilities … large centers with 17 buildings and complete athletic facilities have been planned on three sites in the division area."

The centers would serve various recreational and athletic activities. They were also designed to be within commuting distance of division soldiers. "On two of the sites, giant 40' x 100' quonsets are under construction by division engineers. These buildings will be used as gymnasiums and will be put into operation as soon as they are completed."

Other quonsets would contain a "chapel, a PX, a theatre, a snack bar, and a service club," as well as other miscellaneous activity areas. Areas were to be prepared for football fields, baseball fields, and courts for tennis and volleyball.

Capt. Lucien P. Ordoyne told *Army Times* the centers were expected to be completed by the end of the year.

Army Times newspaper from 27 February 1954 (70) reported on Big League baseball teams scouting Military Service League players ("Service Baseball Talent Hunt").

> With the cooperation of Major League teams already assured, *Army Times* along with *Air Force Times* and *Navy Times* - will conduct a "Service Baseball Talent Hunt" for promising Major League prospects this year. The talent hunt aims to bring all promising players, not owned by a professional team, to the attention of Major League scouts.

"Everyone" was urged to notify the *Times* of any outstanding free agent player.

Thirteen Major League teams promised the data provided by *Army Times* would be provided to their scouting staff; "The teams will then scout the players in action when possible. In some cases, trials will be arranged."

The paper advised they would post tryout times throughout the year.

Baseball players could not be signed to a professional contract until they had been discharged, though football players could. However, if a professional baseball team was interested in a service player, they could sign the player upon conclusion of their military service.

Below are selected quotes from professional baseball team personnel regarding the Service Sports baseball player talent hunt:

Art Ehlers, general manager of the Baltimore Orioles, said, "We ... assure you that if he has any ability at all, we shall give him every opportunity to get started in professional baseball."

Carl Hubbell of the New York Giants said the Giants would be "very happy to have our scouts look over any service players you may recommend as having professional possibilities ..."

Roy Harney, assistant general manager of the New York Yankees "expressed keen interest in the program," and said that the Yankees were "very much interested in the talent hunt."

Fresco Thompson of the Brooklyn Dodgers said, "I am quite certain that your sports desk could undoubtedly serve as a clearinghouse for information on outstanding players in military service who have not as yet had an opportunity to try out for professional baseball ..."

John J McHale, Director of the Minor League System for the Detroit Tigers said, "We are extremely interested in any young players who have not been signed to professional baseball contracts and who are now playing in the Armed Forces."

The Chicago White Sox baseball team offered an opportunity for discharged servicemen to try out at one of their minor league spring training camps in Hollywood, FL; Fort Lauderdale, FL; or Madisonville, KY.

Army Times noted that,

> Although most players on the stronger service teams are already owned by a major league club, *Army Times* believes that there are many unsigned and unknown. A few months ago, for example, the Phils signed a tremendously promising pitcher named Paul Penson who was a standout in the 1953 All-Air Force baseball tournament. Penson had never played pro ball before, but he did not need a pro contract to throw his fastball by many a famous pro in service ball. In 480 innings with Eglin Air Force Base, Penson had 669 strikeouts and an earned run average of 0.83.

In case there is any question about the level of talent in Military Service Sports in the mid-1950s, there is a small note in the 6 March 1954 *Army Times* (71) stating:

Willie Mays, New York Giant outfielder, was discharged here (Fort Eustis) this week. He spent his entire 21-month Army career at Eustis. With the Eustis baseball team, he hit .420 in 1952 and .389 in 1953.

Correspondence dated 1 May 1954 (72) from Major Maurer on behalf of Brigadier General Whitcomb to the commanding officer of the Inchon Military Post is titled "Recreation Facilities," and discusses the merits of developing recreation centers within Japan given "the present curtailment and future uncertainty of the Japan Rest and Recuperation program."

Major Maurer said that "headquarters will continue to urge maximum allocation for Japan R&R for personnel of this command," but that "it is desirable that any locations in Korea susceptible of (sic) development in recreation centers be located."

A 4 May 1954 communication labeled "Korean Communications Zone Track and Field Meet" says that the track and field meet would be held in Taegu, Korea, on 13 June 1954, with the Commanding Officer, Taegu Military Post, as host.

> The Commanding General, Korean Communications Zone, will select outstanding participants from this meet to participate in the All-Far East track and field meet to be held in Miyaginohara Stadium, Sendai, Japan 25-26 June 1954.

> Each Military Post Commander will be limited to one team not to exceed eighteen (18) individuals, including coaches, trainers, and officer in charge. All members are eligible to participate. Military Post Commanders will submit a roster of their teams to the Commanding Officer, Taegu Military Post, APO 234, ATTN, SSO, prior to 5 June 1954, with information copy to the Commanding General, Korean Communications Zone, ATTN, CZSS.

Team rosters will include name, grade, service number, hometown, and organization of each member. This roster is exempt from reports control under the provisions of paragraph 17K, AR 335-15.

Responsibility of Host Command: The Commanding Officer, Regional Camp Schimmelpfennig, APO 547, is designated as host and will be responsible for the conduct of the meet, including the administration, publicity, billeting, and messing for all participants. Request that addressee commands submit team roster, to include name, rank, service number, organization, name of officer-in-charge, mode of travel and expected date and time of arrival at Camp Schimmelpfennig, APO 547, to this headquarters prior to 5 June 1954.

Conduct of competition: Competition will be conducted in accordance with 1954 National Amateur Athletic Union rules. The team will not exceed eighteen (18) individuals, including coaches, trainers, and officers-in-charge. All members are eligible to participate.

Each team may enter a maximum of three (3) contestants in each individual track and field event, but only one (1) team in each relay event. Individuals participating may enter a maximum of five (5) individual events, plus one relay event. All track events will be measured by the metric system. The sequence of events for the meet will be in conformance with NAAU track and field meets, wherever practicable.

Trophies: Appropriate team and individual awards will be made by headquarters AFFE to the championship and runner-up teams and to the individual champion and runner-up of each event.

Track and Field events: 100 meters, 200 meters, 400 meters, 110 meters high hurdles, 200 meters low hurdles, 800 meters, 1500 meters, 3000 meters, 400 meter relay, 800 meter relay, 1600 meter relay. Field events: Pole vault, high jump, broad jump, 16 pound shot put, discus, javelin.

Temporary duty: Team members will be placed on temporary duty with 8017th AU, Camp Schimmelpfennig, APO 547, For the necessary period of time for travel and participation. Reporting date will be not earlier than 18 June 1954, nor later than 20 June 1954. Travel by rail will terminate at Sendai, Japan. Travel by air will terminate at Matsushima Air Base. Coaches meeting: A representative coach from each command will meet at the Camp Schimmelpfennig Special Services Office at 1400 hours 21 June 1954 for the purpose of discussing rules and regulations which will govern the competition. All correspondence in connection with this meet will be addressed to Commanding General, XVI Corps, APO 14, Attention: Special Services Officer.

An 8 May 1954 article in *Army Times* newspaper by Tom Scanlon (73) asked, "Is Army Coddling Sports Stars?" Mr. Scanlon reported there would be a Congressional investigation into possible preferential treatment for famous athletes in the Army. Mr. Scanlon said the matter would be reviewed by the House Armed Services Subcommittee led by Rep. William E. Hess. The hearing would address "inside, rather than outside, pressure," and the service experience of ten athletes would be examined.

Mr. Scanlon noted, for example:

> Although he has long since been out of the Army, one of these big name (sic) athletes will be Sugar Ray Robinson, former welterweight champ. The other nine, according to advance information, are baseball players Willie Mays, Whitey Ford, Billy Martin, Alex Konikowski and Dick Brodkowski,

basketball's O'Brien twins, and boxers Sandy Saddler and Chico Vejar.

The belief of the subcommittee was that the athletes "had been kept off overseas orders or KP or guard duty or afternoon duty or some other duty in order to play on post teams (or fight professionally, as in Vejar's case)."

The Army claimed that no famous athlete would receive preferential treatment (DA Circular 101, 16 October 1953); "Hess said that there is no indication any of the athletes themselves asked for preferential treatment ... Hess wants to see that famous athletes drafted into service are trained and treated like other men."

Brig. Gen. H. C. Powell told the committee that "the Army's position on Army athletics is definitely geared to intra-mural sports activity. This is in line with the Army's 'Sports for All' program."

We have discussed the high level of sports quality in the various Military Service Sports programs, spurred by a plethora of talented athletes, including some who were under professional sports contracts, or who would see action in their professional sport of choice post-service obligation. As noted, Willie Mays, "back with the New York Giants this year," had starred in baseball at Fort Eustis for two years; he was released from service three months early based on a ruling from the Army.

Also, "The subcommittee claims to have found numerous instances where post commanders have kept big-name athlete trainees at their posts while fellow trainees got shipped out, often overseas."

Maj. Gen Robert McClure admitted he had retained some athletes at Fort Ord following basic training. He gave the example of All-American and All-Pro fullback Ollie Matson, "star of the powerful Fort Ord team," noting that the Fort Ord team "fulfilled an entertainment function for soldiers," and that they "played to big crowds and went on to win the nation's service championship."

The article went on to say that Gen. McClure denied star second baseman Billy Martin's request for a hardship discharge. It was noted by Gen. McClure that Martin "*came to camp driving a baby blue Cadillac. Anyone with a car like that can't be broke* (it. added)."

The *Army Times* said that "If posts are to continue to have teams … the best ball players on post will continue to play on them. This would necessarily mean release from duty for the ball games."

The 15 May 1954 *Army Times* has a follow-up article titled "Coddling Probe Proves Little". The article said, "little was proven because the subcommittee headed by Rep. William E. Hess (R. Ohio) relied upon only ten individual cases … moreover, half of those ten cases fizzled."

And in the last-word department, *Army Times* columnist Tom Scanlon on 5 June 1954 (74) wrote: "If Army commanders in the field are beginning to wonder just how Congress expects them to handle big-name athletes, no wonder. Soon they may feel themselves to be in a bind, namely: If a big name athlete plays on a post team it will be called 'coddling' and if he doesn't it will be called 'discrimination'."

The 8 May 1954 edition also had a photo caption story which read,

> Bobby (Doc) Brown, medical officer (1st Lt.), arrived back in the States with his wife Sara and 19-month-old son Pete last weekend. The former New York Yankee third baseman will probably not return to the majors following his release from service now because he intends to become a full-time doctor after July. Brown spent nine months in Korea as medical officer for the 160th FA Bn., 45th Inf. Div.

Military.com had an archived 6 October 2021 article about Bobby Brown, titled "Korean War Veteran Bobby Brown was also a

Cardiologist and World Series Champion" (75). Despite the photo caption noted above, and this article, there is no clear indication that Bobby Brown played baseball in Korea despite having "spent 19 months in service on the Korean Peninsula with the 160th Field Artillery Battalion aid station, the 5th Regimental Combat Team and the 8225th Mobile Army Surgical Hospital."

The *Military.com* article continued: "Bobby Brown was a hero long before he shipped off the fight in the Korean War ... He was a student at Stanford University when he rescued a member of the Coast Guard." He was drafted into World War II, but was able finish his pre-medical courses while in a naval unit at UCLA. The Navy sent him to medical school at Tulane, but he did not finish medical school before the war ended.

"Before the United States joined the war, Brown was already an accomplished athlete. In high school in San Francisco he was noticed by a baseball scout with the Cincinnati Reds, and he was invited to try-out."

He also tried out for the Tigers, Yankees, Brooklyn Dodgers, and A's. In the meantime, he played baseball at Tulane. The Yankees signed Brown upon discharge from the service. He received a three-year contract "with a bonus that was the highest ever in professional baseball at the time."

Brown was "already a two-time World Series champion" by the time the Korean War started in 1950, and he participated in winning two more before being sent to Korea. Following his service in Korea, he was sent to work with Tokyo Army Hospital in Japan.

Brown returned to the then-struggling Yankees in 1954, but then retired, whereupon he "went into Cardiology and opened his first practice in Texas in 1958." However, his connection to baseball continued, as he was named president of the Texas Rangers in 1974 (which lasted one year) and later became the American League president for ten years.

Dr. Brown wondered how well he may have done in baseball had he not had 2-3 years interruption for military service. He died at age 96 in Fort Worth, Tex. RIP, hero.

An article in the 22 May 1954 *Army Times* (pg. 30) discusses "Improved Sports Program Underway for 1st Cavalry":

> SAPPORO, Hokkaido - The jam-packed sports program is gaining momentum with the advent of warm weather on Japan's northernmost island of Hokkaido, home of the 1st Cavalry Division.
>
> To introduce some new faces to Cav boxing fans a change has been made in the regular Hokkaido Boxing Conference rules. There is no limit on the number of men that can make up each of the division's six off-season boxing teams.
>
> As the troopers gain in experience, they will be matched with veteran scrappers to give variety to the schedule. Any squad desiring to book fights with the "First Team" can do so by contacting the division's Special Services Office.
>
> A card of ten fights is planned for every week until August.
>
> In addition to boxing there is volleyball, table tennis, badminton, horseshoes, handball, and softball, all on the company level, which gives every man in the division a chance to compete.
>
> Handball is on the official schedule for the first time this season. Two single wall courts will be constructed at Camp Crawford and two at Chitose.
>
> Tennis, golf, and track and field squads are shaping up for the coming season, while the division's six baseball teams recently began play.

Last year's Cav performances will be hard to beat. A look at the records show that division teams were XVI Corps volleyball champions and runners-up in the AFFE meet, All-Japan small games titlists in badminton singles and doubles and ping pong singles, All-Japan Army kings in swimming and golf, (and) Corps bowling champions.

The XVI Corps skiing team, with two 3d Cav men, swept to the AFFE ski championship. Nine of the Cav boxers won Corps titles, and one, Bob McHugh, won the AFFE light welterweight crown. In basketball, Chitose Special Troops won the AFFE crown last year, and Divarty the All-Japan title this winter.

Records like these spring from the very heart of 1st Cav. A competitive spirit that drives every trooper from the rifleman in the line company to the CO, Maj. Gen. A. D. Mead, permeates the three Hokkaido camps.

Confined as the "First Team" is to the island of Hokkaido, where off-post recreational facilities are limited, an intensive sports program for Cav troopers is vital.

The 12 June 1954 *Army Times* had a small article regarding "Army Sports Stars" (76). The entry for a "star" from AFFE read:

Lou Gage, former Far East Command welterweight champ who lost a close decision in the 1952 All-Army tournament before willing a place on the U. S. Olympic team, is now a pro, fighting out of San Francisco.

8th Army track results were discussed in a 3 July 1954 *Army Times* article (77), which said that Seoul Military Post (SMP) "completely dominated" (9 firsts and 85 5/6 total points), and IX Corps finished second with 63 1/3 points at Seoul City Stadium.

SMP's overwhelming strength in the field events and sprint races overshadowed the double victory performance of Olympic star Bob McMillan. McMillen, co-holder of the Olympic 1500 meter mark, waltzed away from the field in winning his specialty by 150 yards over second place Gary Eyre of I Corps. McMillen's winning time was 3:56.2. The I Corps star came back 30 minutes later to win the 800 meters in 1:55.1.

The article said that Lee Calhoun (SMP) was also a double winner; "The lanky speedster won both the 110 meter high hurdles and the 200 meter low hurdles." IX Corps' Willie Atterbury passed Sherm Miller of the 24th division for a surprise win in the 400 meters (:48.4). SMP also won two out of three relay events.

Author note: Interestingly, I was able to locate only one reference to Seoul City Stadium pertaining to 1954, and it was within a photo caption (78). The photo itself (licensing not allowed by AP) shows a large crowd at what was purported to be Seoul City Stadium on 18 November 1954, just months after the above-mentioned track meet at the same location. In fact, the track lanes can be seen in the forefront of the black and white photo.

The lengthy photo caption read:

> Twenty-thousand Koreans swarmed into the Seoul City Stadium, Thursday, Nov. 18, 1954 to 'denounce' a British-Canadian election plan for unifying North and South Korea. The demonstrators demanded United Nations supervise elections in North Korea alone as provided under South Korea constitutional procedures. Britain and Canada have proposed a compromise formula in the United Nations assembly. It would involve a mixed supervisory commission, including communist, and would involve elections throughout the divided peninsula (AP Photo).

Stars and Stripes also reported 20 July 1954 that the Far East Command Interservice Sports Council announced the FEC Japan Football Championship would be decided in a three-game series of All-Star games rather than contests between interservice champions. The first of the three games was to be played in Tokyo Stadium on December 18 and would feature Air Force vs. Navy in the Torii Bowl. On December 19th, the Army would meet the Marines in the Sukiyaki Bowl.

The two winning All-Star teams would then meet for the interservice championship in the New Year's Rice Bowl (79). Chairman of the Intersports Council, G. Ott Romney, said that decisions on All-Star player choices would be up to the individual services involved. The article said that football was the only interservice sport playoff scheduled for 1954.

The Sports Council had been created as an advisory body for sports within the Command. It was made up of FEC representatives, and from representatives of each of the four main services. Its duties included formulation of eligibility rules, scheduling, officiating, publicity, and "the general management and conduct of the contests.

Stars and Stripes reported on 21 July 1954 that 105 Army and Marine coaches attended a five-day AFFE coaches football clinic at the Fryar Gym in Yokohama, Japan. The instructors were listed as Rip Engle from Penn State, Jess Hill of Southern California, and Thad (Pie) Vann of Mississippi Southern (80).

The opening day curriculum included fundamental offensive and defensive drills, football organization, physical and mental conditioning, and offensive and defensive strategies.

Col. Paul A. Jaccard, Commanding Officer at Camp Yokohama, welcomed the students.

The article went on to say that Mr. Hill reviewed USC's single wing phases of the multiple offense which he had employed in a victory over Wisconsin in the 1953 Rose Bowl. Mr. Vann explained Mississippi Southern's "T" formation offense.

Mr. Engle was said to have had a 28-12 record during four years of coaching, and he discussed offensive and defense drills.

The 27 July 1954 *Stars and Stripes* provided additional reporting on coaches clinics: "100 Coaches Graduate From Clinic" (81). The article said that at the conclusion of the clinics, one hundred Army, Navy and Marine students "were presented with qualifying coaches cards at graduation exercises of the five-day 1954 AFFE Football Coaches Clinic at Fryar Gym." Lt. Col. Moe Burford presented coaching cards to the graduates and "sent them back to their installations to prepare teams for the approaching season."

Topics discussed included pre-season football organization, conditioning, drilling, and offensive and defensive strategy. The coaches also discussed good sportsmanship and the use of college football as a path to an education.

Coach Engle from Penn State reviewed offensive and defensive drills and "explained Penn State's great pass offense." Coach Vann, whose Mississippi Southern team had beaten "major powers" Alabama and Georgia the previous year, discussed the importance of scouting your opponent prior to the game. Coach Hill's Southern California Trojans were noted to have beaten Wisconsin in the 1953 Rose Bowl. Coach Hill discussed defensive tactics against the single wing offense.

Coaches used "numerous films" to help explain fundamentals of the game.

In the 27 July 1954 edition, also on page 12, was a report that "FEAMCom to Start Pigskin Practice Sessions Aug. 2." The 6400 Air

Depot Wing "Marauders," with Capt. Joe Drach as head coach, were expecting a big turnout. FEAMCom had a record of success, as the paper took note of their 49-17-1 record through the previous seven seasons.

The previous year, Air Force had been divided into two conferences – Northern and Southern; "Misawa took the Northern Conference championship with a 3-1-1 record, and Nagoya won the Southern Conference with five wins and no losses."

The 1954 season would see conferences merge into one, representing twelve bases: FEAMCom, Misawa, Brady, Itazuke, Itami, Shiroi, Yokota, Ashiya, FEAF, Nagoya Johnson, and Tachikawa.

The 28 July 1954 *Stars and Stripes* reported that Marines called for players to fill seven football squads (82). 3rd Division Marines were recruited to play for four regimental teams and three "camp squads." The regimental teams would be under control of the Marines and the Camp teams would be under control of the Army: "The Camp Fuji 3rd Marines and McNair 12th Marines will enter teams in the Central Command League, while the 4th Marines from Camp Nara and the 9th from Camp Shinodayama will compete in the Southwestern Command League."

It had not yet been decided whether the Camp teams would be referred to as an Army or Marine team; it would likely depend on how many from each branch were on the team. "Meanwhile, each of the five sports sectors of the division will send five men to the AFFE Football Officials School in Yokohama, Aug. 2-6."

The Officials School would cover the updated 1954 rule book and would focus on current rules and regulations. Once complete, Marine Division Officials graduates would then be able to officiate the Central and Southwest Command Leagues.

31 July 1954 *Army Times* reported that "It's Pigskin Time Again in Korea" (83):

> With football again looming as a major service sport in the Far East, the 7th Division Special Services office is making an all-out attempt to uncover the division's top pigskin talent.
>
> Capt. Lester R. Dillon, division Special Services officer, opened tryouts for the division team this week at Bayonet Field. All personnel interested in playing football this fall have been encouraged to workout. The team will carry 30 uniformed players and five coaches.
>
> The Bayonet 11 will participate in the Eighth Army League, scheduled to begin on Sept. 18 and continue through Oct. 30. With eight division size teams, the league should produce some top flight competition and promises a winner in the Far East Championships.
>
> This will be the first year since before the Korean War that the game has been played on a major scale on the peninsula. During the occupation period prior to 1950, American service teams in Korea, Japan, and China clashed each fall for the All-Far East honors. With the war, however, the sport was abandoned until this year.

The *Army Times* newspaper of 31 July 1954 described the 7th Infantry Division's "Korea Rest Camp" (84). The article calls it a "Bayonet rest camp," and said that it was "fast becoming the most popular spot in the division." 1500 soldiers per month utilized the camp as a supplement for "regular rest leave to Japan."

Oversight of the camp was assigned to 1st Lt. James M. Betteker, assistant division Special Services officer. The three-day stays were apportioned on a quota basis, and soldiers rotated through.

The camp provided "athletic equipment for baseball, softball, volleyball, basketball and other sports," and "those who prefer doing nothing get their wish." Their time was their own.

The library and hobby shop allowed for less strenuous activity, should that be desired. There was a swimming pool and a dining hall; "Best chow I've had in the Army," according to PFC Glenn Zachow. PFC Carl R. Ebersold told *Army Times* that "There's nothing like it. I never had it so good."

The *Stars and Stripes* reported 1 August 1954 on an AFFE "Grid Clinic" given by Pacific Coast Loop officials in Yokohama, Japan (85). The article said two Pacific Coast Conference officials arrived to instruct approximately one hundred Army, Navy, and Marine students from Japan, Korea and Okinawa at the Fryar Gym. The instructors were Edward Wagner from Long Beach, CA, and James Cain from Seattle, WA.

Mr. Wagner was described as a former football coach at Long Beach College in California, where he was "the Dean of Men." He had had 14 years of refereeing experience, including several Rose Bowls. He was a former football star at the University of Colorado, where he was an All-Conference fullback (he was also All-Conference in baseball). He had been captain of both the baseball and football teams.

Mr. Cain was described as a sixteen-year official in the Pacific Coast Conference, where he had worked four Rose Bowls and eight East-West Shrine Bowl games. He had received honorable mention as an All-American player while starring at the University of Washington.

Two 13 August 1954 memos describe two different sessions for the 1954 Basketball Officials Clinics at the Seoul Military Post (86).

Quality coaches led to quality Service Sports in the Far East in the mid-1950s. The 6-10 September Clinic would feature Forrest Twogood, head basketball coach, University of Southern California; Everett Case, head basketball coach, North Carolina State College; and Howard Hobson, head basketball coach, Yale University.

Mr. Twogood's obituary (87) said that he died on 26 April 1972. He coached USC from 1950 to 1966, and he had been a star at the University of Iowa in the late 1920s. In 1929 he signed as a baseball pitcher with the St. Louis Cardinals, for which he played seven years.

Mr. Twogood previously coached basketball at the University of Idaho in the 1930s, and the University of San Francisco in the 1940s. "He leaves his wife, Eleanor."

Mr. Hobson's obituary from 10 June 1991 said he was born in Portland, Oregon, died at age 87, and had been a "basketball pioneer" (88). The article said Howard (Hobby) Hobson coached the University of Oregon basketball team to the first NCAA basketball championship in 1939. He died of congestive heart failure.

"Mr. Hobson coached the 'Tall Firs' to a 46-33 victory over Ohio State in the first N.C.A.A. title game at Northwestern University on March 27, 1939," following a 29-5 season. He was admitted to the National Basketball Hall of Fame in Springfield, MA.

The 11-15 October 1954 Basketball Officials Clinic at Seoul Military Post (86) would feature instructors Erving Dolmer from San Francisco, California, and Elling Okland from Ellensburg, Washington.

The memo said that "Each commander will be limited to the following number of participants: Commanding General, Pusan Military Post, seven (7); Commanding Officer, Taegu Military Post, five (5); Commanding Officer, Inchon Military Post, two (2); Commanding Officer, 5th Regimental Combat Team, one (1)."

"Personnel attending the clinic will have in their possession the following additional clothing and equipment: One sweat suit or similar type clothing, gym shoes, one towel, one athletic supporter, and one pair of athletic socks."

Participants would receive a current rule book. Qualifications for attending the clinic included interest in participating in the program, professional or amateur experience in the activity, and sufficient time remaining in their current tour of duty for the duration of the basketball season (Ending approximately 1 March 1955).

The 14 August 1954 *Army Times* reported on AFFE boxer, PFC Charles Drakeford's, success (89). Drakeford had "climbed to the top rung of the service boxing ladder." He was an All-Army champion of both the Eighth Army and Far East.

> Currently serving with the 2d Div., Drakeford punched his way through four major overseas tournaments beginning with the civilian title and continuing on to IX Corps, Eighth Army and finally the Far East. He hold (sic) a fantastic record of 58 wins in 60 starts, including both military and civilian fights as an amateur.

Drakeford was knocked out of contention to participate in the Olympics by Nate Brooks, who went on to win the Olympic title and had become the North American bantamweight champ.

Drakeford was said to have had an "unorthodox style" and had a "switch hitter's versatility." The article suggested that Drakeford would switch his tactics and attacks depending on who he was fighting, which served to baffle the opponent.

Drakeford was a former New Jersey Golden Gloves champion, 11th Airborne Division champion, and Second Army and All-Army champion. With a few adjustments, Drakeford felt he had a future in boxing: "If I could gain 10 or 15 pounds … I may turn pro."

On 21 August 1954, *Army Times* reported (90) on Second Division baseball, "2d Div. Stars Touring Korea":

> A 2d Division all-star team of 18 players is currently on a 45-day tour of Korea.
>
> Selected by managers of the five teams in the 2d Division baseball league, the Indianhead team will meet every major service team on the Korean Peninsula in August and September.
>
> Stars of the team include Jim Orr, Philadelphia Phil bonus baby; Don Hopp, lanky strikeout artist under contract to the Portland Beavers of the Pacific Coast League; and Jack Gore, former Texas League and Southern Association third baseman now owned by the Atlanta Crackers. Gore is managing the team.

There is a 24 August 1954 memo to the Commanding General of the Eighth United States Army regarding "Roster for Basketball Coaches Clinic" (91):

> In compliance with paragraph 4, Letter AF 353.8 KSS, Headquarters, Eighth United States Army, 3 August 1954, subject: Sports Clinic (Basketball Coaches), the following roster of the Korean Communications Zone personnel to attend the Basketball Coaches Clinic is submitted:
>
> Capt. Paul Davis, US 0527787, KMAG
>
> 2d Lt James Frank, US 04016988, 60th Engr Co
>
> Cpl Arthur Owen, US 04016988, HQ KComZ
>
> Cpl Buazzo Benedict, US 51213424, 226th O.B.D.
>
> Cpl Marvin Defort, US 55372591, 60th Engr Co
>
> Pfc Gilbert M. Rommalfinger, US 56196426, 32nd QM Gp

> Pfc Clyde E. Fleagle, US 52247030, 21st Station Hospital
>
> Pfc John Nevers, US 55394294, KMAG
>
> Pfc Robert S. Thomas, US 52284638, Hq Co 21st Port
>
> Pvt Roy M. Green, US 54133860, Hq KComZ
>
> Pvt John E. Moschele, US 51273695, Hq 772nd MP Bn
>
> Pvt James Thompson, US 51224634, Med Co 5th RGT
>
> Pvt Emanuel K. Kennedy, US 51259340, 507th Sig Co
>
> Pvt Joseph S. Clark, US 55442631, 7th Transport Comd
>
> Pvt E. W. Warren Jr., US 54135192, Hq Co 21st Port

The 11 September 1954 *Army Times* reported on "2d Div. All-Star" Chet Pleszaj (92): "Hard-hitting shortstop owned by the St. Louis Cardinals, has joined the 2d Division All-Star team for its current 45-day barnstorming tour of Korea."

The same edition (pg. 30) reported that,

> The 2d Division's war-enforced absence from the gridiron will end this fall when it will field its first football team since 1949. Second Lt. Bill Carey, former Michigan State end and twin brother of All-American Bob Carey, will coach the Indianhead team. The Warriors will open against the 25th Div. Oct. 3 and will finish the season Nov. 14 against I Corps.
>
> Carey, drafted by the San Francisco 49ers, is expected to blend several of Michigan state's many formations – including Charley Bachman's famed "Flying Z" - into the offensive punch.

Army Times newspaper reported on 18 September 1954 there were "Three Major Sports Dropped – Four Inter-Service Tourneys, including Boxing, Next Year" (93), noting that,

> Inter-Service championship competition in baseball, basketball, and track will be dropped next year in favor of bowling, golf and tennis. Boxing would not be affected. Brig. Gen. John S. Hardy explained that there was a new emphasis on individual sports which would be open to servicemen of any rank or age.

There was an additional concern about time spent away from the home post with team sports if an inter-service tournament was added to the already busy schedule. "A spokesman pointed out … We have orders to get behind track and field and to make certain we are well represented in the Pan-American and Olympic Games."

It was further noted that "the Army's sports chiefs in Washington are preparing the All-Army program for 1955. This year seven All-Army tournaments were held. It is expected that ten will be held next year."

Army Times on 16 October 1954 recounted five-time All-American football legend Col. Charles D. Daly's experience and memories of the game (94):

> A man who reveled with football in its brawling youth and then guided it through the maturing years at the turn of the century recalled part of that colorful story here this week.

> Col. Charles D Daly (Ret.) started playing football for Harvard when the Flying Wedge was the game's most feared offensive weapon and the forward pass was a thing used only by wild young teams such as Notre Dame and the Carlyle Indians.

> Col. Daly is here now visiting his son, Col. John Daly, head of the Department of Materiel.

The elder Daly's impact on the game has seldom been equaled: All-American selection five times while playing for both Harvard and the United States Military Academy.

Coach of three undefeated West Point teams in seven years.

Charter member of the modern National Football Rules committee.

Founder and honorary president of the NCAA National Football Coaches Association.

Charter member and only Army player in football's Hall of Fame.

Selected as quarterback on Walter Camp's 1910 All-Time, All-American team.

Daly's toughness led him to be known as "The Scourge of the Gridiron." He played for Harvard three years and graduated in 1901, having been named as an All-American. After Harvard he played for West Point, where he was again named All-American.

Following his stint at West Point, Daly turned to coaching and "as assistant coach he came up with a unique four-man tandem which made full use of the old rules allowing the ball carrier to be pulled or pushed by his team mates (sic)."

Apparently old-style football was "almost a war of physical combat." Daly had been concerned about the number of injuries, however, and, as a member of the rules committee along with other luminaries such as Amos Alonzo Stagg and Walter Camp, they "moved decisively" on making meaningful changes to the game, which included increasing the number of officials to four and changing the game length to sixty minutes, with a "10 minute rest between halves."

Also, "a neutral zone the length of the ball was enforced between the opposing lines." They approved forward-looking techniques, such as the forward pass and onside kick. They outlawed "crawling, hurdling, tripping and illegal use of hands and arms."

Col. Daly said, "I was a bit dubious when I voted for the forward pass, and when I see how it dominates the game today, I still wonder if it shouldn't be curtailed some."

The 9 October 1954 *Army Times* reported (95) –

> Did Ya Know? A Serviceman assigned to a post or installation of another service may represent the service to which attached in all athletic competition, up to and including Inter-Service play.

The 23 October 1954 *Army Times* (96) included a photo of Yokohama halfback Gus Cueto doing an end run against Camp McGill for a nine-yard gain. The photo caption noted that Yokohama won the Central Command game 6-0.

In the same edition and on the same page appeared an article concerning the revision of Post Team sports schedules:

> All post sports officers now scheduling games for their post basketball teams had better revise their plans.

> The Army TIMES learned this week that post basketball teams will not be allowed to play more than 30 games during the regular season. This 30-game figure does not include post-season tournament games.

> At the same time the army (sic) is also limiting post baseball teams next season to 50 regular season games.

> The new policy will be announced officially to the field through a new DA Circular stating the change and outlining the All-

113

Army program. The Circular was expected to be published soon, possibly this week.

Post basketball teams normally schedule around 50 games a season. The Fort Meade schedule for this season, for example, lists exactly 50 games. The Meade schedule, like many others, will have to be revised because of the new army ruling.

The new ruling also cuts down travel distance for post teams. Teams will be restricted to playing other teams from their own command except that they may play teams in adjacent commands if the round-trip travel distance is less than 500 miles. (In this regard, MDW is considered as Second Army).

This means that a team from the Third Army area may play a team from the Second Army area as long as the distance between the two posts is not more than 250 miles. In any event, a team from the Third Army area cannot play a team from the First Army area.

The new ruling does, however, leave a loophole … exceptions to the 500 mile round-trip travel distance may be made by the commanding generals involved if they so desire it.

Whether or not similar travel restrictions will be placed upon post football teams next year is not yet known or decided upon. But these travel restrictions will not in any way affect current football schedules.

The restrictions were apparently made to encourage more lower-level sports activity and to decrease the emphasis on "spectator" sports, since a big post team exists primarily for off-duty entertainment purposes.

Critical comment from some posts can be expected.

Also in the 23 October 1954 edition of *Army Times*, on page 28, is an article discussing All-Army tournament schedules for 1955 (97). Selected portions are reproduced below:

> Ten All-Army sports tournaments will be held next year, with competition on installation, regimental and battalion levels.

> Following a year's absence, golf and tennis are back on the All-Army slate and volleyball has also been added.

> G-1 has approved the program and DA Circular outlining the program was to be published as Army TIMES when to press …

> … All-Army competition in softball on a regiment level and in volleyball on a battalion level was added to the All-Army program this year to encourage wide participation in company-level sports.

> (Selected) All-Army tournaments for 1955 with dates and host commands:

> BASKETBALL – April 4-9, Third Army. This will be on an installation (post team) level as before. Championship oversea (sic) command teams must represent a unit of not more than 25,000 men.

> TRACK & FIELD – June 18-19, Fifth Army. The All-Army TRIATHLON will be held in conjunction with the Track & Field meet. The triathlon will again serve to discover new talent for the United States pentathlon team …

> … Sites of tournaments will be determined by the commands involved.

> Championship teams and individuals in five of the All-Army events will go on to the Inter-Service competition…

115

… Inter-Service competition in baseball, basketball, and boxing was dropped in favor of bowling, golf and tennis by the Inter-Service Sports Council.

Army Times reported on 30 October 1954 (photo caption) concerning, "Notre Dame Back in Korea" (98). The photo showed a football quarterback behind the center; the caption stated:

> Gene Gribble, former West Point and Notre Dame back, is now playing ball for the I Corps Bullseyes in Korea. Here's Gene in the quarterback slot, about to receive the ball from center, Milton Jones, who formerly played for Virginia Union University. Gribble is with the 1169th Engineers. Jones is with the 96th FA Bn.

Another article on the same page (pg. 31) of *Army Times* reported, "Over 150 Coaches Expected To Vote in the All-Army Poll." The article said the poll was open, and that 150 Army coaches had been expected to participate. There would also be input from 50 Army sports writers; "All head football coaches in the States, Europe and the Pacific … can expect to receive a ballot …"

Moreover, "because of the vast number of Army football coaches – all coaches of strong regimental league teams as well as post teams" were eligible to participate. Also, to "assure outstanding players on smaller posts a better chance for All-Army recognition, the fans were not allowed to participate in the current poll, which was a change from the past."

Players selected would receive Zodiac watches in addition to the recognition. "The Army TIMES All-Army football poll is recognized nationally as the definitive poll of its kind."

In Tom Scanlon's column, "Second Guess", also on page 31, he discussed CONUS football – though, as previously noted, the focus of this book is Far East football, Mr. Scanlon's article merits a mention here based on included information concerning "All-Navy" and "All-Marine":

> Last year at this time any informed football fan had little trouble picking the team which would be hailed as the nation's top service 11. The Fort Ord Warriors -- boasting a grade line, depth, and backs such as Ollie Matson, Dave Mann, Bud Roffler, Don Heinrich, and Larry Segovia -- were loaded, and almost everybody knew it.
>
> Ord went on to prove to any skeptic that they were indeed the nation's best in post season games. In December, Ord walloped the All-Marine champs from Quantico, 55-19, in the Poinsettia Bowl. On New Year's Day in the Salad Bowl, Ord toyed with the All-Navy champs from Great Lakes, 67-12.
>
> But this year things are different. Only time will tell which service team is the best. And perhaps, eventually, the honorary championship will be heatedly disputed.
>
> In the East, Bolling AFB, Fort Belvoir, and Fort Jackson appear to be the best with Fort Lee and Quantico close behind.
>
> In the middle west, there is Fort Sill, Fort Carson and Great Lakes Naval Training Center. Fort Hood also has a fine team.
>
> In the far west, Fort Ord is once again the top team although the Navy PhibPac team is not to be over-looked.
>
> It is known that eight service teams have already received "feelers" from the Poinsettia Bowl Committee of San Diego, Cal. The Poinsettia Bowl is theoretically a contest between the top service teams in the nation (roughly on an East-West basis), and since neither Sill nor Carson face Fort Ord this year the selection of a Western representative could be become

confusing. (Carson, incidentally, has already lost a close one to Great Lakes in the season opener, 14-7, but Belvoir will meet Great Lakes, and a defeat for the Navy team in that one could throw the sailors out of Poinsettia Bowl contention).

The key game coming up in the east would seem to be the coming Bolling-Belvoir game late November. Here's why: Bolling is undefeated but tied (by Fort Jackson last week). Fort Belvoir is undefeated but tied (by Fort Lee two weeks ago).

Jackson would seem to be out of it because of a 14-9 defeat by Belvoir early in the season. Quantico has beaten by both (sic) Belvoir (16-6) and Bolling (25-14). Fort Lee tied Belvoir (7-7) but lost to Bolling (27-0). All clear?

A glance at the Fort Sill games to date (including a 7-0 win over Fort Hood and a 23-20 win over Brooke Medical Center) is deceptive because the present Sill team is much stronger than the one which played these early season games. Since then Oklahoma All-Americans Billy Vessels and Buck McPhail, and Marv Matuszak, All-Pro defensive lineman with the Pittsburgh Steelers, have been added, among others.

Fort Ord has been something of a surprise this year. Matson and Mann and Heinrich and Roffler and Segovia are gone, and the backfield cannot compare with the 1953 unit.

But, as popular 26-year-old coach Bill Abbey told Ord sports columnist PFC Larry Cahn recently, "Defensively we are not as strong as last year, yet no one is scoring off us. We don't have nearly the backfield strength that we did but yet we are scoring more points than our championship club did last year. I am sure that our opponents are not any weaker - we are a lot stronger than I ever thought we would be."

The top service team in the nation? You figure it out. I pass.—
TOM SCANLON.

A 5 November 1954 correspondence from Lt Col Kleiman, addressed to
various Commanding Generals, discussed "Special AFFE Boxing
Tournament" (99). The letter said that the United States Olympic
Committee would conduct a tournament in February 1955 for the
purpose of selecting the United States boxing team for the 1955 Pan-
American Games. In January 1955, the Department of the Army
established a training squad of boxers and selected the team to represent
the Army in the Olympic Committee's tournament.

Also, a special United States Army Forces Far East Boxing Tournament
was to be held 16-18 December 1954 in Fryar Gymnasium at Camp
Yokohama, Japan, to select boxers nominated by Department of the
Army. All United States Army personnel were eligible to participate in
the AFFE tournament.

There is a note which says, "Commands should enter only outstanding
boxers in the tournament; no team championship will be determined."

The correspondence further said, "Publicity is deemed essential to the
success of the tournament and participating commands should be urged
to submit complete information concerning their entries … in time for
use in pre-tournament releases an inclusion in the tournament program."

The tournament weight classes were flyweight, bantamweight,
featherweight, lightweight, light welterweight, welterweight, light
middleweight, middleweight, light heavyweight, heavyweight.
Participating commands would provide boxing trunks, robes, shoes,
competitive headguards, hand wraps, foulproof protective cups, and
teeth protectors. The tournament was to be single elimination. Also,
contestants would be required to present a "Statement of Amateurism"
in triplicate.

Army Times on 6 November 1954 (100) quoted Marvin Matuszak, the "Great All-Pro defensive lineman for 'Pitt' Steelers" and Fort Sill's "220 lb former All-America from Tulsa U" as saying he "thinks Army ball is really top notch!"

The Indiana Football Coaches Association's Indiana Football Hall of Fame (101) says that Marvin H. Matuszak played football for the University of Tulsa, earning Team MVP and All-American honors. He later played professionally for the Pittsburgh Steelers through 1956, the Green Bay Packers in 1958, the Baltimore Colts through 1961, the Buffalo Bills through 1963, and the Denver Broncos through 1964. He was said to have earned All-Pro honors several times.

Mr. Matuszak's career "was interrupted with service in the Army where he was able to play football," earning All-Army honors while serving in 1954 and 1955. He served as a coach with multiple NFL teams following his playing days. (*Note: Despite speculation, online sources indicate that he was* not *related to NFL great, John Matuszak*).

The 13 November 1954 *Army Times* newspaper discussed formation of an "All-Star Service Cage Team" (102). The team would be comprised of the "Top Army amateur basketball players," and would participate in the Mexico City Pan-American Games, 12-27 March, though the plan had not yet been given the go-ahead. Major Army commands had been requested to provide names of top players.

The plan was for the U.S. basketball team to be comprised of "five men from the Armed Forces, five from AAU teams (based on last year's AAU tournament) and four NCAA players." The five service members would be picked from an all-star Armed Forces team which would compete against "college, AAU, and strong service teams in January and February."

Proceeds from games played would be donated to the Olympic Committee.

Marvin H. "Marv" Matuszak (1931-2004) - Find a Grave
Memorial

The 20 November 1954 *Army Times* reported "close" All-Army early poll results (103): "Early returns in the Army Times 1954 All-Army football poll indicate that a close fight will be waged for all positions on the annual mythical eleven."

Polling for backfield positions was particularly close; backs who had already received votes were: "Jim Powers, Fort Ord; Leo Miles, Fort

121

Lee; Rick Casares, Fort Jackson; Dune McCauley, Fort Hood; Bob Haner, Fort Belvoir; Billy Vessels, Fort Sill."

Other backs receiving votes were: "Billy Sanders, Brooke Medical Center; Roy Garland, Fort Lewis; Dan Page, Fort Sill; Sam Baker, Fort Ord; Don Engels, Fort Belvoir; Henry Mosely, Fort Jackson; Henry Vance, Fort Eustice; Ray Huff, 37th Engr. Gp. Pioneers (Main Conference, Europe); and Don Stiles, 39th Inf. Regt. (Southern Conference, Europe)."

Linemen "prominently mentioned" in ballots were: "Winifred Tillery, Brooke Medical Center end; Jimmy Johnson, Fort Jackson center; Joe Tyrell, Fort Belvoir guard; Wayne Martin, Fort Sill end; Rudy Feldman, Fort Hood guard; Hal Mitchell, Fort Lee tackle; George Tarasovich, Fort Belvoir end; Gerry McGinley 4th Recon Bn. end (USFA Command); Pat O'Donahue, Camp Zama end; Andy Makay, Fort Richardson center; and Len Deutscher, Fort Lewis tackle."

The 20 November 1954 edition, also on page 35, had a photo caption which said the *Army Times* poll began in 1951, and that "66 players have received Zodiac watch awards for making All-Army."

Outstanding players of the past were listed as Arnold Galiffa, Andy Hillshouse, Ted Daffer, Mike McCormack, Ollie Matson, Dave Mann, Larry Coutre, and Gerald Weatherly.

> Galiffa, QB, made it in 1952 … with the Hqs Service Command team in Japan. Hillhouse, Daffer, and Coutre made it two years in a row. Camp Polk's Hillhouse, an end, was selected in 1951 and 1592 (sic). Daffer, Fort Eustis guard, was selected in 1952 and again last year. Coutre, backfield star for Camp Breckenridge, was honored in 1951 and 1952. Fort Sam Houston's Gerald Weatherly was All-Army guard in 1952. McCormack, star tackle for Fort Leonard Wood, was named last

year, as were Mann and Matson, Fort Ord backs. Matson was also named Most Valuable Player on the 1953 team.

The 20 November 1954 *Army Times* reported on football and track star SFC Alex Litman, he of "brilliant touchdown runs and still-unbroken track records," who would be reporting to AFFE "in the near future" (104):

> The product of the indestructible legs of SFC Alex Litman -- will soon be only memories to Brooke Army Medical Center sports fans. The 34-year-old athlete is now on leave and will report for duty with the Far East Command in the near future.
>
> Fondly referred to as "The Ghost" for his sudden appearances out of nowhere holding the pigskin, Litman has scored 42 points in the five games he has played this season for Brooke. He averages better than 12 yards per carry.
>
> An all-around athlete, he is probably best known as an All-Army dash star -- the same steam engine drive and lightning speed which were successful in sending him across the football goal line untouched enabled him to break track tapes far ahead of the pack.
>
> Litman, who runs 5 miles before reveille everyday "for exercise," is probably the oldest active sprinter in the nation. Boasting a two year edge on Olympic ace Mal Whitfield, Litman has been running in and winning military and Amateur Athletic Union track meets since entering the Army in 1940.
>
> Halfback Litman has seen twelve seasons of Army football. He threw the 1954 Brooke Comets grid machine into high gear when he streaked into the end zone 3 times in the first game of the season against Southwest Texas.

He also beat Olympic stars Ollie Matson and George Brown at the All-Army track meet at Fort Devens, Mass., last spring. He broke two of his old records at the tourney -- setting a 9.6 mark in the 100 yard dash and a 21.5 record in the 220 yard dash. He was named All-Army for these performances.

In May, Brooke fans saw him voted the outstanding athlete of the Fourth Army Conference track meet at Fort Sill, Okla., where he rewrote the dash books.

He won the Fourth Army 220 title in 21.5, putting in a 21 second performance during the trials of the meet, and swept the 100 yard dash championship in 9.6 seconds. Litman was a member of the Brooke relay team which set a Fourth Army record for the half mile of 1:29.6.

From the All-Army meet, the career soldier went on to compete in the annual AAU meet in Saint Louis, Mo., and the All-Service meet at Camp LeJeune, N. C. Running against the best the Army, Navy, Air Force and Marines could muster at the LeJeune meet, Litman took second in both the All-Service 100 and 220.

Second Lt. John P. Walter, Brooke track coach and former track captain at Michigan State College, calls Litman "One of the greatest and certainly the hardest working athletes I have ever seen."

Walter, who led the Medical Center Cindermen to the Fourth Army championship, should know about such things because he was a member of the Spartan's 1952 cross-country team, the 1st in history to win the Big Ten, IC4A and NCCAA titles in the same year.

Litman, five feet, ten inches tall and weighing 185 lbs, worked as a technician in a dispensary at Brooke's Medical Field

Service School prior to his alert for overseas. During War II (sic), Litman served in the South Pacific, and he holds the Philippine Liberation Medal with one battle star and the Occupation of Japan Ribbon.

A 10 December 1954 memo listed participants in the December 1952 Special AFFE Boxing Tournament for the Korean Communications Zone (KComZ). The participants were:

Cecil D. Watson, Capt(OIC), Hq KComZ; Robert Ranck, 1st Lt, 167th Trans Bn; Edward T. White, Sfc, Hq KComZ; George Harrell, Sgt, 52nd Sig Base Depot; Henry Aragahi, Cpl, 60th Med Depot; Robert W. Savage, Cpl, 8057th A.U.; Denny Dockery, Pfc, 21st Fort Comd B; Psolo Frank, Pfc, 50th Engr Co (Const); William Fulwood, Pfc, 8113rd A.U.; Howard Millsap, Pfc, 1st 90mm AAA Bn; Eli Scott, Pfc, 21st Fort Comd B; Palacio De Leo, Pvt, 388th Engr Co (P/L) (105).

The 1954 All-Army poll results were published in the 11 December 1954 *Army Times* newspaper (106). All First and Second Team honorees are only from CONUS teams. The article appears to suggest that *talented Far East players may have been shortchanged due to the lack of response from their coaches to the selection committee* (It, added).

Army Times said on page 28 that "Fifteen coaches of Far East teams were invited to forward nominations. *Nominations were received from five* (It. added)." The five coaches' Far East nominations had been augmented by an "informal poll" of Central Command coaches and sports writers. Eighteen coaches from Europe participated in their portion of the polling.

Army Times provided biographical summaries of the selected players:

The <u>First Team</u> All-Army 1954 players named:

Pos.	Rank	Team	College	Pro Rights
E	PFC Dan McBride	Fort Carson, Colo	Iowa	n/a
E	Pvt. Geo. Tarasovich	Fort Belvoir, Va.	LSU	Steelers
T	2d Lt. Hal Mitchell	Fort Lee, Va.	UCLA	Giants
T	Cpl. Len Deutscher	Fort Lewis, Wash.	Mich. State	n/a
G	2d Lt. Rudy Feldman	Fort Hood, Tex.	UCLA	n/a
G	2d Lt. John Michels	Fort Eustis, Va.	Tenn.	Eagles
C	Pvt. Bob Lusk	Fort Lee, Va.	Wm. & Mary	n/a
QB	Pvt. Jim Powers	Fort Ord, Calif.	USC	49ers
HB	2d Lt. Billy Vessels	Fort Sill, Okla.	Oklahoma	Edmunton (sic)
HB	PFC Bobby Haner	Fort Belvoir, Va.	Villanova	Redskins
FB	2d Lt. Buck McPhail	Fort Sill, Okla.	Oklahoma	Colts

The <u>Second Team</u> All-Army 1954 players named:

Pos.	Rank	Team	College	Pro Rights
E	Pvt. Winifred Tillery	Brooke Medical	NC St. Col.	n/a
E	Pvt. Stan Wacholz	Fort Ord, Calif.	San Jose St.	49ers
T	PFC Frank Monti	Fort Carson, Colo.	U. of S.F.	n/a
T	Pvt. Bob (Tiny) Goss	Brooke Medical	SMU	Browns
G	PFC Joe Martone	Fort Monmouth, N.J.	Tenn.	n/a
G	2d Lt. Joe Ramona	Fort Sill, Okla.	Santa Clara	Giants
C	Cpl. Jimmy Johnson	Fort Jackson, S.C.	Ga. Tech	n/a
QB	PFC Don Engels	Fort Belvoir, Va.	Illinois	n/a
HB	2d Lt. Leo Miles	Fort Lee, Va.	Va. State	Giants
HB	Cpl. Billy Sanders	Brooke Medical	SW Texas	n/a
FB	Pvt. Rick Casares	Fort Jackson, S.C.	U. of Fla.	Bears

The <u>Third Team</u> All-Army 1954 players named:

Pos.	Name (rank unk.)	Team	College	Pro Rights
E	Gerry McGinley	4th Recon. Bn. USFA	Penn State	n/a
E	Pat O'Donohue	Camp Zama, Far East	Wisconsin	n/a
T	Ben Donkerly	14th A/C Europe	West Va.	n/a
T	Dexter Poss	Fort Jackson, S.C.	Georgia	n/a
G	Joe Tyrrell	Fort Belvoir, Va.	Temple	n/a
C	Bob Baldwin	Fort Wood, Mo.	Trinity	n/a
QB	Ed Soergel	Fort Carson, Colo.	East Ill.	n/a
HB	Henry Vance	Fort Eustis, Va.	n/a	n/a
FB	Dunc McCauley	Fort Hood, Tex.	Houston	n/a

Army post and regimental league coaches from CONUS, Hawaii, Alaska, Europe, and the Far East contributed nominations. Select comments on nominees from the coaches are included below:

From Bill Abbey, Fort Ord Coach:

Jimmy Powers – "*His knowledge of the game and ability to pick the opponent's defense apart has enabled us to move as we have this year. He is outstanding on defense as halfback or linebacker.*"

Stan Wacholz – *"Best offensive end we have ever had at Fort Ord."*

From Bob Cook, Fort Lewis Coach:

Len Deutscher – *"The type of player who always gives his best. Could make any college team in the country. An inspirational leader who has earned the complete trust and respoect of the coaching staff."*

From Cpl. Al Thomy, *Jackson Journal*:

Rick Casares – *"Casares has been everything to Fort Jackson this season -- runner, tackler, blocker, punter, extra point and field goal kicker. Also a fine passer but hasn't been called upon to throw. Defensive play has been vicious. Gained 85 yards against powerful Bolling AFB. There's not a better back in the country."*

Jimmy Johnson – *"A tremendous linebacker. One of our boys, who played football for Oklahoma before entering service, says Johnson is the best linebacker he has seen. He hits hard and true."*

From Leaton Cofield, Brooke Coach:

Billy Sanders – *"One of the best offensive and defensive backs in football today he has two years of college eligibility left and any college would be proud to have him."*

From PFC Geo. E. Egofske, *Brooke Roundup*:

Billy Sanders – *"Stood out above all other players, even above such former All-Americans as Vessels, Heath and McPhail. No Sanders (sic) ability well because I also play on the Brooke team."*

From Robert L. Snell, USFA Area Cmd Coach:

Gerry McGinley – *"In the 12 years that I have been associated with football on the college level and in the Army this player is without a doubt one of the finest I have seen."*

Guard John Michels was described as a *"Hustling guard and co-captain of Fort Eustis Wheels. Starred for Tennessee before playing a year of pro ball with the Philadelphia Eagles."*

Photo: All-Army 1954 picks, https://archive.org/details/sim_army-times_1954-12-11_15_18/page/27/mode/1up?view=theater

John Michels' obituary (107) says that he had been a College Football Hall of Fame player and served 27 seasons as a Minnesota Vikings assistant football coach.

He worked for the Vikings from 1967 to 1993, and was the "longest-tenured coach in franchise history." Most of his offensive line coaching was under legendary head coach, Bud Grant.

Mr. Michels had NFL playing experience with the Philadelphia Eagles in 1953 and 1956. He later played for Canadian Football's Winnipeg Blue Bombers. He also assisted with Texas A&M for one season.

John Michels played guard on Tennessee's 1951 National Championsip team and was voted All-American honors in 1952. He was inducted into the College Football Hall of Fame in 1996, and into the Tennesee Sports Hall of Fame in 1999.

In a tribute to Coach Michels, Vikings.com (108) says that he served as a First Lieutenant in the Army from 1954 to 1956. He was "undersized," but was a "great player … what made him great was his competitiveness." Bud Grant said that players loved to play for Coach Michels, because "Many times he competed harder as a coach than the players did, and they recognized that." Hall of Fame football star and former Vikings great, Ron Yary, said that Coach Michels "led in a way that was perfect for me. He had high expectations and set a high standard."

John Michels - Rest in Peace, hero.

A 16 December 1954 letter from Headquarters, Korean Communications Zone, sent by G.C. Maxwell to the Commanding Officers of Pusan Military Post APO 59, Taegu Military Post APO 234, and Inchon Military Post APO 971, discussed a "Korean

131

Communications Zone Basketball Tournament" for February 1955 (109).

The letter stated,

> The Korean Communications Zone Basketball Tournament will be conducted in Inchon, Korea, during the period 8 - 12 February 1955. The Commanding Officer, Inchon Military Post, will act as host.

> Outstanding players will be selected to represent the Korean Communication Zone in the All-Far East Basketball Tournament to be held at Camp Otsu, from 8 through 12 March 1955. Each military Post Commander was allowed to enter two teams composed of a maximum of 13 players to include a coach and one Officer-in-Charge. Team rosters would be submitted to the Commanding Officer. The rosters would include name, grade, service number, organization and home town (sic) of each member.

Major Commanders were authorized to issue travel orders covering travel of participants to the tournament.

The basketball players would be placed on TDY (temporary duty) for approximately 8 days with Headquarters 21st Port Command B, Inchon Military Post; upon completion of the tournament, the players selected would be placed on temporary duty for approximately 35 days.

Teams were to be composed of both officers and enlisted men, however, "at least 50 per cent (sic) of the players on the court at any one time must be enlisted men." The memo further stated that teams would represent a regimental combat team or units of comparable size, and that grouping together of small units with an aggregate strength not to exceed 5000 men was authorized.

Major Commanders would provide their team members with all necessary equipment and supplies except tournament game balls, which would be furnished by the host command. Awards/benefits included: A team plaque to winners and runners-up, individual awards, $7.50 per man to "competent officials." Tournament results were to be submitted by "electrical means" to the Military Post Commanders.

An 18 December 1954 *Army Times* column by Tom Scanlon (110) discussed the 1954 *Army Times'* All-Army football team:

> Speaking of Army Times' All-Army football team, as we hope you've been doing since the team was announced in last week's paper, we think the 1954 All-Army squad is the best balanced and most accurate yet.

> Only 22 players could win berths on the first two All-Army teams, however, and this automatically kept many a fine ballplayer off the squad.

> Fullback Duane McCauley, for example, has certainly been playing All-Army grade ball for the Fort Hood Tankers this year. But in the All-Army poll he had the misfortune of competing against Fort Sill's Buck McPhail and Fort Jackson's Rick Casares for the top two fullback berths. Belvoir's Jerry Lodge and Fort Ord's Sam Baker, two other fullbacks who had great years, were in the same boat ... picking an All-American team, which is dangerous business as we all know, is a snap in comparison to picking an All-Army team ... it's a big Army and Army ball is played on various levels.

> How do you compare players on a regimental league team with players on one of the strong post teams? The nearest analogy to the predicament is the "All-American" rating of players with small college teams. Although a good number of pro stars come from small colleges, it is seldom that any of these players

133

receive the "All American" credit due them when they are in college …

It's good, too, to see many of our former All-Army players doing well in pro ball. Our Most Valuable Player of '53, Ollie Matson, is probably the best example. Used only on defense by the Chicago Cardinals before going into service he has proved an offensive star for the Cards this year as he was with the Fort Ord Warriors last year.

Another example is Ted Daffer, two-time All-Army guard who has made good as a defensive end for the Chicago Bears this year … incidentally, Ted likes pro ball and tells us that he's found the spirit of the players in pro ball as high if not higher than in college ball. Here are a few of Daffer's comments on pro ball:

"Pro ball is different. All the players are big, strong and fast. Their spirit and love for football is as great or greater than that of college players. Don't work as hard and practice as we did in college but when the games come along every guy is out there to win.

I don't believe the game is any dirtier than college ball, but it is much rougher. I think the Bears this year are one of the best clubs I've ever seen although we did not win the championship. The spirit on our club can only be found on the best of ball clubs. We want to beat the Lions on Sunday."

The 18 December 1954 edition of *Army Times* also included a brief article on the "All-Army Sites Set for 1955" (page 32):

Basketball – Fort Benning, Ga., April 4-9; Track and Field – Fort Riley, Kan., June 18-19; Boxing – Fort Ord, Calif., April 11-16 (only selected sports noted for this publication).

Page 32 also included an article about Fort Richardson, Alaska, basketball coach, Capt. Henry E. Rainbolt, who had won 127 games and lost only 15 games in his career. Capt. Rainbolt had a connection to AFFE sports in Korea:

> Capt. Rainbolt went to Korea in 1948 and coached the 7th Divarty team to the 7th Division championship. He was later picked to head the All-Star team from the 7th Division in a game against the Korean hoop aggregation that had placed eighth in the 1948 Olympic Games in London.
>
> With such stars as Glen Davis, West Point All-American football star of 1944-46, Capt. Rainbolt lost out to the Koreans in a best two-out-of-three series. Davis, according to Rainbolt, was one of the best basketball players and all-around athletes that he has ever coached*.
>
> In March of 1949, the captain led the 555th FA Bn. squad to the finals in the All-Korea basketball championships, only to lose out to a team that eventually won the Far East Command title, and went on to the States to participate in the All-Army Basketball Championships at Fort Dix, N.J., losing out in the finals of that important tournament to Brooke Army Medical Center of Fort Sam Houston, Tex."

Note: Glenn Davis was a phenomenal all-around athlete at West Point, during which time he was awarded the Heisman Trophy.

The 10 December 2014 *Army Times* discussed Davis's legend in an article titled, "Mr. Inside and Mr. Outside: Army Football's Golden Age" (111), which in turn referred to a book by Jack Cavanaugh: "Few teams have glory days as glorious as Army football, a point that veteran sportswriter Jack Cavanaugh drives home in *Mr. Inside and Mr. Outside*, a book chronicling a three-year stretch in the mid-1940s during which West Point compiled a 27-2-1 record, claimed at least a share of three straight national championships, and saw two legendary players earn Heisman Trophies."

Glenn Davis was "Mr. Outside" and Felix "Doc" Blanchard was "Mr. Inside." These two men were popularly believed to be "possibly the greatest backfield tandem in college football history." Glenn Davis had been a "high school super-athlete from Southern California who began rewriting the Army offensive record book in 1943."

In an interesting side note, it was claimed that "Army regularly played to massive crowds at Yankee Stadium, outdrawing NFL games with ease."

Lastly, there was another small article on page 32 regarding Ed Stoken, "Seoul Military Post's star punter," who "may have set some kind of service record with a 104-yard kick against the 1st Marine Div. in a Korean Football Conference Game this year. Stoken, a defensive end, made the long boot late in the 4th quarter to help his mates to a 16-14 upset over the Marines."

The 25 December 1954 *Army Times* reported, "Eighth Army Basketball Aces Get All-Star Team Tryouts" (4). Eight "outstanding Army basketball players" were to go to Wright-Patterson AFB in Ohio on 28 December, "to begin practice for the all-star Armed Forces team." The article said that "all are former college stars," except for Don Byrd of Fort Belvoir, who was "an outstanding player for Fort Leonard Wood, Mo."

> The selection of the 20-year-old Byrd will come as no surprise to those who have seen him perform on a basketball court. Before coming into the Army, Byrd had played only high school ball in Cleveland, Ohio, but during the past two years in Army ball he has held his own against such nationally famous stars as Paul Arizin, Maurice (The Magnificent) Stokes, Ernie Beck, Art

Spoelstra and Dick Knostman. He plays best when he is playing against the best.

Some said he had been "destined for basketball greatness."

The other selections were:

- 2d Lt. Frank Guisness, Fort Lee, Va., "The University of Washington's second highest all-time scoring leader." Guisness was said to have been named to the "Helms Foundation All-American team while with the University of Washington." He was player-coach of the Fort Lee team.
- 2d Lt. Cecil (Pete) Silas, Fort McClellan, Ala., "A star with Georgia Tech and the nationally famous Phillips Oilers." Silas had earned "Tech's all-time scoring mark."
- PFC Robert Peterson, Fort Ord, Calif., "All-Coast at the University of Oregon."
- 2d Lt. Robert Speight, Fort Bliss, Tex., "North Carolina State star."
- PFC Will Wilfong, Fort Leonard Wood, Tex., "Big Seven All-Conference choice at the University of Missouri."
- Pvt. Walter Walowac, Fort Knox, Ky., "Marshall College star."
- PFC Jack Williams, Eilson AFB, Alaska, "Wake Forest star."

Also, "Fifteen players will be chosen from those drilling at Wright-Patterson for the Armed Forces team. A final series with the selected AAU team will determine the players making up the U.S. team which will go to the Pan American games in Mexico City next March." Five players were to be chosen from the Armed Forces team and five from the AAU team; there would be four additional players selected from colleges "to complete the U.S. team."

Included among the ten Air Force players selected for tryouts with the Armed Forces team are three from the 1952 Olympic team, Bob Kenney and Dean Kelley, former Kansas players now at Andrews AFB, Md., and Kerwin Englehart of Yokata AB, Japan.

Other Air Force personnel selected were Bill McCullum, Lockbourne AFB; Bob Williams and Billy Hogie, Sheppard AFB; Gil Roark, Warren AFB; Barry Porter, Kirtland AFB; John Clune, Dover AFB; Earl Redwine, Walker AFB; John Wilson, East Illinois State College; Gill Reich, Lake Charles AFB, and Bradley's Dick Estergard of Furstenfeldbruch AB, Germany.

Maj. Roy P. Johnson, Hq USAF, Special Services branch, said that "The tentative plan is for the team to appear in preliminary games on the same card with pro and college teams."

Army Times reported on 25 December 1954 that Hal Mitchell, All-Army MVP had "only hoped to make the team" (*Ed. - humble!*).

Burly, friendly Hal Mitchell grinned from ear to ear when informed that he had been named the Most Valuable Player on the Army Times All-Army football team last week.

"This certainly comes as a surprise and an honor to me. I was just hoping to make the team again," the 240 pound, former New York Giant, exclaimed.

Asked if he would return to the Giants when his service hitch expires next spring, the former UCLA star remarked, "I really don't know. What I'd like to do is get a high school coaching job in California. If the price is right, I'll go back to pro ball. Then again, I might take a shot at the Canadian brand of football, which is a lot easier than our game and pays a lot more."

Mitchell, the first lineman ever to win MVP honors, considers this as his top thrill in football. Others that stand in his mind were being named to the first string All-Star team in Chicago in 1952 and when Steve Owen had him in the starting lineup against the Browns in 1953.

29 December 1954 correspondence from G.C. Maxwell, Lt Col, AGC, Asst AG, discusses the "Korean Communications Zone 1955 Boxing Tournament" (112). The correspondence said the tournament would be held 24-26 February 1955. Winners of the tournament would represent the Korean Communication Zone in the All-Far East boxing tournament in Japan, 16-20 March 1955.

To paraphrase the communication, teams would be composed of United States Army personnel located within the geographical limits of the Korean Communications Zone; "A boxing team consisting of a winner in each weight class may be entered from each sports conference."

The host command (not yet named) would have various duties, including designating the tournament site, advise participating conferences of procedures, arrange for suitable billeting and messing, furnish facilities and equipment, and so on. Weight classes:

Flyweight 112 lbs

Bantamweight 119 pounds

Featherweight 125 lbs

Lightweight 132 lbs

Welterweight 147 lbs

Light Middleweight 156 lbs

Middleweight 165 lbs

Light Heavyweight 178 lbs

Heavyweight Over 178 lbs

Furthermore,

> Each team will be authorized one coach, one trainer, and an officer in charge. The commanders of units to which the individual participants are assigned will provide boxing trunks, robes, shoes, competitive headguards, foul-proof cup protectors, and teeth protectors. Each contestant will be required to present a "Statement of Amateurism" sworn before a summary board officer, upon reporting at the tournament site … The tournament will be on a single elimination basis, without seeding.
>
> National Amateur Athletic Union Boxing Rules, as defined in the 1954 Official Rule Books will govern, except that, as a protection against eye cuts (and) ear and head injuries, a light weight headguard will be worn by each participant. The head guards will provide a protective covering at least 1/2 inch in thickness, covering the ears, eye ridges, temples, and back of the head.
>
> Also, team awards would be presented on the basis of the following: Five points for each championship, two points for each bout won, one additional point for each bout won after bye, one point to each contestant entered in the tournament. Further, each contestant will be required to weigh again and be examined physically prior to each event in which he competes. The results of physical examinations and weigh-ins will be recorded by the officer-in-charge of the tournament.

Tournament officials would be paid $10 per day for the referee, $5 per day for each of the three judges, and $5 per day for one timer.

Photo: Camp Zama, year unknown, b2wblog20.blogspot.com

1955

The 1 January 1955 *Army Times* had a photo and caption on page 27 presenting "Far East Command Stars" (113):

> Three of the most outstanding players in the Far East this year, from left: Cpl. Phil Gillis, PFC Charlie Black and Cpl. Jim Davenport. Gillis, All-American and from the University of Washington, starred for Camp Tokyo.
>
> Black, a fullback with the 7th Cavalry, was a first team berth on the Army's team in the Far East bowl game ahead of such stars as Camp Tokyo's Dan Schriebman and Camp McGill's Willard Ellard. Davenport, a quarterback, led Camp Otsu to an undefeated season in the Southwest Command.

Far East Command Stars

THREE OF THE MOST outstanding players in the Far East this year, from left: Cpl. Phil Gillis, PFC Charlie Black and Cpl. Jim Davenport. Gillis, All-American end from the University of Washington, starred for Camp Tokyo. Black, a fullback with the 7th Cavalry, won a first team berth on the Army's team in the Far East Bowl Game ahead of such stars as Camp Tokyo's Don Schriebman and Camp McGill's Willard Ellard. Davenport, a quarterback, led Camp Otsu to an undefeated season in the Southwest Command.

Photo: https://archive.org/details/sim_army-times_1955-01-
01_15_21/page/27/mode/1up?view=theater

Also on page 27, a short article called "Korean Conference Coaches Select All-Star Eleven" in which the eleven Korean Football Conference All-Star players were named:

> Ends – Merrill Jacobs (FMD) and Bill Carey (24th Div.).
>
> Tackles – Tom Roche (FMD) and Harley Martin (SMP).
>
> Guards – Jim Pozza (FMD) and Tom Roggeman (FMD).
>
> Center – George Boyer (7th Div.).
>
> Quarterback – John Cahill (FMD).
>
> Halfbacks – Tom Hinson (SMP) and Gene Gribble (I Corps).

Fullback – Tie between Pete D'Alonzo (7th Div.) and Joe Coppola (SMP).

Honorable Mention – Ends Dean Hamilton (SMP), Ed Stoken (SMP), and Don Taylor (FMD). Tackles Jim Walker (7th Div.), Alfred Rogers (7th Div.), and Jim Gregory (I Corps). Guards Jim Eberle (24th Div.) and Joe Salafia (7th Div.). Center Jim Erkenbeck (FMD). Backs Sal DiGiorgi (SMP), Fran Trusky (SMP), and Charles Desadier (FMD).

More on page 27: "AFPS All-Servce (sic) 11," the First and Second and Honorable Mention All-Service teams were named:

> **FIRST TEAM:** Ends Frank McPhee (Camp Pendleton) and Bernie Flowers (Great Lakes). Tackles J.D. Kimmel (Fort Lee) and Dave Suminski (Fort Belvoir). Guards Steve Eisenhauer (Quantico) and Bruce Halliday (Fort Ord). Center Jerry Hilgenberg (Hamilton AFB). Backs Tommy O'Connell (Bolling AFB), Billy Vessels (Fort Sill), Bob Meyers (Camp Lejeune) and Rick Casares (Fort Jackson).

> **SECOND TEAM:** Ends Charlie Jones (Bolling AFB) and Bucky Curtis (San Diego NTC). Tackles Bob Gain (Nagoya Japan AFB) and Jim Mahoney (Little Creek Navy). Guards Rudy Feldman (Fort Hood) and Joe Tyrrell (Fort Belvoir). Center Ronnie Zatkoff (Newport NS). Backs Bobby Williams (Bainbridge NTC), Gene Filipski (Quantico), Bill Boller (Keesler AFB) and Buck McPhail (Fort Sill).

> **Honorable Mention:** Verl Scott (Fort Carson), Hal Mitchell (Fort Lee), John Gramling (Shaw AFB), Pat Sarnese (Fort Belvoir), Jim Eberle (24th Div., Korea), J.D. Smith (Pensacola Navy), Fred Pancoast (Parris

143

> Island), Bill Reichardt (Bolling AFB), Jim Golliday (6th Inf., Germany), John Wheat (Hamilton AFB), Jim Cauthron (San Diego Marines), Ted Marchibroda (Fort Lee) and Billy Cox (Amphib Force Pacific Fleet).

All-Service First-Team center Jerry Hilgenberg's obituary and the *Iowa History Journal* site combine to show the blue-blood football lineage of the Hilgenberg family.

His 16 January 2024 obituary (114) says:

> Former University of Iowa All-American Jerry Hilgenberg has passed away at the age of 92 … Hilgenberg started at center for three seasons for the Hawkeyes (1951-53). He was a first-team All-American and All-Big Ten honoree his senior season. Hilgenberg, and guard Cal Jones, were Hall of Fame coach Forest Evashevski's first All-Americans.

> Hilgenberg led the Hawkeyes to a final national ranking of No. 9 in 1953, the program highest final ranking since 1939. He also excelled in the classroom, earning Academic All-District and All-Big Ten accolades as a senior. Hilgenberg was invited to play in two post-season all-star games after his senior campaign, the East-West Shrine Game and Senior Bowl.

> "Jerry Hilgenberg was a first-class individual," said University of Iowa Moon Family Head Coach Kirk Ferentz …

> A native of Wilton, Iowa, Hilgenberg also lettered in baseball in 1952 and 1953 …

> Hilgenberg was drafted in the fourth round of the 1954 NFL Draft by the Cleveland Browns but did not play professionally, as he was also drafted by the U.S. Air Force.

> (He later helped coach Hawkeye teams to National Championships and Rose Bowl appearances).

Hilgenberg was able to coach his younger brother Wally, who was an All-Conference performer, and ultimately played in four Super Bowls with the Minnesota Vikings …

Hilgenberg was inducted into the Iowa University Club Hall of Fame in 1995.

The *Iowa History Journal* (115) adds:

He was the first of six members of his family – all linemen, mostly centers – to play for the Hawkeyes, as younger brother Wally, sons Jim, Jay, and Joel, and Wally's son, Eric, all followed in his path.

Between them, players-named-Hilgenberg won 19 varsity letters at Iowa. Jerry, Wally, and Jay were named to First Team, All-Big Ten. Joel was a two-time Second Team, All-Big Ten pick. They combined to play 39 seasons in the National Football League, starting 375 games and playing in five Super Bowls and eight Pro Bowls.

The 1 January 1955 *Army Times* edition also included (page 27) Tom Scanlon's "Second Guess" column, which discussed *Fort Jackson Journal's* ("One of the best sports sections of any post paper that comes across our desk") anxiety over the fact that Rick Casares, Jackson's great fullback, "could place no higher than second on the All-Army team."

Former Oklahoma All-American, Buck McPhail, had taken the first-place fullback position. McPhail was been the most valuable player on the Fort Sill Cannoneers championship team.

"The *Jackson Journal's* gripe over the matter began two weeks ago and became more adamant last week following the announcement of the Armed Forces Press Service (AFPS) All-Service selections. On the AFPS squad, Casares was on the first team and McPhail was on the second."

Mr. Scanlon wrote that "From our view it sounds like quibbling; in the first place, we have never proposed to draw a heavy line between players on the first All-Army team and players on the second All-Army team. All 22 receive about equal play in our paper and all 22 receive Zodiac watches."

Also, "*Jackson* may be interested to know that Casares probably would have been on the first All-Army team had it not been for competition in the East from fullback Jerry Lodge of Fort Belvoir. Lodge played great ball for Belvoir this year and several opposition team coaches and writers in the *Army Times* poll ... favored Lodge over Casares. Like Casares, Lodge is considered top-grade pro material."

Mr. Scanlon said, "Our system of selecting the All-Army team is far from perfect but we think it's the best that's been devised yet."

The observation that Mr. Casares was "pro material" was spot-on, as he had fact been selected 18th overall in the 1954 NFL draft (116). He was drafted as a fullback and played for the Chicago Bears (1955-64), Washington Redskins (1965), and Miami Dolphins (1966).

> (Mr. Casares) scored on a long touchdown (81 yards) on his first career carry. He led the Bears in rushing each season from 1955 through 1960 and topped NFL in rushing by a wide margin in 1956 when he amassed 1,126 yards good for 4.8 yards per carry. Casares also led the league that year with 14 touchdowns and 12 rushing touchdowns. His yardage total was just 20 yards shy of the NFL single-season rushing record and the Bears won the Western Conference.

> Casares spent 10 years with the Bears and was the team's all-time rushing leader with 5,657 yards until Walter Payton. He made five consecutive Pro Bowl appearances, and was first team all-pro in 1956 and a second team all-pro several other times.

Mr. Casares' obituary was published in the *Tampa Bay Times* (among other outlets) on 14 September 2013 (117). He was 82 years old at the time of his passing. His wife found him deceased while he was "researching this weekend's football games."

Casares was born 4 July 1931 in Tampa. In high school, he played football, baseball, and basketball. In 2007, "The Florida High School Athletic Association ranked him among the top 100 greatest football players in state history."

> The Korean War ended Mr. Casares' collegiate career early. He was drafted into the service, and was in the Army in 1954 when he was drafted again, by the Chicago Bears. Mr. Casares was a bruising runner – at 6 feet 2, 225 pounds he was large for a running back in the 1950s and NFL … Mr. Casares is still the No. 3 all-time rusher in Bears history.

The very busy 1 January 1955 edition of *Army Times* (page 28) also has an article titled "Army Sports Year in Review," with accompanying photos of football players Hal Mitchell, Alex Litman, Billy Vessels, and others.

Hal Mitchell's daughter, Beth Stephenson, writing for the *Oklahoman* newspaper on 5 September 2016, discussed "memories of columnist's dad" (118). She wrote,

> I grew up in a football household. My dad, Hal Mitchell, was an all-star at UCLA and went on to play a season as a tackle for the New York Giants. When he was hurt in spring practice and cut from the team, he was immediately drafted into the Army. He told the story of showing up at Fort Lee in Virginia. He gave his name. The receiving officer asked him, "Are you THE Hal Mitchell, the football player?"
>
> "Yep."

"Report to the field house"

In those days, each branch of the military had their own team. They were not quite pro, but more like semi-pro.

"I can't play football. I have a knee injury."

The officer apparently looked him over. "Lieutenant, either report to the field house or go to Korea. It's up to you."

He was the captain of the Army football team … he designed a knee brace/pad that would protect his particular injury. The knee healed … He patented the pad system and eventually sold it to Rawlings Sporting Goods.

After the Army, he turned to coaching after turning down a contract from the Washington Redskins, and eventually earned Western Athletic Coach of the Year while at BYU. He also had business success, being named "Head of research and development for Rawlings."

Hal Mitchell passed away on 27 November 1993. Rest in Peace, hero.

The previously mentioned 1 January 1955 "Year in Review" article says that "Nineteen fifty four was an interesting year in Army sports." *Army Times* noted that a team without stars won the All-Army basketball title and that "stars" in several sports were selected for Pan Am Games representative teams. Furthermore, seven All-Army and four inter-service tournaments were held, and the Army "laid down a new set of rules … for post baseball and basketball teams."

Camp Chaffee's basketball team earned a "surprising" All-Army victory at Fort Lewis, Washington:

The hustling underdog Chaffee team of comparative unknowns, organized only a month and 13 games before the All-Army event took place, walloped teams staffed with nationally known big name stars, and went through the tournament undefeated …

148

the speedy Fourth Army champions were led by Indiana's Phil Buck, J.C. Maze, Washington University's Gary Moore and Chuck Stickles, a Little All-American from Hastings College ... the post's All-Army victory pointed up the value of a strong post regimental league.

Army dominated the inter-service tournament in track and field, held at Camp Lejeune, N.C. - "The Army's team won ten events and rolled up a total of 113 points ... the Army's 440 relay team set a new tournament record of 41:4." In boxing, "Third Army – led by Fort Bragg fighters – won the most convincing team victory in All-Army boxing tournament history by taking six individual crowns ... Middleweight champ Roscoe Elliott of Fort Bragg won the tournament 'outstanding boxer' award."

Flyweight Preston Jenkins of the European Command and bantam George Davis retained their All-Army crowns.

The 8 January 1955 *Army Times* newspaper (119) contains a letter from Maj. Gen. F.C. Holbrook, Commanding General, Fort Lee, discussing All-Army Awards:

> The Staff and personnel of the Quartermaster Training Command have noted with great pride the selection of three Fort Lee football players to the Army Times "All-Army" teams. We are especially proud of Lt. Hal Mitchell who has been chosen the "Most Valuable Player." We all know that a good athlete is a good soldier and I can assure you that this is borne out by Lt. Mitchell, Pvt. Bob Lusk and Lt. Leo Miles.
>
> I wish to compliment the Army Times for initiating your splendid program for recognizing outstanding athletes. It is a significant factor in the promotion of Army sports competition and participation.

There is little recompense for Army athletes except the admiration of one's comrades-in-arms. I have observed the tremendous interest of both players and readers in your over-all selections and I compliment you on this assistance in furthering the Army athletic program.

At the annual Fort Lee Fall Sports Dinner I had the honor of presenting the three watches awarded by the Army Times to our Fort Lee football players. I assure you that they were received with great appreciation by the players and with enthusiasm by the entire Sports Group.

Another letter, by "Football Fan" in the same edition of *Army Times* asked if it would be a good idea to rate (Service Sports) football teams as college teams are rated by Associated Press and United Press. He said he "never sees any service teams ranked."

The *Army Times* Sports Editor responded by stating:

We have not started such a rating list because we do not think such a list could be fair and accurate. Frankly, we have never thought much of the wire service college football ratings which receive so much space in the daily newspapers during the football season. Post-season games frequently show up the foolishness of the whole scheme and we can't help but think that it is kinda silly to call one team 89.7 and another 89.6, for example.

The only nationally known service football rating list is put out by Williamson. The final Williamson ratings found the Fort Sill Cannoneers on top but only by two-tenths of a point over Bolling AFB, the team Sill defeated with little trouble in the Poinsettia Bowl, 27-6.

The final complete Williamson service football (stateside only) ratings follow:

1. Fort Sill, 94.2
2. Bolling AFB, 94.0
3. Fort Belvoir, 93.2
4. Quantico, 93.0
5. Fort Jackson, 92.5
6. Fort Lee, 92.2
7. PhibPac, 92.0
8. Fort Ord, 91.7
9. Shaw AFB, 91.5
10. Fort Eustis, 90.7
11. Bainbridge, 90.4
12. Pensacola, 90.3
13. Fort Hood, 90.2
14. Brooke Medical Center, 90.1
15. Keesler AFB, 89.9
16. Parris Island, 89.8
17. Fort Monmouth, 89.4
18. MCRD, 89.2
19. Little Creek, 88.6
20. Camp Pendleton, 87.8
21. Camp Lejeune, 87.6
22. Great Lakes, 87.0
23. Camp Carson, 86.2
24. Hamilton AFB, 86.0
25. San Diego Naval Air 84.7
26. Cherry Point, 83.7
27. San Diego NTC, 82.7
28. Eglin AFB, 82.7
29. Sheppard, 83.3

30. Norfolk Navy, 82.2
31. Fort Lewis, 80.3
32. Tyndall AFB, 86.7
33. Alameda Naval Air, 76.3
34. Fort Leonard Wood, 75.5
35. Long Beach Navy, 75.2
36. Barstow, 74.7
37. Point Mugu, 74.4
38. Memphis Naval Air, 73.1
39. Edward AFB, 71.1
40. Treasure Island, 70.7
41. Fort Meade, 70.0
42. Presidio, 69.6
43. Amarillo AFB, 67.6
44. Charleston AFB, 65.4

The 15 January 1955 *Army Times* (120) reported on the Army screening of boxers for the Pan-American Trials:

> The Army's talent hunt for top amateur athletes who can help Uncle Sam bring home the bacon in the Pan-American games continues.

> Sixty boxers were evaluated for fitness for the task. The Pan-American games were to be held in Mexico City in March; it was considered preliminary to the 1956 Olympics. At the time of the article, the Army was focusing on boxers, baseball players, and wrestlers. Tryouts for basketball, track and field, and other sports were already underway.

About half of the Army's top amateur boxers would be invited to Fort Sam Houston, Tex., for "training and elimination" matches. Twenty of those boxers would be sent to Lackland AFB, Tex., for national tryouts.

From there, the top boxers, including civilians, would make up the U.S. boxing team for the Pan American Games.

The article said that it is more difficult to determine the top baseball players, "because most all of the better players in the Army are under some kind of pro contract." The plan was for the U.S. Baseball team to be made-up of "six college players, six American Legion players and six servicemen."

Also, "The Armed Forces basketball team includes 9 Army players ... According to the Grapevine, biggest need of the Armed Forces team at present is a good pivot man."

Another article in the same edition, on page 29, discussed "Seven Servicemen on Pan-Am Cagers":

> At least two more slots have been opened for armed forces players on the basketball team which will represent the United States in the Pan American games in March ... the NCAA, however, has decided not to recommend names of college players to the basketball committee, so the four NCAA slots will be filled by two from the armed forces and two from the AAU.

> There is a possibility that as many as three of the extra slots will go to the armed forces, giving them eight places on the team. Selection will depend on the tryouts now under way.

> First game for the armed forces players -- organized into a team at Wright Patterson AFB, Ohio -- was to be played this week against the Bradley University freshman team.

> The service team will play at Madison Square Garden on Jan. 18 against Andrews AFB, Md., last year's inter-service champions. This game will be a preliminary to the annual East-West professional all-star game.

The service all-stars will also play at Fort Myer, Va., Jan. 21, or meeting their first major college opposition, Rice Institute, on Feb. 22. They are also scheduled to play in a preliminary to a Harlem Globetrotters exhibition in Chicago on Feb. 28. Opposition for this one will either be an AAU team or an outstanding service team.

Nine army players are trying out for the Armed Forces team. The two latest being PFC Jim Paxson of Fort Knox, Ky., and Pvt. Donald K. Lance of Fort Bliss, Tex. Others are 2d Lt. Frank Guisness, Fort Lee, Va.; Pvt. Don Byrd, Fort Belvoir, Va.; 2d Lt. Cecil (Pete) Silas, Fort McClellan, Ala.; PFC Bob Peterson, Fort Ord, Calif.; PFC Will Wilfong, Fort Leonard Wood, Mo.; Pvt. Walt Walowac, Fort Knox; and PFC Jack Williams, Eielson AFB, Alaska.

No definite steps will be taken regarding the basketball team which will represent the U.S. in the 1956 Olympics until the Olympic Basketball Committee meets at Denver, Colo., June 23.

One of the above noted basketball selections, Cecil (Pete) Silas, of Fort McClellan, Ala., was a highly accomplished person, as is depicted in his obituary of 18 December 2014 (121).

Mr. Silas played basketball at Georgia Tech on a full scholarship, where he received a B.S. degree in Chemical Engineering. And not only did he play Service Sports basketball while serving in the U.S. Chemical Corps, the "six foot, six inch" Silas "played on the army basketball team that went on to win the Pan American games in Mexico City in 1955." He later "joined the Phillips 66ers (professional) basketball team."

Following his service, Mr. Silas rose in corporate ranks to become the Chairman and CEO of Phillips Petroleum, whereafter he retired in 1994 at age 62 following his 41-year career. His obituary reflects that he had been a very involved and valuable member of the community in Oklahoma prior to his passing.

Not Far East, though a Service Sports quality-topic - the 22 January 1955 *Army Times* reported on a "Big League" Baltimore Orioles' scout praising the quality of Army baseball in Europe (2):

> How good is Army baseball in Europe? Well, Freddy Hofmann, scout for the Baltimore Orioles, thinks it is very good. And with Hoffman, it isn't just talk.

> As a result of his scouting trip in Europe last year, six former servicemen are now in the Baltimore farm system.

> Story of Hofmann's scouting trip is told in the current issue of *The Sporting News*.

> "They really have some fine ball players over there," says Hofmann. "People in this country have no idea of the recreational program in our Army and Air Force overseas. And baseball people have no idea as to the caliber of service baseball. From the armed services tournament in Rhein-Main, I easily could have picked two ball clubs capable of playing Class A ball in the United States."

> Players now in the Oriole organization because of Hofmann's spade work in Europe are infielders John Robert Davies and Jesse James, pitcher Earl Hatter, outfielder Charles Maguire, catcher M. E. Hudnall, and shortstop Wesley Swanson. Hofmann thinks most of these men are good enough for Baltimore's San Antonio farm in the Texas League, where Davies has already been assigned.

> All were signed after being released from service. A player cannot be signed to a professional baseball contract while in uniform.

Hofmann highly praised the Army's athletic program in Europe.

The 22 January 1955 *Army Times* edition also discussed 29 Army Boxers that had been invited to Fort Sam Houston, Tex., for Pan-American Games qualifications (pg. 32); "As many as 20 (two for each division) may be sent to the national tryouts … at Lackland AFB, Tex., Feb. 24-26." The two coach-trainers were Second Army's Pat Nappi and Fourth Army's Gunner Lowenstein.

The 29 boxers were selected through "careful screening of command recommendations by the Office of the Adjutant General's sports branch."

Five of the athletes were from the 82d Airborne Div. at Fort Bragg, and "last year the 82d won five Third Army titles and two All-Army titles as Third won the most convincing team victory in All-Army tournament history." 82d Middleweight Roscoe Elliott and lightweight Leon Upsher "are the two All-Army champs," both having had a long list of accomplishments.

> (The Far East was represented with) eight boxers in the Pan-Am list. They are: Bantam Elie Scott, San Francisco Golden Gloves champ in 1953 and Far East champ last year; featherweight Rubin Burns, New York Golden Gloves runner-up in 1950-51 and Far East Runner-up in 1953-54; lightweight Howard Moore, Sixth Army runner-up in 1952 and Far East runner up in 1953; light-welter Leon Watkins, Far East champ last year and National AAU runner up in 1952, welterweight Ray Gil, former 6th Army champ who won nationwide attention for his string of victories on the TV *Meet the Champ* series a few years ago; middleweight George Harrell; light-heavy John James; and heavyweight Bob Ranck, who was 1951-52 NCAA champ while with Wisconsin University and runner-up at the 1952 Olympic Trials.

Georgie Davis, "one of the most famous fighters in the Army was among those selected." He was from Fort Meade and had been All-Service and All-Army champion for two years running. He was previously Second Army champion and European champion.

The article said that "other services will also send outstanding fighters to meet top civilian amateurs in the Pam-Am trials at Lackland AFB."

Also in the 22 January 1955 *Army Times* edition (page 32) was a report on the Armed Forces All-Stars vs. Andrews AFB basketball game in Madison Square Garden, noting that the AF All-Stars were beaten by Andrews AFB (18th straight win) 84-75; "The Air Force team has beaten college and service teams alike and the win was expected. Last year, Andrews won the all-service title."

Lou Tsirorpoulos from Kentucky was the high-scorer for Andrews with 20 points; Cliff Hagen and Dick Knostman both helped lead Andrews to victory with 18 points each.

Bob Kenny from the All-Stars scored 12 points, "after starring for Andrews last year," and "Don Byrd led the All-Star team with 16 points."

While Navy and Marine players were not on the team at the time, they had been expected to join the All-Stars soon thereafter; "Seven, and possibly eight, will be chosen from this team to play on the U.S. team in the Pan-American Games."

The post-cut players remaining with the team were:

> Fort Belvoir's Don Byrd, Walter Walowac and Jim Paxson of Fort Knox, Alva Wilfong of Fort Leonard Wood, Don Lance of Fort Bliss, Cecil (Pete) Silas of Fort McClellan, and Jack Williams of Eielson AFB, Alaska.
>
> Others still with the team ... are: Mel Kelly and Bob Kenney, Andrews AFB; Bob Williams and Billy Hogue, Shepard AFB;

John Clune, Dover AFB; Dwane Morrison, Stead AFB; and Barry Porter of Kirtland AFB.

Armed Forces All-Star Jim Paxson made his mark on basketball beyond his Army days; *Dayton Daily News* reported on 28 October 2014 that "UD (University of Dayton) basketball legend Paxson Sr. dies at 81" (122).

In fact, the Paxson family made their mark on basketball, Jim Sr. played professionally with the Minneapolis Lakers and the Cincinnati Royals. Son John Paxson played professionally with the San Antonio Spurs and the Chicago Bulls. Son Jim Jr. played professionally with the Portland Trail Blazers and the Boston Celtics. Son Michael played basketball with the University of Wyoming and Ohio University.

"He was very proud of those kids and rightfully so," said WHIO broadcaster, Bucky Bockhorn.

Dayton basketball teammate, and later Dayton's all-time winningest coach, Don Donoher, said that Jim Paxson Sr. was "a hell of a teammate, the leader of a great basketball team and a lot of people will miss him."

Jim Sr. was drafted into the Army during the Korean War, and played with the Armed Forces All-Stars, "who won the Pan-Am Games in Mexico in 1955 before returning for his final season (at Dayton) in 1955-56. He averaged 15.5 points per game as a senior "as the Flyers went 25-4 and lost to Louisville in the NIT championship game."

Jim Sr. was also very respected in the community; "If we needed something done, we knew we could call on Jim," said Gary McCans of Dayton University.

Rest in Peace, hero.

The 21 January 1955 *Army Times* (123) reported that Rick Casares "signed with the Chicago Bears this week. Rick's former coach, Bob Woodruff of the University of Florida, calls him one of the greatest pro football prospects he has ever seen." Also signing with professional football was Dune McCauley, another All-Army star from Fort Hood, who was picked up by the San Francisco 49ers. Mr. McCauley had previously played with the Washington Redskins.

The same article noted that twelve men were in Fort Sam Houston to try out for the pentathlon event at the Pan-American Games, and that among them was John E. McMullen with the 8th Cav. Regt., Camp Whittington, Japan, representing the Far East.

An interesting article also on page 32 discussed "World Series hero in 1953 with the New York Yankees," PFC Billy Martin, was "the newest member of the Fort Carson basketball team." The article said, "Billy, who was quite a player in his high school days in Berkeley, Calif., has one of the best one-handed shots on the team."

Coach Dick Swan said Mr. Martin "can be a big help to us once he gets rid of the tightness through the back and arms." Martin was expected to be "separated from the service during the middle of the summer and plans to rejoin the Yankees." Mr. Martin also planned to manage the Carson baseball team (as player/manager), "one of the best service teams in the country last summer, and expected to be even stronger this year."

The 29 January 1955 *Army Times* newspaper reported on the "Service Stars" basketball team's progress; they beat Fort Belvoir 88-77 for their sixth win in eight games (124). "The Stars were led by Bob Kenney of Andrews AFB, Bob Williams of Shepard AFB and Don Byrd of Fort Belvoir. Kenney had 17 points, Williams had 10 and Bryd had 15."

The article went on to note that "Belvoir's star," Dick Groat, was high scorer with 30 points. The All-Star team's only losses were to Andrews AFB ("One of the greatest non-professional teams in the country"), and to "Bradley Frosh."

Seven of the twelve All-Star players would go to the Pan-American Games with the U.S. team, and two additional players from the Service would be selected from AAU, which was allowed seven slots on the Pan-Am team. The two players were Jim Hoverder from Central Missouri University, "high scoring center for the Parris Island Marines, and San Diego Navy's Ken Leslie. Leslie played on the U.S. team in the 1951 Pan-American Games."

Also, "Johkn (sic?) Silk, from last year's Quantico Marine team, currently stationed in the Far East, is on orders to report to Wright-Patterson AFB to try out with the service all-stars." Silk had been an All-American at Boston College and was a pro draft choice of the Syracuse Nets.

There was another *Army Times* article, same edition, page 33, on the great Dick Groat ("You Can Spell Groat with an 'e'"). While Mr. Groat was not in the Far East, he had participated on the All-Army baseball team and the Army All-Star basketball team, and therefore there is some "jurisdiction" to include him in this book. Plus, he was just great:

> Cpl. Richard Morrow Groat, one of the nation's finest combination professional athletes in action today, becomes Mr. Groat, a professional baseball and basketball player, via his separation from the Army on Feb. 11.
>
> His many followers at the army engineer center are not too happy about Groat's departure. Dick built a wonderful reputation at Belvoir both as a soldier and athlete.
>
> Groat's future is a ripe topic of conversation in sports pages throughout the country ... On March 1, Dick leaves for Fort Myer, Fla., and the Pittsburg Pirates training camp.

There, Groat renews his major league Baseball career with the Pirates. This will be the fiery shortstop's first return to the big time since he led the team in hitting with a .284 average in 1952.

Rumor has it that Dick is through as a professional basketball player. It's not true. Pirate owner Branch Ricky and Fort Wayne's Fred Zollner, Groat's pro basketball boss, made a vague agreement to have Dick forgo the National Basketball Association season this winter.

Groat, of course, complied. The truth is Dick doesn't know himself if he's done as a basketball player.

"It all depends on the coming baseball season ... have a good year, I may give up basketball." Groat averaged 13 points a game for the Fort Wayne Pistons and made the NBA All-Rookie team in 1952.

Choosing between sports, Dick does have a favorite. "Baseball is my bread and butter game. Basketball is my first love ... I've never played baseball without a strenuous basketball season before it in my life," Dick said ... That doesn't mean Groat has lost his basketball touch. In fact, the former Duke All American is playing the best basketball of his career right now ... a few weekends ago, Dick scored 115 points in three games playing for three different teams in the space of 24 hours ... Dick's Army athletic doings are strictly in the sensational class. In two baseball seasons, he batted .362 and .377. He personally led the 1953 Belvoir baseball team to the All-Army championship.

The story is the same in basketball. Groat is nearing the 2000 point mark at Belvoir. He also was one of the key men responsible for Belvoir's All-Army basketball crown in the 1952-53 season. Dale Seymour ... coach of this year's Belvoir basketball team, says: "I'll have to revamp the whole team when he leaves. He can't be replaced."

The 24 year-old Groat is probably at the prime of his career right now. Just how long his legs will hold up under the strain of two sports as debatable … for the record, he doesn't drink or smoke.

While not directly AFFE sports league related, there was an interesting letter to the Sports Editor in the 12 February 1955 *Army Times* regarding the Fort Dix basketball team and the level of recognition of a post team versus "other service teams on the East Coast," and which sheds some light on the general status of Service Sports as a competitive entity (125):

> In regard to the question in your 'Second Guess' column as to "Why the Fort Dix basketball team isn't rated higher in the East Coast poll of sports writers," the biggest reason is that Dix, as a post team, does not play the kind of schedule played by other service teams on the East Coast.
>
> Here at Dix our biggest responsibility is to the regimental sized unit. We have seven regimental teams playing a double round robin in a post regimental league. Games are played on Tuesday and Thursday evenings. Our post team is made up of the better players in the regimental league and the post schedule is made up around the regimental league schedule.
>
> Our post record (as of Feb. 4) is 8 wins and 1 loss. This includes two wins over St. Peter's College, three wins over Camp Kilmer and one win over Fort Monmouth. Our lone loss to date was to a great Andrews AFB team by 13 points.
>
> We have great expectations of showing our "stuff" in the forthcoming First Army and All-Army tournaments. We hope to be able to justify a higher rating for our "team of captains" at

the conclusion of these tournaments – 1st Lt. Francis S. Thomas, Sports Officer.

As a side note to the above letter, there is an obituary for Kenneth Murray, Jr., age 80, dated 17 June 2008 with some tie-ins to both CONUS and AFFE competition (126). The obituary noted Mr. Murray's playing history in college, in the military at Fort Dix in New Jersey and at Camp Drake in Japan, and his experience in professional basketball:

> Kenneth Murray Jr., 80, NBA player, school coach … of Bloomfield died on Sunday, June 15, 2008 … He served in the United States Army from 1951 to 1953. He was a physical education teacher at West Orange Mountain High School in West Orange … as well as basketball coach there for many years … He played at St. Bonaventure University from 1946 to 1950, where he captained the team for four years and held the all-time Saint Bonaventure scoring record. He was All-American in 1950, Sporting-News-Player-of-the-Year in 1950, and Catholic All-American.

> Mr. Murray played with the National Basketball Association from 1950 to 1955, and was selected Rookie of the Year in 1950-1951. He was a player and coach at Fort Dix from 1951 to 1952, being the first Army Champions, the Northeastern Inter-Service Champions and All-Army Semi-Finalists. He was also a player and coach at Camp Drake in Japan in 1952 to 1953, Central Japan Champions and the Finalists in the Far East Tournament. Mr. Murray was one of the initial members of the West Orange Sports Hall of Fame.

Rest in Peace, hero.

An 4 April 1955 Circular 735-28 (127) stated that "Special Services supplies and equipment will be issued to T/O&E and to T/D units and organizations to the extent authorized by the Special Services Officer …

Supplies issued to troops normally will consist of those items of basic sports equipment required to support minimum essential free-time recreational programs."

The Circular further said:

> Supplies and equipment are procured and issued for the welfare of members of the Armed Forces. They are issued to regional post Special Services officers for utilization in recreational facilities, such as service clubs, field houses, sports fields, libraries, crafts shops, music and entertainment activities, and implementation of the overall Special Services program as approved by the Commanding General, United States Army Forces, Far East and Eighth United States Army.

The 22 May 1955 *Army Times* (128) includes a "Letter to the Sports Desk," in which "An Interested Party" claimed physical conditioning requirements were lacking. The anonymous letter writer implied that routine physical conditioning as a part of regular duty obligations would improve combat and Service Sports effectiveness and readiness:

> FAR EAST COMMAND. – The importance of physical conditioning to military personnel was adequately described by Field Marshall Montgomery when he said, "Battles are won by the troops who can take one more step." Using this as a criterion we could ask ourselves how many battles troops in the Tokyo – Yokohama – Zama area could win at the present time?

> From my observation the answer would be not many, and this is not the fault of the troops, who at any time may be asked to climb Korean mountains or endure tropical heat.

> Special Services provides many fine athletic plans and programs and the equipment to keep us in good physical trim, but we are not making the most of it.

The fault lies with the present system of taking responsibility for this program away from unit commanders and centralizing the program in a regional office.

This centralization has resulted in the following:

- Although physical training is considered training it is a rarely found item on unit training schedules. In over a year with my unit it has not appeared once.

- If PT is a training function, it should be done during duty hours, not on a voluntary after-duty basis, yet one of the highest headquarters in this area has a record of discouraging men from participating in present programs because it takes as few as one man from the office.

- The centralization of the program's administration has resulted in many adverse situations. One is that few unit commanders know enough about the program to even complain because centralization has shifted all information and responsibility to regional offices.

- In the Tokyo, Yokohama, Zama areas, military personnel continue to change but civilian advisors remain. Although excellent administrators of tournaments, these men have had to assume unit commander's responsibility for all physical training. Thus decisions are arbitrarily made as to who may compete and how the units compete.

- Instruction in various sports is almost totally lacking in some regions. Personnel are detailed to the athletic office who have neither the interest nor the knowledge to conduct the program. An understaffed regional office cannot handle instruction for several thousand troops.

Troops from this area were called upon once to assume combat responsibility. It might happen again. Let us be ready with physical conditioning provided on a maximum participation basis, with the unit commander responsibility backed up with an A&R officer supervising an athletic program within the training schedule. Also, a fair share of welfare funds should be made available to all units to assist their A&R program and wherever regional officers carry personnel as instructors, let's require them to instruct. And when officers are given an afternoon off for athletics, let's see them in the gym or on the playing field. We enjoy the spectator sport program, but will it make us combat ready?

Army Times pointed up the value of a strong company-battalion-regimental athletic program while discussing Camp Chaffee's All-Army basketball victory. Such a program would have merit here.

Author's note: As a matter of policy and interest, the letter writer's concerns appear to be well-intentioned, but I do not accept his premise or implication that AFFE Service Sports were lacking in quality or effectiveness, particularly during the mid-1950s. I believe the evidence presented in this book speaks for itself.

The 4 June 1955 *Army Times* reported, "Tatum Among Noted Coaches Coming to Far East Clinics" (129):

With the name of Maryland football coach Jim Tatum added to a roster of prominent coaches and officials, the Far East program of sports clinics for coaches, officials and competitors is ready to move into high gear during the next four months.

Hailed as a big factor in contributing to the high level of Far East sports competition and officiating, the series of clinics will open June 13, with a four day session on boxing.

Herbert Kreeton, producer of champions at West Point, Roy Simmons of Syracuse University, and Frank Young of University of Idaho will conduct the classes.

In July, Coach Tatum, along with Michigan State's head coach Hugh Daugherty and Texas A&M's Paul Bryant, formerly at Kentucky, will discuss the fine points of the grid game from the 11th to the 15th.

A special clinic for football officials is set to run from Aug. 15-19 under the direction of James M. Cain and William G. Fisher, noted officials of the Pacific Coast Conference.

Basketball coaches come in for attention in early September when the schedule calls for John Friel of Washington State College to lead a four day instruction period on the court game from Sept. 5-9.

Now in the fourth year of operation, the clinics are open to all members of the Armed Forces and to all civilians working for the Armed Forces.

During the first three clinics held in 1955, an estimated 700 persons turned out for instruction on baseball, umpiring, and field and track.

The 1954 program attracted 1400 persons to seven clinics.

The centrally located Yokohama sports center is the site for the clinics which run throughout the year and are held about two months prior to the start of league competition.

Among the famous sports figures who have helped the Army sports programs through the clinics are: Track and field coaches Chuck Werner and Larry Snyder, PCC football officials James Cain and Ed Wagner, baseball coaches Lee Ellbracht and Jack Baer, PCC basketball officials Ervin Delman and Erling Oakland and former National League umpire George Burr.

Photo: Paul W. Bryant in Japan. Courtesy of Brad Green, Curator, Paul W. Bryant Museum, Tuscaloosa, Alabama 2025

Photo: Paul W. Bryant in Japan. Courtesy of Brad Green, Curator, Paul W. Bryant Museum, Tuscaloosa, Alabama 2025

Photo: Paul W. Bryant in Japan. Courtesy of Brad Green, Curator, Paul W. Bryant Museum, Tuscaloosa, Alabama 2025

Photo: Early Paul W. Bryant photo, middle. Others unknown. **Sheet Film 1525: Football team: St. John back for Pre-Flight School.** *P0027 Series 1. United States Navy Pre-Flight School: General Scenes, 1942-1945. Permission: The Louis Round Wilson Special Collections Library. University of North Carolina at Chapel Hill.*

Stars and Stripes reported 12 July 1955 that football coaching instruction had begun at the Fryar Gym in Yokohama, Japan, for 115 Army, Navy, and Marine students. The event was described as the AFFE/Eighth Army clinic for potential gridiron mentors.

Students traveled from units in Korea, Okinawa, and Japan to hear instruction from "Three of the finest football coaches in the U.S. collegiate circles" (130). The trainers were listed as Jim Tatum from the University of Maryland, Hugh Daugherty from Michigan State, and Paul Bryant from Texas A&M.

Mr. Tatum was "Coach of the Year" in 1953, and he talked about his "famed split T formation." He also discussed stance, blocking and passing, with emphasis on offensive ends during an "aerial attack." Paul Bryant was described as "The man who put Kentucky on the football map before going to Texas A&M." Mr. Bryant discussed the kicking game, drills, and coaching techniques.

Mr. Daugherty was said to have begun his instruction with defensive line drills and the pass protection "used by his club against Big Ten foes. He was expected to concentrate on his multiple offense as the clinic gets away from fundamentals." The three "grid mentors" would be expected to later travel to Haneda in Tokyo to tutor the FEAF clinic from July 18-22.

Stars and Stripes reported 16 August 1955 that 150 men from all parts of Japan attended the 1955 AFFE/8th Army football officials clinic in Yokohama (131). It was noted that attendance was the largest since the first official's clinic in 1951. James Cain and Bill Fisher were the instructors.

James "Jimmie" Cain's obituary (RIP) is a fountain of biographical information. Mr. Cain died on 26 August 2007 in Rancho Mirage, CA (132). The obituary said that Mr. Cain was quite an accomplished athlete and person in general. He was described as a former Washington Huskies football star, an insurance man, and a charitable volunteer. He was born on 5 September 1912 on a farm in Paris, Arkansas, but he grew up in Oklahoma.

Mr. Cain had achieved the academic honor roll and excelled and lettered in football, basketball, baseball, and track. In 1932 he was named "Outstanding Oklahoma High School Athlete of the Year." He was recruited by Jimmy Phelan to the University of Washington in 1932 and was given a full scholarship after an "All State" high school career as running back.

171

At Washington, Mr. Cain started on both offense and defense and was named the Most Valuable Coast Player in 1936. He played in the All American-All Players Liberty Bowl game in 1936. In 1937 he played in the Rose Bowl against Pittsburgh (online records show attendance of 87,196). The *Spokane Spokesman Review* newspaper reported on 2 January 1937 that Washington was held scoreless against Pittsburgh, "stunning the capacity crowd." Mr. Cain was listed as a halfback in the game.

Mr. Cain's obituary further says that he played on the College All Star team and had been drafted by the Redskins, with whom he played a short time. He graduated from the University of Washington and married Grace Weir Dolan in Seattle.

Mr. Cain's accomplishments continued post-college. He was a Husky assistant football coach in 1937 and was a finalist for Seattle's Sportsman of the Year in 1948. He later became president of the Washington Athletic Club and the UW Alumni Association. He was involved in numerous philanthropic organizations. In 1996 he was honored as a "Husky Legend," and has been inducted into the State of Washington's Hall of Fame.

Mr. Cain went on to referee football, including spending twenty-five years working the Pacific Coast/Pac-8 Conference; he also became the only football player to both play in the Rose Bowl and to referee it. Mr. Cain was a patriot, serving in the Coast Guard Auxiliary and the U.S. Army Reserve. In the 1950s and 1960s, he worked with the Armed Services setting up football programs on military bases overseas.

The 24 September 1955 *Army Times* (133) reported that the "second All-Korea boxing tournament will be held at Ascom City Gym by Inchon's Replacement Depot on Sept. 27-29. All UN boxers are invited to enter."

The scheduled competitors were:

George Moore, 3d Inf. Regt., "who won the All-AFFE light-middleweight title for three consecutive years, 1951-53. He has won 72 service bouts and in 1953 was voted the outstanding boxer in the Far East."

Solomon Boysaw, 31st Inf. Regt., "Eighth Army lightweight champ and All-AFFE runnerup (sic) last year."

John James, "also of the 31st, All-AFFE light-heavyweight champ in 1954 who was also named the outstanding boxer in the command last year."

Jerry Hargrove of Ascom City's 181st Signal Co., "recent loser by decision to the most highly regarded heavyweight in the Far East, Henry Holley of Japan."

On 26 September 1955, the *Pacific Stars and Stripes* reported a 7th Division victory over Seoul Military Post (SMP), 25-0 (134); "The 7th Div. scored in every quarter to beat Seoul Military Post 25-0 at Yongsan Field here Sunday."

180 pound quarterback Dave Kempker (also acting as kicker), threw eight completed passes for 193 yards, and propelled the 7th Division to fourteen first downs. The Bayonet's performance was so dominant, they resorted to their second and third string players for the final period.

Players with exceptional performances included center George Boyer, weighing in at 220 pounds, and "line ace" end John Sebich, who was the recipient of several Kempker passes. There were no fumbles with carries from halfbacks Glenn Petty and Homer Young.

The 7th Division team was noted to have been "one of the lightest in Korea's Army football," but were also "the fastest and best drilled to date."

7th Div. Bayonet players, 1955. Left: Joseph D. Mergest and Willie C. Leffall. Right: Armando Scogna. Jerry G. Kingrey personal collection. © All rights reserved

The same edition, same page, reported from Kadena AB, Okinawa, that the Air Base Gp. Tigers defeated the 1982nd Braves in Okinawa Air Force League play. Tiger's halfback Mack McDaniels scored from 24 yards in the first quarter, and Braves running back Bob Rowell had a nice 26 yard run in the second quarter, but was stopped on the four-yard line where the drive "stalled." The final scoring play for the Tigers was a 79-yard run by Bob Cremont, though the extra point was missed.

Rushing yardage was lopsided, according to the Stars and Stripes, with just nine yards for the Braves and 228 yards for the Tigers.

Other games reported in the same edition on page 21 included the "Defending champion Yokosuka Seahawks" 40-6 victory over Yokohama Engineer Depot (YED) Dozers at Saigami. Yokosuka quarterback Jerry Smith threw two touchdown passes to end Leo Hudson for the win in the first Central Command game of the season.

Another Yokosuka score came from halfback Jim Hart, who ran one into the endzone from three yards. Fullback Bill Phillips was the only scorer for YED.

A standout for Yokosuka was former Purdue All-American, Bernie Flowers, who at the end of the first half scored on a 26-yard run. Yokosuka's Bob Michaels ran an interception into the end zone for the last Yokosuka touchdown of the game. Yokosuka halfback Charlie Foster contributed a five yard touchdown run in the third quarter.

Also on page 21 was a report of the Camp McGill Marines' victory over the Atsugi Flyers, 18-0. Marines quarterback Van Crooms, end William Holt, fullback Robert Garvey, running back John Orton, end Harvey Warren, halfback Marvin Huston, and quarterback Byron Hand all contributed to the Marines' victory.

More action reported on page 21 included the Johnson Invaders' rout of the Shiroi Rockets on Johnson Air Base in the Japan Air Force league in front of 2500 "attentive fans." Standout players included Ramon Rhinehart, who intercepted a Rockets pass, and Invaders' Jim Small, who returned a punt 55 yards for a touchdown.

Page 21 was loaded with football outcomes information. Central Command's Tokyo Bulldogs defeated Camp Zama at Camp Drake, 19-7. In attendance were 5000 spectators, who watched halfback Bill Jones return a kickoff 102 yards for a touchdown in the second quarter. Jones also put points on the board with two other touchdowns in the game. Zama scored when Bob Ansett intercepted a Don Maxwell pass and gained 37 yards. The article said that "fumbles, pass interceptions and heavy penalties were prevalent in the game …" Fullback Ralph Paolone ably contributed by adding Bulldog yardage to help set up the first Bulldog score on a Jones run.

The Football season was in full swing by 3 October 1955 when the *Pacific Stars and Stripes* reported on multiple AFFE football game results (135):

Tokyo 13	Yokosuka 6
McGill 12	Yokohama 0
Zama 6	Fuji 0
Itazuke 38	Chitose 0
Iwakuni 14	YED 0
Johnson 20	SMP 13

Photo: I Corps HQ circa late 1950s, permission from Bruce Richards, https://www.qsl.net/wd4ngb/crc1.htm

A "small crowd" of 2000 fans braved the rain and cold in Yokosuka to witness the action: "Tokyo Stuns Yokosuka in Rainy Upset 13-6 – Seahawks' Unbeaten Record Broken After 2-Year Domination of CC."

Reporting from a "rain-soaked field" in Yokosuka, the Tokyo Bulldogs "surged from behind" in the second period and then stopped a drive by Yokosuka on Tokyo's 11-yard line. The "defending titlist" Seahawks had not been beaten in two years.

Ralph Paolone ran for a 28-yard TD following a Yokosuka fumble recovered by Jim Brown. Herm Niederhelman provided the other scoring run from 15 yards, contributing to the Bulldogs' 113 yards rushing total for the game. Yokosuka only managed 55 yards and one score, when "Frank McKay intercepted a Herm Niederhelman jump-pass and broke into the open and raced 55 yards" for the touchdown (*Author note: It's not clear how the 55-yard run would have been the only rushing yardage achieved by Yokosuka, but that it what the article appears to have implied*).

The Chitose Bears were destroyed by the Itazuke Green Wave in the Air Force Conference Game at Chitose Air Base, Japan. Stars for Itazuke included Lloyd Ransom, who scored three touchdowns, and John Polk who scored twice. Horace Morrison started for Itazuke as quarterback, but was said to have later caught a screen pass from Walter Schanubel for a score.

Not only did Ransom run for touchdowns, but he also intercepted a Bear pass and scrambled for 93 yards, the longest run of the game. Itazuke completed six of fourteen passes, and Chitose completed five of sixteen passes.

Zama Ramblers' defeat of Fuji Marines came on a "late TD," with a run in by Joe Belack in rainy and slippery conditions. Interceptions by Zama's Sam Kapogiannas and John Gill contributed to Zama's scores and success in defeating the Marines. In other action, Yokohama

Engineer Depot's (YED) thrown interceptions contributed to their loss to the Iwakuni Toriis.

There was more action on page 23, as the I Corps' Bullseyes defeated Ascom City 27-6 in front of 2000 fans at Jackson Field. Outstanding players of the game included I Corps' John Hogue, who had taken a handoff from Ron Brown and scored on the right side in the opening period. However, a short while later halfback Jerry Hargrove threw a fifteen yard scoring pass to Ascom City star Alex Litman (6', 194 lbs) out of San Angelo, Texas.

Ascom's Jessie Butner was singled out for playing "top notch defensive ball," and "New Orleans halfback Al DiCarlo of I Corps played with Ascom like a kid with a new electric train at Christmas," throwing touchdown passes in both the second and third periods.

Starring for Johnson Invaders at Johnson AB, Japan, was halfback Jim Small, who scored all three touchdowns on a "rain-soaked" field in the 20-13 victory over Seoul Military Post (SMP). SMP fullback Horace White earned a 70-yard touchdown on the first play of the game. Notable players included Raymon Rhinehart, who had run for 32 yards in the second quarter to set up one of Small's touchdowns.

In another competitive match, the Manila Air Force Depot Wildcats beat the Clark AFB Thunderbirds at Clark AFB, P.I. 8-0. Notable Wildcat players of the game were Howard Futter, Ernie Brantley, and Dill Gamble. "Highly touted" Clark player, Ike Williams, was trapped by the Wildcats' "wall" in the end zone for a safety in the third quarter. "Coach Ralph Cavalucci's defensive units repeatedly blasted Thunderbird ball carriers for big losses."

Army Times newspaper published an 8 October 1955 article (136) by Tom Scanlon, discussing nine scheduled tournaments (various sports) for 1956 in light of 1956 being an Olympic year.

As previously noted, while this book focuses on AFFE sports, there are situations involving some crossover with the CONUS military sports programs – All-Army competitions are one such instance.

Army Times reported: Five of the nine All-Army championship sports tournaments next year are certain to receive nation-wide attention due to the upcoming Olympics. The five sports were basketball, track and field, swimming and diving, triathlon, and boxing. The All-Army championships would serve as qualifying rounds for the Olympics, per Mr. Scanlon.

Mr. Scanlon further noted that, "In basketball, the Army has arranged a program which will enable outstanding players to get a shot at making the Olympic team without interfering with their activity in command and All-Army tournaments.

Following the All-Army tournament, the Army All-Star team of amateurs will be chosen to compete against Air Force, Navy and Marine teams in what will be known as the Armed Forces Olympic Basketball Elimination Tournament.

He continued,

> Following the Armed Forces tournament, seven players from the winning team and seven players from the other three service teams will be named to an Armed Forces team which will compete against a college all-star team and two National AAU teams in the final Olympic trials April 3-4 in Kansas City.

The Air Force, on the other hand, provided a different path to the Olympic trials. Air Force was to choose a team of amateurs early in the season, which would then play a series of games to determine qualification. This was noted to have been a similar method in which the Air Force chose their Pan-American team. Mr. Scanlon thought the Navy and Marine path would closely resemble the Army's program.

Mr. Scanlon said that the success of the 1956 Olympic basketball program "depends largely upon full participation of the commands in the All-Army tournament," noting that if a command did not participate, then individual players would have no shot at making the team, though there was discussion of a command championship to provide additional opportunity.

The 8 October *Army Times* also noted that Jack Shanafelt, All-American tackle at Penn in 1953 joined the 24th Division football team. *Pennathletics.com* documents that Mr. Shanafelt is in the Penn Hall of Fame Class IX (137). The biography says, "In an era when the Penn football program consistently took on national football powerhouses such as Notre Dame, Michigan, Wisconsin, Ohio State, Georgia, Navy, Army and Penn State, Jack Shanafelt was a standout tackle for the Quakers."

Mr. Shanafelt "was the last Penn football player to earn Division 1 first-team All-America honors." The article said that he was also "a member of the Army All-Star football team in Japan." He was later elected to the Ohio Sports Hall of Fame.

The 10 October 1955 *Stars and Stripes* (138) continued the ongoing AFFE football season coverage with a story about the Tokyo Bulldogs' 51-0 defeat of Yokohama Engineer Depot (YED) at Camp Drake. The Bulldogs had been unbeaten in the Central Command Football Conference going into the game, which attracted 4000 fans. Twenty first downs and 430 yards later, the Bulldogs added to their victory total. Bulldog standouts included halfback Norman Grady, who scored two touchdowns, quarterback Herman Niederhelman, end Gus Simmons, fullback Ralph Paolone, and halfback Ezra Nelson.

On the other side, YED's Arthur Taylor "made several fine tackles" when he was the only one standing between the ball and the end zone.

Other Bulldog strong contributors were center Roy Miller, guard Thomas Mull, guard Richard Barbeck, tackle Joe McLaughlin, tackle Marine Rosa, end Charlie Broxmeyer, and end Al Zampino.

In other football action on page 21, "Zama hands McGill 1st CC Loss As Eliott Paces Defense 7-0" at Zama. Wingback Ed Elliott and John Quinn contributed heavily to the Ramblers' win in front of 4000 fans over the Marines, who had not been scored on to that point in the season.

Quinn scored the Ramblers' only touchdown on handoff from Greg James, and defensive specialist Elliott broke up several plays and intercepted a pass while frustrating the Marines' scoring efforts. In fact, Elliott intercepted two passes and knocked down another, helping the Zama offense claim favorable field position.

At Camp Fuji (3rd Mar. Regt.), the Fuji Marines battled the Yokosuka Seahawks to a 13-13 tie, leaving both teams with one win, one loss, and one tie. Fuji standouts included quarterback Bill Drebushenko, end Bob Warren, quarterback Joe Johnson, and fullback John Callard. Fighting for the Seahawks was ex-Purdue All-America Bernie Flowers, quarterback Jerry Smith, and halfback Alvin Hall.

The 15 October 1955 *Army Times* reported on a New York Yankees visit to Sendai, Japan on 25 October for a New York Yankee-Tokyo All-Stars Baseball Game (139).

The 25 October game was "reserved for servicemen and their families in the Northern Command Area. The tickets cost 1000 yen each," and 5000 were available. After the game at Miyagi Stadium in Sendai, the Yankees would appear in Hokkaido, playing in Sapporo on 26 October.

The 22 October 1955 *Army Times* reported on the great All-Army teams of the past several years and also opened ballots for the "All-Army 1955" football selections (140).

This was the 5th annual *Army Times* All-Army Football Poll, and "Last year only Army football coaches and sports writers were permitted to participate in the world-wide poll. This year any reader of the Army Times may vote."

Poll instructions stated that a person may vote for any player on any Army football team, except for "flag" or "touch" football teams, and that results would be announced in December.

Players picked for the first and second All-Army teams would receive engraved wristwatches from *Army Times*.

The article continued:

> We hope that voters will not overlook the player who was not a 'big name' star in college or pro ball. In the past, several 'unknowns' have won All-Army recognition … The important thing, of course, is how good a player is in Army ball.

> The player with the most press clippings is not necessarily the most ball player (sic) in the Army. We hope that the real standouts in Army football, whether they were known for their football activity before they entered the Army or not, will be the 1955 All-Army players.

Stars and Stripes newspaper published a photo 28 October 1955, showing I Corps quarterback Ronald Brown throwing a pass in a recent AFFE football league game against the 24th Infantry Division, "however, the play was broken up by the Taromen's alert defense." The caption said the 24th "won 15-7 for the fourth straight victory in league competition" (141).

The 29 October 1955 *Army Times* reported, "24th Division Looks Like Team to Beat in Far East" (142):

> With three weeks of the season gone, three games have been played, three games have been won, and the 24th Div. Taromen are in first place in the AFFE/Eighth Army football league.
>
> Opening the season in Korea, the men in blue dumped Ascom City 19-6 in a ball game that saw them lose their rugged guard, All-Big Ten Dick Barnhart from Indiana. Barnhart has now joined the coaching staff.
>
> The following week, the 24th met the powerful 7th Div. Bayonets, and in a first half surge scored 26 points, then held the 7th to 14 in the second half to win.
>
> In their game against Seoul Military Post, the Taromen scored at will. They downed SMP 48-6.
>
> Halfback Ron Fontana, workhorse of the squad, is leading the team in scoring. The high stepping powerful back had scored four touchdowns in the three games.
>
> Sig Howerton is second with one touchdown and nine extra points. Fullback Ron Wislinski is third with two TDs for 12 points.
>
> Seven men have a touchdown apiece: Halfbacks Jesse Allen, John Cooper, Bob Gribble, and Charlie Lax; ends Marv Gregory and Jim Starkey; and quarterback Don Walsh.

The 13 November 1955 edition of the *Stars and Stripes* reported on a game between I Corps Bullseyes and the 7th Div. Bayonets; the Bullseyes upset the Bayonets 19-13, ruining the Bayonets' division title hopes (143). The article pointed out that the Bayonets' loss moved 24th Inf. Div. into first place.

In game action, Bullseye center Tom Capozzoli intercepted a pass on the Bayonets' 25 yard line, setting up a touchdown score by John Hogue on a pitchout from quarterback Burley Crawford. Bayonets' Homer Young blocked the extra point.

Crawford and halfback Tom Crowder contributed to the next score for the Bullseyes. Bayonet quarterback Bill Lugar and Mike LaSorsa added points for the Bayonets, and Gerry (*Ed.* - *"Jerry"*) Kingrey blocked a Bullseye extra point, but the Bayonets were unable to overcome the deficit, and the game went to the Bullseyes.

Stars and Stripes reported 9 December 1955 from Camp McGill, Japan, regarding the Marine Corps' All-Star football team's mascot, "Corporal Earthquake," a "ferocious looking 60-pounder" purebred English Bulldog. Corporal Earthquake attended daily practice sessions at the 3rd Marine Division's training site at Camp McGill. The mascot was promoted to Corporal due to his "outstanding service and conduct."

With a win in the Torii Bowl, Corporal Earthquake hopes to earn his third stripe. He promises to be in "top competitive condition and spirit for the battle" (144).

Stars and Stripes also reported 9 December 1955 from Sendai, Japan, that the football game between the 24th Infantry Division and the 1st Cavalry would be broadcast via shortwave to Korea Far East Network. The game was to be played at Brown Field, Camp Schimmelpfennig.

Stars and Stripes further said on 9 December 1955 that three backs had joined the Army All-Star roster during the second week of practice (145). New talent included Don Driscoll, Zama's 160-pound quarterback, Tokyo halfback Ed Collins, and halfback Don Edgar of Zama.

There was a "surplus of heralded backs," causing a problem for Mike Sabrinsky to pick a backfield. The article said that for fullback, his choices were Paolone, Homer Young, Tom Davis, and Ralph Compton.

Paolone had the running edge, but Davis was probably the best punter on the team. It was noted that quarterback was a weak spot and the five men competing for the slot were Don Walsh, Burley Crawford, Driscoll, Lee Boyd, and Don Maxwell. There was parity: "All five are capable passers."

Eleven men were trying out for the halfback slot, but Joe Platt, Gerry Robinson, Jim Moore, Ron Fontana, and Bill Jones "seem to have the inside track."

In a side note, Bill Jones was said to be a talented singer who had received offers to appear on TV upon his return to the states, giving him a plausible career if football didn't work out. Ralph Compton was said to be badly limping from a "charley horse."

Army Times dated 10 December 1955 reported, "Far East All-Stars Gather for Torii Bowl in Tokyo" (146). A 45-man Army All-Star football squad - one with high hopes of getting a crack at the All-Far East service championship in the Dec. 31 Rice Bowl Classic - has reported to head coach Mike Sabrinsky at Camp Drake." The Army team was "one of the finest ever assembled in the Far East," and had been preparing for the big game.

Coach Sabrinsky and assistant coach Bill Webb selected players based on coaches nominations from the AFFE/Eighth Army League (Korea) and "the RyCom league in Okinawa, and the Central Command and Northern Command Conferences in Japan."

"Star" players noted were Art Hunter and Ralph Paolone of Tokyo Bulldogs (see recap of Torii Bowl game below), and Jack Shanafelt of the 24th Inf. Div.

Shanafelt was described as "an All-American tackle and twice was named lineman of the week in national polls." Al Zampino of the Tokyo Bulldogs was noted to be an "excellent blocker and a fine defensive wingman."

Joe Platt of I Corps was said to have played in the Cotton Bowl when Kentucky defeated TCU 20-7 in 1952. Army guard James Starkey (7th Division) played with West Virginia in the 1954 Sugar Bowl. John Savanich, also from the 7th Division, had been the leading punter at Purdue. 7th Division Max Kitzleman played for the University of Nebraska at 230 pounds.

The list of stars continued. Two Green Bay Packers players, Mike Takacs and James Jebb, were on the roster. Running back James Moore of Div. Arty. played for the Chicago Bears in 1953. "He was the leading scorer in Korea" while with the 24th Inf. Div. The article said that "only three players on the squad have no college experience."

An accompanying article in the same edition said that Michael Sabrinsky, the Tokyo Bulldogs coach, was a former Villanova halfback and would coach the Army All-Stars in their game against the Marine All-Stars at the 17 December 1955 Torii Bowl in Tokyo, Japan.

Sabrinsky's assistant coach, Bill Webb, played as a guard on two West Point National Championship teams. Sabrinsky had previously coached an All-Army team which won the Hawaii Inter-Service Championship in 1949. Sabrinsky took the Tokyo Bulldogs to an 8-1 record, and, "he considers Ralph Paolone as the finest football player he ever coached."

Army Times of 31 December 1955 (147) reported that 25,000 fans watched the Far East Football game between Army and Marines in the Torii Bowl at Meiji Stadium, Japan; Army All-stars beat Marines 20-6. The Army line averaged 217 pounds per man, and Army had "piled up 257 yards rushing and another 55 through the air."

Army plays described included 1st Cav Div Arty's Tom Davis's pass to former Notre Dame All-American, Art Hunter (Camp Zama) for a touchdown. Tokyo Bulldogs' Ralph Paolone was described as a "former University of Kentucky star owned by the Philadelphia Eagles."

The victory was claimed to "be revenge for the Army who had dropped a 27-13 decision to the Marines in the Sukiyaki Bowl last year."

Following the Army game, Gen. I. D. White spoke to Army players, saying, "The Army was proud of you men today … let's do it again for the Rice Bowl."

The "Bowl Jottings" section said Army and Marine troops had paraded onto the playing field before game time. The Army had 3500 marching troops, and the Marines had 3000, and the "only American Bagpipe band in the Far East" provided music for the drill team. The pipers and drummers from 1st Cav. Div. paraded out in kilts … The 80-piece Army band consisted of musicians from the 56th Band of Camp Zama and the 293rd Band from Tokyo.

Army's win entitled them to meet Air Force at Meiji Stadium on 31 December 1955 for the "Rice Bowl Crown."

1956

A 20 February 1956 memo from CG One CavDiv, Sendai, Japan, reported that Central Command handed RYCOM an 80-64 basketball loss, and Korea defeated Southwestern Command 98-63 "in the second day of the 1956 AFFE/ARMY-EIGHT Basketball Tournament at Camp Shimmelpfennig today" (148). Central Command had been "sparked by the fine playmaking of guard Ralph Beard, former Kentucky All-American."

Ralph Beard had an interesting life story, having gone from hero to apparently reluctant involvement in scandal per the *Los Angeles Times* of 30 November 2007 (149):

> Ralph Beard, a three-time All-American guard for the University of Kentucky in the 1940s and a figure in college basketball's biggest betting scandal, died Thursday. He was 79.
>
> Beard, who helped the Wildcats win national championships in 1948 and 1949 under coach Adolph Rupp, died at his home in Louisville, Ky., his son Scott said. After a series of illnesses in recent years, Beard died from heart failure, his son said.
>
> A speedy, 5-foot, 10-inch guard, Beard was among Rupp's famous "Fabulous Five," along with Alex Groza, Wallace Jones, Cliff Barker and Kenny Rollins.
>
> The Wildcats finished 36-3 in 1948, beating Baylor 77-59 in the final of the NCAA tournament. That summer, Rupp and the five starters teamed with Amateur Athletic Union champion Phillips Oilers to win the Olympic gold medal in London, and then won another NCAA title the next season.
>
> Beard was the school's first four-time All-Southeastern Conference selection and finished with 1,517 points, currently 14th on Kentucky's scoring list. His No. 12 jersey was retired and hangs at Rupp Arena.
>
> He moved on to the National Basketball Assn., where he played for and became a part owner of the Indianapolis Olympians, a new franchise. He was chosen as one of the starting five for the NBA All-Star game his second season, 1950-51.
>
> Before the start of the 1952 NBA season, Beard and Groza were among several players involved in a point-shaving scandal that rocked college basketball. They received suspended sentences

but were banned for life from the NBA. When Beard tried to play professional baseball, he was told he was barred from that sport too.

"It ruined my life as I knew it," he told the *Louisville Courier-Journal* last year. "All I ever wanted to do was play basketball."

Beard admitted taking $700 from gamblers but repeatedly denied shaving points.

"I was wrong," Beard told the *Chattanooga Free Press* in 1996. "But it was so different then. I had no money. I didn't even have money for a haircut. I grew up in a slum in Louisville. My father left us when I was 7, and my mother worked two jobs from then on."

The *Police Gazette*, dated March 1953, discussed the scandals (150). Writer Ben Gould described "Front Man" Eli Kaye's (aka Klukofsky) actions: "He was drawn into the betting circle after losing huge sums of money on Kentucky fixes, notably the biggest one of all, the Kentucky-Loyola upset in Madison Square Garden in March 1949." *Author's note: This is NCAA basketball; there is no evidence or even implication of any wrongdoing in Service Sports.*

THE "FIX" WAS ON — L. I. U.'s Sherman White (20), Adolph Bigos (right foreground) and Leroy Smith (61) watch Kansas State's Ernie Barrett (center) and ball at Madison Square Garden, New York, Dec. 2, 1950. L. I. U. trio were charged with taking bribes. Kansas State players were not involved.

IS THE FIX STILL ON
IN BASKETBALL?

ELI KAYE, indicted in the basketball scandal, confided to the Police Gazette writer that games are still being fixed.

The smell of tainted money once again hangs over the nation's

Photo: Police Gazette, March 1953

A 21 February 1956 Memo from CG One CavDiv, Sendai, Japan, reports:

> Cav Div comeback cagers entered the finals of the 1956 AFFE Basketball (sic) as they bounced Northern Command from the running 95-85 at Camp Shimmelpfennig today. It will be Korea, champion of the loser's bracket, versus Central Command, winner of the winner's bracket in the finals tomorrow. Should Korea, who already has 1 loss in Tourney Play, win the all-important tilt, then a final play-off game will be held Thursday afternoon.

If Central Command emerges victorious, then they will be the AFFE Champions and will travel to the All-Army Tournament at Fort Leornard (sic) Wood, MO, March 1-7. The game today was close all the way, with Korea pulling away only in the last minute and half of play. With Northern Command forward Ed Raber and Korea guard Johnny Alviggi playing the starring roles for their respective teams, the lead changed hands 10 times before Northern Command went ahead at the half, 48-47.

Korea, behind the fine shooting of Bo Erias, got hot as the 2d half started and had a 75-63 lead with 12 minutes left (sic) with 12 minutes left to play.

Northern Command, with guards Bill O'Brien and Bo McLemore leading the way along with Raber, came back 85-84 with 2 and a half minutes remaining. Erias, a 6 ft 4 inch sparkplug, hit 2 field goals and 2 free throws in quick succession to put the game on ice for Korea, with a final score reading 95-85. Erias led both teams with 32 points while Alviggi of Korea and Raber of NorCom tossed in 23 apiece (151).

There is a 24 February 1956 memo from Colonel Roy. N. Walker, ACC Adjutant General, to Mr. Frank Brickey, assistant basketball coach at the University of Utah, naming "outstanding" basketball players who would represent Army Forces Far East and the Eighth United States Army in the All-Army Basketball Championships, 11-17 March (152).

The players named were,

> 2d Lt. John Alviggi, guard, 5 feet, 11 inches, 170 pounds, 24 years old, hometown: West Orange, New Jersey, 3 years varsity at Lafayette College, Easton, Pennsylvania; Specialist Second Class, Jack R. Houston, forward, 6 feet, 4 inches, 185 pounds, 24 years old, hometown: Pearson, Georgia, 4 years at Mississippi State, All-State selection; Specialist Third Class

191

Carl B. Wells, 5 feet 9 inches, 160 pounds, 23 years old, hometown: Gary, Indiana, 4 years at Wabash College, Indiana; and Private E2 Baltico S. Erias, forward, 6 feet, 3 1/2 inches, 195 pounds, 23 years old, hometown: Astoria, Long Island, New York, 4 years at Niagara University.

There is a 2 March 1956 Track and Field Coaches Clinic memo/itinerary, which said "The Department of the Army has made available the services of Mr. Lawrence N. Snyder of Ohio State University and Mr. Charles Werner of Pennsylvania State University to instruct in the 1956 FEC Track and Field Coaches Clinics" (153).

The estimated arrival date in Tokyo, Japan was 8 March 1956.

The itinerary included escort to the "Sanno Eotel" (sic) in Tokyo, preparation of clinic curriculum the following day, visiting the Tokyo-Yokohama area 10-11 March, "Instruct at first clinic to be conducted at Camp Drake 0830-1600 hours daily," visit Hakone area 17-18 March, instruct second clinic at Fuchu 19-23 March, and depart Tokyo on 24 March. The "project representative" was Mr. Clarence J. Koehler.

Some of the biggest names in sport participated in coaching clinics overseas for the soldier-athletes. Coach Snyder (Lawrence N. Snyder) was no exception. Coach Snyder's achievements had been noted by *CantonRep.com|The Repository* on 15 March 2016 (154). His legacy included winning the Western Conference Medal for scholarship and track achievements at Ohio State, from which he graduated in 1925.

Coach Synder was hired by Ohio State as a track coach in 1932, and coached Jesse Owens, Glen Davis and Gene Albritton. He "led 15 athletes to Olympic medals including eight golds." He served as Head Coach of U.S. Track and Field in the 1960 Rome Olympics, where Americans earned the top three places in four events. He coached Ohio State until 1965, and his athletes included *52 All-Americans and 14*

World Record holders (it. added). He was inducted into the USA Track and Field Hall of Fame.

Coach Snyder passed away on 25 September 1982. Jesse Owens said of Coach Snyder, "He gets more out of you than you ever dreamed you had ... At the Olympic Games, he had me so fired up I couldn't miss."

Army Times newspaper reported on 3 March 1956 that "The Seoul Military Post team from Korea came back after an opening round loss to win the 1956 Armed Forces Far East basketball tournament here by beating Central Command in the finals 75-68" (155). The Seoul Military Post (SMP) coach was Don Spike, "former Wisconsin University star."

SMP lost to Rycom in the first game, but the tournament was double-elimination, and Seoul advanced to the finals by beating Southwestern Command, Rycom, and Northern Command. Bo Erias, a 6'4" forward from Niagara University, and Don Johnson, a 5'9" guard "enabled the Korea champs to down previously undefeated Central Command 75-62 to force the tournament into a final playoff."

The play of Ralph Beard, a former Kentucky All-American, shone for Central Command, and Central Command entered halftime with the lead; however, in the second half Burt Spice from Korea scored multiple "push shots," and Korea took the lead and "never trailed after that."

Mr. Erias was voted the tournament's outstanding player and outstanding sportsman awards. Players selected to travel to the All-Army tournament (11-17 March 1956) included 6'3" forward Ed Raber of Northern Command and 5'8" guard Carl Wells of Rycom.

A 5 March 1956 memo from Col. Roy N. Walker relates a 29-30 March 1956 meeting of the AFFE/8A (Rear) Sports Council at Camp Zama, Japan, to discuss possible revision of the sports play letter, discussion of AR 28-52, "nr of entries for comd level tournaments," and general details relative to the sports program (156).

A 6 March 1956 memo from Col. Roy N. Walker said that the baseball coach from Ohio State University, Marty Karrow, had recently conducted an FEC Baseball Coaches Clinic (157), and he offered to have his baseball team tour military installations of the Far East for six weeks, from July to August, "under the same cond as Univ of Southern Calif baseball team tour in summer 55."

Army Times newspaper reported 31 March 1956 (158) that three Army basketball players had qualified for Olympic Trials:

> In an unusual tournament, the Air Force team won the Armed Forces Olympic Basketball Trials event here last weekend … the Air Force, Marines and Army finished the tourney with 2-1 records, but the Air Force team took the title on a point-spread system … Air Force won the championship by way of a 19-point spread, compared with the Marines at minus-five and the Army at minus-14.

> Navy lost all three games but the sailors came within quarter of an inch of pulling the biggest upset of the tournament and knocking Air Force out of contention … Navy took possession of the ball trailing by one point against the Air Force … there were only five seconds remaining when James Young arched the climatic (sic) shot from 30 feet out. The ball hit the rim and bounced once, wavered, and as the 2800 fans sat frozen in their seats, rolled off. Wayne Ingram … fouled on the last play, hit a free one (sic) after the game was over.

The article said the 14-man Armed Forces Olympic Trials team would include three Army players at Kansas City: Albert Bianchi (Bowling Green University), Texas; Larry Dugan (Pepperdine College), Kentucky; Clarence Hannon (West Point), Washington.

Also, "By winning the tournament, the Air Force team won seven berths on the Olympic Trials squad: Bill Evans, Gilbert Ford, Thomas Fuller,

McCoy Ingram, Bernard Janicki, Ronald Domsic and Frank Warren. Others on the team are Donald Lange, James Bingham, and Richie Guerin of the Marines, and Navy's Stanley Kernan."

Guerin and Evans tied for the tourney's Most Valuable Player award.

Others named to an 11-man all-tournament team (not to be confused with the Olympic Trials team named) by sportswriters and tournament officials: soldiers Dick White (Fort Jackson, S.C.), Dugan and Sam Jones (White Sands Proving Ground, N. M.); Marines Jim Bingham, Don Lange and Cordell Brown; the Navy's Kiernan; and Ingram and Warren of the Air Force. Bruce Drake, former Oklahoma University coach who coached the Air Force team, would direct the service team in the Olympic Trials.

Lastly, the article related that the Marines star, Richie Guerin, had an amateur standing that was "under a cloud" (Though the article was silent as to the nature of the cloud).

On 10 March 1956, *Army Times* reported on "17th Infantry Champs" (159), stating that

> Hqs. and Hqs. Cp., fighting an uphill battle for almost 4 full periods, came from behind in the final minute of play to upset Service Co. 66-65, to win the 17th Inf. Regt. Provisional Basketball League. The thrilling and hard fought game was played after both teams finished the regular season with identical 7-1 records.

The article went on to say the game-winning "foul shot" (free throw) was made by Dwain Correl with eight seconds left in the game. Prior to the foul shot the game score had been evened up on James Owens' tying basket.

The caliber athlete of some of the soldiers was particularly high. For example, on 9 April 1956, Lt. Col. Hugh T. Paris sent a memo to the

Commanding General of the United States Army Forces, Far East/8th U.S. Army discussing consideration of 2d Lt. Henry Darlington as a candidate for the 1956 Olympic Track and Field Team. He requested duty accommodation for his training and trials, which included a two-hour daily workout (160).

The 5 May 1956 *Army Times* (161) reported that 400 soldiers had been seeking Olympic Team berths:

> More than 400 athletes in the Army have applied for Olympic tryouts in hopes of landing a berth on U. S. Olympic Team. The Olympics will be held at Melbourne, Australia, Nov. 22 - Dec.8.
>
> All-Army Track and Field events will be held at MacArthur in early June and participants will remain there in training until Olympic Trials in Los Angeles later the same month.
>
> Boxers will come to Fort Myer for the All-Army Tournament during the first week of October with Olympic trials scheduled to be held on the West Coast later the same month. Army tryouts and Olympic trials for the Modern Pentathlon will be held at Fort Sam Houston.
>
> Soldier athletes comprised about 25 percent of the U. S. Olympic Team in the recent VII Winter Games held at Cortina, Italy. Twenty percent of the U. S. Team at the 1955 Pan-American Games in Mexico came from the Army. Indications now are that the percentage of Army personnel on the U. S. Olympic Team in Australia will be as high if not higher.

An 8 May 1956 memo from Sam C. Russell, Brigadier General, to the Commanding General of the United States Army Forces, Far East, Eighth United States Army (Rear), discussed Army participation in the Sports Program (162). Brig, General Russell stated he agreed with the policy that Army personnel should not participate in sports competition as members of an Air Force team when such teams compete with Army teams. He noted, however:

> Participation of antiaircraft troops in Air Force sports activities has done a great deal to further the good relations which are essential to the performance of the antiaircraft mission, and to the morale and well-being of antiaircraft troops stationed on Air Force bases.

> Continuation of a limited form of participation by antiaircraft troops is considered desirable. There appears to be nothing objectionable in antiaircraft personnel stationed on Air Force bases joining Air Force teams when such teams are competing with other Air Force teams only.

> This Brigade plans to enter a team in each of the major sports conducted by AFFE/8A using the best qualified personnel available. The limitation on the number of players authorized for any one particular team requires the elimination of some very well qualified athletes from competition.

> Due to the tactical mission of this Brigade, interbattery competition is not feasible. Therefore, personnel eliminated from the brigade team are denied an opportunity to take part in any organized sports program unless they are permitted to participate on Air Force teams.

> In view of the above, it is requested that those athletes unable to play on the 40th AAA Brigade team be allowed to participate on Air Force teams except when the Air Force teams are competing with Army teams.

An 8 May 1956 memo from C. J. Koehler, GS-12, Dir, Sports Branch, said that Mr. Harold Anderson, Bowling Green State University, had accepted an invitation to conduct a basketball coaches clinic along with Mr. Ray Oosting and Mr. Kenneth Loeffler (163).

There is a 9 May 1956 memo from DA WASHDC stating that Clifford Wells accepted and then declined an invitation to conduct a 10 October 1955 Basketball Coaches Clinic. The *College Basketball Experience* website provided a short biography of the esteemed Mr. Wells; he had been a big-time ball coach (164):

> Born and raised in the basketball-rich Hoosier state, Wells became known as the "Dean of Indiana High School Coaches." His career included 30 years of successful Indiana high school basketball coaching, including more than 50 regional, district, and invitational titles and two Indiana State Championships. Clifford was Head Coach at Tulane University from 1945 until his retirement in 1963.

> From 1963 to 1966, he was an enthusiastic Director of the Naismith Memorial Basketball Hall of Fame. Clifford has conducted scores of clinics, written numerous articles, and was an active participant in the NABC where he held many administrative positions including president (1958) and executive officer (1966)." Mr. Wells passed away on 15 August 1977.

A 10 May 1956 memo from Louis J. Aleman, II, Maj AGC Chief, Recreation Division, included an interesting report which listed the number of participants for various sports and activities from 1 Jan 1956 to 31 March 1956 (165).

For example, under "All" activities (including sports, library, entertainment, service clubs, and others) there were 1141 military participants and 1755 civilian participants. There were 232 participants from the military in sports, and 329 civilians participating in sports. The participation figures were broken out, showing the number of officers and the number of enlisted personnel, as well as other sub-categories.

These numbers were for Q1 1956 - there is a breakout of teams in team sports, and, plausibly due to the season, there were none listed for football. However, it appears there were 213 basketball teams, with the number of games played given as 1268 (*Note: though this doesn't appear to be consistent with the number of personnel listed*)!

The above report was updated 4 August 1956 (166), and showed the period 1 April 1956 to 30 June 1956 (Q2 1956). The "All" activities number was now 1244 military participants and 1898 civilian participants.

There were 314 military participants in sports and 402 civilians participating in sports. This Q2 report listed 59 basketball teams (334 games) and only 2 football teams (again, not in season). Interestingly, there were listed an incredible 511 volleyball teams with 3740 games played!

A 7 June 1956 memo from Samuel J. Gormly, Jr., Colonel, USAF Commander, regarding Army participation in Air Force Athletics states that in reference to the 7 May 1956 memo, he recommended rescission of the policy prohibiting Army personnel from participating in Air Force inter-base athletics.

The memo further said there was no competitive league or conference in the area for Army athletic teams, and that sports facilities within the command could provide participation in intramural sports only for Army personnel under cited policy. Specially gifted and qualified athletes of Army units were deprived of adequate utilization of their respected skills.

Authorization for Army men to participate in team play was proposed for inter-base Air Force conference competition only. In the event such individuals were selected for All-Star squads, each would compete with his own service.

Colonel Gormly ended by saying that maximum participation in all sports activities, including inter-base competition, had been in the best interest of the services concerned (167).

Heartbreak: A 7 June 1956 memo from James L Glymph, Lt Colonel, AGC, Exec Officer, SpSerDIV, discussed 2d Lt David C. Epperson, who competed in the high jump event of the AFFE/8th Army meet in Korea. Lt. Colonel Glymph noted that 2d Lt Epperson did not meet the "established standard of 6'2" (jump) as outlined in paragraph 15c, DA Circular 28-17, 12 September 1955."

He further wrote:

> It is the opinion of this office that each major command should endeavor to select the team which can best represent that command with reference to point scoring; therefore, an individual, unless particularly outstanding in a single event, should be entered in at least two events to adequately represent his command.
>
> In view of the fact that you did not meet the required standards, your request to compete in the All-Army Track and Field Championship could not be given favorable consideration (168).

There is a 12 June 1956 memo from Curt S. Riggs, GS-12, NAF Administrator regarding "Reimbursement for expenses incurred during the Torii and Rice Bowl football games" (169). A check was attached in the amount of $4360.47, representing "reimbursement as requested."

There is a 14 June 1956 memo from Colonel Curtis L. Frisbie, USAF, who said that he agreed with the 7 June 1956 letter from Col. Gormly (above), noting that "many fine athletes are stationed with Army units on AF bases," further stating,

> This headquarters recommends the reconsideration of existing policy along the lines outlined in the basic letter and that reconsideration pertaining to all areas of Japan and South Korea (170).

A memo dated 26 June 1956 discussed "Application for Olympics" (swimming) for Breckinridge D Greene of the Hq _Hq Co, 31st Infantry Regiment, 7th Infantry Division, APO 7, Korea. The memo is signed by Donald Lasley, Major, Infantry (171):

1. "Reference: AR 28-50
2. a. Name: Breckinridge D Greene
   b. Grade: Pvt-2
   c. Service Number: US 56264438
   d. Age: 22
   e. Organization: Hq _Hq Co, 31st Infantry Regiment, 7th Infantry Division, APO 7, Korea.
   f. Date Basic Training Completed: 20 November 1955
   g. Date of Completion of Current Enlistment: 19 September 1957
   h. Suitability of Training Facilities: None
   j. Qualifications:
   (1) Played forward at Stockton College in Junior Division. Team was 2nd in tournament in 1951. Pvt Greene was selected on the All-Northern California Team in 1952.
   (2) Played forward and guard at College of the Pacific. Team was 3rd in tournament in 1953 and 1954. Pvt Greene lettered in water polo for four straight seasons and was selected on the All-Northern California team in 1954.

(3) Pvt Greene was named on the All-American Swimming Junior College Team while at Stockton College, both in 1952 and 1953. He swam the 50 yd sprint, the 100 yd sprint, the 4 man relay, and the 3 man medley. At the College of the Pacific he swam the 50, 100, and 220 yard sprints.

(4) Before induction into the Army, Pvt Greene was affiliated with the Olympic Club of San Francisco for tryouts for the Olympics.

3. Pvt Greene volunteers to participate in training and if selected, to represent the United States in international competition.

4. Attached is an affidavit of amateurism.

A supplemental memo notes that Pvt Greene was currently on TDY to Hq Btry in Mara, Japan to participate in an AFFE/8A (Rear) Swimming and Diving meet.

Breckinridge D Greene's obituary, dated 16 November 2007, at *Legacy.com*, says that he lived from 9 July 1933 to 9 November 2007 (172), and passed away from a "long illness." The obituary says that Mr. Greene had been born in San Francisco and was raised in San Carlos.

The article also said "he was an All-American Junior College Swimmer at Stockton College, and he was a member of Omega Phi Alpha, and excelled in swimming and water polo at College of the Pacific. Following graduation from college, Breck served in the U.S. Army with a tour of duty in Korea. He spent a lifetime in Food Brokerage and Direct Sales of food products."

Thank you for your service, Mr. Green.

A 27 June 1956 memo from C.J. Koehler furthers the subject of Army personnel participating in Air Force athletics. C. J. Koehler, GS-12, Dir, Sports Branch, stated that,

CG AFFE/8A established participation policy that Army would not represent Air Force or Navy in any sport. This policy was established April 1956 in reply to ltr FFPPS, Hq FEAF, 23 Feb 1956, and was reemphasized in reply to ltr of 8 May from Gen Russell, CG 40th AAA Brigade.

A memo of the same date from Captain Robert J. Reynolds said that the sports participation policy of AFFE/8A is that Army personnel represent *only* the Army when participating in sports events:

> It is considered that this policy will be of considerable value in building esprit-de-corps and developing leadership in the lower echelons of command. In view of the foregoing, the request contained in paragraph 2, preceding indorsement (sic), is not favorably considered (173).

A 27 June 1956 memo from S. Rubinton, Lt Col, AGC, covers "Itinerary for FEC Football Coaches Clinic Instructors (VIP)" (174):

> 1. Department of the Army has made available the services of Mr. James Owens, Texas A&M College; Mr. Hal Herring, Auburn (Alabama Polytechnic Institute) and Mr. John Hooper, Upsala College, New Jersey, to instruct in the 1956 FEC Football Coaches Clinics. Mr. Owens, Mr. Herring, and Mr. Hooper are scheduled to depart Travis Air Force Base, on or about 1 July 1956; estimated time of arrival Tokyo, Japan, is 4 July 1956. The itinerary for these instructors while in this command is as follows:

4 July	Arrive Tokyo International Airport. To be met by Mr. Clarence J Koehler, Sports Director, AFFE/8A (Rear), processed through customs, and escorted to Dai Iti Hotel, Tokyo.

203

5-6 July	Preparation of clinic curriculum at Special Services Office, HQ AFFE/8A (Rear)
7-8 July	Visit Tokyo - Yokohama area.
9-13 July	Instruct at first clinic to be held at Camp Drake, 0830- 1600 hours daily.
14-15 July	Visit Hakone area.
16-20 July	Instruct at second clinic to be held at Yamato Air Station (Fuchu), 0830-1600 hours daily.
21 July	Depart Tokyo International Airport for Hawaii.

2. Instructors will be billeted at the Dai Iti Hotel upon arrival and during their stay in Japan.
3. Mr. Clarence J Koehler, Sports Director, AFFE/8A (Rear) Special Services Office, has been appointed project representative of this headquarters for all coordination and may be reached at Zama 3-1390 or Sagami-hara 2518.

An attached "MEMO FOR THE RECORD" states that "FEC Sports Clinics for 1956 estb 8 FEC Sports Clinic (sic) with outstanding coaches and officials from colleges and universities in the CONUS to instr, ea of whom will spend aprx 18 days in the Tokyo-Drake area while conducting the clinics."

A brief 28 June 1956 memo from DA WASHDC to CGAFFE/ARMYEIGHT (REAR) CP ZAMA JAPAN (175) concerned Ohio State baseball:

Req Marty Karow, Ohio State Baseball Team, advise this office via TWX thru ofl chan of game scores to date and results fol this date weekly. Unusual interest on Ohio State campus and in Ohio newspapers.

There is a 2 July 1956 correspondence regarding qualifications for the 1956 US Olympic Track and Field Team (176). The correspondence is addressed to: CHOSA WASHDC, DA WASHDC, ARMY TIMES WASHDC, CGARMYONE FT JAY NY, CGARMYTWO FT MEADE MD, CGARMYTHREE MT MCPHERSON GA, CGARMYFOUR FT HOUSTON TEX, CGARMYFIVE CHGO ILL, CGARMYSIX SFRAN CALIF, CGAFFE/ARMYEIGHT (REAR) CP ZAMA JAPAN, CGUSAREUR HEIDELBERG GER, CGUSAARAL FT RICHARDSON ALASKA, USARCARIB FT AMADOR CZ, CGUSARPAC FT SHAFTER TH, COM WEBB AFB TEX.

The correspondence discussed the results of the 1956 US Olympic Track and Field Team Trials from 29-30 June at the Los Angeles Memorial Coliseum. Seven U.S. Army athletes qualified for the Olympic team: Pvt Lou Jones, Pvt Tom Courtney, Pvt Ira Murchison, SP3 Bennett "are Melbourne bound," and Lt Kenneth Reiser, SP3 Willie Hollie, and Pvt Martin Engel had earned alternate positions.

> One of the greatest track performances of all times was turned in by Jones in the 400 meters when he sped to a new world record clocking 45.2 seconds.

> The old mark, set in 1955 by Jones, was 45.4 seconds. Jones streaked out of the blocks at the start of the one lap race, eased up a little in the backstretch and then picked up around the final turn and speed (sic) home across the finish line in front of Jim Lea of the (AF? – illegible).

It was further noted that Courtney "edged his old rival Arnie Sowell in the 800 meter run and in so doing set a new American record of 1:46.4 seconds, breaking his old standard of 1:46.6 seconds."

Bennett became the first man at the Los Angeles Coliseum to jump a distance of over 25 feet in the broad jump, three times. Also, "Little Ira Murchison tied the world record of 10.2 in the 1st heat of the 100 meter dash trials."

Engel, "a member of the 1952 Olympic team, emerged with a fourth place slot among some torrid competition in the hammer throw. The burly private hit a distance of 194 ft 4 inches, one of his best tosses of the season, which gave him his alternate berth."

A memo of 9 July 1956 from Roy N. Walker, Colonel, AGC, (177) stated, "This comd concurs with proposed DA plan to send baseball team to Australia. If appr rep quota of players and proportionate shares of expenses for ea svc be estb by your hq."

The original memo on the subject was from Clarence Koehler, GS-12, Dir, Sports Branch, who wrote, "Mag DA 432583 (LRN 609586) to CINCFE outlines proposed plan for FEC to organize, equip, train, and transport amateur baseball team to participate in 56 Olympics at Australia and req concurrence and/or comment ASAP." He said the "Baseball Tournament is scheduled 25-29 Aug at Cp Zama and will not conflict with proposed baseball tour in Nov 56."

There is a 10 July 1956 memo from M.E. Perry, Captain AGC, Adjutant, to Commanding General United States Army Forces, Far East and Eighth United States Army (Rear), regarding "Camp Zama Football Team."

The memo said:

1. Request the following named members of your command be excused from their military duties 1300-1700 hours Monday through Friday active 16 July 1956 for the purpose of trying out for the Camp Zama Post football team:

IRVING, Steven G	Pvt	US 53232650	M/C
OUTZ, John R	Sgt	RA 14255938	AG-CA
WRIGHT, Olen C Jr	Pvt	US 56267899	G-2

2. Personnel not selected will be returned to duty as soon as practicable after determination of unsuitability. Your command will be furnished the effective date of release.

Stars and Stripes reported 11 July 1956 from Camp Drake, Japan, that "AFFE football coaches clinic moved into high gear here Wednesday, with sessions slated on aerial tactic and defense" (178). *More than 110 prospective coaches from Japan, Korea, and Okinawa attended* (it. added). The instructors were Jim Owens of Texas A&M, John Hooper of Upsala College, and Hal Herring (*Ed. Note: the article spells the name "Harring" and "Herring"*) of Auburn.

The opening day program included demonstrations, reviews of the kicking game, belly offense, Split T, and punt and kickoff returns. It was said that "The three instructors present (sic) a well-rounded view of football." Mr. Herring was a former defensive captain of the Cleveland Browns and "was responsible for the play which made Auburn first in the Southeastern Conference and fourth in the nation defensively last season."

Mr. Owen had been a two-way player at Oklahoma, and he had coached the line which "sparked Texas A&M to a surprising 7-2-1 record in 1955."

There is an 11 July 1956 joint memo from E.H. Koreman, Lt Col, AGC, and T.L. Eastmond, Lt Col, AGC, pertaining to men available for football camp (179). Lt Col Koreman wrote:

1. Request your comment as to the availability of following named personnel 1300-1700 hours Monday through Friday,

effective 16 July 1956, for the purpose of trying out for the Camp Zama Post football team:

NAME	RANK	SN
IRVING, Stephen G	Pvt	US 53232650
OUZTS, John R	Sgt	RA 14255938

2. Personnel not selected will be returned to duty as soon as practicable after determination of unsuitability.

Lt Col Eastmond responded by stating:

1. Pvt Irving was interviewed and volunteered the information that he was not interested in trying out for the post football team.
2. Sgt Ouzts is not assigned to this division.

There is a memo dated 11 July 1956 from Roy N. Walker, Colonel, AGC, to H. S. Whiteley, Col, GS, Actg ACofS, G2 (180), regarding "Camp Zama Post Football Team," as follows:

1. Request your comment as to the availability of Pvt Olen C. Wright Jr, US 56267899, 1300-1700 hours Monday thru Friday for the purpose of trying out for the Camp Zama Post football team.
2. Personnel not selected will be returned to duty as soon as practicable after determination of unsuitability.

Col Whiteley responded:
Concur.

A 12 July 1956 memo from CG AFFE/ARMYEIGHT KOREA (181) to CGAFFE/ARMYEIGHT (REAR) CP ZAMA JAPAN, reads:

> This Hq has been invited to participate in an international baseball tournament at Seoul City Stadium, Korea, 11-12 Aug 56. Tournament is being jointly sponsored by the *Chosun Ilbo Newspaper* of Seoul and the Korea Baseball Association. AFFE/8A will enter one team and has been requested by the sponsors to extend an invitation to a leading Far East Air Force team stationed in Japan.
>
> Request that your Hq extend the invitation to the Air Force team. Further request that full publicity material on team chosen be forwarded to this Hq not later than 28 July for dissemination to Korean newspapers.

A 17 July 1956 follow up states:

> Ref msg CGAFFE/ARMYEIGHT (KOREA) KA 33184 SS (LRN 611607) outlines details of international baseball tournament sked 11-12 Aug 56, at Seoul City Stadium and sponsored by *Chosun Ilbo Newspaper* and the Korea Baseball Association. Msg req that invitation be extended to FEAF team to participate.

There is a 12 July 1956 memo from (182), to V. R. Fegley, DAC, regarding "Camp Zama Post Football Team" as follows:

1. Request your comment as to the availability of Sgt. John R. Ouzts, RA 14255938, 1300-1700 hours Monday thru Friday, effective 16 July 1956, for the purpose of trying out for the Camp Zama Post football team.
2. Personnel not selected will be returned to duty as soon as practicable after determination of unsuitability.

V. R. Fegley, DAC, responded:

Subject enlisted man will be made available for the tryouts.

A 14 July 1956 *Army Times* article (183) discussed spending $800,000 for recreational expansion (*Author note: Roughly over $9,000,000 in 2025 dollars*). The 24th Division in Korea appropriated the money for construction of bowling alleys and service clubs at "Recreation Centers."

The money would be sourced by the AFFE/8A (Rear) major command welfare fund. The plans included hobby shops, 17 athletic fields, 10 gymnasiums, and other recreational structures. Sodding and drainage of the football field at Recreation Center One was also slated as part of the improvements.

The 14 July *Army Times* edition (pg. 51) also reported, "21st Boxing Team Tops in Far East":

> WITH THE 24TH DIV. IN KOREA.-- The 21st Infantry Regiment boxing team won three individual open crowns and route to its eighth straight Far East-Eighth Army boxing championship at I Corps' Jackson Compound recently.
>
> Most impressive of the Gimlet victors was light-heavyweight Roscoe Elliott, who evened an old score with the 32d Infantry's Jim Mann by gaining a split decision in a bruising match. Mann holds an earlier verdict over Elliot this year.
>
> Elliot, 1954 All-Army middleweight king, stalked Mann, an All-Army light-heavyweight semi-finalist last year, throughout the three rounds of boxing. Elliott's heavy body attack paid off with the decision.
>
> Former All-Army bantamweight runner up Sammy Price also turned in a good win for the 21st Inf. squad when he battered

Paulino Villaneuva, 17th Inf., for the better part of three rounds before being awarded a TKO 2:25 of the third.

The successes of middleweight Joe Biggers, featherweight Arcadio Cabato, light-welterweight Bill Eldridge, flyweight Ed Taira, welterweight Lewis Stewart, and light-middleweight Eudell Davidson were highlighted. Also, "Newcomer Otis Goodwin, 31st, pulled one of the surprises of the open tourney when he decisioned the 21st Infantry's Harry Bray, one of the outstanding lightweights in Korean boxing circles."

There is an 18 July 1956 memo from B. R. Watson, Major AGC, Asst AG (184) to Headquarters AFFE/8A (REAR) regarding the "Camp Zama Post Football Team."

1. Sgt Outz and Pvt Wright are available as requested.
2. Pvt Irving has volunteered the information that he is not interested in trying out for the post football team.

A 20 July 1956 memo from CGAFFE/ARMYEIGHT (REAR) CP ZAMA JAPAN to CGUSARPAC FT SHAFTER TH reads as follows:

Football coaches instructors Mr Herring Mr Owens and Mr Hooper sked to dept 1400 local, 21 July on MATS Flt Nr 340. Req coord with Hickam AFB on exact time of arr.

MEMO FOR RECORD:

1. FEC Football Clinic Instructors Mr. Hal Herring, Mr. James Owens and Mr. John Hooper are sked to instruct a clinic in Hawaii 25-27 Jul. The instructors conducted Football Clinics in Japan 9 – 13 Jul (Army) and 16-20 Jul (Air Force) and are sked to depart 21 Jul for Hickam AFB, Hawaii.
2. This msg self-explanatory.
3. Not a reply to an incoming msg.
4. G/S coord not nec. CofS appr not rqr.

5. No Comd program action rqr.

6. Not a journal item.

On 23 July 1956, Colonel Roy N. Walker announced the final point standings for the AFFE/8A Commander's Cup (185):

> Final pt standings for the AFFE/8A Commander's Cup for pd 1 Jan – 30 Jun are as fol: 1st Place 1st Cav Div (Inf) 481 pt; 2d Place AFFE/8A (Korea) 466 pt; 3rd Place RYCOM/IX Corps 439 pt. Perpetual Cup will be retained by 1st Cav Div until 31 Dec 56.

A 24 July 1956 memo from Roy N. Walker, Colonel, AGC, to DA WASHDC (186) discussed the Ohio State University baseball tour of Japan results:

18 Jul	Ohio State 1, Ritumei University 1 (tie)
19 Jul	Ohio State 1, Kwansai University 2
21 Jul	Ohio State 20, Iwakuni NAS 0
22 Jul	Ohio State 19, Ashiya AB 0

A 26 July 1956 letter from John D. Williams, Major, Artillery, Adjutant (187), to Commanding General, 1st Cavalry Division discusses "Report of Far East Command Football Coaches Clinic" as follows:

1. In accordance with AFFE/Eighth Army (REAR) ltr AFFE AG 353.8 SS-RX, subject: Far East Command Sports Clinics for 1956, the enclosed report concerning the Football Coaches Clinic conducted at Subcamp Drake 9-13 July is submitted.

2. Narration of Events: The class consisted of seventy-seven members, fifty-eight of which were from Korea, seventeen from Japan and two from Okinawa. After a briefing of clinic regulations and a resume of the post facilities the clinic was formally opened by Colonel John J Agoa, Commanding

Officer of the Camp Drake Personnel Center. Colonel Agoa welcomed the participants of the clinic on behalf of Major General E. J. McGaw, Commanding General of the 1st Cavalry Division, and wished them luck in the coming football season. The instructors, Mr. James Owen of Texas A&M, Mr. Hal Herring of Auburn and Mr. John Hooper of Upsala were then introduced and the first session of classroom instruction got underway with Mr. Hooper lecturing on weekly organization and preparation. Classroom instruction continued throughout the week from 0830 to 1130 and 1300 to 1600 daily with a break for lunch 1130 to 1300. Instruction consisted of lectures as outlined in the enclosed schedule of classes supplemented by chalk talks and motion pictures of football games and drills. Graduation ceremonies were completed by 1400 on Friday 13 July and after the class had presented the instructions (sic) with gifts of appreciation all members were released to return to their units.

3. Evaluation of instruction: An overall evaluation of the instruction would be from fair to good depending, of course, upon the subject matter and the instructor involved. Mr. Owen was considered the best instructor, presenting his material in a amnner (sic) that was both interesting and instructive and held the attention of the group. Mr. Herring was equally as interesting but his presentation was not conducive to overcome the handicaps of warm weather and apparent lack of interest on the part of a portion of the students. Mr. Hooper, although the most enthusiastic of the instructors, lacked the maturity and experience necessary to impress the students. The fact that he represented a small college few had even heard about also hindered his contribution to the success of the clinic.

Correspondence from 27 July 1956 discussed the 1956 Company Level Volleyball League (Men's), while referencing a 10 May 1956 communication concerning the "1st Cavalry Division 1956 All-Japan Army Sports Program." The correspondence noted that the Camp Zama Company Level Volleyball League would begin play on 15 August 1956. There would be two conferences, the Camp Zama Conference and the Camp Fuchinobe Conference.

A double-elimination tournament (1–6 October 1956) at Fuchinobe Gymnasium would decide the Camp Zama Area Championship. It was noted that 1956 United States Volleyball Association rules would apply (188).

Correspondence dated 31 July 1956 from L. W. Jackson, Colonel, AGC, Chief, Special Services Division, to Commanding General U. S. Army Forces, Far East and Eighth U.S. Army (Rear), discussed Olympic Boxing Trials (189):

1. The Army is authorized to enter a full team in the Olympic Boxing Trials. This team will be selected at the conclusion of the All-Army Boxing Championship which will be conducted at Fort Myer, Virginia, 24-29 September.
2. The Olympic Boxing Committee in conjunction with the AAU and other authorized agencies will conduct a series of Regional Boxing Trials on dates and places shown below:

Albany, New York	22-23 August	Mr. Ben M. Becker
		50 Rosemount Steet
		Albany, New York
Louisville, Kentucky	17-20 September	Mr. Bill Moore
		City Hall
		Louisville, Kentucky

Lackland AFB	20-22 September	Mr. E. F. Pohl PO Box 1716 San Antonio, Texas
Stockton, California	11-12 October	Mr. A. L. Sandell 61 Grove Street, San Francisco, California

3. Winners in each of the ten weight classifications from each of these regionals are qualified to compete in the United States Olympic Finals to be held at San Francisco CA, 18-20 October 1956.

4. Commands are encouraged to afford individuals the opportunity to enter these trials. Such participation will insure (sic) that all personnel are afforded 2 or more opportunities to qualify for the Olympic Boxing Team. In these competitions, commands should consider entering command champions as well as talented individuals who have been unsuccessful in Army Area Championships or those who are unable to compete in the regular program due to duty assignment or location.

5. The provisions of paragraph 7d, AR 28-52, 1955, permit the waiving of headgear requirement for these authorized competitions.

6. Expenses incurred while participating in area eliminations and Final Olympic Trials, if contestant is selected to represent a region, will be the responsibility of the respective commands. An individual who qualifies through any of these regional trials and also is declared an All-Army Champion or is selected to be a member of the All-Army Team will be sponsored by the Department of the Army and the Final Olympic Trials.

7. Identification of contestants in trials as personnel of the United States Army is essential.

Correspondence from 1 August 1956 regarding "Ref Basketball Coaches Clinics" (190) states:

> Mr Raymond Oosting requested and was granted permission to depart CONUS 7 days early for purpose of visiting business associates in Hawaii prior to conduct of USARPAC Clinic 21-23 August 56. Mr Oosting will depart CONUS 10 August 56 and is not eligible for per diem allowances during period of delay enroute (sic).

Correspondence from 2 August 1956 from A B McEowen, Capt AGC, Asst AG, to various Commanding Generals regarding an AFFE/8th Army Baseball Tournament (191) said that the tournament would be hosted by Camp Zama, which would appoint a Host Commander "comprised of three unbiased individuals not affiliated with any of the teams entered in the tournament."

Teams were to submit rosters which would include name, rank, service number, organization, position, uniform number and hometown of each individual member.

The correspondence further noted that "Individuals will report to Camp Zama not earlier than 0800 hours, 19 August 1956, nor later than 0800 hours, 24 August 1956 ... A Pre-tournament banquet will be held at 1830 hours, 24 August 1956 at the Camp Zama NCO Open Mess. Personnel will attend the banquet in Class A uniform."

There are 3 August and 8 August 1956 memos regarding "Camp Zama Post Football Team" (192) which read as follows:

To: Commanding Officer, Camp Zama, APO 343

Pfc James W Keller, US 51338069 and Pvt Anthony S Camerera, US 54172293 are available as requested.

And,

1. The following named enlisted men of your command have been selected as members of the 1956 Camp Zama Post Football Team:

CAMERERA, Anthony	Pvt	US 54172293	AG-EB
KELLER, James W	Pfc	US 51338069	AG-EAD

2. Request they be excused from section duties at 1300 hours Monday through Friday and all day Saturday and Sunday. In the event duty occurs at unusual hours, i.e. 2400-0800 hours, these hours can be changed to 0800-1200 hours daily.

    FOR THE COMMANDER:

    Robert W. Shults
    CWO W-3, USA
    Asst Adj

    Concur in Comment 1, except personnel who are selected for organized athletic teams will be expected to work not more than a four hour tour in this headquarters. For example, these personnel will be assigned office hours from 0800 to 1200 hours and will be released after that time to participate in athletics.

Roy N. Walker, Brig Gen, United States Army Forces, Far East and Eighth United States Army

An 8 August 1956 memo from Roy N. Walker, Brigadier General, United States Army Forces, Far East and Eighth United States Army, Adjutant General, to DA WASHDC, proposed initiating a contest "whereby a serviceman or servicewoman would be selected from FEC attend (sic) coming World Series in CONUS" (193). He said that all expenses would be covered by Pan American World Airways and A G Spaulding Sporting Goods Co. He wanted to know whether or not the plan would be viable.

In case you were wondering how "personnel" on sports teams financed their travel expenses, there's a memo for that! S. A. Hajjar wrote on 10 August 1956 concerning expenses and expense reimbursement (194):

1. Personnel representing this command on sports teams competing in AFFE/8A (Rear) tournaments often are required to spend personal funds for expenses incurred for travel, billets, messing and cleaning or repair of equipment in connection with competition and practice.
2. Upon their return to this command, these personnel report that other commands furnish funds to teams for this purpose.
3. Request that your Headquarters set a definite amount of such expense money that may be furnished sports teams personnel on TDY from all commands.

There is a 13 August 1956 memo from (195) to CGAFFE/ARMYEIGHT (REAR) CP ZAMA JAPAN regarding "Sports officials clinics." There had been a wire received from Mr. Ken Loeffler saying, "Deeply regret health prohibits my participation in Armed Services Far East Basketball Coaching Clinic this September."

The memo further said, "Since Harold Anderson and Raymond Oosting have already accepted and due to time element involved, recommend that no effort be made to procure substitute for Loeffler. Request concurrence."

In a follow up memo from Roy N. Walker, Colonel, AGC, dated 17 July 1956, he said, "This hq does not desire sub basketball instructor."

A 23 August 1956 correspondence from V. H. Krulak to Commanding General, AFFE/8th Army, discusses "Recreation at Fuji Camps" (196). One wonders why war hero Krulak is being troubled with bowling alley allocation and relocation, but here it is:

1. This Headquarters recently received information indicating what appears to be an inequitable allocation of recreation facilities between the three (3) camps in the Sub-Camp Fuji area.
2. It appears that the recreation facilities at South Camp Fuji consist of a Service Club, a Library and a Craft Shop. North Camp Fuji has all these facilities plus a well equipped (sic) gymnasium, a swimming pool, a football field, a track and a bowling alley. The facilities at Middle Camp Fuji are somewhat less than those at North Camp Fuji.
3. Approximately 1,300 troops are stationed in South and Middle Camps, well about 1,800 are stationed in North Camp. This distribution, plus the recent removal of two (2) bowling alleys from Middle Camp Fuji to North Camp Fuji, has resulted in a dearth of recreation facilities for personnel stationed in the South Camp and Middle Camp areas.

219

4. Since the number of troops billeted in South Camp Fuji is approximately the same as the number in North Camp, it appears that North Camp has a disproportionate share of recreation facilities. It is therefore requested that a minimum of one (1) four-lane-alley bowling facility be provided at South Camp Fuji, and it is recommended that two (2) alleys be provided at Middle Camp to replace those removed to North Camp Fuji.

A 25 August 1956 correspondence from CGUSARPAC FT SHAFTER TH to CGAFFE/ARMYEIGHT (REAR) CP ZAMA JAPAN (197) states: "Attn SSO Mr Ray Oosting and Mr Harold Anderson scheduled to depart Hickam Field 1820 hours 26th August, MATS Flight 339."

Sometimes the recreational sports offered were not traditional, and instead had a very militaristic twist. A 6 September 1956 letter regarding the Camp Zama Small Games Tournament (3 – 6 October 1956) describes one of the included sports as hand grenade throwing (198).

The rules described the targeting area, and the equipment was noted as a "standard weight practice hand grenade." The participants were to throw six grenades from the kneeling position and six grenades from the prone position. The closer the impact to the inner circle of the target the better the score. Some may be disappointed to learn these were *not* live grenades.

There is a 6 September 1956 "Report of Far East Command Football Officials Clinic," from John D. Williams, Major, Artillery, to Commanding General, 1st Cavalry Division (199). The report reads as follows:

1. In accordance with AFFE/Eighth Army (Rear) ltr, AFFE AG 353.8 SS-RX, subject: Far East Command Sports Clinics for 1956, the enclosed report of the Far East Command Football Officials Clinic, conducted at Subcamp Drake, 20-24 August, is submitted.

2. Narration of Events: Seventy-two army (sic) personnel reported to Subcamp Drake over the week-end of 18-19 August for the clinic that was to open 0800 hours on the 20th. The class was composed of fifty-three men from Korea and nineteen from Japan. There were no representatives from Okinawa. After a briefing of clinic regulations and a resume of post facilities, the clinic was formally opened by Colonel John S. Zimmerman, Commanding Officer of Subcamp Drake. Colonel Zimmerman welcomed the participants of the clinic on behalf of Major General E. J. McGaw, Commanding General of the 1st Cavalry Division. The instructors, Mr. James Cain and Mr. William Settle, both of the Pacific Coast Conference Football Officials Association, were then introduced and the first session of classroom instruction got underway with Mr. Cain lecturing on the 1956 changes of the NCAA football rules. Class room (sic) instruction continued throughout the week, 0830 to 1130 and 1300 to 1600 daily. Practical work was conducted outside when permitted by the weather. Motion pictures were shown during the afternoon sessions to supplement the lectures. Two written examinations were given during the morning of the last day with scores ranging from 83 to 99 for one exam and 64 to 100 for the second. Both examinations showed a preponderance of marks of 90 or better, indicating excellent presentation and assimilation of the lecture material. Graduation ceremonies were completed by 1430 hours Friday and after the instructors were presented with gifts of appreciation by the class, all members were released to return to their units.

3. <u>Evaluation of Instructors</u>. This was the most successful of all the clinics conducted at Subcamp Drake to date. The clinic was successful not only from the standpoint of the instructors, who were most enthusiastic and interesting in their lecture and practical work, but also from the standpoint of the students, who, by their attentiveness and engaging questions, brought out the best efforts of the instructors. Mr. Cain covered the NCAA football rules, and was considered a "walking rule book," and try as they may the students were unable to stump him with their questions. Mr. Settle conducted the outside practical work and lectures on the mechanics of officiating and his intense interest in the clinic promoted a determination for better officiating. Both instructors are considered outstanding officials in the Pacific Coast Conference and officiating in the Far East will benefit from their efforts.

A 13 September 1956 memo from M. E. Perry, Captain, AGC, to Commanding General, (203), regarding "1956 Camp Zama Post Football Team," says,

1. Request the following named and listed man of your command be excused from his military duties 1300-1700 hours Monday through Friday effective immediately for the purpose of trying out for the Camp Zama Post Football Team:

   William O Williams   Sp3   RA 23859022   AG-EB.

2. Personnel not selected will be returned to duty as soon as practicable after determination of unsuitability. Your command will be furnished the effective date of release.

A 14 September 1956 letter from Charles A. "Rip" Engle, Head Football Coach at The Pennsylvania State College (204), to Commanding

222

General, U. S. Army, Far East and Eighth U. S. Army (Rear), reads as follows:

> Dear Sir:
>
> I would appreciate it greatly if you would add my name to your list of football coaches willing to serve in your summer clinic work for the Armed Forces in any area you may need an instructor. Three years ago I helped conduct the clinics in Japan and I found it to be great experience. Not only did I get a deep satisfaction out of the experience but I also got an appreciation of the fine work being carried out in your athletic programs for the Armed Forces.
>
> I would appreciate any suggestions you may have that might further my chances of being selected on your clinic staff for the summer of 1957.
>
> Sincerely yours,
>
> Coach 'Rip' Engle
>
> Charles A. 'Rip' Engle

A 14 September 1956 memo from (205) to CGAFFE/ARMYEIGHT (REAR) CP ZAMA JAPAN states:

> For SS. Re TELECON this date, Football Coaches of 2 RYCOM Army League teams are: Team AAA Gunners, Lt Samuel H Fycock and CWO Ancel E Williams. Team RYCOMMANDOS, Lt Vernon P Eschenfelder Jr.

A 20 September 1956 memo from CGAFFE/ARMYEIGHT KOREA to CGAFFE/ARMYEIGHT (REAR) CP ZAMA JAPAN (206), announced football results:

> Results of football games played in this command on 15-16 Sep 56: 17th Inf Regt 49, Seoul Area Comd 6, 21st Inf Regt 13- (sic)

223

24th Div Arty 6, 32d Inf Regt 31- I Corps Gp 0, 34th Inf Regt 43- I Corps Arty 0, 7th Div Arty 30- Pusan Area Command 0, 19th Inf Regt 52 – Ascom City Area Command 0.

Brigadier General Roy N. Walker on 21 September 1956 (207) proposed a Sports Conference on 8 and 9 October "at the SPS Ofc, Hq AFFE/8A (Rear)." The purpose of the conference was to "discuss the Sports Program of 1956 and to formulate plans for the Sports Program of 1957."

The proposed agenda was to include discussion of the scope of the AFFE/8A 1956 Sports Program and "participation in All-Army tournaments." They would discuss numbers of tournaments and the level of participation. Also on the agenda was "Feasibility of holding all AFFE/8A sports clinics and tournaments at Cp Zama." Discussion of pay and awards and administrative details had been included in the docket. A representative from each command would be chosen.

A 24 September 1956 memo from CGAFFE/ARMYEIGHT KOREA to CGAFFE/ARMYEIGHT (REAR) CP ZAMA JAPAN discusses "Results of football games" for "2d week of play" (208):

22 Sep 56, 4th Div Arty 34 to SAC 2;

22 Sep 19th Inf Regt 6 to 34th Inf Regt 2;

22 Sep I Corps Arty 47 to Pusan 0;

23 Sep 21st Inf Regt 60 to Inchon 0;

23 Sep 17th Inf Regt 27 to I Corps Gp 13;

23 Sep 31st Inf Regt 20 to 7th Div Arty 13.

A 25 September 1956 memo from Headquarters Subcamp Drake to Commanding General AFFE/Eighth Army (Rear) reports on the recent Far East Command Sports Clinics (209):

> 1. In accordance with AFFE/Eighth Army (Rear) ltr AFFE AG 353.8 SS-RX, Subject: Far East Command Sports Clinics for 1956, the enclosed report of the Far East Command Basketball Coaches Clinic, conducted at Subcamp Drake, 10-14 September, is submitted.
>
> 2. Narration of Events: 52 Army men and one from the Marine Corps attended the Basketball Coaches Clinic that was conducted 10-14 September, at Cornelius Field House, South Camp Drake. The class was composed of thirty two (sic) individuals from Japan and 21 from Korea. There were no representatives from Okinawa. After a briefing of clinic regulations and a resume of post facilities, major Henry F. Erfurt, Special Services Officer of Subcamp Drake, welcomed all participants on behalf of Major General E. J. McGaw, Commanding General of the 1st Cavalry Division. The instructors, Mr. Harold Anderson of Bowling Green University and Mr. Raymond Oosting of Trinity College were then introduced and the first session of classroom instruction got underway. Class room (sic) instruction continued throughout the week from 0830 to 1130 and 1300 to 1600 daily. Practical basketball court work and motion pictures supplemented the lectures. During the last afternoon of the clinic a practice game was played, and after graduation ceremonies, personnel from Korea were instructed to report to the Camp Drake Personnel Center, 1200 hours, Monday, 17 September for return transportation to their units.

A notice from 29 September 1956 from CGAFFE/ARMYEIGHT KOREA to CGAFFE/ARMYEIGHT (REAR) reads as follows (210) says,

> Following individuals are available for Olympic baseball tryouts:
>
> 2d Lt John L Iley,
>
> Patrick Keefe,
>
> Kenneth Cochran,
>
> James L Grant,
>
> SP2 Boffie G Britt,
>
> PFC Kenneth E Lowe,
>
> Pvt Alvin C Pfeffer,
>
> Jack A Benfro,
>
> Richard K Griesser,
>
> George J Zucca.
>
> Due to the fact baseball facilities are being used for football in Korea request that authority be given this headquarters to place personnel on TDY to Camp Zama immediately for training prior to tryouts.

A 3 October 1956 document regarding Olympic Baseball Team tryouts (211), says,

> From SS ref your msg KA 36128 EKSS-R NOTAL. Appr granted for TDY eff immed for tng prior to tryouts for Olympic Baseball Team. Desire Indiv listed on ref msg be placed on 90 days TDY with Hq Co, Cp Zama (8030), APO 343 for purpose of tng and competing in 1956 Olympic competition. Orders will spec that pers are to tvl under orders but not on public business,

that such tvl and dy constitutes dy of a type contemplated by para 6454, JTR, and expenses incd to tvl will be borne by nonappropriated funds.

Indiv will have in their possession a statement signed by their Co Comdr that Indiv is of high moral character and has been free of (illegible) convictions of any type for the past year. Comdr will indo Indiv conduct and character are above reproach, and conduct during past yr has been suf high to meet rqr of good citizenship and conduct at home or abroad. Each Indiv will rept with baseball shoes and glove in their possession. Indiv desiring pay while away from their home sta should have pay records in their possession.

3 October 1956 correspondence from CGAFFE/ARMYEIGHT KOREA to CGAFFE/ARMYEIGHT (REAR) CP ZAMA JAPAN announced Service League football results:

Results of Football Games for third week of play and league standings 29 Sep.

19th Inf Regt 68 to Pusan 0; 31st Inf Regt 26 to I Corps Arty 7; 29 Sep, I Corps (Gp) 12 to 24th Div Arty 33; 30 Sep, SAC 16 to Inchon 0; 30 Sep, 17th Inf Regt 22 to 32nd Inf Regt 21; 1 Oct, 34th Inf Regt 39 to ASCOM City 0.

Doughboy League standings:

19th Inf Regt	3-0
31st Inf Regt	2-0
34th Inf Regt	2-1
7th Div Arty	1-1
I Corps Arty	1-2

| ASCOM City | 0-2 |
| Pusan | 0-3 |

Commando League standings:

17th Inf Regt	3-0
21st Inf Regt	2-3
24th Div Arty	2-1
32nd Inf Regt	1-1
SAC	1-1
Inchon	0-2
I Corps (Gp)	0-3

A 5 October 1956 letter from Capt T G Schulz to Mr. Charles A. Engle, Pennsylvania State University, discussed "Next year's football coaches clinic" (212):

Dear Mr. Engle:

Reference is made to your letter concerning next year's football coaches clinic. You have been recommended by this headquarters as one of the three instructors to attend.

A list of recommended instructors for the 1957 clinics is being sent to the Department of the Army. They will render an invitation to each acceptable instructor. If the Department of the Army accepts our recommendation, you should receive an official letter sometime in November inviting you to instruct in the Football Coaches Clinics.

The clinics are tentatively scheduled for mid-July 1957. After acceptance, pertinent processing instructions will be furnished.

It is planned that the 1957 Football Coaches Clinic will be held in Japan from 8 – 12 July for the Army and in Hawaii 15 – 19 July for the Air Force. I mention this to give you an idea of the time so you can plan accordingly.

I hope this information will be beneficial to you in making tentative plans for the future. We appreciate your interest in our sports program and sincerely hope that you will be with us next year.

The 9 October 1956 *Stars and Stripes* reported, "7th Inf. Div. Holds Cage Carnival" (213), which said, "More than 250 soldiers from the 32nd Inf. Regt. participated in a pre-season basketball carnival being held at the Buccaneer Gymnasium under the sponsorship of regimental Special Services. Teams representing each company vie for trophies in the single elimination tournament.

The competition is under the direction of 2nd Lt. Ronald K. Marciel, Honolulu regimental A & R Officer."

The 9 October 1956 edition also discussed nine AFFE/Eighth Army baseball players from Korea traveling to Japan on October 15th:

(The players will) vie with 30 other players from Japan and Okinawa for a berth on the Olympic baseball squad. The Korean nine was picked by EASCOM Special Services for outstanding play during the baseball season here. A final 18-man Olympic squad will be picked from the men at the Japan tryouts by Sgt. Walt Koziatek, who will manage and coach the team traveling to Australia.

The players were listed as, "Lt. John Riley, third baseman, Seoul Area Command; Lt. Kenneth G. Cochran, a catcher; Pvt. Alvin Pfeffer, a

229

second baseman; Lt. Patrick Keefe, Pvt. Jack Renfro, and Pvt. Richard Griesser, all outfielders, will represent the 24th Div. Lt. James Grant, a first baseman; PFC Kenneth Lowe, a catcher, and Pvt. George J. Zucca, a second baseman, will represent the 7th Div."

In other 9 October 1956 news from *Stars and Stripes*, page 22, it is reported that "American Football Confuses, Thrills Hongkong (sic) Spectators." *Stars and Stripes* sportswriter Lee Kavetski said that 18,000 fans watched American football "for the first time in the Crown Colony's history."

Mr. Kavetski wrote that the Johnson Vanguards defeated the "Chinese" (*sic: Chitose*) Bears 13-6 in an Air Force Japan Conference game at the Hongkong Stadium. Broadcaster John Wallace said, "You can't anticipate the direction in which that odd shaped football will bounce. I was impressed with the spectacle and pageant. It puts our rugby in the shade." Mary Chang, a tourist guide from Hongkong, said, "The boys were so big. Football is too rough. I was scared."

In other football news, the 17th Infantry Buffaloes' quarterback commented on his team also in the 9 October 1956 edition of *Stars and Stripes*:

> Don Ross, a veteran of four football years at Clemson College and now the top 17th Inf. Quarterback, summed up his impressions of the Buffs during an afternoon practice session here.
>
> "Quite a few of the non-college ball players have looked pretty good," Ross said, "but we're a little more fortunate than some of the other teams we've faced lately inasmuch as all of our line has had college experience."
>
> Ross may shift from quarter to left half. "Our line has been holding tight on almost every play and it can open a good sized

hole when we need it, but I played left half at Clemson and I think I'd probably feel more at home at that spot," he said.

Ross, who starred at defensive left half for the Tigers, pointed to guard Bob Schaffer and tackle Ed Gossage as two of the mainstays on the Buff line.

"I played against Gossage in 1953 when he was at Georgia Tech and I'm not kidding when I say that nobody-nobody- ran over Gossage in that game. After the first quarter when all our backs tried Ed's side of the line, they finished the rest of the game by hitting the other side of the line.

As for Schaefer, he was top man on the 7th Div. team last season so you can understand how much of an asset he is on our line. I haven't seen a team that could really beat us unless we're having an off day. With a little luck, not too much, though, we could make it all the way to Japan," he finished, holding up a hand with fingers crossed.

Football game previews and summaries from the 9 October 1956 *Stars and Stripes* edition:

Atsugi Flyers to Host Zama in All-Japan Tilt – The Atsugi Flyers will play host to the Camp Zama Ramblers in an All-Japan conference game in Reid Memorial Stadium … the Flyers will try to regain the Honeybucket trophy which is given annually to the winning team … Atsugi will be represented by a strong 11 this Sunday sparked by … backs Don Webster, and Earl Ramsey and the accurate passing of David Nelson, Sal Centeno and Frank Lee to ends Mervin Houston and Carlos Pinyan …

Sukiran Marines Wallop RyCommandos 39-0 – KUE FIELD, Okinawa. The powerful Sukiran Marine Streaks chalked up their second win of the young Okinawa Interservice League season Saturday afternoon routing a hapless army RyCommando eleven 33-0 before 2500 fans at the Kue gridiron … the Marines displayed 60 minutes of impressive, hard, fundamental football, plus swift halfback Don Carter who continually plagued the Army squad with his deft breakaway running.

Other notable players were Sukiran's Art Craig, who recovered an Army fumble, and H. H. Towle, who blocked an Army punt.

The 9 October 1956 edition also reported on a football game on Guam between the Naval Stations Sou'westers and the Army Pioneers which resulted in a 13-6 Navy victory, but not before Army halfback Olson "went straight down the middle of the field for 71 yards and an Army score," following a five yard offsides penalty.

The 10 October 1956 *Stars and Stripes* further reported on the service league football game between Johnson's Vanguards and the Chitose Bears at the Hong Kong Football Club (214). This was "Hongkong's first glimpse of American Football."

The game was described as having been played in humid 80-degree heat, and the field had been coated with white paint for visibility, but the paint made the surface slippery. Reserve Johnson quarterback Rudy Mendez, who had 15 years of service football experience, was asked if he would play under those conditions again, and he responded, "Heck yes, those Hongkong fans never stopped cheering from the pre-game warmups to long after the final gun."

After the Vanguards defeated the Bears 13-6, Johnson coach Jerry Oliva said, "We played the best team in the loop. That's my only comment." Chitose coach John Rathgerber said, "We weren't outplayed. Our lack of depth and experience was simply magnified in that humidity." Also, "Both teams lauded the exceptional play of Chitose left guard Joe

Schultice. He repeatedly broke up Johnson's offensive stabs through the line and caught the eye of all Hongkong (sic) sports reporters."

Notably, "*Stars and Stripes* coverage of the Hongkong (sic) game was transmitted around the world to Tokyo and picked up several errors en route. *Associated Press* wired the story via London, New York, and San Francisco to Tokyo. Somewhere along the line a digit was dropped from the 18,000 attendance figure, which was received in Tokyo as 1800."

Below are photos of James M. Brock and the Chitose football team. Mr. Brock's obituary says that he passed away 8 March 2024 in Tallahassee, Florida (215).

The obituary read, in part: "He enjoyed playing sports in school, especially football and basketball ... He enlisted in the United States Army in 1953 ... and soon after began his military travels with three years in Japan. J.M. received the Bronze Star in Vietnam for meritorious service in a combat zone, served as the Senior Enlisted Advisor to the Director of the National Security Agency, and retired as a Sergeant Major in 1979 ... He treasured visits with family and connected with grandchildren through his love of history, sports, music, and animals. Most of all, J.M. had a great love for the Lord and for his wife of 33 years, Carolyn."

Photo: Chitose Bears 1955,
https://www.angelfire.com/fl2/altha11/5510chitoseAFBfootballteam.jpg

Photo: https://asachitose.com/FP301.jpg

Photo: Chitose Bears 1955 (subjects not identified),
https://www.angelfire.com/fl2/altha11/Taytelwar551115.jpg

From Jim Brock: "Chitose played the Champs. We didn't do all that bad as the score was much higher against some teams in the past. One thing we can say is we played hard and had fun. The championship banquet that night was the greatest. Misawa's player/coach Dick Heatly, University of Oklahoma 1950, right halfback to Billy Vessels at left halfback, invited me to sit at the head table. What an honor that was. Sat by Dick Heatly and had a very interesting conversation. Dick went to Washington St as a coach when he left the Air Force. I tackled him from linebacker and I must have hit his knee coming forward with my helmet because it was down over my eyes with all straps broken in the top of it. I think I was out for less than a minute, but they took me out for a play and I got a different helmet from one of the subs. Only time ever that I lost memory for a moment or knocked out at all. Great team, great game and even greater banquet."

Athletes Of 8612

☆ ☆

O'BRIEN

LOOKS AT

THE

STARS

☆ ☆

O'Brien

Tom Lawler

The man who has been chosen by The Chitose Confidental Sports Staff as October's Athlete of the Month needs no introduction to the men of the Chitose sports world. Here's a re-cap of Chitose's own star of the sports parade, SP3 Tom Lawler. Tom, who makes his home in the city of Rome, New York, earned ten letters for sports during his high school "tour" at Rome Free Academy. Four of the letters were earned on the baseball diamond as he did the honors at third base. He also gained three more letters for his exploits in football at RFA. His 5 foot, 9 — 180 lb frame assured him a starting position on the gridiron and and he also gained the position as wingman on the academy's hockey team where he chalked up another 3 letters.

Tom in Action at 8612

Since his arrival here early in 1954, Tom has added to his reputation in the sporting field by starring at third base for the unit softball team and twirling a few gnatty games on the mound for Trick #3.

Hockey in the Orient

Tom, who distinguished himself by setting an entire far eastern hockey league (featured by another unit) virtually on its ear with a brilliant performance which resulted in a trip to Korea for further hockey competition.

On Chitose's Gridiron

Tom is presently quarterbacking his way through a thusfar unbeaten season with the unit's well-known top football squad, Trick 3. Before long, however, New York State's St Lawrence University will be the new home of Tom Lawler, one of our finest athletes. Tom plans to begin a course in Business Administration in College when he finishes his Army tour. The 8612 Bears, stars of Chitose, will be hard-pressed to replace Lawler for the third base slot in next year's games, but all sports Next Years of Camp Chitose wish this amiable fellow the best results possible in his future role as student.

Photo: https://www.angelfire.com/fl2/altha11/lawler55.jpg

Photo: Jim Brock, Chitose Bears Football, ca. 1955

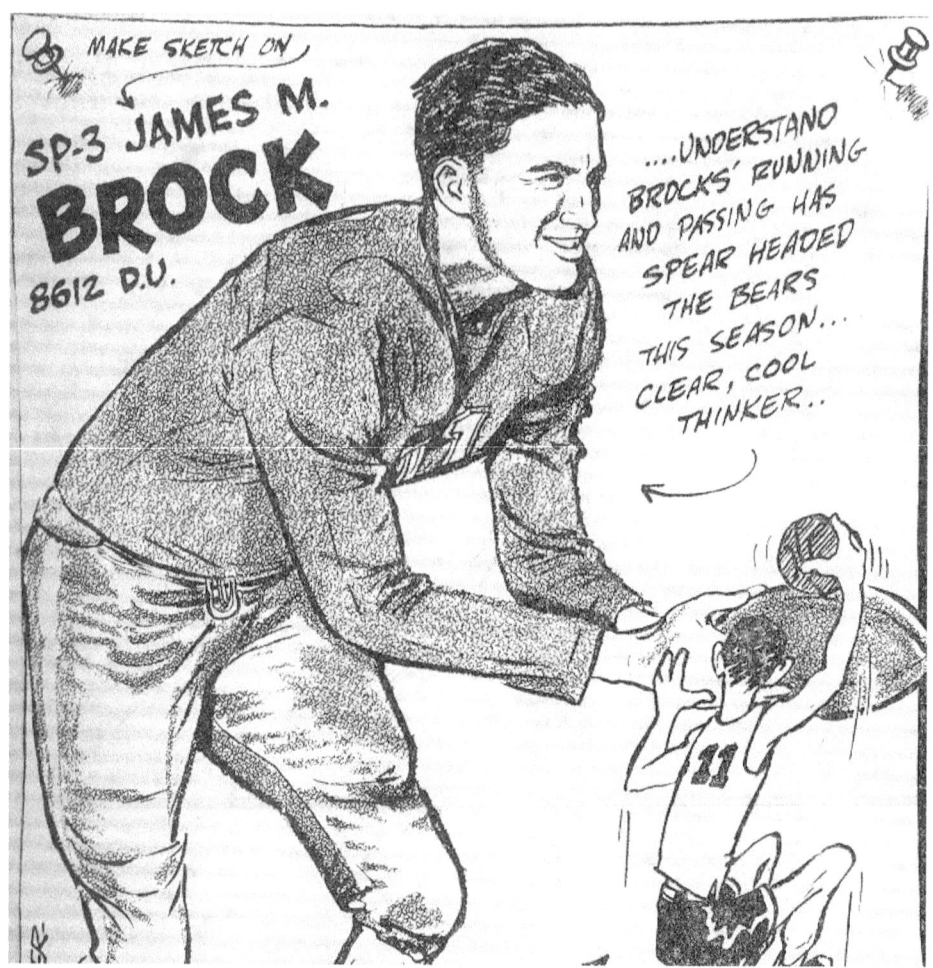

Photo: Jim Brock sketch, https://www.angelfire.com/fl2/altha11/5509brock.jpg

Photo: https://www.angelfire.com/fl2/altha11/551024yokotagame.jpg

GREEN WAVE FULLBACK, Jay McPherson (33), carries for 12 yards before being stopped by Jim Brock (11). Earl Warner (20) moves in from the rear. Hull (10) on the ground. The Bears lost 38-0. Chitose meets FEAF-TIA next on the opponents gridiron. *GAZETTE Photo by Golas*

Photo: "Things got better as time went on. Especially when we got down south with the big boys and the cheerleaders and bands showed up for the games ...
This game was Chitose VS Shiroi AFB "The Green Wave."
https://www.angelfire.com/fl2/altha11/551010greenwave.jpg

Page 6   November 22, 1955

Bears End Football Season By Loosing To Champs 32-0

Misawa's championship football squad handed Chitose a 32-0 defeat last Saturday on the Jet gridiron before an estimated crowd of 1500. The game brought a close to the Chitose football season.

The scoring started when the Jets received the opening kick off and moved down to the one yard line on seven plays. HB Bernell Anderson carried for the score. The Bears took over and moved the ball back to their 47 before the Jets took over on downs. Misawa scored another quick TD when QB Mashburn passed to FB George Hahn on the 12 yard line and Hahn went over.

The Bears defense led by Schultice, Jacobs, Schneider and Teller settled down after the TD and held the Jets scoreless during the second quarter while the offensive action see-sawed back and forth. Half time score : 12-0.

The Jets came back in the third quarter to score twice when HB Anderson skipped around end for 27 yards and pay dirt, and a fumble recovery in the end zone by End Carl Morgan. They added another TD in the fourth on a 15 yard pass from QB Paul Shook to End James Graijan.

Offensively for the Bears Brock handled the quarter backing with Moore, Webb and Hull rounding out the backfield. 'Mutt' Schultice handled most of the Bear kicking and ends Golston and Fitspatrick did most of the aerial receiving. Brock threw 23 passes and hit for eight and a total of 93 yards. The Bears also gained 113 yards on the ground, had eight first downs, and lost five yards on penalty. Jet statistics show they had 16 first downs, threw 10 passes and hit for six while intercepting four Chitose heaves. They also lost 30 yards on penalties.

Misawa's football team had all the backing needed to make winners out of them. Looked just like a college game complete with football programs to female cheerleaders and a Japanese band.

https://www.angelfire.com/fl2/altha11/551122chitosevsmisawa.jpg

There is an 11 October 1956 memo from CGAFFE/ARMYEIGHT KOREA to CGAFFE/ARMYEIGHT (REAR) CP ZAMA JAPAN (216) regarding football results for the fourth week of play:

6 Oct.　　　　ASCOM City 25, Puson 12

I Corps 71, Inchon 6

19th Inf 12, 31st Inf 7

21st Inf 45, SAC 6

32d Inf 19, 24th Div Arty 0

7th Div Arty 25, I Corps Arty 6.

Doughboy:

19th Inf 4-0,

34th Inf 2-1,

7th Div Arty 2-1,

31st Inf 2-1,

ASCOM City 1-2,

I Corps Arty 1-3

Pusan 0-5,

Commando:

17th Inf 3-0,

21st Inf 3-0,

32d Inf 2-1,

24th Div Arty 2-2

I Corps 1-3,

SAC 1-3,

Inchon 0-3.

There is a 16 October 1956 memo from CGAFFE/ARMYEIGHT KOREA to CGAFFE/ARMYEIGHT (REAR) CP ZAMA JAPAN (217) regarding football results:

Results of AFFE/8A football games for week 13-14 Oct.

32nd Inf vs Inchon 38-0,

21st Inf vs I Corps (Gp) 7-6,

31st Inf vs Ascom City 44-6,

19th Inf vs 7th Div Arty 44-0,

34th Inf vs Pusan 46-0,

17th Inf vs 24th Div Arty 7-7,

SAC vs I Corps Arty (exhibition game) 6-0.

Doughboy League:

19th Inf 5-0-0

34th Inf 3-1-0

31st Inf 3-1-0

7th Div Arty 2-2-0

ASCOM City 1-3-0

I Corps Arty 1-3-0

Pusan 0-5-0

Commando League:

21st Inf 4-0-0

17th Inf 3-0-1

32d Inf 3-1-0

24th Div Arty 2-2-1

SAC 1-3-0

I Corps 4-1-0

Inchon 0-4-0

Correspondence of 17 October 1956 from CGRYCOM/NINECOR OKINAWA RI to CFAFFE/ARMYEIGHT (REAR) CP ZAMA JAPAN (218), states, "This hqs has none deemed adequately qualified to act as head coach for Army All-Stars in the inter service football games."

Correspondence from 19 October 1956 by CGARMYSIX SFRAN CALIF to a number of commands and news sources, including DA WASHDC and *Army Times*, discussed second night results for the 1956 Olympic final boxing trials:

(Ed. note – all punctuation, or lack thereof, reflects the original).

Following are the second night results of the 1956 Olympic final boxing trials being held at the Cow Palace in San Francisco. 6th Army boxers have advanced into the semifinals of the final Olympic boxing trials as a result of their performance in the 2nd (sic) night of competition in the 3 day tournament. Jose Torres Ft Meade; Sgt Edward Crook USAREUR; PFC Richard Lee USAREUR; 1st Lt Pearce Lane Ft Polk; Specialist 2nd Class James Boyd Ft Benning and 1st Lt Pete Rademacher Ft Benning will all compete Friday night at which time the semifinals and finals of the tryouts will be held at the Cow Palace.

Torres started off the Armys (sic) winning ways when he slugged his way to a 3rd round TKO in the 156 lb class division. Early in the round inter service champion floored his opponent with a right cross to the face and seconds later assaulted him with a barrage of hooks as the referee halted the bout. Crooks

243

(sic) foe was also the victim of a TKO being subdued after just 34 seconds of fighting in the 2nd round. A hard right hand hook to the face was the proving blow in a shortened bout. Boyd after boxing a cautious primary round came back strong in the 2nd round and landed a solid KO right cross to the jaw to send his foe to the canvas for a full count. The inter service lightweight scored his knockout in one minute and fifty five seconds of the 2nd round. Lee scored repeatedly with solid blows to the stomach scored a 3 round unanimous decision to win laurels in his middle weight bout of the evening.

Rademacher in one of the best and also closest fights of the evenings card charged his way to a 3 round split decision over his Army mate Sgt John Johnson USAREUR. The 1956 inter service champion proved too aggressive for his rugged for (sic) in the highly applauded heavyweight match. Pearce Lane earned his decision of the evening the easy way as his opponent James Mackey Ft Ord came up with an injured jaw from the previous nights (sic) bout and was forced to default.

PFC James Harrison stationed with the 550th AAA Bn at Norfolk Virginia was the victim of a split decision in another very close match. Other Army losses during the second night of competition included SFC Leon Upshur 3rd Army 82nd Air Borne Div SP-3 Francis Okuda Hawaii and Sp-2 George Davis Ft Meade. All losses were decisions.

Following are the summaries of the Army competitors in the 2nd night of competition. Flyweight Ray Perez Hawaii decision Okuda Ft Shafter bantam weight David Abeyta Idaho State College decision George Davis Ft Meade. Light welter weight John Granger Messena NY split decision Upshur 3rd Army. Welter weight Lane Ft Polk default over James Mackey Ft Ord.

Light middle weight Torres Ft Meade TKO over Phillip Moyer Idaho State; Crook USAREUR TKO over Bill Branch Carleton Mich Middle weight Dick Lee USAREUR decision over Harold Butler Washington DC; Harrison 550th AAA lost split decision to Douglas Jones New York. Lightheavy (sic) weight Boyd Ft Benning KO over Willie Richardson Oregon. Heavy weight Rademacher Ft Benning split decision over Johnson USAREUR.

A memo dated 20 Oct 1956 (219) discussed 1957 baseball coaching and umpire clinic requirements:

Request 57 clinic requirements for baseball coaches and baseball umpires be submitted NLT 15 November 56. Reply should include dates and sites of clinics, date departure from US (sic), date departure from command, rate of per DM, and civilian employee rating desired while in your command. Letter regarding other sports clinics being dispatched 19 Oct 56.

A 23 October 1956 memo from CGAFFE/ARMYEIGHT KOREA to CGAFFE/ARMYEIGHT (REAR) gives the football results from the period 20-21 October 1956 (220):

Ascom City 27, 7th Div Arty 14   32nd Inf 13, 21st Inf 7

I Corps 28, SAC 0   17th Inf 70, Inchon 0

19th Inf 53, I Corps Arty 6

34th Inf 13, 31st Inf 2

Doughboy:

19th Inf	6-0-0
34th Inf	4-1-0
31st Inf	3-2-0
Ascom	2-3-0
7th Div Arty	2-3-0
I Corps Arty	1-4-0
Pusan	0-5-0

Commando:

17th Inf	4-0-1
21st Inf	4-1-0
32nd Inf	4-1-0
24th Div Arty	2-2-1
I Corps	2-4-0
Inchon	0-5-0

A 25 October 1956 correspondence from Roy N. Walker, Brigadier General concerns a meeting for head football coaches to discuss assembling of the Army All-Star Football Team for the Inter-Service Championship (221):

> Req head football coach of each Army team of your comd report to this hq 2460 T-142, Cp Zama, NLT 1000 hr 6 Nov 56 for a one day meeting. The purpose of this meeting is to discuss the assembling of the Army All-Star Football Team to represent this comd in the Inter-Service Championship. Each coach will be

prepared to present his list of candidates for tryouts for this team. Recommendations for the head coach and his assistants will be made as a result of this meeting. Notification of time arrival req.

An attached letter from Harry Halldow, Major, Inf., reads:

M/R

a. In view of the Commanding General's personal interest in the Army football team, which will participate in the interservice bowl games in December, and in view of last years (sic) experience in selecting the Army team, it is considered desirable to hold a coaches conference at this headquarters in order to make proper selections for all positions.

b. Nominations for the 1955 Army football team were made by radio with each subordinate command being given an opportunity to select their outstanding players. This action resulted in some positions being over subscribed and others not adequately filled. Therefore, it is believed that a conference by all coaches presenting the qualifications of candidates for the various positions and by comparison and discussion, outstanding players will be chosen.

c. In order to reduce the number of personnel brought to Japan for the tryouts, thereby saving travel cost, it is more economical to have a conference of coaches select minimum number of candidates for positions, yet ensure that no outstanding player is not selected and that the Army team is adequately filled.

d. As a result of the conference, a recommendation for the head coach and his assistants will be made to the Commanding General for approval.

A 25 October 1956 memo from James L Glymph, Lt Colonel, ACG, (222) reads:

1. This office has received a letter from Mr. W. R. Bentley of the Southeastern Conference Football Officials Association in which he volunteers an "Officials Team" from that conference to conduct Officials Football Clinics in overseas commands (Incl 1).

2. As you will note, Mr. Bentley offers the services of this team with the understanding that transportation only will be provided. No per diem is expected or required.

3. While Mr. Bentley's offer is most generous toward providing this valuable service to the Army, it is the recommendation of this office that the per diem and allowances be continued and that the gratuitous performances of the individuals be all that they provide. To allow this excellent program to be manned on a "best offer basis" might have a detrimental effect.

4. Request your acceptance or rejection of this offer as soon as practicable in order that Mr. Bentley may be informed.

There is correspondence dated 29 October 1956 (223) from CGAFFE/ARMYEIGHT KOREA to CGAFFE/ARMYEIGHT (REAR) regarding the AFFE/8A Football Conference final week results:

27 Oct 56   I Corps Arty 14, Ascom City 12;

34th Inf Regt 34, 7th Div Arty 7;

21st Inf Regt 13, 17th Inf Regt 7.

28 Oct 56   31st Inf Regt 96, Pusan 0

32d Inf Regt 48, SAC 6

24th Div Arty 60, Inchon 6.

A 29 October 1956 memo from CG AFFE/ARMYEIGHT KOREA (224) to CGAFFE/ARMYEIGHT (REAR) gives the final standings of the AFFE/8A Football Conference Doughboy and Commando Leagues:

> Following are the final standing (sic) of the regimental leagues in AFFE/8A Football Conference: Doughboy League: 19th Inf Regt 6-0-2 (winner), 34th Inf Regt 5-1-0, 31st Inf Regt 4-2-0, I Corps Arty 2-4-0, Ascom City 2-4-0, 7th Div Arty 2-4-0, Pusan 0-6-0. Commando League: 24th Div Arty 3-2-1, I Corps (GP) 2-4-0, SAC 1-5-0, Inchon 0-6-0.

There is a group of correspondence regarding "Voluntary Services of Southeastern Conference Football Officials Association." The grouping starts (in order of documentation as received from the National Archives II) with a 2 November 1956 letter from T. G. Schulz, Captain, AGC, to "The Adjutant General, Department of the Army, Washington, D. C. ATTN: AGMS" (225). The letter reads as follows:

> 1. The generous offer outlined in the basic communication has been evaluated by the Special Services Office, this headquarters. From an economy viewpoint, it appears unfeasible to recruit more than two instructors, especially from the East Coast, considering the costs involved. During the past five years, instructors for the Football Officials Clinics conducted in this command were provided by the Pacific Coast Conference. This method has proved very satisfactory, therefore, it is planned to utilize the Pacific Coast Conference officials again for the 1957 Clinics.
>
> 2. This headquarters appreciates Mr. W. R. Bentley's interest in our Army Sports Program, however, in view of the above, his offer cannot be favorably considered at this time.

M/R:

    a.   Ltr, AGMS 353.8, TAG, (Undated), subj: "Voluntary Services of Southeastern Conference Football Officials Association," states that Mr. W. R. Bentley (Southeastern Football Conference) has offered a team of six (6) officials to conduct clinics in this comd.

    b.   This 1st Ind informs DA that economy wise it would not be feasible to recruit a team of officials from the East Coast. Furthermore, instructors for previous AFFE/8A Football Officials Clinics have been provided from the Pacific Conference with a considerable savings of non-appropriated welfare funds, since we offer 1st Class Air Travel in CONUS for clinic instructors."

C. J. Koehler, GS-12
Sports Director
1 Nov 56, Ph 3-1390

There is also a letter attached to the 2 November 1956 package written by W. R. Bentley on 9 October 1956 to the Adjutant General, Department of the Army, Chief, Special Services Division, as follows:

Sir:

Some time ago I brought to the Adjutant General's Office, Army Recreational Service Branch, a proposal for putting it on a football officiating clinic anywhere needed in the European or Pacific area.

Since that time I have had correspondence from the Special Service Officers, U.S. Army Europe, on two or three different occasions, and so far this year I have offered my services for the next summer clinic.

As a spokesman for the Southeastern Conference Football Officials Association, I would like to submit the following proposal:

We football officials comprising the Southeastern Conference Football Officials Association would like to have the opportunity of putting on one of our clinics for the benefit of the men who are needed in the European or Pacific area.

It would be our proposal to use the same required crews as are used in nearly all of the conferences covering the United States, that is to say, a six man crew comprised of Referee, Umpire, Judge, Back Judge, and a Rules Co-ordinator (sic), who we use for rules discussions and interpretations.

Our further proposal would contain a proposition of using our entire crew and moving them from their homes in the Southeast to the European Area where needed and back to their respective home after they have completed their work.

As far as the per diem expense for those six men while on theis (sic) mission, I can tell you that our selected crew would waive the per diem allowance, if necessary, and would only expect the transportation as mentioned above, together with the necessary transportation within the area to which they were sent.

We feel like we have the best officiating in any Conference in the United States, and your inquiry would certainly find that these statements being made by me are correct. Most of our men are men who own their own businesses, and others are professional men who are, so to speak, their own particular bosses, and, therefore, we feel that we would be doing the Army a service in making this sort of proposition, and in making the suggestion of a full crew we feel that we could do you the best job you have ever had in this line of work.

Of course, we know that you will want to think the matter over, but because of the fact that our men would necessarily have to make certain arrangements sometime in advance before departing, if we were selected, we would like to have a commitment of acceptance of this proposition as soon as possible.

You can rest assured that the six man group that would form this mission would be men of the highest caliber and all of whom would be possessed of 20 to 25 years actual active football officiating experience.

We could cut the size of this crew to three man, if necessary, but we believe that you are entitled to a perfect clinic, and with the above stated number, we feel, as mentioned above, that we would give you a most thorough job which would warrant your looking into the future of inviting other solid crews to put on the same sort of clinic.

I mentioned the fact that our men would waive the per diem expense because I would rather have one of our complete six man crews go, and waive the per diem, in order that we could do you a more thorough job, and the expense would be reduced to some extent by our waiving the per diem expense.

Our crew would be subject to your instructions anytime between the date of June 1st and August 1st, 1957, or between other dates, if these dates did not concur with the dates that you so choose.

We have had visitors to our clinic from numerous other conferences all over the United States, and we feel mighty proud of the work that we have been able to do, and, therefore, this is the reason, again I say, that we would like to offer you this service.

It would give me a great deal of pleasure to hear from you at your earliest convenience as to our proposal in this matter.

/s/ W. R. Bentley

A 29 October 1956 memo from M. E. Perry, Captain, AGC to the Commanding General United States Army Forces, Far East and Eighth United States Army (Rear) released two players from duty to attend tryouts for the Camp Zama Basketball team (226). The players were Robert Godwin, Pfc, US 55526618, AG-EA; Gerald Saperstein, Pfc, US 55537129, Office of the CG.

A 5 November 1956 memo from (227) to CGAFFE/ARMYEIGHT KOREA discusses Army All-Star Football:

In view of the intense overall comd interest in assembling the strongest Army All-Star Football squad to represent this comd in the Interservice Bowl series it is considered that the best qualified indiv should personally present recm for outstanding candidates. Acd (sic) it is considered highly essential that the head coach of each team that played in league competition and a qualified representative of SPS Ofc, your hq, attend the one day meeting on 6 Nov as previously proposed.

There is another memo in the same attached communications, as received, from National Archives II from Herbert G. Sitler, Col, INF, Special Services Officer, regarding "Selection of All-Star Football Team and Coaches" dated 1 November 1956. The memo reads as follows:

1. This headquarters dispatched to subordinate commands 25 Oct, a message requesting the head football coaches of each Army team within the respective commands of 1st Cavalry Division, AFFE/8A, Ryukyus Command/IX Corps, and Camp Zama to be present at a meeting on 6 Nov, for the purpose of proposing nominations for the Army All-Star squad (TAB A).

2. CG, AFFE/8A, in response to above message interposes strong objection to sending coaching staffs on proposed date (TAB B). This decision is made in view of all-star games of the two presently organized leagues scheduled for 17 Nov and final championship game on 22 Nov.

3. However, in view of this commands intense interest in the All-Army football team, it is considered that this headquarters should affirm its original plan for head coaches of All-Army teams that played in league competition to assemble at this headquarters for a one day meeting on 6 Nov, for the purpose as stated in paragraph 1. It is not considered that absence of such short duration as required to fulfill this highly important mission could be dilatorious (sic) to the conduct of the football program of all-star teams due to play in Korea on 17 Nov. Accordingly, it is recommended that this headquarters request attendance of head coaches of all teams of AFFE/8A and a representative of Special Services Office, AFFE/8A, has the best action to take in achieving the maximum results. It is further recommended that proposed message be dispatched (TAB C).

4. Concurrence: G-1 (Concur)

Herbert G. Sitler, Col INF

The final memo attached to the above is dated 30 October 1956, and it is from CGAFFE/ARMYEIGHT KOREA to CGAFFE/ARMYEIGHT (REAR) CP ZAMA JAPAN; it reads as follows:

> Coaching Staffs of All-Star Football teams of this command cannot be spared from meeting in Japan on 6 Nov. Strongly recommend that this command be authorized to send representative group to Japan for selection of candidates for Army All-Star Team.

Some might be surprised to learn that of all possible recreational activities to include on a U.S. military base in Japan so soon after Korean Armistice (pursuant to the United States-Japanese Security Treaty), the seemingly-impractical activity of bowling was included. In fact, a series of memos obtained from National Archives II in College Park Maryland, describe efforts to build two additional bowling lanes at Middle Camp Fuji and add four bowling lanes at South Camp Fuji (228).

The initial correspondence (in this archived grouping) was from Herbert G. Sitler, Col, Inf, Special Services Officer on 17 October 1956. The response (denial) from Major General Pierson was dated 5 November 1956 (*The reader may recall that Gen. Krulak appears to have previously decided this issue on 23 August 1956; see previous entry*).

Col Sitler indicated the "problem" was to determine the "number of bowling lanes that are required at North, Middle, and South Camp Fuji …" He noted that a total of six bowling lanes were already in operation at the same locations. Major General Pierson denied two additional bowling lanes at Middle Camp Fuji, as the existing lanes were not being fully utilized. He denied the request for four bowling lanes at South Camp Fuji, "because of the relatively small strength to be served and the proximity to the bowling center at Middle Camp." He also noted there was a "current suspension in Japan of all nonappropriated fund construction" due to pending command reorganization.

There is a 5 November 1956 memo from M. E. Perry, Captain, AGC to Commanding General, United States Army Forces, Far East and Eighth United States Army (Rear), regarding basketball team participation (229), as follows:

1.   Request the following personnel be released from duty at 1200 hours Monday through Friday and all day Saturday and Sunday, effective 9 November 1956, to participate with the Camp Zama post basketball team:

2.

GODWIN, Robert	Pfc	US 55526618	AG-EA
SHAGOOL, Richard	Pfc	US 55527042	PIO

3.   Further request personnel not assigned evening or night duty.

There is an 8 November 1956 memo from Lt Colonel James L. Glymph, AGC, Exec Officer, SpServDiv, TAGO (230), which requested a list of instructor requirements for the 1957 AFFE Sports Clinics no later than 1 January 1957. The information requested included name of instructor, alternate's names, civilian employee rating, per diem allowance, proposed sites and dates, departure schedules, and excess baggage allowances.

The personnel selected by the command would be offered to conduct similar clinics on the return trip from Japan, pursuant to established arrangements from 1953. The memo includes an attached list of interested individuals and clinic dates for 1957:

CLINIC	DEPARTURE DATES	NR OF INSTR	RECM INSTR
Softball Coaches & Officials (combined) 15-26 Apr	CONUS – 7 Apr Japan – 27 Apr	3	Request (illegible) select two coaches and one official.
Football Coaches 8-19 Jul	CONUS – 30 June Japan – 20 July	3	Charles "Rip" Engle, Pa State Univ; Bill Orwig, Univ of Neb; Buck Shaw, Air Force Academy. Alternates: Jess Hill, Univ of So Cal; Murray Warmath, Univ of Minn.
Football Officials 5-16 Aug	CONUS – 28 Jul Japan – 17 Aug	2	James M Cain and William J Settle, Pacific Coast Conference. Alternates: Ed Wagner, Los Angeles FBO Assn; Robert (illegible) Jones, Big Ten.
Basketball Coaches 9-20 Sep	CONUS – 1 Sep Japan – 21 Sep	3	Jerry Bush, Univ of Neb; Ray Oosting, Trinity College; Harold Anderson, Bowling Green. Alternates: "Bud" Foster, Univ of Wis; Cliff Wells, Tulane Univ.
Basketball Officials 23 Sep – 4 Oct	CONUS – 15 Sep Japan – 5 Oct	2	William Haarlow and John Norlander, Big Ten. Alternates: John Pace and Chuck Taylor, Big Ten.

Boxing Coaching & Officials (combined) 28 Oct – 8 Nov	CONUS – 20 Oct Japan – 9 Nov	3	(illegible), Wash State College; Al York, Univ of Va; John O'Donnell, Davenport, Iowa. Alternates: (unreadable), USMA, West Point; Vern Woodard, Univ of Wis; Roy Simmons, Syracuse Univ.

The memo said clinics would be in the Tokyo area and that instructors should not leave CONUS early or late, as "earlier or later departures may tend to complicate arrangements." Per diem expenses were to be paid from "nonappropriated welfare funds of this headquarters." Lastly, air transportation between CONUS and Japan would be handled by MATS (Military Air Transport Service) out of Travis Air Force Base.

An 8 November 1956 memo from Roy N. Walker, Brigadier General (231), to CG ONE CAVDIV TOKYO JAPAN (COURIER), reads as follows:

> FM 630681 from SS. Reference letter AFFE SS-RX 353.8 AG, HQ AFFE/8A, 18 Oct 56, subject: 1956 Far East Command Football Championship.
>
> In accordance with paragraph 3 above reference request necessary Technical Support be provided to ensure successful administration and conduct of these events. Appropriate committees should be appointed and be composed of officers whose normal duty includes supervisory responsibility of a function comparable to their committee assignment. Committee organization should include: Publicity, administration, transportation, control of VIPs, ceremonial activities, and other assignments deemed appropriate. All details concerning football

bowl games will be coordinated with Special Services Officer, this hq.

A 16 November 1956 memo from G. Willoughby, Maj, Acn 0, G3 O&T, stated it is a "MEMO FOR RECORD." The subject was: "AFFE/8A Drill Team (U)." The memo stated:

1. BASIC: D/F, SpS to G3, 9 Nov 56, subj as above.
2. REFERENCE: Ltr, AFFE AG 353.8 SS-RX, AFFE/8A (Rear), 6 Oct 55, subj: AFFE/8A Drill Team Competition.
3. DISCUSSION:
    a. By basic, SpS req G3 to arrange for a drill team from Korea to participate in the halftime activities at the Inter-Service Football bowl games in Tokyo (Korakuen Stadium) on 15 and 30 Dec 56. SpS advises that the GC has approved the selection of a team from Korea. Basic informs that 1st Cav Div will billet the team during the period of 9-31 Dec and SpS will coordinate the details on the half time (sic) activities with the OIC of the team.
    b. Subj team for the 1955 bowl games was selected in accordance with the procedures outlined in ref. Time precludes competitive selection of the team by this hq. Inst acn auth AFFE/8A req general rather than specific guidance in these matters.
    c. SpS informs that arrival in Japan on 9 Dec coincides with the arrival of the band--also provided by AFFE/8A.
    d. Inst acn otherwise self-explanatory.
    e. CofS approval not required.
4. COORDINATION: G3 AFFE/8A (K) (Col Wansboro & Lt Col Rogers, 51-603) G3 1st Cav Div (9-266-2226) (re para 3, 4 & 6) SpS (Mr Koehler, 3-1390) (re arrival date)

5. ACTION: G3 fwd ltr thru G1 and SpS to AG for signature and dispatch.

6. ADMIN INSTR:

    a. Complete acn on G3 case #11-2172.

    b. Unclassified.

    c. No comd program acn required.

Correspondence dated 19 November 1956 from M. E. Perry, Captain, AGC (232), said:

1. Request the following individual be released from duty at 1200 hours Monday through Friday and all day Saturday and Sunday, effective immediately, to participate with the Camp Zama post basketball team:

    GODWIN, Robert   Pfc   US 55526618   AG EC

2. Further request individual not be assigned evening of night duty.

There is a 20 November 1956 letter from Clarence J. Koehler, GS-12, Dir, Sports Branch to CGAFFE/ARMYEIGHT KOREA, CGRYCOM/NINECOR OKINAWA RI, CG ONE CAVDIV TOKYO JAPAN, CG FOURZERO AAABRIG HIYOSHI JAPAN, CO CP ZAMA ZAMA JAPAN (COURIER) regarding the football program (233), subject: 1956 FEC Football championship. The letter includes names of those trying out for the 1956 Army All-Star Football Team and names of managers and trainers (*in block format as it originally appeared*):

Fol players have been selected to tryout for the 1956 Army All-Star Football Team: AFFE/ARMYEIGHT (KOREA): 1st Lt Robert V Joslin, 04034276, 24th RCN Co; 2d Lt Vernon E. Kraft, 04027947, Hq I Corps (Gp); 2d Lt James Doughan, 04053106, Hq 24th Inf Div Arty; 2d Lt Robert R Fraley, Hq 34th Inf; 2d Lt Walker E Gossage, Jr, 04028625, Hq & Hq Co, 17th Inf; 2d Lt

Joe Mehalick, 04034675, 514th Trans Co; 2d Lt Marion J Minker, 04035148, Co B, 13th Eng Bn (C); 2nd Lt Godwin Ordway, 072182, Co G, 34th Inf; 2d Lt Jerome Passafiume, 04036437, Co B, 34th Inf; 2d Lt Donald H Ross, 04058762, Co C, 17th Inf; 2d Lt Robert H Schaeffer, 04018373, Co F, 17th Inf; 2d Lt Charles T White, 04035372, Hq Co, 19th Inf; 2d Lt Gene C White, 04059100, 21st Inf; Sgt Lonnel Coats, RA 14395941, Co F, 32nd Inf; SP2 Bobbie Gean Britt, FR 18387877, Hq & Hq Co, 17th Inf; Cpl William P McCormick, US 56266563, Co D, 728th MP Bn; SP3 Stanley W Hosking, RA 15529175, Btry B, 13th FA Bn; SP3 Ronald K Spangler, Hq 24th Div Arty; PFC Ronald A Billings, US 56253072, Btry B, 13th FA Bn; PFC Rick M Bingham, US 56261788, Co I, 32nd Inf; PFC Thomas M Breatz, US 55496820, Hq & Hq Co, 19th Inf; PFC Stephen H Brozina, RA 13548641, Hq & Hq Co, 31st Inf; PFC Donald J Cole, US 54172088, Co A, 32nd Inf; PFC Johnnie J Collier, US 53229477, Svc Co, 34th Inf; PFC Ronald F Earl, US 56256545, Co D, 32nd Inf; PFC Charles D Lewis, US 55526640, Med Co, 32nd Inf; PFC Ralph M Mueller, US 51363234, Hq & Hq Co, 34th Inf; PFC Jerry L Ogle, US 56240828, Co A, 19th Inf; PFC James E Shoultz, Jr, US 54168201, Hq 24th Div Arty; PFC George Walker, US 56230625, Co B, 32nd Inf; Pvt Richard L Herman, US 56265332, Hq 34th Inf; Pvt Charles W Ratliff, RA 19534892, Hq & Hq Co, 31st Inf; Private Clifford A Straka, US 55515333, Hq & Hq Co, 19th Inf; Self (first name not aval), Hq 31st Inf; CG ONE CAVDIV: 1st Lt Edward J Kauchick, 02004703, 583rd Air Sta; 2d Lt Robert Antkowiak, 04036057, 70th Tank Bn; 2d Lt Robert E Laya, 04048707, Hq Btry Div Arty; Sgt Henry L Rhodes, RA 18297171, Cp Drake (8002); Sgt Thurmon Toliver, RA 18335530, Yokohama Sta Complement (8064); PFC Charles L Black, ER 56198225 (illegible); PFC Tommy Davis, RA 18205686, Btry D, 29th AAA Bn; PFC (illegible) ER 14467794, Co A, (8235); Pvt Jim Mongelluzo, US 51364195, Btry C, 29th AAA Bn; Pvt Ted Mullen, US 55539349, Hq Btry, 583rd FAB; Pvt William E Perrin, RA 17437358, 517th MP Co; FOURZERO AAABRIG: 2d Lt William Bradshaw, 0434917, Hq 40th AAA Brig; Pvt Fred Maten, US 55549265, Hq 753rd AAA Bn; Pvt Leon Poole, RA 17436053, 97th AAA Bn; Pvt John Price, US 54171994, Btry B, 37th AAA Bn; CP ZAMA: Sp3 Edmond D Hayes, RA 56130770, Japan Signal Bn (8047); SP3 James V Sides, US 53258880, Co D, (8247); SP3 Clyde W Sweeney, RA 13505915, 392nd MP Co; PFC Tony L Aloisio, RA 15534659, Japan Signal Bn (8047); PFC John F Roth, Jr, US 56252885, Cp Zama (8030); PFC Larry B Schrecengost, RA 13539462, 392nd MP Co; Pvt Billy R Boyd, US 54171013, Cp Zama (8030); Pvt Larry Hartshorn, RA 17448961, Japan Signal Bn (8047); Pvt George S Robinson, US 54175273, 392nd MP Co; Pvt Olen C Wright, US 56267899, Hq AFFE/8A (Rear)(8000); RYCOMNINECOR: SFC Bryant K Cranshaw, Hq RYCOM and PFC James Matthews, Hq RYCOM. Coaching staff selected are: Head Coach Maj Michael J Sabrinsky, Hq 1st Cav Div; Line coaches, 1st Lt Lloyd Hill, Cp Zama and 2d Lt Edgar O Willhelm, 19th Inf Regt, 24th Div; Backfield coaches, 2d Lt Martin C Hodges, 32nd Inf Regt, 7th Div and 2d Lt Vernon E Weber, 17th Inf Regt, 7th Div. Managers and trainers are: PFC Regis J Eiben, 96th MRU, Cp Zama; PFC Hugo G Nutini, Co D, Japan Sig Bn (8047) and SFC George Koenig, 15th Med Bn, 1st Cav Div. Above pers will be placed on orders in acd with para 7 of ref ltr and orders will incl statement that travel is of URGENT OFFICIAL nature. Indiv selected will report in Class "A" unif to Sports Officer at the fieldhouse, Cp Zama, Japan, NLT 0900 hr, 26 Nov 1956. Pay record must acmp pers desiring pay while on TDY to Cp Zama. Indiv concerned will bring one pair of shoulder pads, one pair of football shoes and two pairs of sweat socks. Rep SPS Officer, this hq, be informed of firm est time of arrival and method of trv to insure that pers will be met on arrival.

The memo continued by indicating that the coaching staff "was approved by CG" and that "players were selected by coaching staff as agreed at the meeting of head coaches on 6 Nov 56."

A 20 November 1956 letter from Lt Col James Glymph (234) to Commanding General, United States Army Forces, Far East, and Eighth U. S. Army (Rear), concerned the "Conduct of Finals in All-Army Basketball and Baseball in Overseas Commands":

1. The possibility of conducting the finals of the All-Army Basketball and Baseball competition in overseas commands is being explored.

2. A plan to implement such a procedure has been advanced as follows:
   a. Basketball

      (1) Regular All-Army competition to be conducted in CONUS between teams representing USARCARIB, USARAL and USARPAC.
      (2) A team representing USAREUR would not compete in the above competition.
      (3) The team winning the competition in CONUS would be declared the All-Army Champion, Phase I, and the words presented accordingly.
      (4) The winner in CONUS competition would then travel to USAREUR and compete in a best three out of five series or four out of seven series against the team representing

USAREUR. These games could be scheduled at different sites in order to provide maximum spectator entertainment.

(5)   The winner of the above series would be declared the All-Army Champion. Should the team representing USAREUR win this series, the team which had won Phase I will forfeit the All-Army Trophy to USAREUR, and instead, will receive a smaller replica of the trophy to be retained for one year, or until the next All-Army Basketball Tournament. Individual awards will be retained by team members winning Phase I and duplicate awards will be presented to members of the team representing USAREUR provided the USAREUR representative wins the series.

b.   Baseball

A similar plan could be worked out for All-Army Baseball with the following exceptions:

(1)   Phase I competition in CONUS would include teams representing the CONUS Armies plus USAREUR, USARCARIB and USARAL.

(2)   USARPAC and AFFE would not participate in Phase I.

(3)   On completion of Phase I the winning team would travel to USARPAC for a best three out of five series. The winner of this series would then travel to AFFE and play a series of best four out of seven games against the team

representing that command; awards and trophies would be awarded as in basketball.

3. Funds for travel will be provided by major commands to the competition conducted in CONUS. The travels for the team winning Phase 1 to overseas destination and return will be paid by Department of the Army. Travel within overseas commands will be provided by the overseas command in which competition is conducted.

4. Messing and billeting will be provided in accordance with DA Circular 28-26.

5. Request your comments and/or concurrence.

On 5 December 56, C. J. Koehler, in an attached memo, stated, in part, "This 1st Ind concurs with the DA plan."

A 24 November 1956 memo from Roy N. Walker, Brigadier General, to CO CP CAMP ZAMA JAPAN (COURIER) AND CO CP CAMP ZAMA ZAMA JAPAN (COURIER) discussed the Army Band playing at halftime for the Torii Bowl football game at Korakuen Stadium in Tokyo, Japan on 15 December 1956 (235).

（東京名所）後楽園球場   Kora

Photo: Korakuen Stadium, Tokyo, ca. 1960, *https://www.oldtokyo.com*

There is a memo dated 5 December 1956 regarding "Camp Zama Post Basketball Team" (236) which reads as follows:

> The following named enlisted man of your command, member of the Camp Zama Post Basketball Team, will be placed on temporary duty for a period of approximately four (4) days effective 11 December 1956 to Camp Otsu for the purpose of participating in basketball games against the 7th Cavalry regiment: GODWIN, Robert, Pfc, US 55526618.

A 13 July 2024 obituary for Robert T Godwin of Topeka, KS says that he passed away on 10 July 2024 (237). The obituary noted that Godwin served in the Army from 1955 – 1957. He attended Kansas University and graduated from Washburn University; it's confirmed he played basketball for Washburn, but it's not confirmed that he played basketball for Kansas.

Mr. Godwin later obtained his Optometry Doctorate degree in Texas, but ran his practice in Topeka and Holton, Kansas. Further research showed that Dr. Godwin was the top scorer for Washburn University Basketball for the 1954-55 season, averaging 17.0 points per game, for a total of 340 points (238)

There is a memo dated 6 December 1956 C.J. Koehler, GS-12, Sports Director, CGAFFE/ARMYEIGHT (REAR) OF ZAMA, JAPAN (239), discussing the "Fol players … dropped on 5 Dec from the AFFE/8A Army All Star Squad." (Note: Underlines added by author for clarity).

The parties named were:

> AFFE/ARMYEIGHT (KOREA): 2d Lt Robert R Fraley, Hq 34th Inf; SP2 Bobbie G Britt, ER 18387877, Hq & Hq Co, 17th Inf; SP3 Ronal K. Spangler, Hq 24th Div Arty; PFC Johnnie J Collier, US 53229477, Svc Co, 34th Inf; PFC James E Shoultz, Jr, US 54168201, Hq 24th Div Arty; PFC George Walker, US 56230625, Co B, 32nd Inf; Pvt Charles W Ratliff, RA 19534892, Hq & Hq Co, 31st Inf; PFC James H Self, Hq 31st Inf; PFC Wayman Burleson, US 54177071, 19th Inf. ONE CAVDIV (INF): Sgt Thurmon Toliver, RA 18335530, Yokohama Sta Complement (8064); PFC Charles L Black, ER 56198225, Co A, 7th Cav; Pvt Ted L Mullen, US 55539349, Hq Btry, 583rd FAB; Pvt William E Perrin, RA 17437358, 517th MP Co. FOURZERO AAABRIG: Pvt Fred Maten, US 55549265, Hq 753rd AAA Bn; Pvt Leon Poole, RA 17436053, 97th AAA Bn; Pvt John Price, US 54171994, Btry B, 37th AAA Bn. CAMP ZAMA: SP3 James V Sides, US 5325880, Co D, (8247); SP3 Clyde W Sweeney, RA 13505915, 392nd MP Co; PFC Larry B

Schrecengost, Hq RYCOM and PFC James Mathews, Hq RYCOM.

There is 6 December 1956 correspondence regarding "Far East Air Forces 1957 Sports Clinics" (3). The memo says:

> Sports clinics conducted for the past six years by this headquarters have proved to be a definite step towards improving coaching and officiating of athletic teams and contests within the Far East Air Forces. These clinics reduced the number of protested games, increased spectator interest and generally improved the quality of competition.

> To continue this program during 1957, clinics are tentatively scheduled for the following sports on the dates indicated. Exact dates will be confirmed by a wire prior to each clinic.

> Volleyball Coaches and Officials 20 Jan - 25 Jan

> Baseball Coaches 27 Feb – 1 Mar

> Baseball Umpires 24 Mar – 29 Mar

> Softball Coaches and Officials 21 Apr – 26 Apr

> Football Coaches 14 Jul – 19 Jul

> Football Officials 11 Aug – 16 Aug

> Basketball Coaches 15 Sep – 20 Sep

> Basketball Officials 29 Sep – 4 Oct

> Boxing Coaches and Officials 3 Nov – 8 Nov

> Clinic site: All clinics for 1957 will be held at the 6048th Air Base Wing, APO 226. The Commander, Tokyo International Airport, is designated Host Commander, and is responsible for providing athletic facilities, equipment, messing, billeting, and local transportation.

Eligibility: All military and civilian personnel assigned or attached to the Far East Air Forces are eligible to attend, as well as personnel from the Army, Navy and Marines.

Entries: Commanders will send only those personnel who can benefit from the instructions to be received and who are expected to remain in this Command for the duration of the season of the sport concerned. Commanders will submit the following information to Commander, 6048th Air Base Wing, APO 226, with an information copy to this Headquarters, fifteen days prior to the announced start of the clinics:

1) Roster of representatives to include name, grade, AFSN, AFSC and organization.
2) Name and AFSN of OIC of group.
3) Mode of travel and ETA at clinic site.

Orders and reporting: Personnel attending clinics will be placed on TDY with the 6048th Air Base Wing, APO 226, to arrive not later than the time of registration stipulated in paragraph 7 below. Upon arrival, all personnel will report to Commander, Tokyo International Airport, for billeting.

Registration: All personnel will register for the clinic at 1400 hours in the base gymnasium, Tokyo International Airport, Tokyo, Japan, the Sunday prior to each clinic.

Quotas: Coaches clinics: Each base will send a minimum of one and a maximum of three coaches for each base level team and a minimum of one and a maximum of three for each group level team. Officials clinics: Each base will send a minimum of four officials for each base level team and a maximum of two for each group level team.

Equipment: Each person attending the clinics will have in his possession the following:

1) Class A uniform
2) Sweat suit or appropriate substitute
3) Gym shoes (for indoor work)
4) Pencils
5) Whistles (when applicable to the sport)
6) Sufficient funds to defray personal expenses

Certificates and Rule Books: This Headquarters will provide current rule books for each sport. Upon successful completion of the clinics, each student will receive a graduation certificate and card. In the case of officials, only those possessors of such cards will be eligible for reimbursement for officiating at Air Force games within this Command.

Clinic instructors: The men who instruct at the clinics come to the Far East as volunteers on invitational orders shared by the Department of Defense, and are prominent men in coaching and officiating ranks of colleges and professional teams in the United States. These men do not receive any salary and in many cases give up lucrative positions in the States by making the trip to the Far East.

Attendance: This Headquarters will not tolerate absenteeism nor tardiness for sessions, and will not grant requests for passes or time off during clinic hours. Personnel not complying will be returned to their bases. Any reports of violations of clinic rules will be dispatched to the Commander of the person concerned for disciplinary action.

There is a 7 December 1956 memo from (240) to AMEMB HONG KONG, USAIRA MELBOURNE AUSTRALIA, which states:

> For Paul Modic, USCIS, your letter 29 Nov received. U.S. Olympic Baseball Team will arrive Hong Kong as scheduled 22 Dec. Baseball clinics and softball game with Hong Kong team approved 23 Dec.

> Urge special effort be made to secure Kings Park or any public park or area open to general public for intra-squad exhibition baseball match, on 24 Dec or earlier. Game may be abbreviated if necessary. U.S. Team has bases, pitcher's box and home plate and will assist in lining baseball field. Public address system needed. Reasonable reservations desired Golden Gate Hotel for 21 persons.

> For Colonel Weisinger, OIC, U.S. Olympic Baseball Team. Visit to Hong Kong firm. Representatives Hong Kong Softball Association will meet plane on arrival Kai Tak Airport. Confirm ETA Hong Kong during stop in PI. Clinics and softball game with Hong Kong team scheduled for 23 Dec. Intra-squad baseball game may be played on 24 Dec or earlier if efforts to secure an adequate field or area are successful. Suggest results games (sic) in Australia be transmitted this headquarters by radio.

An 8 December 1956 memo from CGAFFE/ARMYEIGHT KOREA to CGAFFE/ARMYEIGHT (REAR) CP ZAMA JAPAN, subject "AFFE/8A Drill Team" stated that a "Drill team consisting of one officer and 38 EM depart Korea 8 Dec 56 for approximately 23 days TDY to represent the command at Inter Service Football Bowl games in accordance with the referenced letter. Exact ETA will be furnished by telephone to Duty Officer 1st Cav Div."

An 11 December 1956 correspondence from (241) to CGAFFE/ARMYEIGHT (REAR) CP ZAMA JAPAN, CGRYCOM/NINECOR OKINAWA RI, CGAFFE/ARMYEIGHT KOREA, says,

> The Torii Bowl football game to be played at Korakuen Stadium in Tokyo at 1300 hours on 15 December 1956 will match the Army All-Stars against the Navy All-Stars.
>
> Only a limited member (sic) of reserved seats are available, therefore, general and flag officers have been invited to sit in the Army team reserved box. In addition, all Army colonels in this area, with one guest each, are being invited to sit in an adjacent reserved section.
>
> All colonels of your command who happen to be in Japan are cordially invited to attend this event and occupy seats in the reserved section for colonels. The wearing of the uniform is desired.

A 15 December 1956 memo from Roy N. Walker, Brigadier General, USA, to DA WASHDC (242), said,

> Know you will be happy to learn that in Torii Bowl Football Game at Korakuen Stadium, Tokyo, this afternoon, Army All-Stars defeated Navy-All (sic) Stars thirty-five to zero. Game played in fine weather before capacity attendance and was in best tradition of interservice contests.

[*Author note: Various sources list seating capacity of Korakuen Stadium (current site of the Tokyo Dome) at 50,000 people, presumably for baseball. It is not clear what the capacity was for football, though it plausibly would have held a large number of people for Service Sport football.*]

The 15 December 1956 *Army Times* newspaper devoted the better part of three pages to 1956 All-Army football selections (243). Players named, as well as coaches who named them, were listed. Complete All-Army Poll results were also provided by position.

> Army football – European style – stole the show in the sixth annual Army Times All-Army football poll. The enthusiasm created by the wide-open regimental level Army leagues in Europe was reflected in the voting as quarterback Vinny Drake, a 25-year-old balding Second Lieutenant who starred for Fordham in 1953, won "Most Valuable Player" honors and four other European players won All-Army berths ... The Far East placed three men on the All-Army team including fullback Tommy Davis of the Tokyo Bulldogs, a contender for Most Valuable Player honors ...

The short bio for Tommy Davis said, "Tokyo fullback – Two years at LSU. Voted top player in 1955 New Year's Day Rice Bowl All-Star game. On Far East All-Army team again this year. In All-Japan Conference, was high scorer with 11 TDs, 16 conversions and four field goals, to lead the Bulldogs to the championship. Also good defensive back. Very popular with Far East coaches in All-Army Poll."

AFFE player Joe Mehalic joined Tommy Davis on the squad. 2d Lt. Mehalic's short bio indicated he had been with I Corps, Korea, and had played tackle at the University of Virginia from 1951 – 1953 where he was an "honorable mention All-American and team captain in 1953." He was drafted by the Philadelphia Eagles and had some exhibition game play with the Eagles, though he was "cut from the squad because of his upcoming service with the Army." Coach Cimakosky approvingly said that Joe Mehalic "... never slows up a minute while in the game." A University of Virginia historical team roster showed #51 Mehalic at the tackle position, 6'1", 215 pounds.

The third AFFE player selected was Pvt. Larry Hartshorn of Camp Zama, Japan, who had played college football with Kansas State, and pro football with the Chicago Cardinals. He was said to have been a "consistently good performer on Far East Army All-Star team."

The remainder of the 22-man All-Army squad was made-up of stateside players, mostly from big post teams. PFC Tommy Davis is listed as having been a fullback with 1st Cav., Tokyo, college – LSU, residence in Shreveport, Louisiana, USA. AFFE players on the honorable mention list were Marion Minker, 32d Inf., Korea; Ed Gossage, 17th Inf., Korea; Bill Bradshaw, 40th AAA, Japan.

AFFE coaches on the selection committee included:

> William A. Burkhardt, 8th Cav. Regt., Japan; 2d Lt. Joseph C. Cimakosky Jr., I Corps Bullseyes, Korea; 1st Lt. Edward S. Conway, 5th Cav., RCT, Japan; 1st Lt. Lloyd H. Hill, Camp Zama Ramblers, Japan; Lt. Martin C. Hodges, 32d Inf. Regt., Korea; Capt. Clinton R. Moorman, Special Services, Yokohama, Japan; PFC Franklin D. Morgan, Sports Reporter, 8th Cav, Regt., Japan; Sgt. Don Perkins, Sports, 7th Cav. Regt., Japan; PFC Alex B. Salazar, Sports Editor, Troopers Tribune, Japan; SFC William C. Shepard, Sports Reporter, Rycom; PFC Sam F. Shawhan, Sports Reporter, 1st Cav. Div., Japan; and 2d Lt. Vernon E. Weber, 17th Inf. Regt., Korea.

An 18 December 1956 correspondence from CG ONE CAVDIV TOKYO JAPAN to CGAFFE/ARMYEIGHT (REAR) CP ZAMA JAPAN, CGRYCOM/NINECOR OKINAWA RI, CGAFFE/ARMYEIGHT KOREA (244), stated,

> The Rice Bowl football game to be played at Korakuen Stadium in Tokyo at 1300 hours on 30 December 1956 will match the Army All-Stars against the Air Forces All-Stars.

274

Only a limited number of reserved seats are available, therefore, General and Flag officers have been invited to sit in the Army Team reserved box. In addition, all Army Colonels in this area, with one guest each are being invited to sit in an adjacent reserved section. All colonels of your command who happen to be in Japan are cordially invited to attend this event and occupy seats in the reserved section for colonels. The wearing of the uniform is desired.

On 20 Dec 1956, the memo was amended: "General officers have been invited to sit in the Army team reserved box."

An 18 December 1956 memo from DA WASHDC to CGAFFE/ARMYEIGHT (REAR) CP ZAMA JAPAN discussed the Army All-Star football team (245):

From CSUSA. Pass to coaches and players, Army All Star Football Team. Sgd Maxwell D Taylor, General, United States Army, Chief of Staff. Hearty congratulations on your decisive victory over the Navy All-Stars on 15 December. The entire Army is proud of your efforts.

A 19 December 1956 memo from Brigadier general Roy N Walker (246), said,

Fol msg received from Gen Maxwell D Taylor, COFS, U.S. Army: "Hearty congratulations on your decisive victory over the Navy All Stars on 15 December. The entire Army is proud of your efforts." A copy of this message has been passed to the coaches and players.

Another 19 December 1956 memo from Brigadier general Roy N Walker (246), discussed the 56th Army Band and plans for the entertainment program of the 30 Dec 1956 Rice Bowl game at Korakuen Stadium, Tokyo, Japan:

Bands should report with Blue Unif and instruments. AFFE/8A Band (Korea) to process thru Cp Drake Center for issue of OD unif … CofS approved the plan to mass the three bands AFFE/8A (Korea), 56th Army Band, and 1st Cav Div, for performances during the football bowl games. AFFE/8A (Korea) Band returned to Korea after the Torii Bowl game on 15 Dec.

Informational correspondence dated 21 December 1956 from James L. Glymph, Lt Colonel, AGC, to Commanding General, United States Army Forces, Far East and Eighth U.S. Army (Rear), stated,

Rule changes made during the 1956 Olympic Games at the International Rules Committee meeting in Melbourne, Australia which have been adopted by the AAU and will be utilized in the 1957 All-Army Wrestling Championships at Fort Bliss, Texas, 10-15 March 1957 are inclosed (sic) for your information and guidance.

Note: The specific rule changes were not attached to the correspondence in the National Archives research.

A 27 December 1956 memo from CG TWOFOUR INFDIV KOREA to CGAFFE/ARMYEIGHT (REAR) CP ZAMA JAPAN (247) stated: "Attn Sp Svc Off. Play 60 minutes of the fine brand of football of which you are so capable and the score will take care of itself. Good luck from the Officers Mess of 24th Inf Div."

There is a 27 December 1956 memo from A.B. McEowen, Capt. AGC, to Commanders, Subordinate Tactical and Area Units, regarding the "1st Cavalry Division 1957, All-Japan, Army Wrestling Tournament" (248) as follows:

1. The 1st Cavalry Division's 1957, All-Japan, Army Wrestling Tournament will be conducted 13-17 February 1957 at Regional Camp Otsu, Japan.

2. The following 1st Cavalry Division organizations will enter 1 Army team and other listed organizations are invited to enter (unreadable):

    a. 1st Cavalry Division Artillery including all non-divisional organizations in the Subcamp Drake area and other Division Artillery personnel stationed throughout Japan.

    b. 5th Cavalry Regiment including all non-divisional units in the Regional Camp Schimmelpfennig Area.

    c. 7th Cavalry Regiment including all non-divisional units in the Regional Camp Otsu Area to include outstanding players from Regional Camp Kobe, Kokura, and Kure and the 802nd Engineer Battalion (Heavy Construction).

    d. 8th Cavalry Regiment including all non-divisional units in the Regional Camp Whittington Area.

    e. 1st Cavalry Division Special Troops at Subcamp Drake, Subcamp Fuji, and Metropolitan Tokyo area. Division Special Troops units stationed in other areas throughout Japan will compete with the local Regimental units team.

    f. Hq 40th AAA Brigade stationed at Camp Moore and 40th AAA Brigade troops stationed throughout Japan.

    g. Camp Zama

    h. Yokohama United States Army Port to include all units stationed at Subcamp Yokohama.

3. The 1st Cavalry Division 1957, All-Japan, Army Wrestling Tournament will be conducted on an individual basis with team scoring. The championship will be conducted as a double elimination type tournament. Freestyle and Greco Roman will be conducted in that order. The 1957 Amateur Athletic Union of the United States Wrestling Rules will govern all competition

277

with the exception that the training headgear will be worn by each competitor, and the team scoring system given in paragraph 6 below. Each participating organization is authorized to enter personnel in each of the following weights:

a. Flyweight   up to 114 ½ pounds

b. Bantamweight   up to 125 ½ pounds

c. Featherweight   up to 136 ½ pounds

d. Lightweight   up to 147 ½ pounds

e. Welterweight   up to 160 ½ pounds

f. Middleweight   up to 174 pounds

g. Light heavyweight   up to 191 pounds

h. Heavyweight   over 191 pounds

4. An individual may represent his organization in both Freestyle and Greco Roman.
5. Each contestant will be examined by a doctor after weighing in on each day of competition.
6. As an exception to the Official AAU Wrestling Rules the team championship will be determined by the following scoring systems:
    a. One point for each match won up to the finals.
    b. Two points for each match won following a bye up to the finals.
    c. Three points for each match won in the finals of each weight class.
    d. One point for each match lost in the finals of each weight class.
7. Visiting team personnel will be placed on TDY to Regional Camp Otsu, APO 9, for the necessary period, to arrive not earlier

than 0800 hours, 11 February 1957 or later than 1700 hours 12 February 1957. Orders will specify that personnel R2 travel under orders, but not on public business, that such travel and temporary duty constitute duty of a type contemplated by paragraph 6454, Joint Travel Regulations, and that expenses incident to such travel and temporary duty will be borne by locally available nonappropriated funds. Orders will further state that if individuals are selected for the 1st Cavalry Division Team, TDY is extended an additional 15 days, and if individuals are selected to represent AFFE/8th Army at the All-Army Wrestling Tournament, TDY will be extended an additional 30 days, and individuals will report to the Commanding Officer, Camp Drake Personnel Center (8042), APO 613, for necessary processing for travel to CONUS.

8. Addressee command will ensure that all individuals have cleared their command, and that each individual has up-to-date personnel records, pay records, and sufficient military clothing in his possession. The person-in-charge of each team will deliver these records to the A&R Officer, Regional Camp Otsu, upon arrival at the tournament site. Visiting teams will notify the A&R Officer, Regional Camp Otsu, of their estimated time and place of arrival at Otsu, and the mode of transportation by telephoning Otsu 5237.

9. Commanding Officers entering teams will submit rosters of their teams, to include the name, rank, service number, organization, wrestling weight, and hometown of each participant, together with the name of the person-in-charge, and two team pictures, to reach this headquarters, Attention: Special Services Officer, not later than 7 February 1957. An information copy of this roster with a team picture will be forwarded direct to the Commanding Officer, Regional Camp Otsu, APO 9, Attention: Special Services.

10. A meeting of all coaches and contestants will be held at 0900 hours, 13 February 1957 at the Main Field House, Regional Camp Otsu.

11. The winner and runner-up of the final bout in each weight class plus a trainer, coach, and officer-in-charge, selected by this headquarters, will comprise the 1st Cavalry Division Wrestling Team, and will represent this command in the AFFE/8th Army Wrestling Tournament to be held at Regional Camp Otsu, 25 – 27 February 1957.

12. The Commanding Officer, Regional Camp Otsu will be responsible for the following:

    a. Providing adequate playing facilities.

    b. Providing suitable billeting and messing facilities for participating officials.

    c. Providing competent medical service during each contest.

    d. Providing comprehensive publicity.

    e. Providing administrative personnel to conduct the competition.

    f. Providing programs for spectator interest.

    g. Sale of refreshments at all sports events.

    h. The conduct of the pre-tournament military to include the weigh-ins, medical examination and pairings.

    i. Providing each competitor with an economical brochure to include rosters of teams, tournament pairing brackets, uniform and post regulations and facilities.

    j. Coordinating the estimated time of travel of visiting teams.

    k. Providing adequate transportation for competitors.

    l. Maintaining close liaison with the Sports Branch, Special Services Section, this headquarters on all matters pertaining to the tournament.

    m. Selection and payment of officials for the tournament not to exceed a total of $40.00 per day.

n. Arranging for the presentation of awards to recipients immediately following the final match at the site of the contest by an officer of Field Grade or higher rank made available for this purpose.

o. Submitting to this headquarters, Attention: Special Services Officer, not later than seven days after the tournament a brief historical resume of the activity to include the following information: (this information is exempt from reports control under the provisions of paragraph 17k, Army Regulations 333.15, 12 March 1953).

    (a) Five copies of tournament brackets.

    (b) Results of each contest.

    (c) Five copies of all action photographs and news clippings.

    (d) Five copies of each program.

p. Appointing a tournament committee composed of three unbiased individuals not affiliated with any teams entered in the tournament.

13. Trophies will be provided by this headquarters to the winning and runner up teams and to the individuals (sic) winners in each weight class.

A 29 December 1956 memo from CG THREE MARDIV OKINAWA RI to CGAFFE/ARMYEIGHT (REAR) CP ZAWA JAPAN (249), stated: "Major General Shapley regrets unable to accept your invitation Korakuen Stadium Rice Bowl game."

There is a game program for the 30 December 1956 Rice Bowl football game at Korakuen Stadium in Tokyo Japan (1300 hours) between "Air Forces" and Army, as part of the "Far East Command Inter-Service Football Championships" (250).

The program opens with comments from General L.L. Lemnitzer, United States Army Commander-in-Chief, who said, in part, "To those of us serving in the Armed Forces, this time-honored sport has a special significance. Football fosters in our youth many of the important qualities so important to success in combat. Among these qualities are peak physical condition, courage, determination, and quick decisive thinking and action under pressure. Above all, football emphasizes and its long, tough training, the type of close effective teamwork that pays off in battle."

General Lawrence S. Kuter, United States Air Forces Commander, said, "In all our training, whether it be military or athletic, we seek one principal result: the skillful accomplishment of an assigned mission."

General I.D. White, United States Army Commanding General, United States Army Forces, Far East and Eighth United States Army, offered: "The 10th annual Inter-Service championships bring to a close another outstanding football season in which military personnel stationed throughout the Far East have once again proved their ability to fight hard and honorably."

The 1956 Army and Air Forces All-Stars were listed on rosters by jersey number, name, position, age, weight, height, team, and hometown (see referenced roster photos below).

The Rice Bowl game program gives an interesting history of Bowl Games:

> At home in the United States during this season, traditional 'bowl' games with all the attendant color and atmosphere surrounding them are being played in various sections of the country. Football classics, such as the Rose Bowl of Pasadena, California; the Cotton Bowl of Dallas, Texas; Miami's Orange Bowl and Sugar Bowl of New Orleans, Louisiana, bring together some of the finest teams in the land in contests which

will determine to a large degree the relative merits of football as it is played in different sections of the United States.

"Bowl" games in the Far East theater were first inaugurated on New Year's Day of 1946. Far East annual bowl affairs presently consist of Japan's Torii Bowl, Sukiyaki Bowl and Rice Bowl; Okinawa's Typhoon Bowl; Guam's Sweat Bowl; Korea's Kimchi Bowl; and the Philippine's (sic) Bamboo Bowl.

The gridiron classic in Japan was originally set up as a service game between All-Star Teams in Korea and Japan. Appropriately named the Rice Bowl, the contest has been the climax to (sic) Far East football since its origin in 1946, with the exception of those games cancelled due to the outbreak of hostilities in Korea.

December of 1952 saw the birth of the Torii Bowl and the following year, 1953 the Sukiyaki Bowl was added making the bowl games an Inter-Service affair with Army, Navy, Marine, and Air Force All-Stars participating.

The 1956 series found the Army All-Stars conquering the Navy All-Stars in the 5th Annual Torii Bowl contest on December 15th, and the Air Forces All-Stars zooming to victory over the Marine All-Stars in the 4th Annual Sukiyaki Bowl held December 16th. Today, December 30th, the winners compete in the 10th Annual Rice Bowl to determine the Far East Football Championship.

Historical outcomes (from the program; *1951 skipped):

TORII BOWL

1952	Navy	20	Air Forces	13
1953	Air Forces	25	Navy	7
1954	Air Forces	50	Navy	47
1955	Army	20	Marines	6
1956	Army	35	Navy	0

SUKIYAKI BOWL

1952	Army		Bye	
1953	Marines	53	Army	6
1954	Marines	27	Army	13
1955	Air Forces	21	Navy	0
1956	Air Forces	29	Marines	7

RICE BOWL

1946	Japan	6	Korea	0
1947	Korea	19	Japan	13
1948	Korea	18	Japan	13
1949	Army	13	Air Forces	7
1950	Air Forces	18	Army	14
1952*	Army	25	Navy	6
1953	Marines	19	Air Forces	13
1954	Air Forces	21	Marines	14
1955	Air Forces	33	Army	14

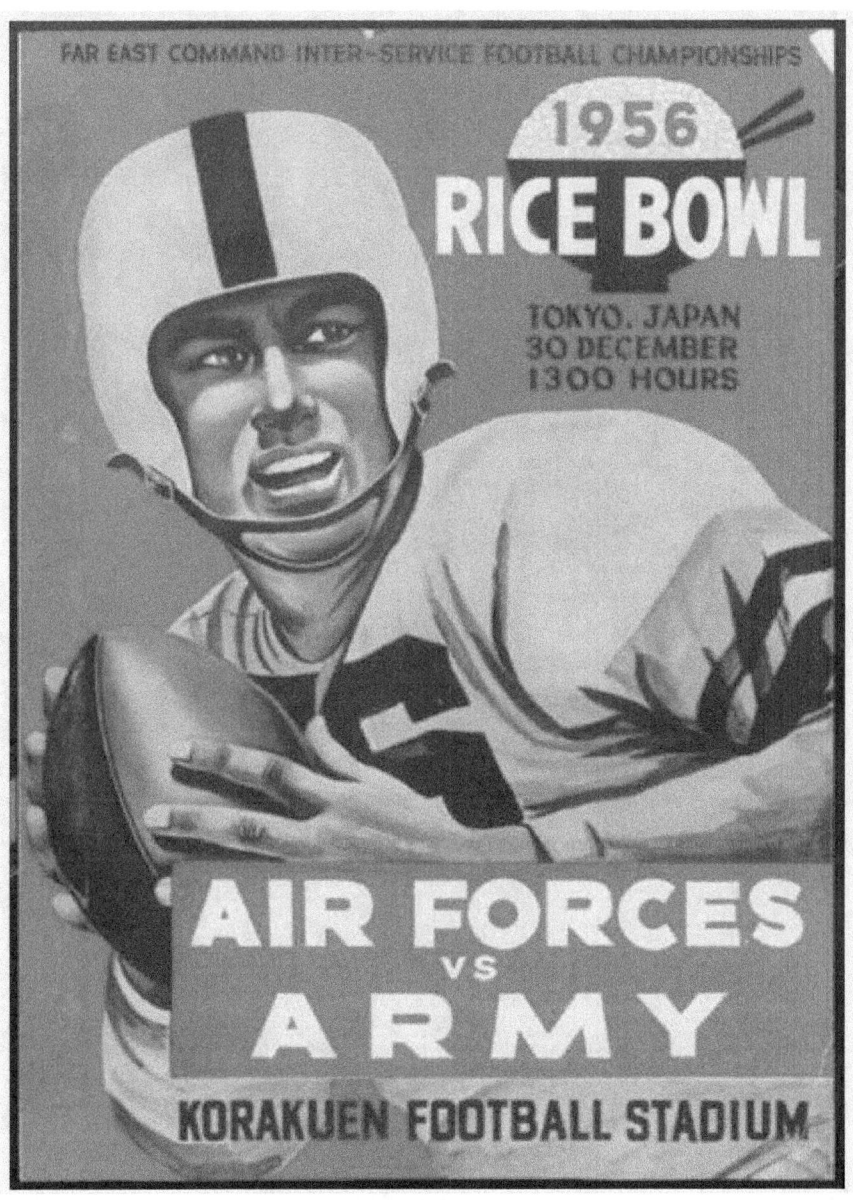

Photo: 1956 Rice Bowl football program cover.

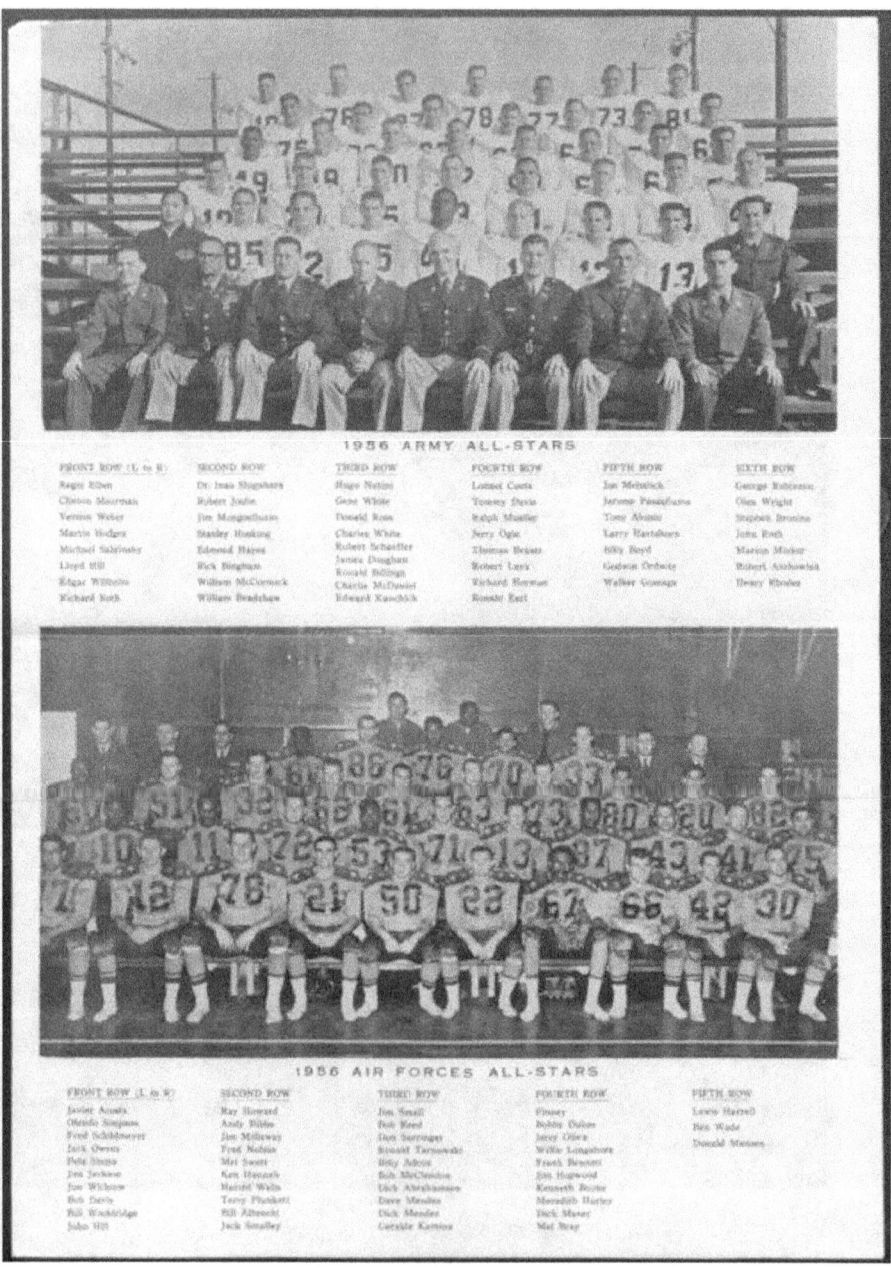

Photo: 1956 Rice Bowl team photos.

Photo: 1956 Rice Bowl team rosters.

Note: There is a similar type program (251) for the 16 December 1956 Sukiyaki Bowl in Tokyo Japan, also at Korakuen Stadium, between Marines and Air Force (winner goes to rice Bowl). See the 1956 Sukiyaki Bowl Marine Corps All-Stars and the Air Force All-Stars rosters below (*Author note: The quality of the originals was somewhat poor, but being that these are rare documents, this is the best we can offer at this time*):

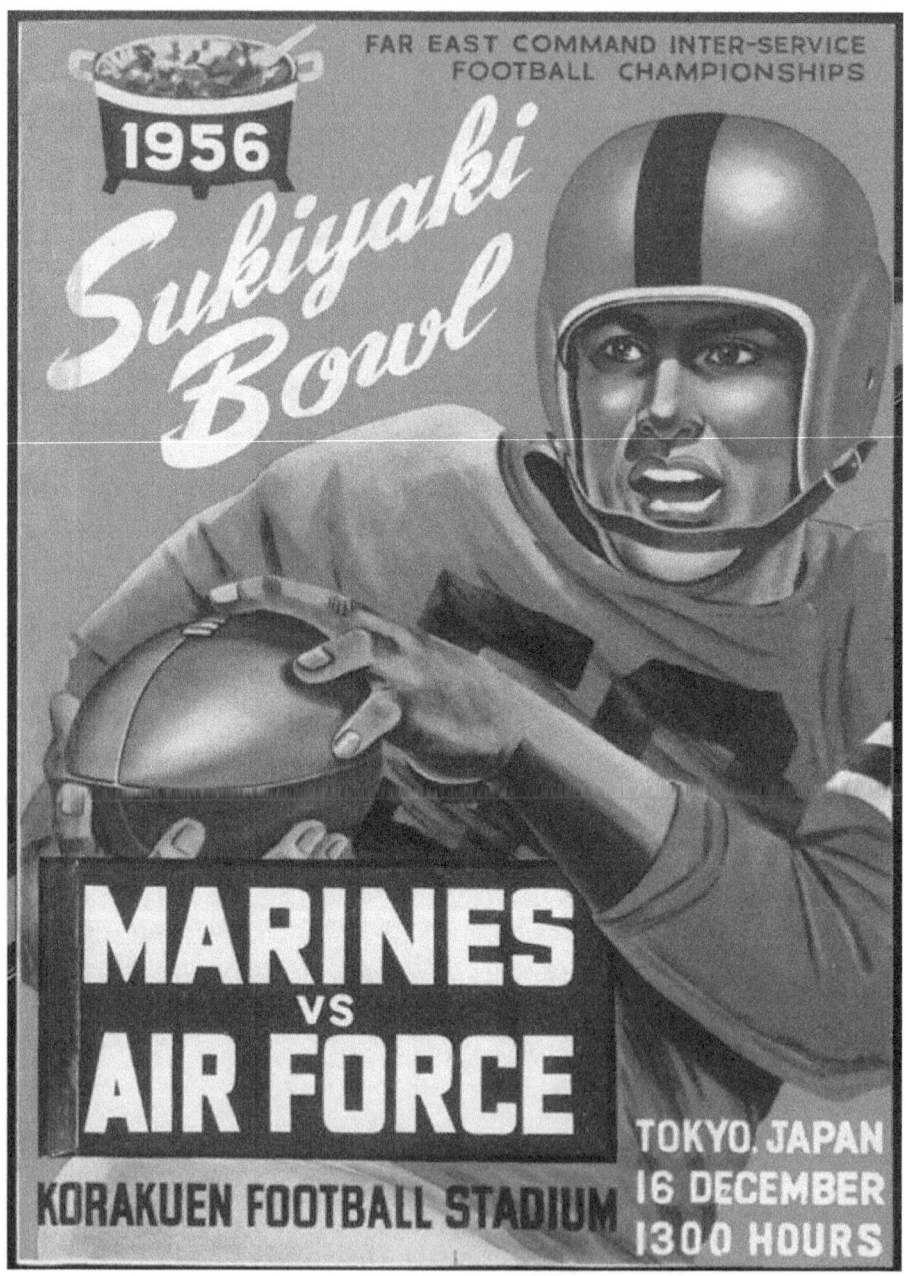

Photo: 1956 Sukiyaki Bowl football program cover.

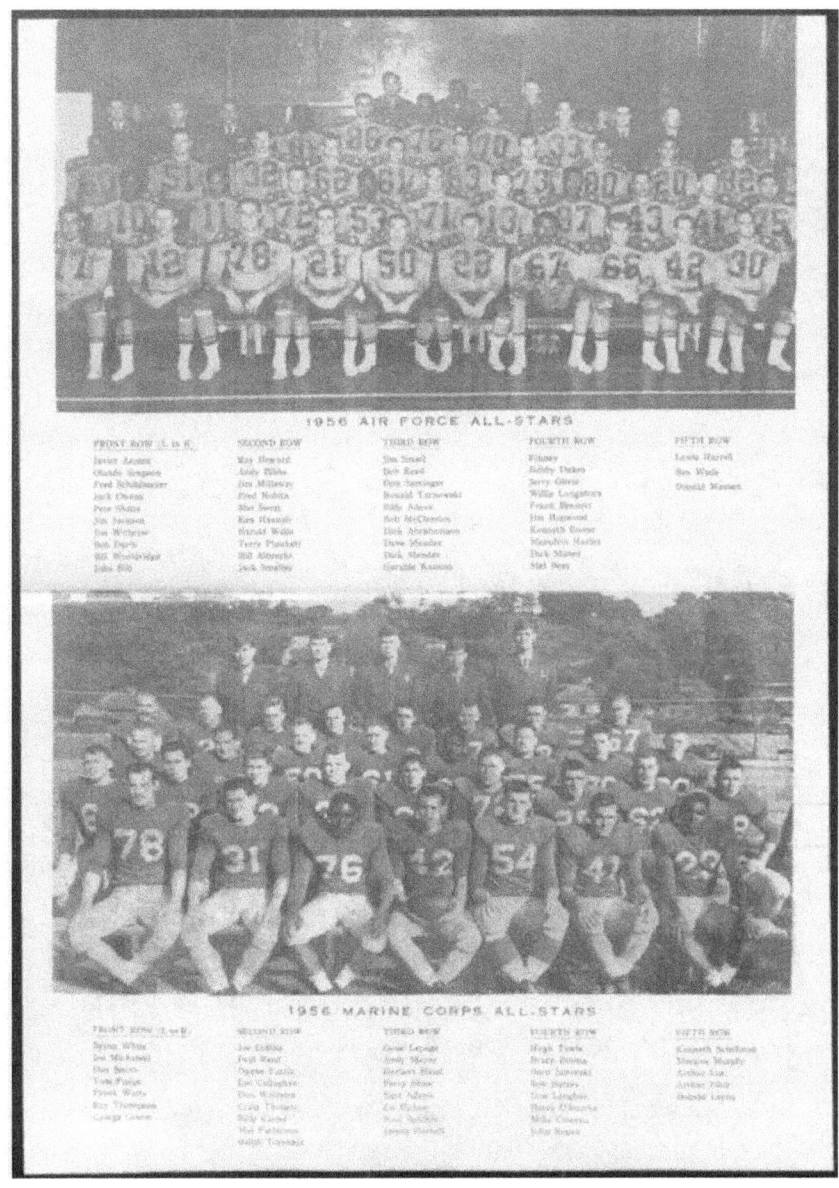

Photo: 1956 Sukiyaki Bowl team photos.

Photo: 1956 Sukiyaki Bowl rosters.

In a tragic twist of fate, Ronald Tarnowski, an Air Force All-Star Rice Bowl participant from Duluth, Minnesota, passed away at age 82 along with his wife, Mary, age 78, according to the *St. Paul Pioneer Press* newspaper (252).

The 8 August 2017 news article described their ordeal; while heartbreaking, it's also a story of love and heroism:

> Decades ago, at age 42, Mary Tarnowski suffered from a stroke that left her paralyzed on the right side of her body, making it difficult for her to move or speak. Her husband, Ron, served as her caretaker for more than 35 years … in recent years, Ron Tarnowski, an Air Force veteran and retired captain of the local fire department, began showing signs of early onset dementia

... suddenly, the tough man with a "commanding presence," adventurous spirit, and the build of a former football player, needed to be taken care of too ... so it was troubling when, on the evening of July 29th, Karl Tarnowski (son) and his wife found the elderly couple's home empty, and their Chevy Tahoe gone ...

For the next 7 days, the family, law enforcement and hundreds of community members in Duluth launched an extensive search effort that covered thousands of miles ... on Saturday afternoon eight days after the couple went missing, the family received their answer and a tragic end to their strenuous search.

A U.S. Border Patrol helicopter found the couple's Chevy Tahoe on an overgrown, abandoned driveway in a swampy area off the road just two miles away from the family's hunting property ... Marie Tarnowski's body was discovered inside the Tahoe, and her husband's body was found outside the vehicle, about 50 feet from the road ... Police think Tarnowski left the vehicle in order to seek help ... Both are believed to have died on July 29th, the day they first went missing ...

Mr. Tarnowski sacrificed himself to find help for his wife; Mr. Tarnowski was an American Hero – Rest in Peace.

Mr. Tarnowski's obituary (punctuation is the original) lists his football history and other accomplishments (253):

Ron 'Bisco' Tarnowski was born on December 29th, 1935 in Duluth to Frank and Marie Tarnowski. He graduated Central High School, where he played football. He joined the US Air Force, serving in the Philippine's, and played football there. After the Air Force, Ron attended UMD and played on their football team.

Ron retired as a captain from the Duluth Fire Dept. after 31 years. He was a member of Saint Joseph's church in Duluth Heights; he was a active member of the Knights of Columbus; member of Minnesota's first snowmobile club, the Turtle patrol; he loved to tinker in his garage; antique cars; spending time at the hunting shack; checking on what the boys were doing and the "Wednesday Night Cruiser Guys". He was buried with Military Honors in Duluth.

A 30 December 1956 memo from CGAFFE/ARMYEIGHT CP ZAMA JAPAN to DA WASHDC (254) states: "It is a distinct pleasure to report that in Rice Bowl football game at the Korakuen Stadium, Tokyo, this afternoon, the Army All-Stars defeated the Air Force All-Stars twenty-one to six."

SECTION SUMMARY

The preceding section functions as somewhat of an encyclopedia and narrative at the same time, providing robust documentation, to the extent possible, of AFFE Service Sports in the 1950s. It's possibly the first time U.S. Military Service Sports in the Far East have been documented to this extent, post-contemporaneous. It is almost certainly the first time that actual military memos and correspondence have been mated with mainstream news accounts to form a more complete picture of Service Sports operations behind the scenes as well as what had been revealed publicly.

The Service Sports program, post-Korean War, appears to have had the full and complete endorsement of top military leaders at the time; they considered these programs part and parcel of military training, particularly football, which had benefits directly applicable to combat applications (strength, leadership, team-building, etc.). While they always seemed mindful to use Service Sports budgets wisely, military leaders generally spared no expense when it came to providing necessary assets to enable superb competition to flourish.

The weight of evidence suggests that Far East Military Service Sports were symbiotic with the local communities; not separate, but integrated. From exhibition football games in Hong Kong (to the delight of many), to giant football championship and All-Star games in Japan, the local community was invited and welcomed.

It was truly a special time.

UNIV. OF ALABAMA BASEBALL IN FAR EAST

13 December 1956 correspondence from Ralph L. Veach, GS-8, to DA WASHDC (255), titled "Offer of University of Alabama Baseball Team" for a Far East tour, says:

> Reply to offer of University of Alabama Baseball Team held in abeyance pndg receipt of add info. Req team record last five years, aprx nr of lettermen rtn from last year's team, and prospect for conference finish next spring. This hq interested in college baseball team to tour next summer, and concur in bringing outstanding teams from different sections of the US. With Jap university teams to be sked and record of last two teams, desire to select a strong team preferably a … conference champion.

> *(Author note: The University of Alabama baseball team in 1955 under Coach Tilden Campbell was 23-6, and was the Southeastern Conference Champion).*

Documents generously supplied by the University of Alabama's Paul W. Bryant Museum provide more context for the Alabama baseball team's 1957 Far East tour. The tour had been approved and arranged, and appears to have been successful, save for a "severe Asian flu siege," which befell members of the team and staff.

Correspondence, undated, but referencing the 25 June to 6 August 1957 trip said, "The University of Alabama's baseball team, annually recognized as one of the nation's finer collegiate clubs, represented well the United States on a six-weeks Far East good-will tour during the summer months of 1957."

Despite the flu having impacted "21 of 24 members," and "some near catastrophic airplane trouble over the Pacific Ocean," Alabama managed to win 15 out of 20 games against U.S. Military bases and Japanese universities.

Miles traveled were said to have been 21,912, which included bus, train, and air travel.

<u>Personnel making the trip</u>:

Head Coach Tilden 'Happy' Campbell

Assistant Coach Joe Kilgrow

Athletic Director Hank Crisp

Athletic Publicity Director Finus Gaston

Photographer Jim Cummings

Trainer David Johnson

Pitcher Frank Roland

Pitcher Bobby Ledford

Pitcher Don Adams

Pitcher Clyde Eurick

Pitcher Gary Freeman

Pitcher Mike Tamucci

Pitcher Pete Reeves

Pitcher Howard Tepper

Pitcher Ralph Blaylock

Catcher Mack Jones

First Baseman Fred Frickie

Second Baseman Chuck Bancroft

Third Baseman Herb Kosten (Captain)

Shortstop Tony Sansome

Left Fielder Norman Koury

Center Fielder Dale Rice

Right Fielder Bill Walker

Escort Officer First Lieutenant Jack Smalley (former star Alabama football player stationed in Japan with the Air Force.)

```
RESULTS   WON 15  LOST 5
```

Team Played	Place	Ala.	Opp.	
Yokasuka NAB	Japan			Rain
Yokahama	Japan	10	0	
Camp Drake	Japan	4	1	
Atsugi NAS	Japan	3	4	
Camp Zoma	Japan	2	1	
Johnson AB	Japan	2	7	
Rikkio University	Japan	0	1	
Tachikawa AB	Japan	4	3	
Fuchu AS	Japan			Rain
Yokota AB	Japan			Rain
Fifth AF	Japan			Rain
Kansai University	Japan	4	1	
Itami AB	Japan	4	0	
Itazuke	Japan	7	3	
Ashiya AB	Japan	11	4	
Osan AB AF All-Stars	Korea	10	1	
Seventh Inf. Div. Stars	Korea	19	0	
Seoul Area Command	Korea			Rain
Korean All-Stars	Korea			Rain
24 Inf. Div. Stars	Korea			Rain
I Corps. All-Stars	Korea			Rain
Okinawa All-Stars	Okinawa	7	0	
Kodena AB	Okinawa	5	1	
Marine All-Stars	Okinawa	20	3	
Army All-Stars	Okinawa	4	0	
Marines	Honolulu	3	4	
Navy	Honolulu	14	1	
Marines	Honolulu	1	10	
		134	45	

Courtesy of Brad Green, Curator, Paul W. Bryant Museum, Tuscaloosa, Alabama 2025

FINAL 1957 BASEBALL STATISTICS FOR 23 GAMES

Hitting	G	AB	R	H	2B	3B	HR	RBI	TB	SH	SB	HP	BB	SO	Ave.	PO	A	E
Adams, p	1	1	0	1	0	0	0	0	1	0	0	0	0	0	1.000	0	1	0
Ledford, p	9	24	9	12	0	0	2	9	18	0	0	0	6	2	.500	3	0	0
Frickie, 1b	23	79	30	32	7	2	1	22	46	4	0	0	17	4	.405	177	16	1
Kubiszyn, ss	23	80	21	28	5	3	3	23	44	5	1	0	15	6	.350	37	66	6
Roland, p	10	24	5	8	2	0	0	6	10	2	0	1	2	6	.333	3	17	3
Freeman, p	2	3	1	1	1	0	0	2	2	0	0	0	0	0	.333	1	3	0
Rice, cf	23	83	15	26	2	0	0	10	35	4	0	0	13	5	.311	29	50	2
Kosten, 3b	23	74	24	23	2	1	0	6	27	3	6	0	21	4	.311	64	52	4
Bancroft, 2b	23	82	13	25	3	3	0	8	34	3	4	0	8	11	.302	50	4	3
Blalock, c	14	43	7	13	3	0	2	11	22	1	1	0	1	0	.286	0	2	0
Reaves, p	3	7	0	2	0	0	0	1	2	0	0	0	1	0	.268	27	4	1
Koury, lf	23	56	15	15	0	1	2	13	23	3	2	2	25	2	.243	40	6	5
Walker, rf	22	70	9	17	4	2	3	17	34	4	1	0	13	4	.167	36	1	3
Jones, c	11	24	5	4	1	0	0	0	5	1	0	0	1	2	.167	0	2	0
Eurick, p	5	6	0	1	0	0	0	0	1	0	0	0	1	1	.143	1	5	1
Tepper, p	5	7	0	1	1	0	0	1	2	0	0	0	0	1	.000	0	0	0
Hoover, p	1	0	0	0	0	0	0	0	0	0	0	0	0	1	.000	0	2	0
Leonard, p	1	1	0	0	0	0	0	0	0	0	0	0	0	0	.000	0	0	1
Tannucci, p	3	1	0	0	0	0	0	0	0	0	0	0	0	0	.000	1	2	0
Sansone, lf	2	1	0	0	0	0	0	0	0	0	0	0	1	0	.000			
	23	667	144	209	34	13	13	129	306	32	15	3	141	73	.313	550	238	32

Pitching	G	CG	W	L	Pct.	IP	AB	R	H	BB	HB	SO	WP	ER
Reaves	2	0	2	0	1.000	12 1/3	41	7	12	6	0	2	0	7
Ledford	7	6	6	1	.857	52 2/3	208	26	43	13	0	43	1	24
Roland	9	6	5	1	.833	61 1/3	221	19	45	12	1	63	1	6
Tepper	5	2	2	1	.667	23	102	10	19	13	2	11	1	6
Freeman	2	1	1	1	.500	7 1/3	28	3	5	3	0	4	1	2
Tannucci	3	0	0	0	.000	5 1/3	21	6	5	4	0	5	0	1
Adams	1	0	0	0	.000	2 2/3	13	3	2	4	1	2	0	1
Leonard	1	0	0	0	.000	2	8	3	1	4	0	1	1	3
Hoover	1	0	0	1	.000	4	18	6	7	6	0	2	1	5
Eurick	4	0	0	2	.000	18	79	19	23	9	1	10	1	15
	23	15	16	7	.696	189	741	102	163	76	5	120	6	18

22

Courtesy of Brad Green, Curator, Paul W. Bryant Museum, Tuscaloosa, Alabama 2025

Orientation material from Far East Command to the baseball team was geared towards "Entertainers" in general, and was quite detailed. Note that visitors were strictly prohibited from participating in "direct action" against the enemy.

ORIENTATION MATERIAL FOR ENTERTAINERS VISITING
THE FAR EAST COMMAND

1. ON BEHALF OF THE COMMANDER-IN-CHIEF, FAR EAST COMMAND, AND THE SPECIAL SERVICES OFFICER, IT IS A PLEASURE TO WELCOME YOU TO JAPAN. FOR MOST OF YOU THIS IS YOUR FIRST TRIP TO THIS PART OF THE WORLD. WE SINCERELY HOPE THAT YOUR TIME HERE WILL BE AS ENJOYABLE FOR YOU AS IT IS FOR US TO BE YOUR HOST. THERE HAVE BEEN MANY ENTERTAINMENT GROUPS WHICH HAVE PRECEDED YOU AND THROUGH OUR EXPERIENCES WITH THEM, WE WILL ATTEMPT TO MAKE YOUR STAY AS COMFORTABLE AS POSSIBLE UNDER THE PREVAILING CIR-CUMSTANCES. WITH YOUR COOPERATION, WE FEEL SURE THAT YOUR TOUR SHALL NOT ONLY BE INTERESTING AND EDUCATIONAL, BUT ALSO AN EXPERIENCE WHICH YOU WILL NEVER FORGET.

2. THE FAR EAST COMMAND INCLUDES ALL MILITARY INSTALL-ATIONS OF THE ARMY, NAVY, AND AIR FORCE IN JAPAN, KOREA, AND OKINAWA AND HAS ADMINISTRATIVE AND COMMAND RESPONSIBILITY FOR ARMY AND AIR FORCE UNITS IN THE PHILIPPINES AND GUAM. THE FAR EAST COMMAND DOES NOT ACCEPT RESPONSIBILITY FOR PERFORM-ANCE OR OTHER ARRANGEMENTS MADE BY MEMBERS OF ENTERTAINMENT UNITS WITH PERSONNEL OR INSTALLATIONS OUTSIDE THE JURISDICTION OF THE FAR EAST COMMAND, NOR CAN TIME OF AVAILABILITY OF UNITS IN THE FAR EAST COMMAND BE CURTAILED TO ALLOW TIME IN OTHER AREAS.

3. YOUR TOUR OF THE FAR EAST COMMAND WILL TAKE YOU TO KOREA, JAPAN AND MIDWAY IF YOU ARE ON THE 16-WEEK CONTRACT WITH USO CAMP SHOWS; TO KOREA, JAPAN, OKINAWA, THE PHILIPPINES, GUAM, AND VARIOUS OTHER ISLANDS OF THE PACIFIC INCLUDING HAWAII IF YOU ARE ON A 20-WEEK CONTRACT WITH USO CAMP SHOWS. UPON ARRIVAL IN THE PHILIPPINES, YOU WILL BE UNDER THE ADMIN-ISTRATIVE AND OPERATIONAL CONTROL OF THE COMMANDER-IN-CHIEF, PACIFIC, WHOSE HEADQUARTERS ARE LOCATED IN HAWAII. THEIR POLICIES GOVERNING YOUR TOUR ARE VERY MUCH THE SAME AS THOSE OF THE FAR EAST COMMAND. YOUR ITINERARY IN ANY ONE OF THESE AREAS WILL BE GIVEN TO YOU BY THE SPECIAL SERVICES OFFICER UPON ARRIVAL. WE DO NOT HAVE ACCESS TO THAT INFORMATION AT THIS HEADQUARTERS.

4. GENERAL INFORMATION:

A. CURRENCY: UPON ARRIVAL AT THE AERIAL POINT OF ENTRY OF JAPAN, YOU ARE REQUIRED TO CHANGE ALL OF YOUR AMERICAN MONEY INTO A SPECIAL MILITARY SCRIPT WHICH IS USED IN JAPAN, KOREA AND OKINAWA IN LIEU OF THE FAMILIAR UNITED STATES "GREENBACK". MILITARY SCRIPT MAY BE USED FOR ALL MILITARY SPONSORED ACTIVITIES OR INSTALLATIONS. YEN IS THE JAPANESE STANDARD CURRENCY. USE ONLY YEN WHEN MAKING PURCHASES ON THE JAPANESE MARKET OR FOR GIVING AS GRATUITIES TO JAPANESE NATIONALS. THERE ARE NUMEROUS PLACES, INCLUDING YOUR BILLET ,

Courtesy of Brad Green, Curator, Paul W. Bryant Museum, Tuscaloosa, Alabama 2025

WHERE YOU MAY EXCHANGE MILITARY SCRIPT FOR YEN. ONCE PUR-
CHASED, YEN CAN NOT BE CONVERTED BACK INTO MILITARY SCRIPT OR
UNITED STATES CURRENCY. UPON DEPARTURE FROM THE FAR EAST
COMMAND, ALL MILITARY SCRIPT (NOT YEN) WILL BE CHANGED BACK
INTO UNITED STATES CURRENCY.

B. UPON ARRIVAL IN TOKYO, YOU WILL BE BILLETED IN AN
OFFICERS' BILLET. IT IS REQUESTED THAT YOU FAMILIARIZE YOUR-
SELF WITH HOTEL REGULATIONS PERTAINING TO CIVILIAN GUESTS.

C. YOU WILL BE ISSUED PX (POST EXCHANGE) CARDS WHICH
WILL AUTHORIZE USE OF POST EXCHANGE FACILITIES FOR THE PURCHASE
(IN MILITARY SCRIPT) OF NECESSARY RATIONED ITEMS ANYWHERE IN
THE FAR EAST COMMAND. SUPPLIES AT THE POST EXCHANGES ARE
LIMITED.

D. CIGARETTES AND THOSE ITEMS DAILY REQUIRED BY MEN,
SUCH AS RAZORS, TOOTHPASTE, TOOTH BRUSHES, ETC., ARE NORMALLY
AVAILABLE IN KOREA. REQUIREMENTS PECULIAR TO WOMEN, PERFUMES,
LOTIONS, BOBBY PINS AND ITEMS OF A PERSONAL NATURE, ARE NOT
ALWAYS AVAILABLE IN KOREA. IT IS THEREFORE NECESSARY THAT YOU
PURCHASE A SUFFICIENT AMOUNT OF PERSONAL ITEMS PRIOR TO YOUR
DEPARTURE FOR KOREA. CAMERA FILM AND OTHER LIKE ITEMS ARE NOT
AVAILABLE IN KOREA, NOR ARE LARGE QUANTITIES OF MOTION
PICTURE FILM AVAILABLE IN JAPAN. YOU MAY BE REQUIRED TO SAT-
ISFY YOUR NEEDS OF THESE ITEMS ON THE JAPANESE MARKET.

E. BILLETS IN THE FAR EAST COMMAND DO NOT FURNISH
TOWELS OR SOAP.

F. ELECTRIC CURRENT IN JAPAN IS 110 VOLTS, 50 CYCLES.
IN OTHER AREAS, INCLUDING KOREA AND OKINAWA, IT IS 110 VOLTS,
60 CYCLES. ELECTRICITY IS AVAILABLE THROUGHOUT THE FAR EAST
COMMAND, INCLUDING KOREA. AMERICAN MADE PRODUCTS OPERATE
SATISFACTORILY ON EITHER TYPE OF CURRENT.

G. MUSICAL INSTRUMENTS OR SUPPLIES ARE NOT AVAILABLE
IN THE FAR EAST COMMAND. THERE ARE, HOWEVER, FACILITIES FOR
MAKING MINOR REPAIRS OF MUSICAL INSTRUMENTS.

5. MAIL

A. YOUR MAILING ADDRESS WHILE TOURING THE FAR EAST
COMMAND WILL BE YOUR NAME, YOUR UNIT NUMBER, SPECIAL SERVICES
SECTION, HEADQUARTERS, UNITED STATES ARMY FORCES, FAR EAST,
APO 343, c/o POSTMASTER, SAN FRANCISCO, CALIFORNIA.

B. ANY MAIL RECEIVED FOR YOU SUBSEQUENT TO YOUR
DEPARTURE OF THE FAR EAST COMMAND WILL BE RETURNED TO USO
CAMP SHOWS, INC., NEW YORK, N.Y., OR TO THE HOLLYWOOD COORDI-
NATIONS COMMITTEE, UNLESS OTHERWISE SPECIFICALLY INSTRUCTED.

2

Courtesy of Brad Green, Curator, Paul W. Bryant Museum, Tuscaloosa, Alabama 2025

C. ALL OF YOUR MAIL WILL BE DELIVERED TO THE PROFESSIONAL ENTERTAINMENT BRANCH OF THE SPECIAL SERVICES SECTION, HEADQUARTERS, UNITED STATES ARMY FORCES, FAR EAST, WHERE IT WILL BE HELD AND FORWARDED, WHILE IN KOREA, TWICE A WEEK TO THE SPECIAL SERVICES OFFICER, WHO IN TURN WILL FORWARD IT TO YOU WHEREVER YOU MIGHT BE.

D. LETTERS AND PACKAGES MAILED FROM THE FAR EAST COMMAND TO THE UNITED STATES REQUIRE THE SAME POSTAGE AS THOSE MAILED FROM SAN FRANCISCO, CALIFORNIA. AIR MAIL STAMPS AND PACKAGE MAILING FACILITIES ARE AVAILABLE AT ALL ARMED FORCES POST OFFICES THROUGHOUT THE FAR EAST, INCLUDING KOREA. YOU, AS A CIVILIAN, ARE NOT AUTHORIZED FREE MAILING PRIVILEGES WHILE ON TOUR IN KOREA. THESE FREE MAILING PRIVILEGES ARE FOR MEMBERS OF THE ARMED FORCES ONLY, AND REGARDLESS OF ANY OTHER INSTRUCTIONS YOU MAY RECEIVE TO THE CONTRARY, FREE MAILING PRIVILEGES DO NOT INCLUDE CIVILIANS IN KOREA.

E. TELEGRAMS MAY BE SENT FROM TOKYO TO THE UNITED STATES, AND OVERSEAS TELEPHONE SERVICE IS AVAILABLE AT THE RATE OF $4.00 A MINUTE (PAYABLE IN YEN). FURTHER INFORMATION CAN BE OBTAINED FROM THE DESK CLERK AT YOUR BILLET. THESE SERVICES ARE NOT AVAILABLE IN KOREA.

F. IT IS REQUESTED THAT AUTHORITY BE GIVEN THE DIRECTOR OF PROFESSIONAL ENTERTAINMENT, HEADQUARTERS, UNITED STATES ARMY FORCES, FAR EAST, TO OPEN ALL TELEGRAMS WHICH MAY BE DELIVERED IN YOUR NAME. IN THE EVENT THEIR CONTENTS ARE OF IMPORTANCE, EITHER OF A BUSINESS OR PERSONAL NATURE, THIS INFORMATION WILL BE FORWARDED TO YOU BY TELEPHONE IMMEDIATELY. IF THEY ARE STANDARD TELEGRAMS OF CONGRATULATIONS, BIRTHDAY GREETINGS AND THE LIKE, THEY WILL BE FORWARDED TO YOU WITH YOUR REGULAR MAIL.

6. SOCIAL ENGAGEMENTS:

A. THIS HEADQUARTERS DOES NOT MAKE ANY SOCIAL ENGAGEMENTS FOR ANY MEMBER OF A UNIT, OR FOR THE UNIT AS A WHOLE, PRIOR TO ITS ARRIVAL FROM THE UNITED STATES. WHILE IN TOKYO, SOCIAL ENGAGEMENTS MAY BE ACCEPTED BY THE INDIVIDUAL CONCERNED OR BY THE UNIT. HOWEVER, IF YOU PLAN TO GO OUT OF TOWN OVERNIGHT, OR WILL BE GONE FOR ANY LENGTH OF TIME, YOU WILL INFORM YOUR UNIT MANAGER WHERE YOU MAY BE CONTACTED. IN THE EVENT THE UNIT MANAGER DESIRES TO GO OUT OF TOWN, OR WILL BE GONE FOR ANY LENGTH OF TIME, HE IS TO NOTIFY THE DIRECTOR OF PROFESSIONAL ENTERTAINMENT WHERE HE MAY BE CONTACTED.

B. WHILE ON TOUR, WHICH MAY BE CONSTRUED TO MEAN WHILE NOT IN THE TOKYO AREA, PROCESSING, OR ON R&R, INDIVIDUALS OF UNITS MAY NOT ACCEPT INVITATIONS FOR SOCIAL ENGAGEMENTS WITHOUT FIRST CONSULTING WITH THE UNIT MANAGER.

3

Courtesy of Brad Green, Curator, Paul W. Bryant Museum, Tuscaloosa, Alabama 2025

c. IT IS RECOMMENDED THAT THE ACCEPTANCE OF SOCIAL ENGAGEMENTS WHILE ON TOUR BE ACCEPTED AS UNIT INVITATIONS ONLY, AND NOT AS INDIVIDUAL. IT IS THE RESPONSIBILITY OF THE UNIT MANAGER TO SEE TO IT THAT SOCIAL ENGAGEMENTS DO NOT INTERFERE WITH THE SCHEDULED ITINERARY OF MOVEMENT OR THE PRESENTATION OF PERFORMANCES.

7. MEDICAL CARE:

A. THERE ARE SEVERAL DISEASES WHICH ARE PECULIAR TO THE FAR EAST AND AT SOME TIME DURING YOUR TOUR YOU WILL REQUIRE MEDICAL ATTENTION, WHETHER IT BE FOR HEADACHES, STOMACH OR INTESTINAL DISORDERS, AND IT IS MOST IMPORTANT THAT IF YOU DO NOT FEEL WELL YOU REPORT TO A DISPENSARY OF THE NEAREST MEDICAL UNIT FOR AN EXAMINATION. DO NOT HESITATE TO MAKE IT KNOWN THAT YOU DO NOT FEEL WELL AND REQUIRE MEDICAL ATTENTION.

B. MEDICAL CARE IS AVAILABLE THROUGHOUT THE FAR EAST AT THE RATE OF $1.75 PER TREATMENT AT THE DISPENSARIES, OR $14.25 PER DAY FOR HOSPITALIZATION. THESE CHARGES WILL BE PAID BY THE INDIVIDUAL AND RECEIPTS OF PAYMENT WILL BE OBTAINED FOR REIMBURSEMENT UPON RETURN TO THE UNITED STATES THROUGH USO CAMP SHOWS, INCORPORATED.

C. EVACUATIONS FROM KOREA OR OTHER AREAS IN THE FAR EAST COMMAND DUE TO ILLNESS OR INJURY, WILL BE MADE THROUGH MEDICAL CHANNELS AND ONLY UPON THE ADVICE OF AUTHORIZED MEDICAL AUTHORITIES.

D. THE UNIT MANAGER WILL IMMEDIATELY REPORT TO THE SPECIAL SERVICES OFFICER, THE HOSPITALIZATION OF ANY INDIVIDUAL IN A UNIT WHICH PRECLUDES THEIR PARTICIPATING IN PRESENTATION OF PERFORMANCES OR CONTINUING THE BALANCE OF THE TOUR.

8. SECURITY:

A. YOU ARE IN AN AREA WHERE TROOPS OF THE UNITED NATIONS ARMED FORCES ARE IN COMBAT READINESS AND IN AN AREA OF A TEMPORARY TRUCE. DO NOT ASK ANY QUESTIONS REGARDING MILITARY ACTIVITIES. THE LESS YOU KNOW THE LESS YOU CAN PASS ON ACCIDENTALLY.

B. DO NOT DISCUSS CHANGES IN ITINERARY, UNIT DESIGNATIONS, TROOP TYPE OR NUMBER, THE AMOUNT OF CASUALTIES, THE DEPLOYMENT OF TROOPS, OR ANYTHING OF A MILITARY NATURE.

C. UNIT MANAGERS WILL RETURN ALL COPIES OF ITINERARIES TO THE SPECIAL SERVICES OFFICER, HEADQUARTERS, UNITED STATES ARMY FORCES, FAR EAST, UPON RETURN TO TOKYO.

D. THERE ARE NO RESTRICTIONS ON TAKING PICTURES IN THE FAR EAST COMMAND; HOWEVER, IT IS REQUESTED THAT YOU REFRAIN FROM

4

TAKING PICTURES OF ARMY, NAVY AND AIR FORCE EQUIPMENT THAT MAY
BE OF VALUE TO THE ENEMY.

9. RULES OF GROUND WARFARE:

A. YOU ARE A CIVILIAN TRAVELING WITH THE UNITED
NATIONS ARMED FORCES AS A NONCOMBATANT; THEREFORE, YOU ARE NOT
AUTHORIZED IN ANY WAY TO PARTICIPATE IN ANY DIRECT OR INDIRECT
ACTION AGAINST THE ENEMY. YOU ARE NOT AUTHORIZED TO FIRE ANY
WEAPONS WHATSOEVER WHILE TOURING THE FAR EAST COMMAND, NOR
WILL YOU REQUEST MILITARY PERSONNEL TO ESCORT YOU TO THE MAIN
LINE OF RESISTANCE FOR THE PURPOSES OF OBSERVING ENEMY ACTION,
NOR WILL YOU ASK ANY PILOT OF LIGHT AIRCRAFT WITH WHOM YOU MAY
COME IN CONTACT TO FLY YOU OVER THE MAIN LINE OF RESISTANCE OR
ENEMY TERRITORY. TO BE ON THE SAFE SIDE, REFUSE ALL INVITA-
TIONS TO PARTICIPATE IN THE ABOVE AS ANY VIOLATION WILL
CLASSIFY YOU AS A PARTICIPANT IN ACTION AGAINST THE ENEMY, AND,
IN THE EVENT OF CAPTURE, YOU MAY BE TRIED BY THE ENEMY AS A
WAR CRIMINAL, OR IF THE ENEMY IS AWARE OF THE FACT THAT YOU
ARE PARTICIPATING IN SUCH, YOU MAY BE TRIED BY PROXY AS A WAR
CRIMINAL.

10. LEGAL STATUS:

A. THE UNIFORM CODE OF MILITARY JUSTICE PROVIDES
THAT ALL CIVILIANS WHILE TRAVELING WITH THE ARMY, NAVY AND AIR
FORCE, ARE SUBJECT TO THE UNIFORM CODE OF MILITARY JUSTICE.
IF A QUESTION ARISES AS TO THE LEGALITY OF A CONTEMPLATED
ACTION, CONSULT THE LOCAL SPECIAL SERVICES OFFICER.

B. WHILE IN JAPAN YOU ARE IN A COUNTRY NOT OUR OWN.
WHEN YOU ARE OFF THE MILITARY RESERVATION, YOU ARE SUBJECT TO
JAPANESE LAW. IF YOU IGNORE OR VIOLATE THAT LAW, YOU ARE
LIABLE TO ARREST BY THE JAPANESE POLICE AS WELL AS THE UNITED
NATIONS MILITARY POLICE, SUBJECT TO TRIAL BY JAPANESE COURTS
AND, IF FOUND GUILTY, SUBJECT TO IMPRISONMENT IN JAPANESE
PENAL INSTITUTIONS. JAPANESE LAWS ARE VERY LITTLE DIFFERENT
THAN THOSE IN THE STATES, AND IT IS EXPECTED THAT YOU WILL CON-
DUCT YOURSELVES WITH PROPER DECORUM IN A MANNER THAT WILL
REFLECT CREDIT UPON YOURSELVES, THE FAR EAST COMMAND, AND YOUR
COUNTRY.

11. PASSPORTS AND IDENTIFICATION:

A. UPON DEPARTURE FROM JAPAN TO KOREA, YOUR PASSPORTS
WILL BE TURNED OVER TO THE SPECIAL SERVICES OFFICE FOR SAFE-
KEEPING WHILE ON TOUR.

B. YOU WILL BE ISSUED NONCOMBATANT IDENTIFICATION
CARDS FOR YOUR TOUR IN KOREA. THIS CARD WILL ALSO SERVE AS
NECESSARY IDENTIFICATION AT ALL MILITARY INSTALLATIONS THROUGH-
OUT THE FAR EAST COMMAND.

5

Courtesy of Brad Green, Curator, Paul W. Bryant Museum, Tuscaloosa, Alabama 2025

C. YOU WILL BE ISSUED A TEMPORARY IDENTIFICATION CARD WHICH WILL SERVE TO IDENTIFY YOU THROUGHOUT YOUR TOUR OF THE FAR EAST COMMAND IN THOSE PLACES WHERE YOUR NONCOMBATANT CARD IS NOT SUFFICIENT. THIS TEMPORARY IDENTIFICATION CARD SHOWS THAT YOU ARE TRAVELING WITH THE ARMED FORCES AND ARE ENTITLED TO MANY PRIVILEGES WHILE IN THE FAR EAST; FOR EXAMPLE, YOU MUST SHOW THIS CARD TO BE ADMITTED TO THE TOKYO POST EXCHANGE. YOUR NONCOMBATANT CARD IS NOT SUFFICIENT IDENTIFICATION.

12. CONDUCT OF PERSONNEL:

A. PRESENTATION OF SUGGESTIVE, OBSCENE OR OBJECTIONABLE MATERIAL IS NOT ACCEPTABLE IN ANY AREA WITHIN THE FAR EAST COMMAND. THE SPECIAL SERVICES OFFICER WILL IMMEDIATELY REPORT TO THE COMMANDER-IN-CHIEF, FAR EAST COMMAND, ANY USE OF SUGGESTIVE, OBSCENE OR OBJECTIONABLE MATERIAL.

B. THE USE OF INTOXICATING LIQUORS BY MEMBERS OF THE UNIT WILL BE KEPT TO A MINIMUM.

13. TRANSPORTATION AND STAGE FACILITIES WITHIN THE FAR EAST COMMAND:

A. ALL MAJOR MOVES IN OR OUT OF JAPAN WILL BE MADE BY MILITARY AIRCRAFT, NORMALLY FOUR-ENGINE AIRPLANES. TRAVEL IN JAPAN WILL BE ACCOMPLISHED PRIMARILY VIA JAPANESE RAILROAD WITH SLEEPER ACCOMMODATIONS FOR OVER NIGHT TRIPS. TRANSPORTATION WITHIN JAPAN FROM TRAINS TO BILLET AND FROM BILLETS TO PERFORMING AREAS WILL NORMALLY BE ACCOMPLISHED BY MOTOR VEHICLE. IN KOREA, EVERY EFFORT WILL BE MADE TO TRANSPORT THE UNIT BY AIRCRAFT. THE LONGER MOVES FROM THE AREA FORWARD WILL BE MADE BY A C-47, C-46, AND THE SHORTER MOVES BETWEEN UNITS IN THE FORWARD AREAS WILL BE MADE BY LIGHT AIRCRAFT PRIMARILY USED FOR ARTILLERY OBSERVATION. TRANSPORTATION FROM AIRSTRIP TO PERFORMANCE AREAS WILL NORMALLY BE MADE BY MOTOR VEHICLE (JEEP, AMBULANCE OR TRUCK).

B. YOU WILL BE NOTIFIED OF YOUR SCHEDULE OF PERFORMANCES, TRAVEL AND PICK-UP TIMES BY THE LOCAL SPECIAL SERVICES OFFICER. EVERY CONSIDERATION WILL BE GIVEN TO ALLOW YOU THE MAXIMUM AMOUNT OF TIME TO SATISFY YOUR PERSONAL REQUIREMENTS. IT IS IMPORTANT THAT YOU BE AVAILABLE FOR TRAVEL REQUIREMENTS AS SPECIFIED IN SCHEDULES. JAPANESE TRAINS RUN ON ACCURATE TIME SCHEDULES AND WILL NOT WAIT FOR PASSENGERS. IN KOREA, AIRCRAFT WILL OFTEN BE DIVERTED FROM THEIR TACTICAL MISSIONS TO ACCOMPLISH THE MOVEMENT OF YOUR UNIT -- THEY MUST NOT BE DELAYED. BE ON TIME.

C. PERFORMING FACILITIES VARY GREATLY THROUGHOUT THE FAR EAST COMMAND. IN JAPAN THERE ARE A NUMBER OF THEATERS

6

Courtesy of Brad Green, Curator, Paul W. Bryant Museum, Tuscaloosa, Alabama 2025

WHICH COMPARE FAVORABLY WITH THOSE IN THE UNITED STATES.
OTHERS HAVE ONLY THE BAREST NECESSITIES. IN KOREA, THE MAJOR-
ITY OF YOUR PERFORMANCES WILL BE PRESENTED OUT OF DOORS.
YOUR STAGE MAY BE WELL CONSTRUCTED, OR YOU MAY BE REQUIRED TO
PERFORM ON THE BARE GROUND IN AN IMPROMPTU PRESENTATION.
PRIVATE DRESSING FACILITIES WILL BE PROVIDED AT ALL LOCATIONS.

14. CLOTHING

A. PRIOR TO YOUR DEPARTURE FOR KOREA, YOU WILL BE
ISSUED ALL NECESSARY CLOTHING FOR YOUR PERSONAL USE, OTHER
THAN THAT REQUIRED FOR STAGE PRESENTATIONS. THIS IS A MILITARY
UNIFORM LESS INSIGNIA, WHICH YOU WILL WEAR AT ALL TIMES WHILE
TRAVELING THROUGHOUT KOREA. YOU ARE RESPONSIBLE FOR THE
CLOTHING ISSUED, AND YOU WILL BE REQUIRED TO PAY FOR ANY LOSSE

B. IT IS ABSOLUTELY NECESSARY THAT YOU TRY ON ALL
CLOTHING ISSUED TO YOU. MAKE SURE THAT IT DOES NOT FIT TOO
TIGHTLY.

C. THE CLOTHING ISSUED YOU WILL BE WORN IN KOREA AND
TO AND FROM AIRFIELDS ENROUTE TO, OR FROM KOREA ONLY. IF WORN
IN JAPAN AT ANY OTHER TIME, YOU WILL BE SUBJECT TO QUESTIONING
AND POSSIBLE ARREST BY THE MILITARY POLICE.

D. IT IS RECOMMENDED THAT YOU TAKE WITH YOU TO KOREA
ONE OR TWO PIECES OF STREET CLOTHING THAT YOU MAY WEAR FROM
TIME TO TIME WHEN NOT TRAVELING OR ON STAGE. THESE WILL COME
IN HANDY WHEN VISITING OFFICERS' OR ENLISTED MENS' CLUBS
DURING YOUR TOUR.

E. STORAGE FACILITIES WILL BE MADE AVAILABLE TO YOU
IN TOKYO TO STORE SUCH CLOTHING AS YOU MAY DESIRE, WHICH WILL
NOT BE NECESSARY DURING YOUR TOUR OF KOREA.

15. BILLETING AND MESSING CONDITIONS:

A. THERE IS A WIDE VARIANCE IN BILLETING FACILITIES
WITHIN THE FAR EAST COMMAND. IN JAPAN YOU WILL BE BILLETED
PRIMARILY IN PERMANENT-TYPE BILLETS. YOU WILL BE BILLETED IN
TENTS THE MAJORITY OF YOUR KOREA TOUR. MARRIED COUPLES WILL
BE BILLETED TOGETHER WHEREVER PRACTICABLE.

D. MESSING FACILITIES ARE PROVIDED AT ALL MILITARY
INSTALLATIONS THROUGHOUT THE COMMAND. THE CHARGE FOR MEALS
IN GOVERNMENT MESSES IS THIRTY CENTS FOR BREAKFAST AND FORTY-
FIVE FOR LUNCH AND DINNER. MESSING SERVICE CHARGES VARY
THROUGHOUT THE COMMAND, RANGING FROM NO CHARGE TO A MAXIMUM
OF TWENTY-FIVE CENTS PER MEAL. THE FOOD WILL BE THE BEST
AVAILABLE AND UNANIMOUS OPINION OF PREVIOUS UNITS TERM IT AS

7

Courtesy of Brad Green, Curator, Paul W. Bryant Museum, Tuscaloosa, Alabama 2025

EXCELLENT. YOU MAY BE REQUESTED TO TAKE YOUR MEALS WITH
ENLISTED MEN OR OFFICERS. THESE INFORMAL VISITS ARE APPRECIA-
TED BY THE MEN AND ARE CONSIDERED AN IMPORTANT MORALE FACTOR.
SOME UNITS IN THE FORWARD AREAS HAVE ESTABLISHED POLICIES
WHEREBY USO CAMP SHOW UNITS HAVE ONE MEAL WITH THE ENLISTED
MEN, ONE WITH THE OFFICERS, AND ONE WITH THE COMMANDING GENERAL

     c. DO NOT CONSUME FOOD OR LIQUIDS PREPARED BY PERSONS
OTHER THAN MILITARY PERSONNEL IN KOREA. USE ONLY WATER
PROVIDED AT MILITARY INSTALLATIONS FOR DRINKING PURPOSES.
UNDER NO CIRCUMSTANCES PURCHASE ANY LIQUOR ON THE LOCAL KOREAN
MARKET AS IT OFTEN CAUSES BLINDNESS AND DEATH.

    16. LAUNDRY AND CLEANING:

     WHILE IN THE TOKYO AREA, 24 HOUR CLEANING FACILITIES
ARE AVAILABLE FOR YOUR PERSONAL WARDROBE AND COSTUMES. IN THE
EVENT YOUR COSTUMES NEED REPAIRING, FACILITIES WILL BE MADE
AVAILABLE TO YOU.

    17. REHEARSAL FACILITIES:

     WHILE IN TOKYO, REHEARSAL FACILITIES CAN BE MADE
AVAILABLE FOR YOUR UNIT, IF REQUESTED, BY THE LOCAL SPECIAL
SERVICES OFFICER.

    18. MISCELLANEOUS:

     A. INQUIRIES AND REQUESTS ORIGINATING FROM INDIGENOUS
SOURCES REGARDING AVAILABILITY OF UNIT PERFORMANCES, INTER-
VIEWS OR OTHER PURPOSES, IN ADDITION TO OFFICIAL DUTIES, SHOULD
BE REFERRED TO THE ENTERTAINMENT BRANCH, SPECIAL SERVICES
SECTION, HEADQUARTERS, UNITED STATES ARMY FORCES, FAR EAST.

     B. ALL PUBLICITY IS THE RESPONSIBILITY OF THE PUBLIC
INFORMATION OFFICE (PIO). YOU ARE REQUESTED NOT TO MAKE
INDIVIDUAL ARRANGEMENTS WITH COMMERCIAL AGENCIES OR PIO WITH-
OUT PRIOR CLEARANCE WITH THE SPECIAL SERVICES OFFICER,
HEADQUARTERS, UNITED STATES ARMY FORCES, FAR EAST.

8

An interesting communication between baseball coaches, wherein Marty Karow from The Ohio State University gave Japan-travel advice based on prior experience to Alabama Head Coach, Tilden "Happy" Campbell:

THE OHIO STATE UNIVERSITY
Novice G. Fawcett, *President*
COLUMBUS 10

DEPARTMENT OF PHYSICAL EDUCATION
Richard C. Larkins, *Director*

March.8,'57

Dear Happy:

I will try and give you the things that I think will help you on making arrangements for your trip which as I told you will be terrific and at the end will be tiresome for both you and the boys.

We took a total of 25 people on the trip one of which was our athletic director and we had to include him on the first 24 men as that is what they wanted us to take only and then after I had begged for that number as Rod Dedeaux took only 22 on his trip so you can judge accordingly. I used the idea that we would need at least 9 pitchers because of the number of games we had scheduled. We played 30 and had some 34 or 36 scheduled.

I don't know but feel that Lt.Col Louis (Lou) Tschudi will be in charge of trip arrangements. He did make a trip down to Columbus and talk the final details over with me and we had a fine time as he is a real Joe. You might ask him to make a similar trip to your place It would be worth while and I sure he would enjoy it. I had him stay at my house.

Mr.Ralph Saylor is in charge of the activities over in Japan and will be the one that will brief your team on their regulations which as I told you must be observed or they would send the team home as they will not permit anything to cause any ill feeling between the people over there and U.S.A. A fellow by the name of Jimmy

Your group will have to get passports and you will have to get birth-certificates on each boy which you send to Washington to have the passports made valid. They will explain this in their letter to you and I suggest that you have you boys start now to get their birth certificates as that takes a long time. If they do not have birth certificates then they can have a Blood relative send them a statement to the effect of their birth and that should be noterized or a copy should be obtained from the court house in the town of their birth where it will or should have been registered. In the case of the Catholic boys they will get a baptismal certificate from their church.

You will also have to get a lot of Shots for the trip and that is a tough job as it does effect some you kids like it did mine and hurt us in a game or two in our conference race as one of them really had a reaction so you had best try to figure out when it would be best to get them and the sooner the better as in the early games they might not mean as much. This information will be sent you so you can start working on it. It is a job so get some one to get on it as soon as you know.

They will send you travel orders which you will have to have the boys carry one set on them all the time and you will need them in the various places that you must give a set for Military Aircraft transportation.

They will fly you into Frisco International airport and from there they will have bus transportation to Travis Air Force Base where you will be put up for the nite depending on your departure date and time. This you must pay for as you leave but you will be reimbursed when you arrive in Tokyo within a few days after you get there so I would make arrangements to take at least $3000.00 along for the expenses that you will have until you get your reimbursement from the Govt. I suggest that you get some kind of book keeping set-up for the one that handles the money and you or some grown man should your trainer as this is a real task to make sure that the kids get their proper allowances as they will give you about 8 or 9 checks which will be in the amount of $1000.00 or more each and of course you will have to pay the boys their Per Diem which is as follows: You will be paid $10.00 (TEN) a day while

Courtesy of Brad Green, Curator, Paul W. Bryant Museum, Tuscaloosa, Alabama 2025

(2)

...the U.S.A. which does not include Hawaii and $5.40 a day while in the far East. This will take care of your actual expenses OK but you will have some things like laundry of uniforms,and other baseball gear.This you also have to pay for as they do not pay for this.All the money you get you must pay for meals,hotel and other expenses it will take care of most of it but you will need money for these incidentals that you have to take care of.I think we spent about $2500.00 of Univ.Money for extra trips not paid for by the Govt. and incidentals.Happy what I did was handle the money myself but it was really a headache.After each week I would give the boys their allowances taking out what I had to pay for like hotel or meals.This way the kids had a little extra for themself and I was sure that I paid for the hotel out of their allowances before I gave them their money that was left.Some times in fact half the time you will be invited to eat with the service teams and in that way you and the boys will have that days allowan- ces for themself.I advise you to make sure that you pay for the expenses before you give the boys their Per Diem for that reason I payed them in weekly instalements and a week late .They of course will have a little money to start with and can carry them over for a couple of weeks and about that time you will receive your checks from the Govt. and the kids will start to need money.The eats and hotel are very reasonable I think we paid aout $21.00 for about 5 weeks or at least 4 weeks and meals a very reasonable.I suggest that you try and eat with as many of the teams you play as possible as it gives the boys extra money to spend.

Happy tell the kids and keep in mind the you can get a lot of things very cheap in Japan and they will want to bring home some things.Cameras,Pearls,Fur Stools or Capes Komonoes,silk,just a lot of things.It wo ld take a book to write about this.If you have something special in mind let me know and I will give you what I think it will cost.

John Scially who is in charge of the Air Force is a swell guy and lives in Tokyo he can really help you get lots of items very reasonable.He will also to a wonderful job in seeing that you have a good trip.Dutch Koehler at Camp Zama is another swell Joe but he is handicapped because he is located so far from Tokyo.

You will travel by plane mostly,bus and train all of which will be arranged for by the people there.You will also have an escort officer who will be with you and in charge if seeing that you are taken care of all the time he gets a real fine vacation and sure is a help as he known where to get hold of people.

Happy,we tried to take a movie of our trip and sorta passed it up because we did not have anyone tha was real good with a movie camera.I suggest that you ask the Military people to give you and Officer who can and would take pictures for you ml one who knows what he is doing you might get a guy who is a photographer as your escort officer that sure would make a fine film of the trip.I wish we would have done that.We spent some $500.00 on film and half of it was no good.

We had our medical staff give the kids the shots required such as Tetanus,Yellow fever,small pox,Typhoid,Typhus,Cholera and Shick Negative.This will keep them well stuck by the time they are thru with them.They must also get pictures of each boy for his passport so suggest that you get them I think they are 2x2" but you had better wait till you get the right size or call down to the immigration dept in town and ask what size so you could staht to get themdlured up.

We also took out insurance on each boy totaled to $50,000.00 each and the Univ. pa id for that it was about $27.50 for each policy that is close to the amount.This I would say be sure and get and those boys who are youngsters we got their parents consent for them to go on the trip.Some insurance Co will be glad to take this to cover the entire you are away from date you leave until you return to Tuscaloosa.

We were allowed 65lbs for each many personal baggage and then were allowed 900 lbs extra for baggage as a sure w ay not to have to pay any money for air shipping and to have a lot left for when you return.We had to take some baseballs along incewe but they will furnish you with balls for games and practice I would still take some so you a can work out if you wish.This extra weight will help you get some of the things you buy back home with out extra cost to the boys or yourself so be sure to ask for plenty and take enough stuff along that you might leave or ship home to have extra weight on the return trip.

Happy,I am sure that there is a lot more but you think of questions and I will be glad to answer all I can.I am enclosing a couple of forms that they gave us do you can get a head start .Well hope you all have a wonderful time and be sure to Give John Scially & his Wife Man & Dutch Koehler my very best wishes.Let me know if there is any more dope you want hope this helps

Sincerely *Marty Karow*

Courtesy of Brad Green, Curator, Paul W. Bryant Museum, Tuscaloosa, Alabama 2025

308

Courtesy of Brad Green, Curator, Paul W. Bryant Museum, Tuscaloosa, Alabama 2025

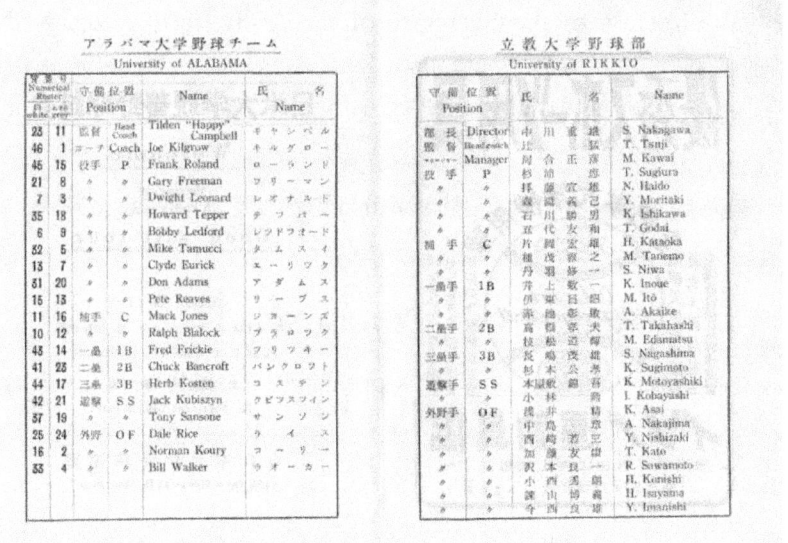

Courtesy of Brad Green, Curator, Paul W. Bryant Museum, Tuscaloosa, Alabama 2025

AFFE SERVICE SPORTS STRUCTURE

Research at U.S. National Archives II in College Park, Maryland, revealed a trove of background information on the structure and governance of Service Sports leagues. The Department of Defense website (256) gives a chronological history of Armed Forces Sports.

The first Inter-Service Sports Council (ISSC) met in 1947, with representatives from Army, Navy, and Air Force, according to the DoD website. The chronology says the ISSC's Articles of Agreement were approved in 1948.

A document from Department of the Army, dated 13 February 1948, discusses "Articles of Agreement Covering the Inter-Service Sports Council" (257):

> The Inter-Service Sports Council, established under the joint direction of the Secretary of the Army, the Secretary of the Navy, and the Secretary of the Air Force, has approved the following Articles the Agreement covering the Inter-Service Sports Council:
>
> ARTICLES OF AGREEMENT
>
> For the
>
> INTER SERVICE SPORTS COUNCIL
>
> SECTION I. Name. This organization shall be known as the Inter-Service Sports Council.
>
> SECTION II. Objects. The objects of this Council are---
>
> 1. To encourage the maintenance of physical fitness by all members of the armed forces through a policy of "sports for all."

2. To promote understanding, goodwill, and cooperation among the Armed Services through inter-service sports championship competitions.
3. To further enhance the Esprit-de-Corps of the individual Armed Services through the development and encouragement of spectator interest sports.
4. To establish and maintain throughout the Armed Services a uniform test of eligibility and uniform rules for the government of all service sports within its jurisdiction.
5. To institute, regulate, and award the inter-service sports championships of two or more of the United States Armed Services.

SECTION III. Members.

1. The membership of this Council shall consist of two (2) representatives from each of the following services.
   a. Department of the Army.
   b. Department of the Navy.
   c. Department of the Air Force.
2. These representatives will serve until such time as relieved by proper authority.

SECTION IV. Duties of the Council.

1. The council representatives shall have power to make all arrangements for the annual inter-service competition sponsored, not inconsistent with any Army, Navy, and Air Force directives in force, and have full power to act on and determine all points that may arise in connection with competitions.

311

2. The Council representative will not exercise any control whatsoever, (sic) over the policy for a sports program which may be instituted by a member service within its own command.

SECTION V. <u>Committees</u>. The Chairman of the Council, with the advice and consent of other Council members shall appoint such committees as may be deemed advisable to further the objectives of the Inter-Service Sports Council.

SECTION VI. <u>Level of Competition</u>. Jurdiction (sic) of the Inter-Service Sports Council will originate at Headquarters, Department of the Army, Headquarters, Department of the Navy, and Headquarters, Department of the Air Force, level and terminate with the conclusion of the inter-service sports championship competition.

SECTION VII. <u>FINANCES</u>.

1. No entry fees will be charged to the teams or individuals in the various sports championships.
2. Expenditures involved in the conduct of the Inter-Service Sports Championship Tournaments (exclusive of travel) will be pro-rated equally among the participating department (sic).

SECTION VII. Amendments. The articles governing this council may ne (sic) changes, amended, added to or altered only by a majority vote of the representatives in charge, which must include the affirmative vote of at least one representative from the Department of the Army, Department of the Air Force, and the Department of the Navy.

The Marine Corps joined the ISSC in 1953.

In 1954, the First Department of Defense Directive 1330.4 was established (*See AFEE Service Sports Rules and Regulations Section/Chapter*).

There is a "General Sports Eligibility Rules" document from Headquarters, United States Army Forces, Far East, dated 7 June 1954, which discusses structure of the Sports Programs (258). This document rescinds Letter AG 353.8 SS-RX 12 January 1954. Major Cowman notes establishment of controls, including:

1. That personnel will not be transferred, placed on temporary duty, or otherwise attached to units for purposes of strengthening sports teams.
2. When a team representing its parent unit or organization is entered in the progressive levels of tournament play to determine the United States Army Forces, Far East Championship team, the personnel of that team will not be augmented or reinforced at any level of play.
3. If a member of a team is transferred, sustains an injury or for military reasons is unable to continue play, the parent unit or organization may substitute a member of that unit or organization to fill the vacancy. The individual substituted must have been a member of that unit or organization prior to the entry of its representative team in the progressive tournament play for the United States Army Forces, Far East Championship.
4. It shall be the responsibility of all sports councils to establish the dates for submission of rosters for appropriate leagues and tournaments in the lower levels of progressive play.
5. An officer authorized by each major commander will certify that his representative team has not been strengthened through personnel transfers or reinforced by the selection of outstanding

individuals from the parent organization as indicated in paragraph 2B above. This certificate will be submitted to reach this headquarters, ATTN: Special Services Officer, at least 72 hours in advance of the opening date of the United States Army Forces, Far East tournaments.

The Eighth Army Blue Book (15) stated that "organized sports shall not be conducted from the hours of 0600-0800 under any circumstance."

There is a 17 June 1954 document from Major Cowman titled "United States Army Forces, Far East Sports Tournaments," which discussed the schedule for the remainder of 1954, and the policies and procedures "by which the applicable sports event will be conducted through 31 December 1954" (259). The lengthy document discussed rules for volleyball, track and field, tennis, golf, swimming, triathlon, baseball, softball, flag football, small games (hand grenade throw, badminton, etc.), and others.

The document included "Administrative Details", summarized below:

1. Entries in the United States Army Forces, Far East tournaments and meets will be indicated in the rules and regulations for specific sports. When appropriate, a tournament, meet or play-off series will be conducted between the representative conferences or teams under the supervision of each addressee command to determine the team or individuals to represent that command.

2. For those sports indicated in enclosure #2, "Rules and Regulations," where only one team will represent Japan in the United States Army Forces, Far East Sports Tournaments competitions, a tournament, meet or playoff series will be established by headquarters United States Army Forces, Far East, to determine the team or individuals who will represent the Army personnel of Japan in such competitions.

314

3. The Commanding Generals of commands designated as host commands for the United States Army Forces, Far East Sports Tournaments as shown in enclosure #1, "Schedule of Events," will be responsible for:

    a) Designating the tournament site and advising participating commands or conferences three days prior to the tournament.

    b) Advising visiting commands as to procedures to be followed in reporting for participation in the tournament and the organization to which personnel will report.

    c) Furnishing playing facilities and tournament balls.

    d) Paying tournament officials.

    e) Arranging for suitable billeting and messing.

    f) Providing competent medical service during all contests.

    g) Arranging for comprehensive publicity.

    h) Submitting results of each day's competition by radio message to commanders concerned, with information copies to headquarters …

        (1) Tournament brackets.

        (2) Results of each contest.

        (3) Two (2) copies of all action photographs.

        (4) Two (2) copies of programs.

    i) Maintaining close liaison with Special Services Officer, this headquarters, on matters pertaining to tournaments, meets or playoffs.

    j) Arranging for the presentation of individual and team awards, which will be provided by this headquarters.

    k) Appointing tournament committee for each event composed of one representative from each team participating in respective tournaments, with a representative of Headquarters, United States Army Forces, Far East, Special Services Section, Sports Branch, as advisor of the tournament committee. These committees will meet at least 24 hours in advance of the opening date and will:

(1)   Establish local rules and procedures for the conduct of each tournament, based on provisions of official rules for respective sports.

(2)   Resolve all protests.

4. Commanders responsible for visiting teams will issue necessary orders placing personnel on temporary duty with host command as instructed. No per diem will be authorized. Host command will be furnished information requested below, a minimum of seven (7) days prior to the tournament …

a) Advance notification as to mode of travel and expected time of arrival.

b) Team rosters, including name, rank, age, height, weight, service number, hometown and designation of military unit to which each member is a sign and players' positions for team sports.

c) Team and individual photographs, together with personal data including previous sports experience for publicity purposes. In this connection, the assistance of local Public Information Offices should be solicited.

5. The Commanding General, United States Army Forces, Far East will provide suitable awards from nonappropriated funds for teams and individuals as indicated …

6. Officials for the United States Army Forces, Far East tournaments and meets will be selected by Headquarters, United States Army Forces, Far East.

7. Transportation: Travel of teams by commercial transportation in Japan is chargeable to locally available nonappropriated welfare funds. Addressee commands are authorized to issue orders directing travel by air, using this letter as authority for members of teams and individuals participating in or necessary to the conduct of these contests. Limitations set forth … "Rules and Regulations," will not be exceeded for inter-island travel. Travel of teams via air within Japan will be on a space available basis. Visiting commands are reminded that teams should not arrive in Japan without sufficient funds to pay commercial transportation costs.

8. It is desired that full promotional effort be utilized in order to sustain high degree of participation and spectator interest in the 1954 United States Army Forces, Far East Sports Program at all levels of command.

A 17 July 1954 memo discussed Company Level Sports eligibility rules (260). The memo is addressed to Commanding General, Pusan Military Post, APO 59; Commanding Officer, Taegu Military Post, APO 234; and Commanding Officer, Inchon Military Post, APO 971.

The KComZ memo says:

> To assure that all teams within the Korean Communications Zone are of equal strength in company level sports, several methods of division have been devised.
>
> Company level teams will be representative of company, battery, or comparable size units. The grouping of smaller units which have an aggregate strength not to exceed 250 is authorized.

Composition of teams for Army units whose strength exceeds 250 authorized personnel, including officers and enlisted men, will be based strictly upon the following criteria:

a) Division of units by the alphabetical system. For example, one team may be composed of personnel with names beginning with "A" through "M" and the other team with names beginning with "N" through "Z". Within the alphabetical brackets the strength will not exceed 250 personnel.
b) Organization of teams by staff sections.
c) Organization of teams by grouping of detachments.

The team roster required by the pertinent sports directive will specify which of the above criteria was used in determining the composition of the team.

Commanders of Army units which fall within the purview of paragraph 3 above will submit in writing to this headquarters the criteria used in determining the composition of their entries in the Korean Communications Zone tournaments. Report will be submitted prior to 1 September 1954.

After appropriate criteria for entry is determined, there will be no change without the written approval of this headquarters.

Lt. Col. Leo Kleiman addressed news coverage of Service Sports in a 29 November 1954 memo titled, "News Coverage of Sports Competition" (261). The memo said:

Sports have a large following among service personnel. In the Far East Command, the athletic program is highly organized and includes thousands of competitors.

Since the purpose of any sports program is to promote unit esprit, as well as fitness and health, it is imperative that commanders publicize their programs to the greatest extent. Sports coverage through the *Pacific Stars and Stripes*, the *Far East Network* and *American Forces Korea Network* as well as unit newspapers stimulates interest in athletics which are an important part of this command's recreation program and assists in the accomplishment of the objectives of the sports program.

Tournaments and sporting events also offer excellent opportunities for wide-spread hometown coverage of benefit to the Army generally as well as to this command and the individual serviceman.

It is highly desirable that adequate coverage be given to major subordinate command's sports competition and *Pacific Stars and Stripes*, the *Far East Network*, the *American Forces Korea Network*, unit newspapers and interested commercial news media.

In order to expedite the flow of news relative to athletic events, it is directed that the most expeditious means of communication, telephone or teletype, be used in transmitting results of games and team standings.

Photographs of athletic events will also be expedited if forwarded by courier. For *Pacific Stars and Stripes*, for example, it is desirable that results of weekend games appear in the Monday edition, necessitating receipt of copy by 07:30 on Monday.

A review of most stories and photographs of sports activities received by this headquarters and the *Pacific Stars and Stripes* reveals extremely poor writing and photographic quality that makes much of the material unusable.

To insure (sic) good copy the sports story follows the same general format as that for a news story. The story must give the who, what, when, where, why and how and be written in thoughtful, orderly sequence. Amplify the key points in the lead and give concise description of the contest as it progressed. Rules apply when the story is telephoned to the *Pacific Stars and Stripes*.

To insure (sic) good quality pictures, it is necessary to follow the general lines of good pictorial reporting. Proper instructions must be given to the photographer, and every effort will be made to shoot pictures of action.

Excellent action pictures can be obtained from the sidelines by waiting for opportunities when the action comes close to the side from which the reporter is working. In preparing pictures for forwarding, it is imperative that a caption containing the pertinent information (who, what, when, where, why, and how) be attached to the photograph.

Within Japan, the sports news of *Pacific Stars and Stripes* (telephone Tokyo 266-2739 during normal duty hours on Saturday and Sunday; after duty hours telephone Tokyo 266-2731-2-3-4 between 1900 and 2100 hours) may be called directly, or the *Japan Teletype Network* may be used, following the procedure outlined in paragraph 12 below.

For units in Korea, sports news may be telephoned to the *Stars and Stripes* Bureau in Seoul or delivered to Public Information Officer, 8th United States Army (fwd) for transmission by teletype as outlined in paragraph 12 below.

Sports news from the Ryukyus Command will be delivered to Public Information Officer, headquarters Ryukyus Command, for transmission by teletype as outlined in paragraph 12 below.

In transmitting sports news by teletype, the following procedure should be used: Transmissions should be sent to Station #742 – FEC PIO News Room. Copy should be marked "Sports News, for Immediate Distribution to (Indicate Media)," and "Info Copy to AFFE/8A PIO Advance."

Due to increasing personnel limitations, it is imperative that the closest coordination and cooperation be maintained between Special Services, Public Information and Troop Information and Education personnel to insure (sic) complete and timely coverage of athletic events.

Recission: Ltr, Hq AFFE, AG 353.8 TI, Subject: "News Coverage of Sports Competition," dated 6 August 1954.

A 5 October 1954 memorandum addressed selection of sports officials; it is titled: "Korean Communications Zone Sports Officials Association" (262):

PURPOSE: To specify procedures for the organization of military personnel who are qualified to officiate at sports league and championship events in the Korean Communications Zone Area.

OBJECTIVE: The ultimate objective of the Sports Official Association program is to guarantee a high degree of sports officiating, increase the interest of spectators, and to elevate the quality of athletic competition in the Korean Communications Zone Area.

ADMINISTRATION: In order to accomplish this goal, the headquarters will conduct a series of sports clinics for prospective officials in the following sports: volleyball, softball, flag football, basketball. In addition, headquarters United States

Army Forces, Far East, will conduct similar sports clinics in the following: football, basketball, boxing, baseball.

To successfully complete each sports clinic, personnel will be required to attend classes of a particular sports clinic and pass a written final examination. Those completing each sports clinic will be issued a sports official's card and will be placed on the list of approved officials for that sport. They will then be eligible to officiate in that sport on all levels of competition.

SELECTION OF PERSONNEL: Commanders who select individuals to participate in these clinics should select only those who are highly qualified. The official is the person who judges the play, enforces the rules, applies the penalties and certifies the outcome of the events. His role affects both participants and spectators. Therefore, the selection of competent officials is a most important part of the process of conducting sports.

Recommended qualifications are: A working knowledge of the sport, either as a former player or official, an active interest in the sports program, sufficient time left in Korea to be utilized as an official.

ASSIGNMENT OF OFFICIALS: Personnel who have successfully completed sports clinics will be issued a Korean Communications Zone Sports Official's Association Card for that sport, and they will be registered on the official's roster of their local special services office.

Personnel who have not attended clinics may qualify as registered officials by successfully completing an examination in each respective sport. Examinations for these applicants will be obtained from the Special Services Officer, this headquarters. Only those personnel who have a Korean Communications

Zone Sports Official's Association Card will be reimbursed for services rendered as outlined in KComZ Circular 108, 1954. The Conference Director will assign sports officials at all levels of competition within his respective conference.

The 11 December 1954 document titled "AFFE/8A Sports Tournaments" is one of the important semi-foundational documents giving us a more complete picture of Service Sports in the mid-1950s. It covered the schedule of tournament events for 1955, rules and regulations, administrative details, and selected sports rules. The document was signed by Leo Kleiman, Lt. Col., AGC (263).

The second page listed the sport, location, host command, and tournament dates for 1955. Sports include skiing, bowling, basketball, boxing, track and field, golf and tennis, swimming and diving, softball, baseball, volleyball, small games, and flag football. We can see that the post-Armistice Sports Program was varied and robust.

Though the major subjects of this book include football and basketball, the football season for 1955 is not included in this particular document (see document in Appendix). The basketball tournament schedule was listed as 8-12 March at Camp Otsu.

There is a 12 July 1956 detailed letter as to objectives, definitions and parameters of the Sports Program (264). The letter is directed to Commanding General, United States Army Forces, Far East and Eighth United States Army; Commending General Ryukyus Command and IX Corps; Commanding General 1st Cavalry Division (Inf); Commanding General 40th AAA Brigade; Commanding Officer, Camp Zama. It reads as follows:

1. a. References
    (1)   AR 28-52.

(2)   AR 210-10

(3)   AR 210-50, AFR 176-1

(4)   AR 28-50

(5)   DA Circular 28-12

(6)   DA Circular 28-17

(7)   DA Circular 28-22

(8)   TM 21-225

(9)   Letter, AFFE AG 353.8 SS-RX, Headquarters, AFFE/8A (Rear), 15 December 1955, subject: "AFFE/8A Sports Tournaments."

(10)   Letter, AFFE AG 353.8 SS-RX, Headquarters, AFFE/8A (Rear), 6 January 1956, subject: "Far East Command Sports Clinics for 1956."

(11)   Letter, AFFE AG 353.8 SS-RX, Headquarters, AFFE/8A (Rear), 25 January 1956, subject: "AFFE/8A (Rear) Women's Sports Program."

(12)   AFFE/8A (Rear) Command Program No. 11C (Welfare and Morale Services), Volume II, 29 April 1956.

b. Supersessions:

(1) Letter, AFFE AG 353.8 SS-RX, this headquarters, 5 October 1954, subject: "United States Army Forces, Far East, Sports Program."

(2) Letter, AG 353.8 SS-RX, this headquarters, 9 February 1955,

subject: "Participation in All-Army Sports Competition."

2. <u>Purpose</u>. This directive establishes a United States Army Forces, Far East and 8th United States Army Sports Program designed to promote comprehensive sports activities at all levels of command, and provides for progression into higher level competitions in certain selected sports.

3. <u>Objectives</u>. The objectives of the United States Army Forces, Far East and 8th United States Army Sports Program are to aid in the mental, physical, and moral development of Army personnel of this command, and to stimulate a high degree of esprit de corps by:

  a. Encouraging maximum participation in wholesome recreative sports during free-time hours on a voluntary basis.

  b. Improving sports skills and techniques through the media of qualified instruction, coaching, and officiating.

  c. Providing incentives for continually increasing competitive and spectator interests.

  d. Fostering international goodwill and understanding by maintaining close relationship with indigenous communities in sports activities of mutual interest and where practicable, competing with and against civilian teams.

e. Coordinating free-time recreational sports with on-duty physical training programs to accomplish complete cooperation in the development of physical fitness and to generate interest in improving sports skills.

Definitions.

f. Intra-Camp Programs are defined as the sports programs conducted at each post, camp, and station.

g. Intra-Command Programs will be those sports competitions between posts, camps, and stations, and/or separate units and organizations within each major subordinate command. These competitions will be designed to determine major subordinate command champions in each sport for entry in AFFE/8A championship events.

h. AFFE/8A Championship Events will be those tournaments and meets scheduled by this headquarters for the purpose of ascertaining champions in certain selected sports.

4. Responsibility. In order to provide continuity and maintain normal command channels, the following responsibilities are announced:

a. Headquarters, United States Army Forces, Far East and Eighth United States Army (Rear) will:

  (1) Exercise command supervision over all phases of the AFFE/8A sports program.

  (2) Supervise and govern an AFEE/8A sports council, subdivided into committees, as shown below, which will serve as advisory groups on related functions.

   (a) <u>Sports Committee</u>, composed of one representative from each addressee command. This committee will recommend and advise on matters pertaining to the AFFE/8A sports program.

   (b) <u>Women's Army Corps Sports Committee</u>, composed of one representative from each Women's Army Corps Detachment in AFFE/8A. This committee will recommend and

advise   on   matters
pertaining   to   the
AFFE/8A   women's
sports program.

(3)   Sponsor official's and coaches
clinics in the major sports.

(4)   Organize and supervise sports
events   conducted   for   the
purpose   of   determining
AFFE/8A   champions   and
entries   in   annual   All-Army
events   sponsored   by
Department   of   the   Army,   as
well   as   competitions   in
connection with the Olympics,
National   AAU   Events,   and
Inter-Service Championships.

b.   Major   Subordinate   Commands.
Commanding Generals, AFFE/Eighth
Army   (Korea),   Ryukyus   Command
and   IX   Corps,   and   1st   Cavalry
Division (Inf) are responsible for:

(1)   Administering   the   sports
program   within   their
geographical   areas   of
responsibility. Personnel of
Camp Zama and the 40th AAA
Brigade   will   be   eligible   to
participate in the 1st Cavalry
Division (Inf) Sports program.

(2)   Establishing a Sports Council
which will be representative of

organizations within respective areas. These councils will serve as the commander's advisory groups on matters pertaining to respective sports programs including joint Foreign National recreational activities. Meetings will be held as frequently as considered necessary, but not less than once every six months. Subject to approval by major subordinate commanders, councils may be empowered to suspend for limited periods of time, players, coaches or officials for unsportsmanlike acts; discuss rules and regulations, within overall policies, covering activities of each area; and will individually promote and encourage maximum sports activities and participation within their own organizations.

(3)   Insure (sic) that sports tournaments conducted by units or commands do not conflict good with the

established AFFE/8A championship events.

(4) Provide supplies and equipment for teams and/or individuals from their commands who compete in AFFE/8A championship events.

5. Operations. Commanding Generals, AFFE/Eighth Army (Korea), Ryukyus Command and IX Corps, and 1st Cavalry Division (Inf) will organize each sports program in order to best accomplish the following:

a. Intra-Camp Programs. Conduct as many company level sports activities as practicable with emphasis being placed on maximum participation.

b. Intra-Command Programs.

(1) Insofar as practicable, conduct inter-post, camp, and station leagues in the major sports, to include but not limited to: football, basketball, and baseball, to ensure maximum spectator interest.

(2) Conduct tournaments and meets in as many other sports, such as boxing, tennis, track and field, swimming, bowling, and golf, as practicable.

    c.   Conduct a Women's Army Corps sports program in those sports in which WAC personnel may compete.

    d.   Provide suitable awards for all competitions so as to encourage maximum participation at all levels.

    e.   Conduct training programs and clinics to continually improve coaching and officiating.

    f.   Promote close relationships with local indigenous communities in furtherance of recreational activities of joint interest.

6.   <u>Participation</u>.

    a.   Participation in AFFE/8A command championships is limited to Army personnel of units assigned or attached to represented commands.

    b.   If the 40th AAA Brigade does not field a representative team, then personnel of this unit will be permitted to participate in the nearest Army unit sponsoring teams and/or individuals in elimination tournaments to select major subordinate command entries in AFFE/8A championships.

    c.   Army personnel will not represent Navy or Air Force in any sport.

    d.   Unit identity and/or distinctive team names should be preserved at all levels of competition in order to sustain organizational esprit de corps. Teams comprised of personnel from two or more units will carry the unit designation of the organization with the predominant number of participants.

e. Commanders are encouraged to invite Department of the Army civilians to participate in intra-command sports programs; however, such personnel are not authorized to participate in AFFE/8A Championships.

f. Army personnel may participate in local international sports competitions at the discretion of the commander concerned.

7. Level of Competition.

a. The level of competition for intra-command basketball, baseball, and football teams may be either regimental or division level at the discretion of the commander concerned. The representative major subordinate command team for AFFE/8A championships may not exceed a representation of more than 25,000.

b. Flag football, softball, and volleyball teams entered in intra-command competitions and AFFE/8A championships will be from companies batteries, or comparable size units. The groupings of smaller units which have an aggregate strength not exceeding 250 men is authorized. Eligibility requirements for these sports only, (sic) will be as follows:

(1)   When a team representing its parent unit or organization is entered in the progressive levels of tournament play to determine the AFFE/8A championship team, the personnel of that team will not be augmented or reinforced at any level of play.

(2)   If a member of a team is transferred, sustains an injury, or for military reason is unable to continue play, the parent unit or organization may substitute a member of that unit or organization to fill the vacancy. The individual substituted must have been a member of that unit or organization prior to the entry of its team in the progressive tournament play for the AFFE/8A championship.

> (3) An officer authorized by each major commander will certify that his team does not exceed company level and has not been strengthened through personnel transfers or reinforced by the selection of outstanding individuals from the parent organization as indicated in paragraph b(1) above. This certificate will be submitted, upon arrival at the tournament site, to the Special Services Officer of the host command.

> c. (For) Individual type sports of boxing, bowling, golf, tennis, swimming, handball, horseshoes, track and field, table tennis and badminton, the most outstanding athletes will be selected on individual merit as team members at all levels of competition.

8. Officials.

> a. Personnel successfully completing courses at schools and clinics will be utilized whenever possible as officials in AFFE/8A championships.

> b. Payment of commissioned officers or warrant officers acting as officials at sports events will be in accordance with paragraph 6c(3), Army Regulations 210-50, 4 November

1953:   "Payment   from nonappropriated   funds   to commissioned officers or warrant officers for services rendered is not authorized, except for personal expenses when voluntarily officiating at sports events or in the conduct of educational,   religious   or entertainment   activities.   Personal expenses may include maintenance of required uniform, necessary travel, subsistence and lodging incident to participation in such activities."

(1)   The following table shows the maximum rates of pay for enlisted and civilian sports officials, the levels at which compensation is authorized, and the maximum number of officials authorized:

SPORT	AUTHORIZED LEVEL OF COMPETITION	MAXIMUM RATE PER GAME	MAXIMUM NUMBER OF OFFICIALS AUTHORIZED
Badminton	Tournaments only	$1.00 per game	1 Referee

Sport	Level	Pay	Officials
Baseball	Battalion Regimental Tournament	$1.00 per game $20.00 per game $25.00 per game	2 Umpires per game 3 Umpires per game 4 Umpires per game
Basketball	Company or Battalion Regimental Tournament	$6.00 per game $20.00 per game $25.00 per game	2 Officials 2 Officials 2 Officials
Bowling	Tournament only or Special Services Leagues	$10.00 per day	2 Foul Judges
Boxing	Tournaments or Exhibitions	$20.00 per day $15.00 per day	2 Referees 3 Judges
Football (11-man)	Regimental	$80.00 per game	4 Officials
Flag Football	Company League Play Tournament	$9.00 per game $15.00 per game	3 Officials 3 Officials

Horseshoes	Tournament only	$1.00 per match	1 Referee
Handball	Tournament only	$1.00 per match	1 Referee
Softball	Company League Play Tournament	$9.00 per game $15.00 per game	3 Umpires 3 Umpires
Swimming	Meet only	$20.00 per day	1 Starter 1 Clerk
Track and Field	Meet only	$20.00 per day	1 Starter 1 Clerk
Table Tennis	Tournament only	$1.00 per match	1 Referee
Tennis	Tournament only	$4.00 per match	1 Referee 1 Umpire
Volleyball	Tournament only	$4.00 per match	1 Referee 1 Umpire

(2)   Other officials, such as timers, linesman, announcers, and scorers, necessary to successfully conduct major subordinate command competitions, may be paid a

maximum rate of $2.00 per official for each game or match at the discretion of the commander concerned.

(3) Officials for AFFE/8A Championships will be paid from nonappropriated funds available to the Special Services Office, AFFE/8A (Rear). Maximum rates of pay may be exceeded when required for AFFE/8A Championships.

(4) Custodians of nonappropriated funds are authorized to make payment to recognized sports official's associations in the Far East for officiating services performed at Army sports contests by members of the associations.

9. Awards. No cash prizes will be awarded any contestant in any sports event. United States Savings Bonds and similar instruments are considered to be cash prizes. Trophies, medals or awards (other than cash), may be awarded in connection with sports events within the following maximum costs:

a. Camp level. Individual awards $7.50; team awards, $15.00.

> b. Major Subordinate Command Level. Individual awards $12.50; team awards $20.00.
>
> 10. <u>Publicity</u>. It is desired that continuing publicity be given to the AFFE/8A sports program through every possible source and that each activity be widely publicized in order for each individual to be completely aware of events being staged and to assure full and active spectator interest.

MEMO FOR THE RECORD:

1. Ref AR 25-52, 3 Jan 56, outlines new sports regulations that are applicable to all major CONUS and oversea commands.
2. This ltr implements AR 28-52 and announces the rules and regulations relative to the AFFE/8A Sports Program. Information contained in this ltr was unanimously recommended by the AFFE/8A (Rear) Sports Council, comprised of sports representatives of the major subordinate commands.
3. G/S coord obtained from <u>HKC for R(?)Z</u> G-1; <u>JRJ for HJVH</u> G-3; <u>JNC for KLS</u> TIE. CofS appr not rqr.
4. No Comd program action rqr.
5. This is a journal item. Corr maybe found in AG and SS files.

The 4 February 1956 *Army Times* (265) addressed the policy for professional athletes playing on post baseball, basketball, and football teams:

> The number of professional players on any Army baseball, basketball or football team, and the number of days given over to Army post teams in boxing, baseball, basketball and football have been limited by AR 28-52, dated Jan. 3, now being

distributed to the field. The new regulation outlines in detail the entire Army sports program.

In baseball, basketball and football, not more than 25% of the men on the team can be what is called "restricted" professional players. In basketball and football, a restricted player is anyone who is or has been under contract to a professional league team. In baseball, a restricted player is anyone who is or has been under contract to a Class "A" league team or any team in a higher classification.

This 25% pro rule will probably affect post baseball teams more than post football or post basketball teams. Few, if any, Army football or basketball squads have been 25% professional. But a number of post baseball teams have been more than 25% pro during the past few years, if one keeps in mind the Class A and above ruling.

As for football, the best example is probably the Fort Ord, Calif., team. Despite a loss to Fort Sill, Ord was generally rated the best Army team in the country last year. Ord began the season with a squad of 39 men including nine pros, which would have been under the new 25% maximum. At the time of the Poinsettia Bowl game, Ord had a squad of 29 men including seven pros, also under the maximum. Since Ord had more professional players than most Army post teams have, the 25% rule would not seem to influence Army football to any great extent.

As for baseball, a number of top Army post teams would have been over the new 25% pro maximum last year, including the All-Army championship team from Fort McPherson, Ga.

The maximum amount of time, including pre-season training, which may now be devoted to the four major sports is as follows: 150 days for baseball, 90 days for basketball, 105 days for boxing and 120 days for football.

These periods of time do not include competition in Army area, All-Army, inter-service, national or international championships. Nor do these time periods apply to regimental level competition. At some posts, a post baseball or basketball team is organized only after regimental league play has been completed. In such cases, no matter how long the regimental league season has been, the time requirement listed above applies only to the post team.

The new regulation repeats the schedule restriction of 30 games for a post basketball team and 50 games for a post baseball team.

On the matter of how many officers may be on an Army baseball, basketball or football team, which has caused some confusion in the past, the new reg spells it out this way: "At least 50% of the personnel of a squad in the Army Sports Program in baseball, basketball, and football will be enlisted persons. In all other sports, teams may consist of officer and enlisted personnel in any proportion."

Use of the word "squad" should clear up any doubt as to whether a basketball team may have three, four or five officers in the game at the same time. If half of the squad is made-up of enlisted men, it's OK to have even five officers on the court at the same time.

The 500-mile round trip restriction for inter-post games which has been on the books for more than a year, in Circular form, is also repeated (sic): "Inter-installation and civilian competitions will be restricted to the geographical limits of the Army area in which the installation is located except installations located near Army area boundaries may travel into an adjacent area providing the round trip does not exceed 500 miles. Exceptions to this may be granted by the major commander concerned" (In regard to this restriction, MDW is considered to be within the Second Army area).

Elsewhere in the regulation, the administrative and financial end of the Army Sports Program is outlined as well as command tournaments, All-Army tournaments, trophies, official, civilian sports directors, etc.

The regulation supersedes AR 680-30 dated (sic) Feb. 23, 1950; Cir. 3 dated Sept. 30, 1954; and DA message 371360 dated Feb. 8, 1955.

A 20 July 1956 memo from Headquarters Eight Army Support Command to Commanding General AFFE/8A (Rear) gives an idea of the various Korea-area Commands that existed at the time: I Corps (Gp), Seoul Area Command, 7th Inf Div, 24th Inf Div, Pusan Area Command, Ascom City Command, Taegu-Taejon Area Command, Inchon Area Command (266).

Correspondence dated 18 August 1956 from Robert J Reynolds, Capt, AGC, to Commander in Chief, Far East Command (267), said:

1. References letter AGJ 334 (25 Mar 54) AJ-S, Hq FEC, 25 March 1954, subject: "Far East Command Inter-Service Sports Council."
2. Lt Col John A Carlson, AGC, Chief, Recreation Division, Special Services Office, Hq AFFE/8A (Rear), will replace Lt Col Donald J. Kievit, CE, as AFFE/8A (Rear) member on the Far East Command Inter-Service Sports Council. Maj Harry Halldow, Inf, Assistant Chief, Recreation Division and Mr. Clarence J. Koehler, Sports Director, are designated alternates.

An attached memo from John A. Carlson, Lt Col, AGC, Chief, Recreation Division, dated 16 August 1956, stated:

1. Ref ltr AGJ (25 Mar 54) AJ-S, Hq FEC, 25 Mar 54, subj: "FEC Inter-Svc Sports Council," established FEC Inter-Svc Sports Council, giving mission, composition, scope and functions, and processing of council actions.
2. This ltr notifies FEC that Lt Col John A. Carlson, this Hq, replaces Lt Col Donald J. Kievit as AFFE/8A (Rear) member of FEC Inter-Svc Sports Council and designates Maj Harry Halldow and Mr. Clarence J. Koehler as alternates.

A 20 September 1956 memo from C. H. Simcox to various commanding generals (268) discussed payments to tournament officials. The memo references letter AFFE AG 353.8 SS-RX, HQ AFFE/8A (Rear), 12 July 1956. The memo notes an amendment as follows: "Payment of commissioned officers or warrant officers acting as officials at sports events will be in accordance with paragraph 6c(3)(a) and (b), Army Regulations 230-5, 18 July 1956. Payments from nonappropriated (sic) funds may be made to commissioned or warrant officers for authorized voluntary services rendered during off-duty hours under the following conditions":

> "Services shall be limited to those to be performed on an intermittent fee basis without direct supervision and control of official superiors, such as officiating at sports events and conducting educational, religious, recreation, or entertainment activities, so that no relationship of employer and employee is created." It is further stated that "engagement for such services shall be in accordance with policy established by the major commander."

There is a 24 September 1956 distributed letter from M. E. Perry, Captain, AGC, Adjutant regarding "Company Level Basketball League," (269) as follows:

1. The Camp Zama Company Level Basketball League will begin play on 28 November 1956. League games will be played Monday, Wednesday, and Friday evenings at the Camp Zama, Fuchinobe and 8169th Hospital Gymnasiums. Upon completion of league play the top four teams will play a double elimination tournament to decide the league championship.

2. Each unit or section desiring to enter a team will submit the team name and officer-in-charge or coach, to the Camp Zama Athletic and Recreation Office prior to 4 November 1956 so that a practice schedule can be arranged. Team rosters containing the name, rank, service number and hometown of each team member will be submitted not later than 23 November 1956.

3. Games will be played in accordance with 1956 NCAA Basketball rules and attached league rules, inclosure (sic) one. The Camp Zama Athletic and Recreation Officer will be the president of the Camp Zama League and will make final decisions regarding league play.

4. Games will be scheduled at 1830 and 2030 hours and may be cancelled for military reasons only.

5. There will be a meeting of team coaches at 1300 hours, 16 November 1956, at the Camp Zama Field House (sic). The league schedule will be distributed to coaches at this time.

6. Two officials for each league game will be assigned by the Camp Zama athletic and recreation officer. The home team will provide the official scorer.

The "CAMP ZAMA Company Level Basketball League Rules" are as follows:

1. RULES: 1956 NCAA Basketball Rules and the following rules will govern league play:

   a. League play will be double round robin. Games will be played as scheduled. The league champion and runner-up will be presented awards upon completion of league play. In the event two (2) teams tie for first or second place, one (1) play-off will be played. In the event three (3) or more teams tied for first or second place a double elimination tournament will be held.

   b. Games will consist of four (4) eight (8) minute quarters with one (1) minute between quarters and eight (8) minutes between the halves.

   c. The team captain is the only man who may talk with an official about his calls. Any other man who does so will be charged with a technical foul. The team captain must call time to discuss play.

   d. The only person who may call timeout is the man who has possession of the ball or a team captain when his team has possession of the ball.

   e. At the end of league play the top four teams will play a double elimination tournament to determine who will represent Camp Zama in the 1st Cavalry Division All-Japan play-offs.

   f. Players are required to be in game uniform. Uniforms will not be changed between players during the game. If this occurs a technical foul will be called and the two (2) involved removed from the game.

g. In the event of similar team colors, the visiting team will draw jerseys from A & R Supply the night of the game.

2. ELIGIBLITY

a. Personnel who are assigned or on TDY orders to the unit or section can play with the team. No person will be placed on TDY or transferred for the sole purpose of playing basketball.

b. Each team may consist of any number of players from their organization or section but only fifteen (15) players and one (1) coach, and one (1) manager may be on the bench and/or court at one time.

c. Any man who is cut from the Post Team prior to 15 December 1956 will be permitted to play company level basketball.

d. Once a player's name has appeared in the official scorebook he will not be permitted to transfer to another team unless he appears on orders assigning him to another unit or a section.

e. Typed rosters to include full name, rank, service number, hometown and position of each team member will be forwarded to this headquarters, Attn: Special Services Officer, prior to 23 November 1956. Team members must be on the file roster by 1600 hours the day of a game.

3. FORFEITS:

a. Any team that does not appear on the court for play fifteen (15) minutes after the scheduled time will forfeit the game.

b. Request for change in the schedule must be agreed upon by both coaches and presented to the A & R Officer for approval 24 hours prior to play.

346

4. MANAGERS AND COACHES
    a. Managers and coaches are encouraged to drop into the A & R Office and read the official NCAA Basketball Guide 1956.

Sportsmanship is essential. Managers and coaches are responsible for their teams actions and conduct well on the court.

There is an 18 October 1956 communication regarding "1956 Far East Command Football Championship" (270) as follows:

1. References:
    a. Letter, AFFE AG 353.8 GA-M, HQ AFFE/8A (Rear), 1 September 1955, subject: "Major Special Services Events."
    b. Letter, AFFE AG 353.8 SS-RX, HQ AFFE/8A (Rear), 15 December 1955, subject: "AFFE/8A (Rear) Sports Tournament," inclosure (sic) 3.

2. The 1956 Far East Command Football Championship will be determined by a series of bowl games to be played 15, 16, and 30 December 1956 at Korakuen Stadium. A drawing conducted by the Far East Command Inter-Service Sports Council resulted in the following pairings:

    a. 15 December (Torii Bowl Game): Army vs Navy,
    b. 16 December (Sukiyaki Bowl Game) Air Force vs Marines,
    c. 30 December (Rice Bowl): Winner of above games.

3. The Commanding General, 1st Cavalry Division (Inf) is responsible for the physical preparation of the stadium for the bowl games. This responsibility will be implemented as applicable in accordance with references listed above and separate instructions as may be issued.

4. General Rules:

    a. The Bowl Games will be played according to the 1956 National Collegiate Athletic Association football rules.
    b. No team may be assembled prior to 26 November 56 for training for the respective Bowl Games.
    c. A maximum thirty-five (35) players plus a five man coaching staff may be included on a squad selected to represent any of the services.
    d. No restriction will be placed on the number of officers authorized to participate.
    e. Only military personnel stationed in Japan, Okinawa, and Korea, who were present as officially recognized members of conference teams during at least two games of regularly scheduled conference play in 1956, are eligible for selection as players on the AFFE/8A All-Star squad.

5. Selection of the AFFE/8A squad.

    a. A head coach and four assistant coaches will be selected by this headquarters.
    b. Players will be selected by head coaches of each AFFE/8A football team at a meeting to be held at this headquarters early in November.
    c. Players selected will report to Camp Zama by 26 November 56 for the purpose of training for the

inter-service bowl games. Final selection of the thirty-five (35) players who will comprise the AFFE/8A team will be announced prior to 12 December 1956.

6. The Commanding Officer, Camp Zama, will act as host for the training of the Army team and will be responsible for the following:

    a. Providing suitable billeting and messing facilities.
    b. Furnishing practice football facilities and necessary uniforms and equipment.
    c. Providing such transportation as may be needed during the training period and bus transportation to the site of the Bowl Games.
    d. Arranging for pre-game publicity material on individuals as requested by this headquarters.

7. Orders. Individuals selected will be placed on fifty (50) days temporary duty with Headquarters Company, Camp Zama (8030), APO 343, for the purpose of training and competing in the 1956 Far East Command Football Championship competition. Orders will specify that personnel are to travel under orders but not on public business, that such travel and temporary duty constitutes duty of a type contemplated by paragraph 6454, Joint Travel Regulations, and that expenses incident to travel will be borne by locally available nonappropriated funds. Reimbursement for such expenses will be made by the Camp Zama Major Command Welfare Fund, AFFE/8A (Rear) Account upon presentation of certified vouchers for expenses incurred.

8. Equipment.

    a. All football players will report to Camp Zama with the following equipment in their possession:

        1. One pair of shoulder pads.
        2. One pair of football shoes.
        3. One pair of sweat socks.

    b. Game uniforms will be furnished by this headquarters.

9. Personnel.

    a. Individuals desiring pay while away from their home station should have pay records in their possession.

    b. Personnel who are scheduled for rotation to CONUS within sixty (60) days subsequent to completion of the fifty (50) day TDY period will not return to their parent unit. All personnel records will accompany individuals concerned.

10. Additional information concerning the 1956 Far East Command Football Championship will be disseminated in subsequent directives.

M/R:

    a. Ltr SS-RX 353.8 AG this hq, subj: "1956 Far East Command Football Championship," informs Subordinate Commands on the 1956 Inter-Service Football Games, stating rules, method of player selection, and responsibility of Subordinate Commands.

b. The Army has been designated the responsibility of host for the 1956 Inter-Service Football Championships. Next year 1957 (sic), the Air Force will have responsibility. The Navy and Marines will not have this opportunity as they will be unable to accomplish this task, due to their strength and organization.

AFFE SERVICE SPORTS RULES AND REGULATIONS

DEPARTMENT OF DEFENSE DIRECTIVE 1330.4

A 4 September 1954 Department of Defense Directive addresses "Participation in International Sports Competitions" (271):

Subject: Participation in International Sports Competitions

References:

(a)   Public Law 159, 8th Congress, approved 1 July 1947

(b)   Public Law 342, 83d Congress, approved 22 April 1954

I.   PURPOSE

The purpose of this directive is to prescribe a Department of Defense policy regarding the participation of Armed Forces personnel in international sports competitions. This policy has particular reference to participation in the Pan-American and Olympic Games.

II.   POLICY

The Congress of the United States, by Public Law 159, 80th Congress, Authorized the direction of the training and attendance of personnel of the Armed Forces in Olympic Games. By Public Law 342, 83d Congress, the President of the United States is authorized and requested to urge all citizens to do all in their power to support the Pan-American and Olympic Games and to insure (sic) that the United States will be fully and adequately represented in these games. The primary training responsibility of the Department of Defense is the training of personnel for the

Armed Forces. In view of the significance attached to full and adequate representation in international sports competitions, the Secretaries of the Army, Navy, and Air Force, consistent with this primary training responsibility, will provide opportunity for Armed Forces personnel who volunteered to train for and compete in authorized international sports competitions.

III. PROCEDURES

A. The Department of Defense Committee on International Sports Competitions will serve as the liaison, coordinating and advisory agency for the Secretary of Defense on international sports competitions. This committee will resolve such matters which, within the stated policy or procedures, cannot be resolved by the Service Secretaries. The committee will make necessary interpretations of, or, when deemed necessary, recommend to the Secretary of Defense proposed changes in, the stated policy.

B. While the provisions of this directive apply primarily to the Pan-American and Olympic Games, the Secretaries may apply applicable portions as a guide for participation of personnel of their respective Services in international sports competitions considered desirable by the respective Secretaries.

C. Upon being selected for a team representing the United States in international competition, Armed Forces personnel will be equipped, transported, and subsisted by the sponsoring agency (United States Olympic Committee, etc.) in the same manner as our civilian members of the team.

IV.   ADMINISTRATION

A. Assignments. Armed Forces personnel who are selected to participate may be placed on duty at such places and for such periods of time as are necessary:

1. To train for and participate in the Pan-American Games, Olympic Games and other authorized international sports competitions.
2. For planning, observing, or coordinating matters pertaining to authorized international sports competitions.

B. Training. Suitable specialized training will be provided separately or jointly by the Services for those members of the Armed Forces qualified to compete in authorized international sports competitions.

V.   REPORTS
Armed Services Directives and regulations implementing this directive will be coordinated to insure (sic) uniformity with respect to methods, procedures and safeguards and forwarded so as to reach the assistant Secretary of Defense (Manpower Personnel) not later than 60 days from the effective date in this directive.

VI.   EFFECTIVE DATE

This directive is effective 4 September 1954.

PUBLIC LAW 11, VOL. 69 – 84th CONGRESS, 1st SESSION, 1955

Public Law 11, as noted on DoD website, "Established authorizing Armed Forces Personnel to train/participate in national and international events."

Per the actual text of law, the Secretary of Defense was authorized to "permit the personnel of the Armed Forces to train for, attend, and participate in the Second Pan-American Games, the Seventh Olympic Winter Games and Olympic Games of the XVI Olympiad, future Pan-American Games and Olympic Games ..." *See Appendix for supporting documentation* (272).

The law also allowed the Secretary of Defense to authorize athletes to participate in other non-specified international sports, and to allow funding and supplies and materials as necessary (but not more than $800,000, apportioned to the various service branches).

FURTHER RULES, REGULATIONS AND PROCEDURES

All rules and procedures stated in paragraph 9, letter, AG 353.8 SS-RS, Hq AFFE, 5 October 1954, subject: "United States Forces, Far East, Sports Program" will apply where applicable except that at the discretion of the addressee commands, teams in basketball, baseball, softball, and volleyball may exceed the maximum levels of competition established in paragraph 9d (1) and (2).

Personnel of other services, on active duty for periods in excess of 90 days, who are assigned or attached to Army elements may participate as members of Army teams at all levels of competition provided that the parent service of individuals concerned will permit said individuals to compete in All-Army championships and in the CONUS.

Addressee commands may enter one team each, with the exception of IX Corps, which will be permitted to enter one team from the Northern Honshu sports conference and one team from Tokyo-Yokohama area conference, in each of the AFFE/8A Championship Tournaments.

Tournament Rules for skiing, bowling, boxing, pistol shooting, and other sports were included.

Basketball tournament rules are as follows:

The basketball team entered may be a regimental level team or a team selected from a combination of units and organizations with a strength not exceeding 25,000. Squads will not exceed twelve men, to include a coach plus an officer-in-charge. The tournament will be double elimination. 1955 official NCAA basketball rules will govern conduct of the tournament. Trophies will be presented the champion (sic) and runner up teams.

Administrative details:

Entries in the AFFE/8A sports tournaments and meets will be as indicated in the rules and regulations for specific sports. When appropriate, a tournament, meet, or playoff series will be conducted between the representative conferences or teams under the supervision of each addressee command to determine the team or individuals to represent that command.

The Commanding Generals of commands designated as host commands for AFFE/8A sports tournaments as shown in enclosure #1, "Schedule of Events," will be responsible for: Designating the tournament site and advising participating commands accordingly, 30 days prior to the tournament; advising visiting commands as to procedures to be followed in reporting for participation in tournaments and the organization to which personnel will report; furnishing playing facilities and tournament balls; paying tournament officials; arranging for suitable billeting and messing; providing competent medical service during all contests; arranging for comprehensive publicity; submitting results of each day's competition by radio message to commanders concerned, with copies to headquarters; tournament brackets; results of each contest; 2 copies of all action photographs; 2 copies of programs.

Furthermore, commanders responsible for visiting teams will issue necessary orders placing personnel on temporary duty with the host command as instructed. Orders will specify that personnel are to travel under orders, but not on public business, that such travel and temporary duty constitutes duty of a type contemplated by paragraph 6454, joint travel regulations, and that expenses incident to such travel and temporary duty will be borne by locally available nonappropriated funds. Host command will be furnished information below, a minimum of seven days prior to the tournament, with information copy to this headquarters, Attention: Special Services Officer.

(The host command will provide) team rosters, including name, grade, service number, hometown, designation of military unit to which each member is assigned, and players position for team sports; team and individual photographs, together with personal data, including previous sports experience for publicity purposes … the assistance of local public information offices should be solicited.

The commanding general, AFFE/8A, will provide suitable awards from non-appropriated funds for teams and individuals as indicated in enclosure 2, "Rules and Regulations." Officials for AFFE/8A sports tournaments and meets will be selected by headquarters AFFE/8A. Transportation: Travel of teams by commercial transportation in Japan is chargeable to locally available nonappropriated welfare funds.

Addressee commands are authorized to issue orders directing travel by air, using this letter as authority for members of teams and individuals participating in or necessary to the conduct of these contests. Limitations set forth in inclosure (sic) 2, "Rules and Regulations" will not be exceeded for inter-island travel. Travel of teams via air within Japan should be on a space available basis. Visiting commands are reminded that teams should not arrive in Japan without sufficient funds to pay commercial transportation costs.

It is desired that full promotional effort be utilized in order to sustain a high degree of participation and spectator interest in the 1955 AFFE/8A Sports Program at all levels of command.

Correspondence from Herbert Nelson, Colonel, AGC Adjutant General, dated 27 March 1956, contains minutes from the 6 March 1956 meeting, as presented by L.A. Weissinger, Colonel, which pertain to the Far East Command Inter-Service Sports Council. The minutes were directed to the Commanding General, United States Army Forces, Far East 8th United States Army (Rear); Commander Naval Forces, Far East; Commander Far East Air Forces; and Commanding General, 3d Marine Division.

Colonel Nelson noted issues related to personnel representing the service of the base or post of assignment, regardless of parent service, in the all-star championship series, and determined the "manner of designating the Home Team that will have the privilege of occupying the west side of the Meiji Stadium" (273).

The council minutes stated, in part:

"The twenty-second meeting of the Far East Command Inter-Service Sports Council was held at 1000 hours, 6 March 1956, in the J-1 conference room, Headquarters, Far East Command."

In attendance were voting members, Colonel L.A. Weissinger, J1, Hq, FEC; Lt. Col. D. J. Kievit, AFFE/8A (Rear); Commander W. M. Cureton, NAVFE; Major E. D. Webber, 3d Marine Division, FMF; and

Mr. John Scially, FEAF. Visitors were Commander A. R. Johnson, J1, Hq, FEC; Major J. E. Hoppin, FEAF.

The football championship series of 1956 was discussed, including the all-star team type of play versus the regular league team play for the championship series. The voting group unanimously agreed with Mr. Scially that the Football Championship Series would be played by all-star teams.

The men also discussed the eligibility of personnel playing on teams representing other than their parent service. The group again unanimously agreed with Mr. Scially that officer eligibility would be set forth in the regulations of the respective parent service. There was further unanimous agreement that *a player must have played in a minimum of two recognized league games to be eligible for all-star championship play (it. added)*.

Mr. Scially's motion that personnel should be permitted to represent the service of the assigned post or base, regardless of parent service, in the championship series was not carried. Lt. Col. Kievit cited the DA Circular 28-22, which said, "Effective with the 1956 season, Army personnel will participate in inter-service championship competitions only as members of an Army team."

The Host Team was responsible for physical preparation of the stadium, and the Home Team would have the privilege of occupying the west side of the stands. There were various proposals as to the basis for determining the Home Team, and no conclusion was reached, though it was noted the Marine Corps had no preference.

The parties agreed that each service would participate equally in the financing of the Bowl Series, and custodianship of the funds would fall to the Host Service.

The Council was to agree on selection of officials, who were to earn $20.00 for field officials, and $10.00 for chain and box officials. The members unanimously agreed on Meiji Stadium as the site of the series. The preliminary games would be held on 15 and 16 December, and the championship game was to be played on 30 December.

A 16 July 1956 Circular (680-10) discussed Special Services Hotels (274). The Circular said the Commanding General, 1st Cavalry Division (Inf), "is responsible for the logistic support of special services hotels in accordance with applicable Army regulations and other current directives." The commanding officer, Special Services Hotel Detachment (8248) would be responsible for maintaining a staff, provide a central agency for receipt of the confirmation of individual and group reservations, maintain records, enforce policies, and other.

Special Services hotels within Japan were established by the Commanding General, AFFE/8A, as off-post military activities, operated on a partially self-supporting basis by the Commanding Officer, Special Services Hotel Detachment (8248). Commanding General, AFFE/8A, had approval authority for discontinuance of a Special Services hotel, acquisition of a Special Services hotel, change in status of a Special Services hotel, etc.

The Circular continued by noting that Special Services hotels would be contracted for and operated in accordance with good business principles. There would be an equitable balance between prices charged guests for services rendered, and operational expenses. Hotels would provide first class accommodation in metropolitan and resort areas.

The Fiscal Officer, Special Services Hotel Detachment (8248), would serve as recorder-custodian of the Japan Hotel Fund, a revenue producing fund established for the administration of monies associated with Special Services hotel operations. The Japan Hotel Fund would be controlled, audited, and inspected as provided in applicable regulations and directives governing nonappropriated (sic) funds. There would be a Hotel Council appointed to oversee operations.

Hotel guests were required to pay billeting fees for personal services, meals, recreational transportation, motion pictures, and other incidentals with military payment certificates only. Hotel guests were to conduct themselves in a manner which would not exceed the limits of good taste or encroach upon or interfere with the pleasure, enjoyment, or rest of other guests. If the officer in charge were to deem behavior "annoying to others," he would take necessary action to restore decorum by the "most prompt and tactful means."

There were enlisted hotels and officer hotels. Priority would be given requests for reservations from personnel for rest and recuperation leave from Korea.

The hotels Circular was signed by Roy N. Walker, Colonel, AGVC, Adjutant General.

There is an 8 December 1956 memo from James L Glymph, Lt Colonel, AGC, regarding boxing protective headgear (275), addressed to Commanding General, United States Army Forces, Far East and Eighth U. S. Army (Rear):

> The Amateur Athletic Union has again failed to approve the optional use of the boxing protective headgear in tournaments sanctioned by that organization. This in no way changes the Army policy in making the use of the protective headgear mandatory in all amateur boxing competitions both military and civilian ... several athletic equipment manufacturers have developed types of boxing protective headgears with various degrees of adequacy. The most prevalent fault of boxing headgears to date has been the tendency to "slip" during competitive bouts. Wilson Sporting Goods Company has recently developed a new protective headgear which, after

361

extensive testing, appears to be adequate. The headgear is listed as Number H 1902 and is priced at approximately $7.45. It is recommended that this headgear or one of equal calibre (sic) be purchased when replacing boxing headgears presently on hand.

ESTABLISHMENT OF SPORTS PROGRAM AND COUNCIL FAR EAST

There is a 12 December 1956 correspondence from D.H. Callahan, Captain, AGC, Asst Adjutant (276), regarding the 1957 Army Sports Program.

1. References:
   a) TM 21-225, the Army Sports Program.
   b) TM 21-220, Sports and Games.
   c) Letter AFFE AG 353.8 SS-RX, Headquarters United States Army Forces, Far East and Eighth United States Army (Rear), 12 July 1956, subject: AFFE/8A (Rear) Sports Program
   d) Letter CZCT-NF 120.1, this headquarters, 21 November 1956, subject: Expenditures from Unit Fund.
2. Purpose: To establish a sports program to promote sports activities at company level and to provide for progression into higher level competition in certain selected sports.
3. Objectives: To aid in the mental, physical, and moral development of Army personnel of this command, and to maintain a high esprit-de-corps by:
   a) Encouraging maximum participation in wholesome recreative sports.
   b) Expanding the opportunity for individuals to engage in sports of their choice.

c) Developing leadership through participation in competitive sports.

d) Improving sports skills and techniques through the media of qualified coaching and officiating.

e) Providing incentives for increasing competitive and spectator interest.

f) Fostering international good will and understanding by maintaining close relationships with indigenous communities in sports activities of mutual interest and, where practicable, competing with and against civilian teams.

4. Sports Council: To provide program opportunity, and to aid and advise the Athletic and Recreation Officer, a sports council composed of the following members is established:

a) Chairman – Executive Officer, Camp Zama.

b) Recorder – A & R Officer, Camp Zama.

c) Members – One officer from each company size unit.

5. Responsibilities:

a) Sports Council:

(1) Conduct Meetings, when necessary, at the call of the chairman.

(2) Assist and advise the Athletic and Recreation Officer in planning seasonal sports programs.

(3) Resolve any problems of a sports nature brought before the council and establish operating policy when required.

b) The Athletic and Recreation Officer will:

(1) Supervise all phases of the sports program.

(2) Act as recorder for the sports council.

(3) Organize and supervise periodic coaches and official's clinics in all major sports.

6. <u>General</u>:
   a) Amateurism:
      (1) Amateurs may compete with and against professionals in all sports except boxing without jeopardizing their amateur standing, provided such competition is in connection with the Army Sports Program.
      (2) Military teams may compete against civilian professional teams without jeopardizing the amateur standing of team members provided the competition is staged by a military organization.
   b) The number of officers competing on teams will not exceed fifty percent of the team strength at any time.
   c) Unit designation and/or distinctive team names are encouraged at all levels of competition.
   d) Levels of competition:
      (1) Flag football, basketball, softball, and volleyball competition will be at company level. Companies, batteries, and/or comparable size units, or a grouping of smaller units, having an aggregate strength not exceeding 250 men are authorized to enter one team. Units and/or grouping of small units with strength exceeding 250 men may field two teams.
      (2) Teams entered in the 1st Cavalry Division All Japan Conference for football, baseball, and basketball will be composed of the outstanding competitors from this command.
      (3) In individual type sports, the outstanding athletes will be selected as team members to participate at all levels of competition.

7. <u>Supplies</u>:
   a) Game balls for league and tournament games will be supplied by the Camp Zama Athletic and Recreation Officer.
   b) Uniforms and practice equipment will be provided by the unit by requisition through normal supply channels or when equipment is not available for issue by using unit funds in accordance with reference 1d.

8. <u>Publicity</u>: Continuing publicity will be given to the Camp Zama Sports Program through every possible media. Each sports activity will be widely publicized in order that every individual will be completely aware of athletic events being staged, to assure full and active spectator interest and player participation.

9. Letter CSZO 353.8, this headquarters, 10 Jan 56, subject: 1956 Sports Program is rescinded.

HISTORICAL NOTES REGARDING CAMPS/POSTS

On 24 August 1953, the AFFE command reported on the length of new Far East duty tours (fixed tours), stating, "The tour for all Army personnel in Korea will be 10 calendar months" (277).

It's instructive to know that "normal" length of Foreign Service Tours (FST) were structured as follows (278):

> Korea (all personnel): 16 months
>
> Japan/Okinawa (all personnel accompanied or subsequently joined by dependents and male personnel without dependents): 36 months
>
> Japan/Okinawa (male personnel who have dependents and whose dependents do not join them): 24 months

The 2 January 1954 *Army Times* (279) reports that "Men in Korea and their families in the States were asking when the Korean duty tour would be shortened to 12 and 14 months." Brigadier General Herbert B. Powell, "the Army's Acting Assistant G-1," said the policy, which went into effect on 1 October 1953, would remain at 16 months; "All constructive service accrued before Oct. 1 is converted to a calendar month basis and is applied against the fixed tour requirement of 16 months."

A major U.S. Military base/camp in Japan, Camp Zama, appears in many sports news stories; here's some background:

A U.S. Government website for U.S. Army, Japan, discusses Camp Zama from the 1950s (280). The history says that U.S. Army Far East Headquarters decided to construct a new headquarters, moving from downtown Yokohama to Camp Zama, following a fire that destroyed five buildings on South Camp Zama, leaving space for the new command. "The command was relocated into Building 101 in October 1953."

Camp Zama "once again became a staging area for troops" on their way to Korea, including the "1st Cavalry and the 7th, 24th, and 40th Infantry Divisions." It had become more common to have family members present, and new accommodation were made accordingly.

"In 1954, IX Corps was assigned to U.S. Army Forces Far East, and an airfield was built on the northwest corner of the installation with a 1,500 foot runway."

From a Service Sports perspective, Camp Zama played an outsized role in supporting and hosting Service Sports and other recreational activities. It's rich history is well-documented in archival records.

Camp Zama wasn't the only beloved U.S. Military Far East facility in the 1950s. United States Forces Korea (USFK) was based at Yongsan Garrison in Seoul; Yongsan held a special place in the hearts of troops and local Koreans alike before it was scheduled to be relocated to Camp Humphries in Pyeongtaek in 2017 (though it appears to have been a very drawn-out process) at a cost of roughly 16 trillion won (281).

There is a 2017 "USA Today" article which interviewed "Korea's godfather of rock," Shin Joong-Hyun, who got his start as a teenage guitarist at the Yongsan Garrison in Seoul, and shared his fond memories of that time (282).

> Concrete walls topped with concertina wire is what most South Koreans only ever see of the Yongsan Garrison, a sprawling U.S. military base in the center of Seoul.
>
> But as a teenage guitarist in 1955, Shin Joong-Hyun remembers the first time he entered the base. He and other local musicians had been hired to entertain soldiers with American songs, which Shin says were all but unheard of to most Koreans at that time.

"I knew nothing about American music then," he says, recalling that he needed to learn jazz, R&B and rock 'n' roll numbers for auditions at the clubs on the base.

By hearing imported records on the jukebox and listening to the U.S. Military's Armed Forces Korea radio network, Shin says he got the hang of it. Soon, he and the others took what they learned inside the base and began playing American music for local audiences.

Shin said Yongsan was like his home, and "without the Yongsan Garrison, it feels like my generation's culture will soon be gone and me along with it." The 2017 article noted that American soldiers were being relocated, and the 617 acres of land would be transferred back to the Korean government, and "… since the Korean War, (Yongsan) had been home to the US Eighth Army and other US units."

In "The History of Korea", author Jinwung Kim (283) described the Yongsan relocation:

In July 2004 South Korea and the United States agreed to move the Yongsan compound, with South Korea assuming the estimated cost of $5.5 billion to relocate the base by the end of 2008. In December 2006, however, it was revealed that the relocation of USFK bases to P'yongt'aek could fall three to five years behind schedule. The Yongsan Garrison was expected to move to the new site by the end of 2011, and the 2d Infantry Division (would move) at the end of 2013. The delay was caused by failure to timely obtain all the necessary land for the transfer of the U.S. bases.

The 6 February 1954 *Army Times* newspaper reported, "No Saddle Shoes at Yong-San U" (284): "School bells are ringing all over Korea for Americans no longer engaged in fighting. One of the many 'universities' set up by the Army in Korea is the one attended by 350 soldier-students at the Eighth Army Hqs. Education Center in Yong-

San." The school had been located at Eighth Army Headquarters outside of Seoul.

The article said there were 72 education centers "spread throughout Eighth Army units to keep American soldiers profitably employed during this post-armistice period." Subjects taught ranged from second grade through college level. There were even courses for "soldiers who have not yet finished eighth grade(!)."

Available courses included philosophy, political science, economics, anthropology, foreign languages, algebra, radio technology, and "slide rule operation."

"This educational program has been called 'one of the most important activities of this post-armistice period' by General Maxwell D. Taylor, Eighth Army Commander, 'who is studying Korean himself.'"

There is a memo from Brigadier General Paul A. Disney dated 26 April 1955 concerning "Guest Privileges in Women's Quarters – Yongsan Military Reservation" (285). The memo granted the privilege of having guests of both sexes in their rooms during certain hours. The "chief consideration" was "the fact that other U.S. agencies employing women personnel in Korea extend this privilege." Brig. General Disney said that the privilege "carries with it the responsibility to guard against its abuse."

Budgets and recreational funds:

The 20 March 1954 *Army Times* (286) discussed frozen funds for recreational facilities. The short article said the Budget Bureau had withheld funds since 1952 due to "no standard criteria."

Once the requirement was met, the Budget Bureau was expected to release the following amounts: Army - $8.6 million, Air Force - $7.2 million, Navy - $1.5 million, and Marine Corps - $0.9 million.

Sometimes life on base was mundane; other times not - miscellanea on supplies, living conditions, fitness, behavior:

A 3 July 1955 memo from Captain Thomas Simmons concerned the waterproofing of Quonset huts; there was an urgent need for "mastic" for waterproofing purposes. He requested assistance from the Commanding General of the United States Army, as he had "no way of obtaining additional supplies" (287).

There are Headquarters, 3rd Battalion, 7th Infantry journals showing a brief glimpse into the soldier's duties/activities in the 1950s. A July 1954 journal entry from Capt. Otto P. Scharth said, "3d Bn, 7th Infantry, continued to occupy and improve area vic CT 503199. Training consisisted (sic) of Preliminary Rifle Instruction, organized athletics, appearance and inspection."

The August 1954 entry says, "3d Bn, 7th Infantry, continued to occupy and improve area vic CT 503199. Training consisted of Command Conference (Atomic Energy – your Future), Rifle Platoon as Advanced Party, Dismounted Drill, Weapons and Appearance Inspection and Organized Athletics. Bn. participated in H & S Security Alert (1603), In position at 1635, alert terminated at 1655."

There were also guideline requirements for full justification of each project, including: Project title, location, troop strength to be served, proximity to other similar facilities, desired completion date, estimated period of usage, estimated cost, rough sketch of project to show general design and dimensions, and a statement regarding availability of funds from other sources, to include appropriated or nonappropriated funds, and whether or not the project could be funded from the Major Command Welfare Fund.

Camp Casey Schoonover Bowl stadium:

The Schoonover Bowl was originally built in the 1950s at Camp Casey, opening in Sept. 1958 as a football field with natural grass turf, according to real property records of U.S. Army Garrison Red Cloud and Area I. The stadium was named after Medal of Honor recipient Cpl. Daniel D. Schoonover (288), and is still in use at the time of this writing, though in updated condition.

Living Conditions:

As a background on past base/camp living conditions, a document from the National Archives II in College Park, Maryland, dated 2 February 1955, discussed health care facilities, noting that "… since the cessation of hostilities (sic) operation has been similar to that of a station hospital" (289). It was noted that personnel were "abundant," and supplies were adequate; "The 44th Surgical Hospital, having remained in the same location for the past four years has had the opportunity to establish excellent facilities and sanitation has been very satisfactory."

The report further said that "There have been no cases of Hemorrhagic Fever or intestinal outbreaks in any of our personnel during the year … rodent control program and destruction of brush in the compound has been vigilantly maintained. Well-constructed latrines are maintained in excellent condition throughout the year." The report said surgeries performed were mostly elective, such as for "circumcisions, hernias, and hemorrhoids."

Apparently, fitness and obesity concerns are not just a modern phenomenon. A memo from the United States Army Forces, Far East, dated 30 December 1955, said that "A large number of officers, enlisted men and women, and Department of the Army civilians on duty in this command are overweight according to standards AR 40-105 … AR 40-100 …" (290).

The memo said that "overweight" was detrimental to good health and a handicap to military personnel on duty. Symptoms included undue fatigue, shortness of breath, and lower efficiency. Accidents were higher, and incidents of medical problems such as heart disease, arteriosclerosis, high blood pressure, etc., were higher. The memo said, "Obesity is not conducive to good military bearing and appearance."

The memo continued, noting the cause of overweight was eating more food than the body could use for "energy and repair." Moderate exercise and the elimination of fatty foods and the reduction of starches, such as potatoes, rice, macaroni and desserts was recommended. Proteins such as eggs, meat, fish and milk were also recommended, as were fruit and vegetables.

The officers were charged with instituting an active program to reduce overweight to conform to standards. A Standards chart of information was attached.

Overweight or not, the troops did not always behave well:

A 7 July 1956 memo (291) from Wilbur McGill, Major, USAF, described poor conduct by personnel at a USO show, stating that "This headquarters has noted the report of the conduct of personnel attending the above subject show (*Ed. - "High Time"*) at the 621-8 AC&W Detachment on 28 May 1956.

Situations as reported reflect with discredit on the unit in question and the Air Force. Request that this headquarters be notified of corrective action taken to prevent repeated occurrence of discrepancies of this nature."

A glimpse into Army life in post-war Korea also comes through a military police "OFFENSE OR INCIDENT REPORT" dated 24 October 1956 (292), in which the incident described was, "Senior passenger in speeding vehicle, on Rt 1, 3 miles south of 24th Div CP."

The "subject" was "Conway, C.C." The complainant was Pvt. Toriello, Frederick, US 52412059 24th MP Co. The "details of offense" stated, "Offender, senior passenger in a 1/2 ton truck, USA 20980225, BM: EASCOM 8020AU-HQ41, driven by Pfc Sandy, Billy D, H&S Co 8020th AU, was apprehended for allowing driver to speed 35MPH in a 25MPH zone." The vehicle was released to the operator, and the offender was "allowed to proceed."

These brief glimpses into military life during the mid-1950s are useful for understanding the environment in which U. S. Military Service Sports occurred.

MY VISIT TO JAPAN, HISTORICAL SITES INSPECTION

In April/May 2025, I visited Japan to see firsthand the area and what historical sites I could see with the limited time I had. The reasons I chose Japan over Korea at this time include the very favorable exchange rate with the US dollar at the time of this writing, but also because although football and other sports had wide participation in Korea, the Service Sports football championship and All-Star games, attended by tens of thousands of fans, took place in Japan.

The downside of visiting Japan this purpose is that only a few of the historical stadiums which existed in the 1950s remain, and one, which I really wanted to see in its original form, Paloma Mizuho Stadium (formerly Nagoya City Mizuho Park Athletics Stadium - 名古屋市瑞穂公園陸上競技場), is currently being renovated for the 2026 Asian Games, and now looks nothing like the original. I just missed it.

It should also be noted that Tokyo of the 1950s and Tokyo of today are two different worlds. Stadiums that existed in smaller towns in the 1950s, if they still exist today, would now be in just one small part of a massive, sprawling metropolis covering hundreds of square miles.

My visit was limited to Tokyo and surrounding areas. Two stadiums that existed and were used by Service Sports in the 1950s, and still exist as of the time of this writing, are in Tokyo and Yokohama – Meiji Stadium, Tokyo (now known as Meiji Jingu Stadium), and Yokohama Mitsuzawa Football Stadium, Yokohama (now known as NHK Spring Mitsuzawa Football Stadium).

I was not allowed to access the interior of Yokohama Mitsuzawa Football Stadium, but I obtained photos of the exterior (which was generally obscured by vegetation and other obstacles).

375

Meiji Jingu Stadium sits on a large property close the newer Japan National Stadium, which fairly recently replaced the old National Stadium (国立競技場).

I visited Meiji Jingu Stadium in the Shinjuku area of Tokyo and was fortunate to be able to attend a college baseball game occurring at the time. With exception of perhaps the lighting, scoreboard, and some other minor details, the stadium appears to be very similar to how it would have appeared in the 1950s.

When historical Service Sports records refer to American football games played at Meiji Stadium, at least in or about 1955, I believe they were referring to what is currently the Meiji Jingu Stadium, which is now used primarily for baseball.

The former National Stadium would have been physically more oriented for football given it's oval shape, but it wasn't built until 1958. Therefore, I believe that the stadium I visited and that is still in existence at the time of this writing, Meiji Jingu Stadium, is the same one used for football championship games in the mid-1950s.

Another stadium frequently used for Service Sports American football in the mid-1950s was Korakuen Stadium, which no longer exists (demolished 1987), and was at the current site of the Tokyo Dome. However, Korakuen Hall, which was opened in the early 1960s, still exists right next to the Tokyo Dome, and I attended a kickboxing match there while visiting the site. The small, intimate venue is still regularly used for sports such as kickboxing, pro wrestling, and boxing.

One of the locations that came up quite frequently for Service Sports in the mid-1950s was Camp Zama, which still exists in the Sagamihara City area.

Photo: Torii Bowl program from 1955; location Meiji Stadium, Tokyo.

I had contacted the Camp Zama library from the United States, and was advised I could visit the library and see if there was anything of use to my project, however when I arrived at Camp Zama, I was not allowed to access the base by Camp Security due to lack of military credentials. However, from outside the base I spoke with Dustin Perry of the Camp Zama Public Affairs Office, who believed there were no currently existing relics or venues from the 1950s. There were no formal archives or historical documents to the best of his knowledge, which is unfortunate because of the rich history of Service Sports at Camp Zama.

Hopefully the findings in this book can help restore some of the Camp Zama-related information from the mid-1950s temporarily lost to time.

I ran out of time to visit the ruins of Camp Drake or legacy site Miyaginohara Stadium in Sendai. Those sites will have to wait for a future visit.

Lastly, another site frequently referenced in historical documents, particularly for player, coaches and official's clinics, was Fryar Gym in Yokohama, which no longer exists (see Yokohama historical maps below for original location). The Fryar Gym site is allegedly the current site of the tallest building in Japan. I wish that more of these older venues had been preserved for history, but progress is an implacable force.

HISTORIC MAPS - JAPAN

CAMP ZAMA HISTORIC MAP

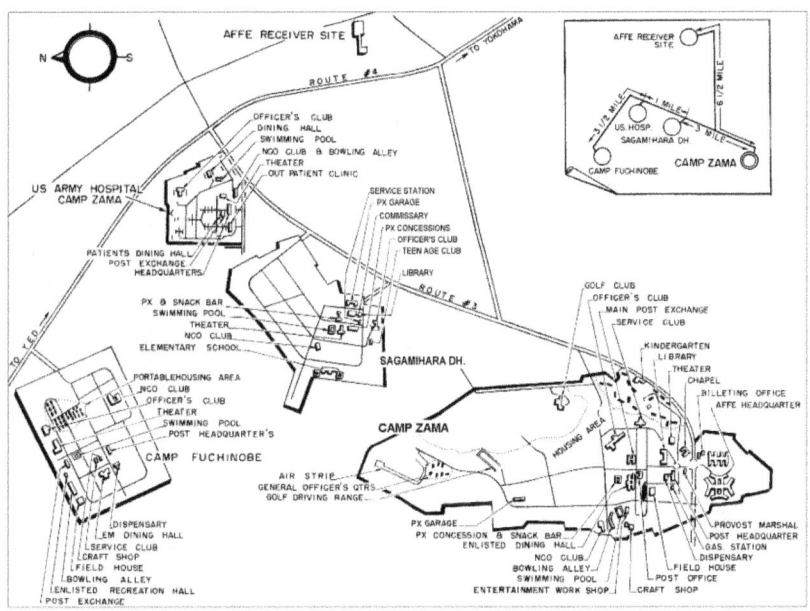

YOKOHAMA AREA HISTORIC MAPS

FRYAR GYM LOCATION

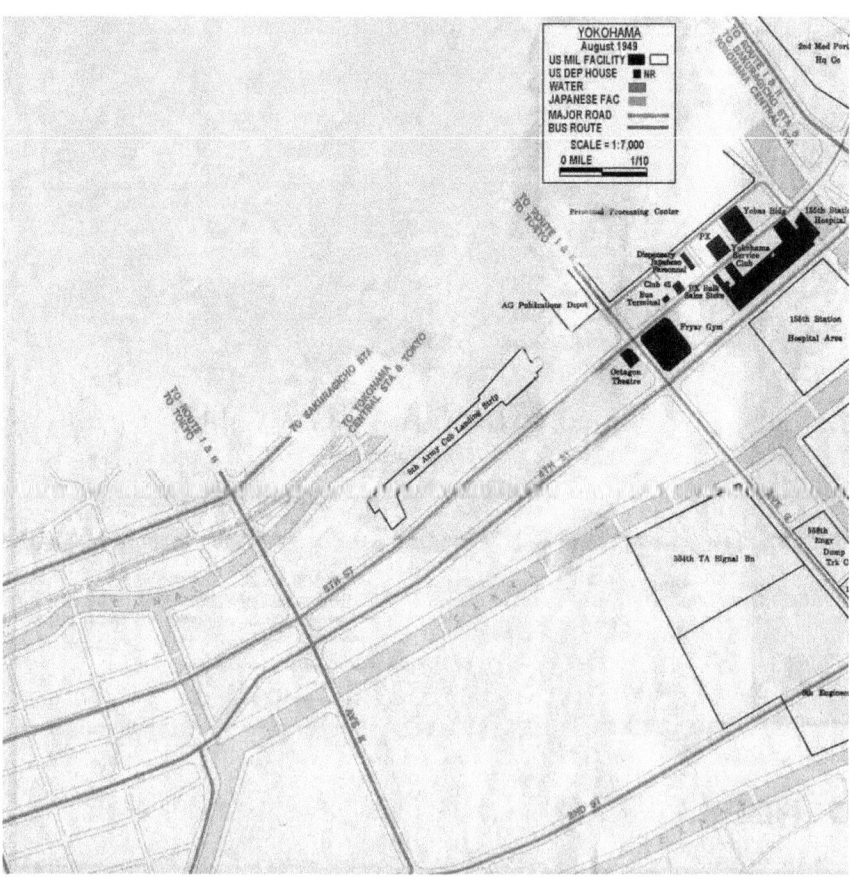

Map: Friar Gym, Yokohama area, https://yohidevils.net/kanto/maps/moremaps.htm

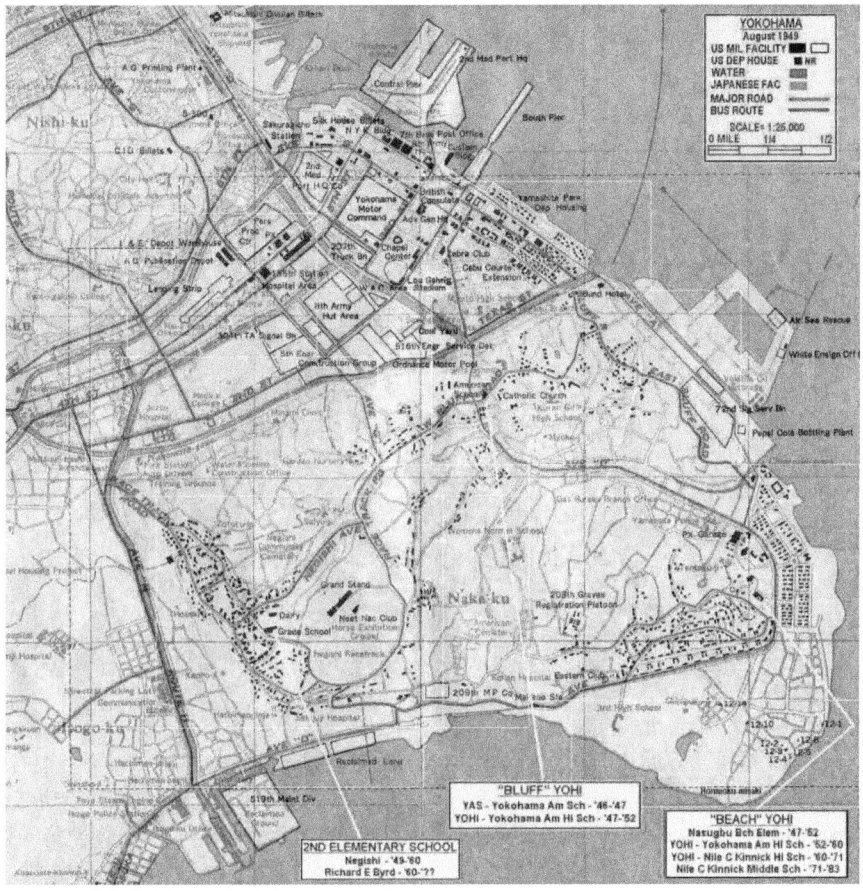

Map: 8th Army HQ, Yokohama area, https://yohidevils.net/kanto/maps/moremaps.htm

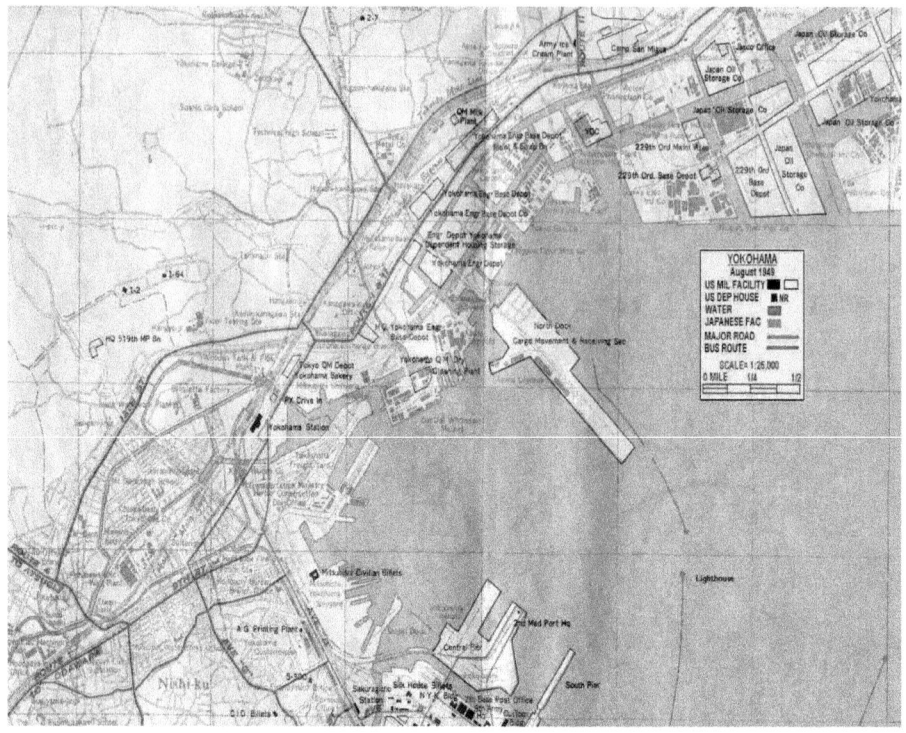

Map: Yokohama area, https://yohidevils.net/kanto/maps/15map02.jpg

ARMED FORCES SPORTS ALMANAC 1954

An amazing publication from 1954, the Armed Forces Sports Almanac, published by Military Service Publishing Company of Harrisburg, Pennsylvania, author C. O. Kates, provides exceptional details on U.S. Military Service Sports players and teams generally from 1951 to 1954 in the Far East, Europe, and CONUS (293). This book is rare; I was only able to identify approximately six or seven copies in America, housed at some universities, military facilities, and at the Library of Congress.

The Almanac is a large book covering many different Armed Forces sports. Christopher Malpass of the Interlibrary Loan and Document Services at UNC Wilmington, North Carolina, graciously provided scanned copies of the 264 pages pertaining to football and basketball Service Sports.

This incredible publication gives team names and rosters, game scores, All-Army team selections, Service All-Star selections, Service All-American selections, and more. Selected pages are reproduced below.

FOOTBALL

SERVICE ALL-STARS

Selected in a poll conducted by the
Armed Forces Press Service
1952

FIRST TEAM:

Offense

Andy Hillhouse, Camp Polk, re
Bill Pearman, Ft. Belvoir, rt
Bob Griffis, NTC San Diego, rg
George Radosevich, Parris Island, c
Ted Daffer, Ft. Eustis, lg
Jim Weatherall, Quantico, lt
Jim Mutscheller, Quantico, le
Al Dorow, Bolling AFB. qb
Bill Hayes, Parris Island, fb
Larry Coutre, Camp Breckinridge, hb
Bill Wade, PhibPac, hb

Defense

Bob Schnelker, Parris Island, re
Jack Stroud, Camp Drake, rt
George Weatherly, Ft. Sam Houston,
   rg
Irv Holdash, Ft. Eustis, c
Joe Palumbo, Ft. Eustis, lg
Don Coleman, Camp Atterbury, lt
Harrison Frasier, Camp Lejeune, le
Verl Lillywhite, NTC, San Diego, qb
Ken Shobe, Ft. Sam Houston, fb
Bob Boyd, NTC, San Diego, hb
Jim Glisson, Ft. Jackson, hb

1953

FIRST TEAM:

Frank McPhee, Quantico, e
Leo Sugar, Ft. Lee, e
Jack Esslinger, NAS, Norfolk, t
Hal Mitchell, Ft. Lee, t
Gil Bucci, Parris Island, g
Don Trevisano, NAS, Pensacola, g
Ray Beck, Ft. Jackson, c
Bob Williams NTC, Bainbridge, b
John Petitbon, Quantico, b
Ollie Matson, Ft. Ord, b
Al Dorow, Bolling AFB, b

SECOND TEAM:

Nick De Rosa, Cherry Point, e
Ed Bell, Ft. Monmouth, e
Gene Lipscomb, Camp Pendleton, t
Jim Mahoney, Little Creek, t
Jim Simmons, Burtonwood AB, g
Joe Skibinski, Ft. Monmouth, g
Paul Hatcher, PhibPac, c
Don Heinrich, Ft. Ord, b
Hank Lauricella, Ft. Belvoir, b
Bob Meyers, Quantico, b
Bill Reichardt, Bolling AFB, b

SERVICE ALL-AMERICAN TEAM

Based upon the Williamson 1953 Service All-American Balanced Poll

FIRST TEAM:

Bucky Curtis, NTC, San Diego, e
Gene Schroeder, Great Lakes, e
Jim Weatherall, Barstow, t
Roscoe Hansen, Quantico, t
Pat Cannamela, Ft. Ord, g
Ted Daffer, Ft. Eustis, g
Glen Graham, Camp Lejeune, c
Billy Wade, PhibPac, qb
John Petitbon, Quantico, qb
Zippy Morocco, Ft. Jackson, hb
Ollie Matson, Ft. Ord, fb

SECOND TEAM:

McPhee, Quantico, e
Jessup, NTC, e
McCormick, Ft. Leonard Wood, t
Boggan, Camp Lejeune, t
Forrester, Hamilton AFB, g
Beck, Ft. Jackson, g
Morris, Ft. Belvoir, c
Bonar, Bainbridge, qb
Smith, Pensacola, hb
Dorow, Bolling AFB, hb
Brunson, Ft. Jackson, fb

THIRD TEAM:

Langas, Ft. Belvoir, e
Martin, Ft. Sill, e
Kimmell, Ft. Lee, t
Anderson, Bainbridge, t
Eggers, Ft. Belvoir, g
Bucci, Parris Island, g
Fuller, Brooke AMC, c
Page, Ft. Sill, qb
Preston, MCRD, hb
Kinek, Cherry Point, hb
Hansen, Little Creek, fb

HONORABLE MENTION:

End: Henke, Ft. Ord.
Tackles: Duca, Cherry Point; Feldner, Ft. Hood; Griffis, PhibPac.
Guards: Kapral, Ft. Sam Houston; Cahill, Little Creek.
Centers: Evans, Barstow; Hatcher, PhibPac.
Quarterbacks: Harding, Camp Polk; Kissel, Ft. Belvoir; Brown, Camp Pendleton.
Halfbacks: Goode, El Toro; Carodine, Camp Pendleton.
Fullbacks: Piscuskas, Camp Polk; Mann, Ft. Ord.

91

384

ARMY

United States

ALL-ARMY TEAMS

Selected by the readers of ARMY TIMES

1951

FIRST TEAM:

Andy Hillhouse, Camp Polk, e
Denver Mills, Ft. Eustis, e
Jack Stroud, Ft. Jackson, t
Joe Mlinarich, 2d Armd. Cav., t
Gerald Weatherly, Ft. Sam Houston, g
John Helwig, Ft. Ord, g
Bob McCullough, Camp Breckinridge, c
Nat Taylor, Ft. Campbell, qb
Red Jenkins, Ft. Jackson, hb
George Fisher, 1st Div Arty, hb
Larry Coutre, Camp Breckinridge, fb

SECOND TEAM:

Harry Kina, Nurnberg, e
Joe Zuravleff, MDW, e
Nick Bolkovac, Ft. Jackson, t
Archie Finn, Ft. Knox, t
Ronald Gonier, Ft. Eustis, g
Joe Ethridge, Brooke AMC, g
Pete St. Clair, Indiantown Gap, c
Bob Elliott, 14th Armd. Cav., qb
Wally Triplett, Camp Polk, hb
George Sims, Ft. Ord, hb
Hercules Harris, Ft. Richardson, fb

1952

FIRST TEAM:

Andy Hillhouse, Camp Polk, e
Frank Rascoe, Ft. Sam Houston, e
Bill Pearman, Ft. Belvoir, t
Tom Palmer, Ft. Jackson, t
Ray Romero, Indiantown Gap, g
Chuck Asher, Camp Breckinridge, g
Clayton Tonnemaker, Camp Drake, c
Arnold Galiffa, HSC, Japan, qb
Larry Coutre, Camp Breckinridge, hb
Sammy Reynolds, Ft. Eustis, hb
George Lagorio, Ft. Ord, fb (Most Valuable Player Award)

SECOND TEAM:

Mike Roarke, Indiantown Gap, e
Barry Deetz, Indiantown Gap, e
Jack Stroud, Camp Drake, t
John Helwig, Ft. Ord, t
Ted Daffer, Ft. Eustis, g
Joe Palumbo, Ft. Eustis, g
Les Richter, Camp Cooke, c
Rocco Calvo, Ft. Lee, qb
Randall Clay, Brooke AMC, hb
Dan Washelesky, Camp Polk, hb
Ken Shobe, Ft. Sam Houston, fb

1953

FIRST TEAM:

Leo Sugar, Ft. Lee, e
Bob Langas, Ft. Belvoir, e
Mike McCormick, Ft. Leonard Wood, t
Hal Mitchell, Ft. Lee, t
Ted Daffer, Ft. Eustis, g
Ray Beck, Ft. Jackson, g
George Morris, Ft. Belvoir, c
Ed Soergel, Camp Atterbury, qb
Dave Mann, Ft. Ord, hb
Billy Sanders, Brooke AMC, hb
Ollie Matson, Ft. Ord, fb

SECOND TEAM:

Ralph Thomas, Ft. Bliss, e
Entee Shine, Camp Atterbury, e
Pat Sarnese, Ft. Belvoir, t
Marion Campbell, Ft. Bliss, t
Pat Cannamela, Ft. Ord, g
Rudy Andabaker, Ft. Lee, g
Harry Riley, Ft. Lewis, c
Dan Page, Ft. Sill, qb
Jim Leftwich, Ft. Belvoir, hb
Jim Roshto, Ft. Sill, hb
Billy West, Ft. Sill, fb

THIRD TEAM:

Wayne Martin, Ft. Sill, e
Cliff Livingston, Ft. Ord, e
Benton Bumgarner, Brooke AMC, t
Stan Campbell, Ft. Ord, t
Frank Kapral, Ft. Sam Houston, g
Bill Pearman, Ft. Belvoir, g
Guy Fuller, Brooke AMC, c
Ron Morris, Ft. Lee, qb
Don Pinhey, Ft. Leonard Wood, hb
Burrell Shields, Ft. Monmouth, hb
Duncan McCaulley, Ft. Hood, fb

ABERDEEN PROVING GROUND, MD.

1953

CO. D, 1st TECH TNG BN
Champions, ORTC

Team

Nick Carchidi, lhb, capt   William Firebaugh, lg
Richard King, le   Ervin Easterling, lg
George Black, re   Pasty Deo, rhb
Lester Grossman, rg   Joseph Policastro, qb
Paul Clements, c   Sylvester Simons, fb
Earl Gerdiman, le

ARMY CHEMICAL CENTER, MD.

1953

Ft. Monmouth 6-47
Bolling AFB 2-51
Ft. Meade 13-8

Team

A. Graham, coach   Dan Earich
George Receveur, qb   Ray Starsinic, re
Tony O'Brochta, rt   John Georges, lhb
(All-American)   Al Lightheart, fb
Joe Carr, lg   Aldo Tremonti, rhb
Bob Prout, rg   Bart Polizzotti, g
Don Molino, c   Herb Cook, le
Cliff Parks   Sam Mullins, lt

Team

Clifford Storm, e	Robert Bowen, e
James Trentman, e	Sam Higa, qb
Wallace Busch, e	Elmo Spann, qb
Joseph Nagroski, e	Thomas Crum, hb
John Huling, e	John Davis, g
John Sims, e, e	Harvey Swanger, hb
Manuel Colston, g	Howard Roberts, hb
John Watson, g	Leon Chappel, hb
Gerald Caldwell, g	Anthony Espoza, hb
Dean Dickey, t	Sam Trankito, fb
Darrell Goeden, t	John Bragoli, fb
Robert Black, t	Sonny Richardson, hb
H. Maldonado, t	Leonard Schieble, g
N. Krooachuck, t	Willie Roberson, qb
James Martin, t	Marlon Bullock, c

CAMP DRAKE, JAPAN (BULLDOGS)
1952

FECOM, Army Champions
Far East Inter-Service Champions

Second Major Port 53-0
Naval Beach Gp 38-0
Yokosuka Naval Base 26-12
Tokyo Ord Depot 66-0
Atsugi Flyers, Navy 60-0
Camp Drew 54-0
Tachikawa 36-0
Tokyo AB 23-0

Team

Rex Henry, coach	Buster Humphreys
Johnny Zeiger, fb	Bill Van Hueit, hb
Pete St. Clair, e	Gene Vargas, g
Bob Krestel, fb	Ronnie Nelson, hb
Clint Moorman, g	Cliff Hooper, e
D. Cavalancia, g	Bruno Andrina, e
Bob Forte, hb	Rodney Rust, e
Percy Bean, hb	Verdese Carter, t
Charles Balcifuis, e	T. Marcovecchio, qb
John Hock, t	Paul Luke, e
Frank Ernaga	Don Hinkle, e
John Cassell	Sam George, hb
Howard Hamilton	Shad Garnett, e
Clarence Stevens	Jim Cunningham, e
Cliff Smith	Mike Boyle, g
Pete Rose	Johnny Baffa, hb
C. Tunnemaker, e	Bill Austin, g
Jack Stroud, t	Paul Phipps, e
Mike Macciola, b	Bill Pitts, hb

CAMP KOBE, JAPAN
1953

Camp Fisher 7-0
Camp Nara 7-6
Osaka Medics 26-0
FEAMCOM 9-26
Camp Eta Jima 6-20
Camp Otsu 7-6
Camp Gifu 0-8

Team

William C. Jones, hb	Luther Washington, e
Ellis Rasberry, hb	Fred Irvin, g
Arthur G. Bass, e	Walter L. Dunford, e
Lester R. McNary, fb	Abraham T. Kapana, g
Robert E. Doyle, hb	Charles J. Earley, e
William V. Regan, fb	Robert L. Gantt, e
Ferdinando Bianco, hb	George H. Maginley, e
Eugana N. Kayal, t	James Leiseberg, e
Howard A. Allen, g	Ellsworth Freeman, e
Jack L. Whithead, t	Wilford Godfrey, e
Mearl E. Pitts, t	George S. Jackson, fb
Richard A. Peterson, e	

CAMP TOKYO (BULLDOGS
1953

Army, Central Command Champion
All-Japan Army Tournament
Champions
9W, 2L

Yokohama Engr Depot 0-32
Atsugi Navy 24-0
Camp Drew 26-19
Camp Yokohama 39-0
Tokyo MPs 25-13
Yokosuka Navy 19-28
Tokyo Arsenal 40-7
FEAF Base 28-0
187th Abn Inf Regt 35-0
XVI Corps 20-0
Camp Fisher 6-53

Team

D. Foldberg, coach (All-American)	H. G. Kurtz, fb (CC All-Star Team)
Edwin E. Ball, e	Eugene D. Lorbeck, e
James Battle, g	Paul A. Luke, e
Lawrence Behrens, e	Donald B. Mancini, e
Harold Brown, t	Donald Martin, t
Joe Butler, e	F. R. Mikulsky, hb
Juan Castillo, g	Roland Nelson, hb
Al J. Caruso, qb	Russell K. Nott, g
Junior R. Cole, e	Ferdinando Papia, g
Charles M. Cravey, hb	James Park, t
Craft A. Edmunds, fb	George Pickett, qb
R. B. Fullerton, c	William H. Reetz, t
George R. Greeno, t	Henry Rhodes, e
Gene A. Jones, t	Bob Saye, t
L. A. Juracic, e	Gerald Shanklin, e
J. Kastan, hb (CC All-Star Team)	Thomas Tyson, t
	Theodore Uphoff, hb
Richard Klinczar, fb	Benjamin Woods, e
Raul Kokolus, g	R. Pakulski, mgr

YOKOHAMA ENGINEER DEPOT
1953

Camp Tokyo 0-32
Camp Drew 12-13
Yokosuka Navy 14-21, 19-14
Atsugi Navy 0-61
Camp Yokohama 15-14
Tokyo Arsenal 19-0
Tokyo MPs 26-19

Team

G. Shumard, coach	Lawrence Weiss, g
C. Perkins, asst coach	Harry Cordray, g
B. Burnett, asst ch, mgr	Bob Glavas, qb
	Bobby Young, fb
Author Taylor, hb	Gary Sites, g
George Roby, e	Frank Luderfinger, t
Joe Jordan, e	Mike Rovnak, e
Erwin Grandy, fb	Bernie Kolb, fb
Ray Cancelliere, g	John Reiker, t
James Irving, g	Joe Calgero, t
D. C. West, e	Rick Dickerson, t
J. Dello-Russo, g	Joe Taylor, t
Gennaro Dibiase, e	John Kashner, t
Don Thompson, e	Mike Crawford, t
Frank Chiappone, e	

1ST CAVALRY DIVISION
1953

SPECIAL TROOPS (CAMP CRAWFORD)
3W, 6L, 1T

8th Cav Regt 0-9, 25-18
Camp Chitose Spl Trps 13-12, 6-7

The Forgotten Athletes of the American Forces Far East

Div Arty 15-0, 13-13
5th Cav Regt 6-20, 12-24
7th Cav Regt 7-13, 7-13

Team

J. Schoff, t, coach
H. Hammond, hb
Arthur Takamori, qb
Robert Dittmar, g
Samuel Taylor, hb
Walter Richardson, e
Bobbie Maggard, hb
James Coffery, qb
Lewis Brash, g
Bobbie Moore, hb
Chesley Manock, hb
Walter Madsen, qb
Richard Hermes, hb
Hand Feil, g
Donald Barnhart, fb
Edwin Hayes, e
Kenneth Hansen, e
Leslie Fambrough, fb
Lewis Burden, e
Edwin Hill, g
Staten Webster, hb
Walter Moses, t
James Smith, g
Andrew Emery, c
James Warbington, fb
Thomas Bowers, t
Richard Beisel, c
Charles Darling, e
Alfred Opunui, e
Donald Rasmussen, t
Leo Palmer, t
Kenneth Gibson, t
George Stitzer, g

5th CAVALRY REGIMENT
1953

Camp Crawford Spl Trps 20-6, 24-12
Division Artillery 19-0, 39-12
8th Cavalry Regt 18-12, 35-6
7th Cavalry Regt 20-15, 6-6
Chitose Spl Trps 20-0, 27-13
*Camp Sendai 27-26
Misawa AFB 0-18
* Exhibition Game

XVI Corps Championship Tournament:

Camp Sendai 2-20

Team

Ollie Colvin, qb
Carl Hallo, hb
William Abbot, hb
Kenneth Keil, g
James Green, t
John Distefano, hb
Maurice Thurmond, e
Calvin Humes, hb
Joseph Klein, c
James Lipp, c
William Williams, e
James Banes, g
Thomas Griffith, g
Harry Parker, g
John Suzeitis, g
Mike Walsh, qb
Rudolph Scott, fb
Elmo Ferrari, qb
J. T. Leitaker, t
Robert Dufallo, hb
Ray Melnik, e
Frank Tate, g
Fredrick Keyes, t
Chester Haydka, e
George Holcomb, fb
George Brown, fb
Willie Wilson, t
Ralph Picklesimer, g
Gerald LaMonica, c
H. T. Pryor, coach
R. E. Rech, line coach
Clyde Bond, mgr
Jim Beavers, mgr
Joe Montalto, mgr

7th CAVALRY REGIMENT (GARRY OWENS)
1953

9W, 1L, 1T

Chitose Spl Trps 36-14, 14-13
Div Arty 34-0, 45-0
5th Cav Regt 15-20, 6-6
8th Cav Regt 13-6, 39-6
Crawford Spl Trps 13-7, 13-7
Camp Sendai 6-0

Team

Larry O. White, coach
L. Carotenuto, asst ch
Joseph Scrivano, mgr
Arthur Worthy, lhb
John Alvarez, qb
Andy Martin, qb
A. Southworth, rhb
Leroy Schoenfeld, e
Dan Vilt, lg
William Fanning, fb
Mike Tiscia, le
Herman Fisher, rt
John Nemet, rt
Bo Atkinson, e
Jere McMiller, fb
Henry Holbert, le
Wesley Myers, lt
Isaac Haney, fb
Rod Thoresun, e
Cloyd Easely, re

James Kelly, lhb
Richard Thompson, e
Van Williford, lhb
B. Deragowski, rhb
John Kucharski, rg
Paul Dearth, qb
C. Van Valkenburg, lg
Thomas Birch, e
Charles Selzle, rhb
Bruce Pritchard, lt
Lou Valis, rg, capt
Fontaine Piland, rg
George Rybak, rt
Louis Massay, rt
Alex Gamberine, lg
George Catherman, le
Norm Heisman, rt
C. Anderson, lhb
Sam Livingston, re
William Regner, le

8th CAVALRY REGIMENT
1953

Camp Crawford Spl Trps 9-0, 18-25
5th Cav Regt 12-18, 6-35
7th Cav Regt 6-13, 6-39
Div Arty 28-12, 26-6
Chitose Spl Trps 13-13, 34-6

Team

P. N. Wandishin, re
R. W. Hobbs, fb
W. W. Swenney, le
R. E. Vaccarezza, c
William W. Blake, rt
H. J. Blackmore, qb
Paul B. Gidich, rg
Thurman Childers, qb
Robert J. Jackson, rhb
G. J. Fennemore, rg
C. L. Fletcher, rhb
Leon J. Irvan, rt
George J. Hemelt, lg
D. W. Greenhagen, qb
Robert L. Sanders, lt
Donnell Horton, lt
Jimmie G. Ritter, le
Frank P. Scrivano, c
Louis S. Kuslo, rt
H. G. Michls, lhb
E. A. Grillo, rhb
James W. Salley, lhb
Max Ross, rg
Graham P. Lowe, re
Melvin D. Adams, fb
J. F. Hmurovic, lg
Leroy L. Young, g
R. J. Schutte, lhb
Dean R. Drager, c
Hibbert J. Manley, g
Lennit Ford, Jr., qb
C. M. Gfeller, t
C. W. Yantz, Jr., fb
Orion Hyde, coach

RYUKUS COMMAND
1951
Army All-Star Football Team

John Lapotka, coach
Steve Ray, asst coach
Leslie Turner, mgr
Peters, aid man
Dupree, aid man
Arthur Robinson, t
Jarrod Richardson, t
Algibiades Cooper, t
Floyd F. Craig, t
Joseph Costello, g
Robert Milton, e
Samuel Reynolds, hb
Colie Abney, e
R. Whetsel, hb
Curtiss King, c
Carl Green, g
Philip Rattenni, g
Ernest Moone, e
R. Tonkovich, hb
James Cary, t
Daniel Hall, hb
Arthur Bernard, g
Joseph Williams, g
Norman Means, Jr., t
Max Kebee, hb
Benny Thorn, g
Eugene Thomas, fb
H. Richardson, g
William Bond, hb
Campbell Denley, e
Eugene Selznick, e
Lowell Buis, g
James Gray, qb
George Kauka, g
William Mitchell, hb
Charles Hubbell, e
George Karazia, e
Alvar Gustafsen, t
Lem Wafer, t
Norman Atkins, e
Charles Allen, t
Granville Chadwick, fb
Wallace Harvey, hb

1952
Army All-Star Football Team

Ray Legenza, coach
C. Allen, asst coach, t
Frank Eckhart, mgr
Eugene Selznick, e
Audrey Brown, e
Jake Williams, e
James McGill, e
Merrill Lindsey, e
Norman Means, Jr., t
Daren Senne, t
Lem Wafer, t
William Knudson, t
Lewis Wright, t
James Thompson, t
Richard Gentzel, c
Robert Copeland, t
Gene Cannon, qb
Armond Papajoe, qb
Orville Gunther, hb
Dave Gibson, hb
Leon Carson, hb
Oscar Younger, hb
Willie Murray, hb
William Wallace, hb
Charles Jones, hb
James Napper, hb
Robert Murad, hb
C. L. Ladner, hb

Harvey Richardson, g
Jesse Wooten, g
Richard Simpson, g
Joseph Costella, g
Maurice Packer, g
Ray La Burge, g
Robert Broadus, g
Joe McGill, e
Nick Floratus, e

Darris Alce, fb
Nat Washington, fb
Ernest Monoe, fb
William Bond, fb
Richard Anderson, e
Jack Beasley, mgr
Charles Smith, mgr
Joe Burgess, mgr

1953 All-RYCOM Team

First Team:

John Simas, Service Command, e
Lou Vedova, 29th RCT, e
Al Sensley, 97th AAA, t
Harry Steuber, 29th RCT, t
Bill Schutice, Port Command, g
Don Wiseman, 29th RCT, g
Ernest Edwards, Service Command, c
Jim Malosky, 29th RCT, qb
John Flemming, 29th RCT, hb
Howard Porsey, 29th RCT, hb
Jim McGill, Port Command. fb

Second Team:

John Busby, 29th RCT,
Ken Darrow, Salisbury Sound, e
Ken Ely, 29th RCT, t
Carl Frudley, 97th AAA, t
Frank O'Malley, 97th AAA, g
Russ Hayward, 29th RCT, g
Jim Arwood, 29th RCT, c
H. C. Bloss, Salisbury Sound, qb
Hal Jackson, 97th AAA, hb
Fred Nissel, Port Command, hb
George Van Zant, Service Command, fb

USARPAC (MUSKETEERS)
1953

NAS, Barbers Point, T. H. 6-0
USMC, Pearl Harbor 7-7
US Navy, Pearl Harbor 7-6
Hawaiian 49ers 0-38
USMC, Kaneohe 13-19
Hawaii U. 6-28
Islanders 44-12

Team

S. Swiatek, coach, fb
J. Scholtz, asst ch, t
F. Dower, asst ch, g
LeRoy Albrecht, g
Herman Clark, t
Gordon Lopes, e
Henry Ahlo, qb, hb
Robert Andrade, fb
Martin Blitzer, c
Edward Borden, e
Augustus Dyson, e
Richard Farias, hb
Sherwin Fellesz, hb
Stanley Fonseca, g
Waldimar Doane, e
Albert Forsythe, hb
Valentine Freitas, fb
Richard Gomard, qb
Howard Han, hb
Edmund Ho, hb
Richard Hokomalia, g
Ben Holt, qb
Allen Irvine, t
Ralph Irvine, t

Eric Kalohelani, hb
James Kennu, hb
Moses Kim, g
Sam Keohokapu, c
W. Carnchan, trainer
Gilbert Koga, g
Roy Langley, e
Stanley Lyons, fb
G. McMillan-Gordon, e
Douglas McQuillin, g
Warren Mitchell, e
John Pang, t
Robert Parks, c
Marvin Pounds, c
Larry Price, t
Eddie Rother, c
Roy Ryder, hb
Elmer Solidum, qb
Joseph Thomas, t
Stephen Vierra, t
Al Wills, t
Granville Wright, e
David Yamashiro, hb

NAVY

ALL-SEA SERVICE TEAMS
1953

Selected in a poll conducted by
NAVY TIMES

First Team:

Eugene Schroeder, Great Lakes, e
William Jessup, NTC, San Diego, e
Robert Anderson, Bainbridge, t
Rex Boggan, Camp Lejeune, t (Player of the Year Award)
Ralph Jecha, Great Lakes, g
Al Viola, Quantico, g
Glen Graham, Camp Lejeune, c
William Bonar, Bainbridge, b
J. D. Smith, Pensacola, b
John Petitbon, Quantico, b
Maurice Bassett, PhibPac, b

Second Team:

John LaTorre, Bainbridge, e
Sam Williams, Pensacola, e
Robert Dees, Great Lakes, t
Robert Griffis, PhibPac, t
James Speight, Bainbridge, g
Jack Lordo, MCRD, San Diego, g
John Bergamini, MCRD, San Diego, c
Junior Arterburn, Great Lakes, b
Ralph Huffman, CG, Cape May, b
Ray Smith, Camp Lejeune, b
Charles Hren, Great Lakes, b

Third Team:

Frank McPhee, Quantico, e
Jack Bighead, NAS, San Diego, e
Howard Heinrich, Pensacola, t
John Feltch, Camp Pendleton, t
Phil Joyce, CG, Cape May, g
William Ward, NAS, San Diego, g
Paul Hatcher, PhibPac, c
Ed Brandenburg, Cherry Point, b
Robert Goode, El Toro, b
James LeSane, Bainbridge, b
John Amberg, Quantico, b

Shore Installations

AMPHIBIOUS FORCE, PACIFIC FLEET USN AMPHIBIOUS BASE, CORONADO, CALIF. (PHIB PAC INVADERS)

11th Naval District Champions: Third Place

8W, 2L

1952

Compton College 40-19
El Toro Marines 53-0
MCRD, San Diego 20-39
USC, Freshmen 26-0
NAS, Alameda 47-20

Newton, le
Blackston, fb
Thornborrow, rt
Keene, rhb
Buttorff, lg
Kundick, re
Cartwright, rg
Schappe, le
Perfetti, rhb
Urlage, rg
Miller, e
Wilke, re

Huff, rhb
Stoup, lt
Kopp, lt
Carter, lhb
Hendershot, ie
Weis, rt
Stone, lt
Singleton, re
Gammel, lg
Johnson, iz
Frain, e

NAVAL AMPHIBIOUS FORCE, LITTLE CREEK, VA. (PHIB LANT-GATORS)
1953

NTC, Bainbridge 14-12
NAS, Norfolk (Tars) 26-6
MCAS, Cherry Point 8-7
Ft. Lee 0-15
Bolling AFB 2-20, 13-22
Ft. Eustis 12-20
Parris Island 28-7
Ft. Jackson 13-22
Morris Harvey College 20-0
Ft. Monmouth 14-26

Team

Phil Bucklew, coach
R. W. Meanix, hb
Howard Irvin, hb
Russel Packer, qb
Stuart Tisdale, qb
Frank Branch, qb
James Davis, hb
George Marinkovich, fb
Vern Wynott, hb
Len Toomey, fb
Edwin Spraker, hb
Noel Schmidt, hb
Howard G. Hansen, fb
John Cahill, g
Gerald Klaus, t
John O'Bar, g
Frank Vitale, g
Roy Robbins, e
Clyde Ross, e

Donald Kelley, e
Jack Love, e
John Schneider, e
Robert Jackson, e
Donald McGin'ey, e
Thomas Martin, e
Charles Gaudet, t
Timothy Tamm, t
James Mahoney, t
(Service-All-Star)
William Wallace, t
Vaughnaa Whitmore, e
Charles Daniels, e
Robert Pryor, t
Josh Oldham, g
Jack Wagner, fb
William Pearson, g
Robert Smith, g
Frank Martin, qb

NAVAL AIR STATION, NORFOLK, VA. (NAVY TARS)
1953

Bainbridge 0-46
Ft. Lee 0-39
Ft. Meade 21-0
NAS, Jacksonville 12-9
Little Creek 6-26
Cherry Point 6-24
Ft. Belvoir 0-54
Quonset Point 26-6
NavRecSta, Anacostia 0-19

Team

Doug Mac Lachlen, e
Jack Esslinger, t
(Service All-Stars)
Max Kidd, g
Ed Holden
Don Daniels
Pete Williams
Bob Baxter
Stewart, t

Mixon, e
Don McCauley
Ed Kavanaugh
Ted Bittner
Jim Jennings
Odie Posey
Sileo
Dick Claypool
Harmon

USS PHILIPPINE SEA
1953

12th Naval District League: Third Place

12th ND Comm 49-13
Treasure Island 25-18
NAS, Moffet Field 19-0
NAS, Alameda 19-8
Western Sea Frontier 7-0 (Forfeit)
NAS, Oakland 39-37
NSC, Oakland 32-32
Marines, S. F. 13-20
Naval Hosp., Oakland 60-18
Marines, Port Chicago 40-6
Mare Island 32-52

Team

Dale Know, b
John Waters, b
Bob Thompson, b
Robert Smith, b
Toby Maes, b
Ed Harper, b
Jim Glerum, b
Dale Courtney, b
H. Moore

Ira Reitz
Richard Speese
Ralph Raffield
Warren Helgerson
Linton Doucet
M. Rentz
W. Isberg
B. Lucas
John Felker

USS SALISBURY SOUND
1953
Team

R. Chase, head coach
L. Dean, asst coach
James E. Miles, e, hb
William C. Stapp, e
Wilfred H. Block, t
Minor N. Mosier, t
Paul E. Neff, g
Oscar Turrantine, g
Leon R. Fice, e
William Jinnings, fb
Herman C. Bloss, qb
Albert I. Dodd, hb
Sterling W. Smith, qb
George Hagar, trainer

Jimmie Potts, fb
Gerald F. Burch, e
Kenneth E. Darrow, e
James W. Riley, e
Kenneth Elliott, t
Billy J. Renick, e, t
James C. Taylor, g
Gerald G. Wester, g
Joe L. Snead, e
Calvin Harrison, hb
Charles M. Turner, qb
Keith L. Nixon, bb
Herbert Severns, fb
Floyd L. Karr, mgr

MARINES

ALL-MARINE TEAMS

Selected by the sports editors of Marine service publications in a poll conducted by LEATHERNECK Magazine.

1952

Offensive:
Jim Mutscheller, Quantico, e
Bob Schnelker, Parris Island, e
Tex Lawrence, San Diego, t
Rex Boggan, Parris Island, t
Al Viola, Camp Lejeune, g
Carl Plantholt, Camp Lejeune, g
George Radosevich, Parris Island, c
Sam Vacanti, Parris Island, qb
Billy Mixon, Parris Island, hb
Tom Carodine, San Diego, hb
Bill Hayes, Parris Island, fb
Defensive:
Jerry Elliott, Parris Island, e
Harrison Frasier, Camp Lejeune, e

Art Davis, Camp Lejeune, t
Roscoe Hansen, Parris Island, t
Dick Lashley, Parris Island, g
Gil Bucci, Parris Island, g
Bob Goode, San Diego, lb
Bob Griffin, San Diego, lb
Orville Williams, Camp Lejeune, db
John Idzik, Parris Island, db
Don Scott, Quantico, safety

1953

First Team:
Frank McPhee, Quantico, e
Rex Boggan, Camp Lejeune, t
Al Viola, Quantico, g
Glen Graham, Camp Lejeune, c
Ray Suchy, Camp Pendleton, g
Sam Duca, Cherry Point, t
Nick DeRosa, Cherry Point, e
Ed Brandenburg, Cherry Point, b
John Petitbon, Quantico, b
Bob Goode, El Toro, b
John Amberg, Quantico, b

Second Team:
Willie Roberts, Camp Pendleton, e
Jim Weatherall, Barstow, t
John Maultsby, Camp Lejeune, g
John Bergamini, San Diego, c
Gil Bucci, Parris Island, g
Ken Huxhold, Camp Pendleton, t
Ken MacAfee, Quantico, e
Ed Brown, Camp Pendleton, b
Ray Smith, Camp Lejeune, b
Reggie Lee, Camp Lejeune, b
Bob Meyers, Quantico, b

Honorable Mention:
Eugene Brooks, Cherry Point, e
Bob Trout, Quantico, e
Walt Viellieu, Quantico, t
Phil Muscarello, San Diego, t
Frank Malack, Cherry Point, g
Tom Roggeman, Quantico, g
Gerald Wenzel, Quantico, c
John Fry, Quantico, b
George Kinek, Cherry Point, b
Arnold Burwitz, San Diego, b
Bob Tougas, Camp Pendleton, b

MARINE DEPOT OF SUPPLIES, BARSTOW, CALIF. (BULLDOGS)

1952

George AFB 28-6
TraPac Navy 27-7
MCAS, El Toro 18-0
Camp Pendleton 13-56
Ft. McArthur 46-7
NOTS, Inyokern 32-6
NAMTC, Point Mugu 6-7
PhibPac 0-53
NAS, Alameda 7-12
NS, Long Beach 20-16
Edwards AFB (Desert Bowl Game) 12-9

1953

NAS, Alameda 20-0
MCAS, El Toro 7-18
Edwards AFB 26-6
NOTS, China Lake 37-0
Camp Pendleton 18-40
NS, Long Beach 19-7
Treasure Island 12-14
NAMTC Point Mugu 6-19
NAD Hawthorne 43-0

Team

Brown, qb, asst coach
David English, qb
Edward McKechnie, qb
Michael Serna, qb
Leo P. Steele, qb
Archie W. Brooks, hb
Edward O. Hicks, hb
John Kabeiseman, hb
Dorsey Lightner, hb
George K. C. Pang, hb
Humberto R. Vega, hb
Jack P. Wages, hb
Avery Burton, fb
Charles S. Cannia, fb
Ray Craig, fb
Robert R. Hessler, fb
Calvin O. Randle, fb
Donald W. Town, fb
M. Lissman, head coach
L. Cunningham, trainer
Bill Fischer, mgr
Dean Winchell, mgr

Thomas G. Ellery, e
Lloyd E. Longino, e
Herbert L. Mundy, e
Stanley E. Reed, e
Anthony Wozniak, e
Clifford Brookshier, t
George C. Matulich, t
Peter P. Salopek, t
Frank P. Turner, t
Weatherall, t line coach
(AB-American; All Marine)
Howard L. Evans, g
Lynell C. Clubine, g
Ernest Cunningham, g
Upton B. Henderson, g
Robert F. Salvidio, g
John K. Ferguson, c
Peter J. Omer, c
Evans, c

MCAS, EL TORO, CALIF.

1953

Phib Pac, Coronado 0-27
Barstow (Bulldogs) 18-6
MCRD, San Diego 16-21
Camp Pendleton 7-34
NS, Long Beach 26-0
Ft. Lewis 19-32
Eagle Rock, Los Angeles 6-13
NAS, San Diego 2-33

Team

Robert A. Carew, hb
Robert L. Goode, hb
Thomas L. Larson, g, t
Walter Riebeling, g, t
Jimmie F. Meza, g, t
Joseph J. Barbagallo, e
James L. Ludlow, g
Leslie G. Cates, t
Daniel J. Labat, t
Allen E. Riser, hb
Scipio Spahn, qb, hb
Gene A. Fodge
Rodney V. Hurich, e
Gerbert H. Price, hb
Lionel A. Sigman, fb
R. Watson, coach, t
George A. Murray, t
Charles E. Ramsey, g
Raphael B. Cooke, e, t

Richard A. Morrow, g
Jack K. Robins, e
Gerald R. Sullivan, e
Dean J. Westgaard, hb
John L. Hilton, qb
Richard L. McKee, t
James J. Davis, g, t
D. Fortenberry, g
Jerry J. Kearney, e
Ivan H. Storer, hb
Robert W. Wofford, fb
Buster W. Chancey, e
Sammy Kahalewai, fb
Sammy L. Brown, fb
Robert G. Denton, t
Gary F. Harvey, g
Jerry A. Matney, hb
Frank L. Strocelius, t

MARINE BASE, CAMP PENDLETON, CALIF.

1952

11th Naval District League: Fourth Place
6W, 4L

Ft. Ord 19-39
Camp Cooke 29-11
Luke AFB 40-20

Camp Kilmer 12-0
Zuni AC 13-0
Rider College 6-27
Wildwood Islanders 15-0
NAS, Chincoteague 27-6
U. of Penn Frosh 0-0
Millville AC 12-6
NAS, Atlantic City 19-0

Team

R. Clark, head coach	Wesley West, b
F. Smith, asst coach	Lynn Streiff, b
Robert Connor, b	Gordon Gobel, b
Allison, e	Bob Stelle, b
Gayle Rowe, e	Dick Kennedy, b
Bill Conley, e	John Lombardi, c
Junie Sica, b	Ross Keith, b
Edward Stevens, e	Drummond, g
Reich, t	Shorts, b
Tom Illi, e	Jacoby, e
Vance, e	Ronald Fluegel, g
Vita Clapp, b	Dan Casey, b
Weingarten, g	Don Legg, g
Maynard Wolfe, b	Bill Hawley, t
Foster Campbell, b	Stephen Dalina, t
Richard Novak, c	Bross, e
Fuller, t	Frank Palmisano, g
Fischer, t	Maropis, e
David Thorne, t	Perrin, g
Smith, g	Goldsmith, b
Harry Slaine, b	

1952 ✗ ✗
7W, 1L
Cape May Rockets 6-0
NTC, Bainbridge 0-27
NSD, Bayonne 19-0
NAS, Chincoteague 27-0
NAS, Atlantic City 29-0
Princeton U JV 19-7
USCG Port Securtiy 38-0
Dover AFB 13-0

Team

R. Clark, head coach	Marcus Hill, e
Norman Cariho, b	F. Smith, asst coach
Anthony Diamente, b	Robert Connor, b
Frank Franklin, b	Joseph Dooley, b
Emund Harvey, b	Carl Gimber, b
Donald Mausfield, b	Peter Longo, b
Guy Railey, b	Billy McKinnon, b
Junie Sica, b	Henry Sorelle, b
Arnie Weber, b	Edward Tuton, b
Alfred Adkins, e	Edward Wieland, b
H. M. Sage, e	Charles Ratway, e
Edward Stevens, e	Arnold Stern, e
John Waggoner, e	Donald Transue, e
James Beckett, t	John Wengrocki, e
Stephen Dalina, t	John Coleran, t
James Whiting, t	Donald Econe, t
Frederick Attebury, g	Salvatore Santaniello, t
William Cronks, g	Harold Wilson, t
Charles Offutt, g	Donald Coleman, g
Russell Adams, c	John Gotich, g
William Bischoff, c	Donald Sullivan, g

1953 ✗ ✗
Cape May Rockets (semi-pro) 6-0
Ft. Dix 7-6
Dover AFB 20-7
Ft. Monmouth 0-33
Princeton JV 13-6
NTC, Bainbridge 14-34
NAS, Atlantic City 7-14
Marine Depot, Phila. 14-6

Team

James Andrews, b	Wells, t
Luther Brinson, b	Beck, g

Mathew Carr, qb
John Fini, b
Ralph Hoffman, hb
(All Sea Service)
Donald Larson, b
Raymond Lewis, b
Billy McKinnon, b
Kenneth Morrow, b
Walter Scheidhauer, b
Glenn Schoeneck, b
Loreto Sica, th, co-capt
Guy Tracy, b
Alfred Adkins, e
Wayne DeGraff, e
Thomas Gilmer, e
John Kirby, e
Thomas Schmidt, e
Edward Stevens, e
Donald Warner, e
Maynard, e

William Bartmess, t
Stephen Dalina, t
James Morris, t
James Northrup, t
Orba Puckett, t
Donald Transue, t
Henry Caruso, g
Philip Joyce, g
(All Sea Service)
Eugene Morahan, g
Curtis Neal, g
Charles Offutt, g
Joseph Salter, g
Rodney Wilson, g
William Craver, e
Wallace Gorr, c
W. Van Derveer, c
F. K. Smith, hd coach
R. Connor, asst coach
V. E. Ziegler, trainer

AIR FORCE

United States

ALL-AIR FORCE TEAM

Selected by the readers of
AIR FORCE TIMES

First Team:

Walt Klevay, Bolling AFB, hb
Bill Reichardt, Bolling AFB, fb
Carl Trippeer, Sheppard AFB, qb
Tom Driscoll, Hamilton AFB, e
Dick Brand, Sheppard AFB, e
Joe Moss, Bolling AFB, t
John Myers, Keesler AFB, g
Girard Oliva, Keesler AFB, c
Bob Cunio, Nagoya, g
John Wheat, Hamilton AFB, t
Glenn Lippman, Eglin AFB, hb (Most
  Valuable Player, USAF)

Second Team:

Leo Martin, Bolling AFB, e
Howard Pierson, Nagoya, e
Robert Martin, Sheppard, t
Don King, Itami, t
Herschel Forrester, Hamilton AFB, g
Don Jackson, Westover AFB, g
Alan Clark, Pope AFB, c
Al Dorrow, Bolling AFB, qb
Billy Tidwell, Keesler AFB, hb
Billy Stevenson, Keesler AFB, hb
Buddy DiMott, Sheppard AFB, fb

Honorable Mention:

Jerome Wilson, Westover AFB, e
Charlie Jones, Bolling AFB, e
Jim Glasgow, Sheppard AFB, t
Dick Adams, Eglin AFB, t
Lonnie Williams, Sheppard AFB, g
Lou Mascola, Hamilton AFB, g
Will Alston, Sheppard AFB, c
Ray Graves, Eglin AFB, qb
John Collis, Westover AFB, hb
Merle Myers, Sheppard AFB, hb
Harry Hugasian, Hamilton AFB, fb

BOLLING AFB, WASHINGTON, D. C. (GENERALS)

1953

Army Chemical Center 51-2
Quantico Marines 12-16
Ft. Jackson 26-20
Little Creek 20-2
Camp Lejeune 27-23
Ft. Eustis 0-7
Ft. Lee 7-14
Ft. Belvoir 19-7
Ft. Monmouth 18-0
NTC, Bainbridge 35-7

Team

J. Poloncheck, asst ch
Roger Antaya, coach
W. Klevay, hb (All-AF team)
Leon Carrica, e
A. Dorrow, qb (All-AF, 2d team)
D. Reichardt, fb (All-AF team)
Don Wallace, hb
Dick McGinley, hb
Charles Jones, e
John Ignarski, g
Hugh Jacobs, c
L. Martin, e (All-AF, 2d team)

L. Moss, t (All-AF team)
Joe Dudeck, g, co-capt
Red Lawson, t
Bob Lega, mgr
C. Dorsey, trainer
Bob Allwine, g
John Lindsay, e
Mel Groomes, hb
D. Fucci, qb, asst ch
A. Miketa, c, co-capt
George Christiansen, t
Allen Boyd, fb
Fred James, hb
Ed Nickla, t
Roy Martine, e

EDWARDS AFB, CALIF. (JETS)

1953

Eagle Rock AC 0-39
NOTS, China Lake 39-6
Point Mugu 0-15, 0-29
NAS, San Diego 0-46
Barstow Marines 6-26
Hamilton AFB 6-39
Spartan AC 14-0
Spoiler AC 33-6
Presidio, S. F. 19-40

Team

John Slupski, hb
Chan Johnson
Jerry McCafferty, b
L. Weaver, qb
Bill Craft

Jack Rose
Winston Baber
Charlie Walzer
Bob Robinson

EGLIN AFB, FLORIDA

1953

Marine Corps Air Station 15-0
NAS, Pensacola 7-27
Shaw AFB 13-2
Sewart AFB 34-0
Tyndall AFB 26-0
Jacksonville Navy 33-0
Ft. Benning 35-13
Great Lakes Navy 28-12
Keesler AFB 19-8, 21-62

Team

Ben Burke, t
Duane Johnson, g
Ray Thibault, e
Walter Gary, c

Clarence Logan, e
Walt Taylor, e
Mike Fornaro, hb
Ernest Childs, e

A. J. Baker, e, fb
Fidell Gander, fb
Demus Jones, g
Glenn Lippman, hb
Brad Nashuum, g
Scotty Kobus, hb
Leonard Travis, hb
Roy Dunbar, g
William Wilson, fb
Richard David, qb
Oliver Agramonte, e
Richard Adams, t
Hugh Meyer, e
Quinten Lanho, t
Charles Light, g
Rocco Calabredta, g
Jack Palizay, hb
Art Bischoff, qb
Pasquell Testa, g
Marciano Duron, hb
James Bradford, t
Charlie Nordman, e
David Karr, c
Leroy Fair, e
William Lewis, hb
Joe Peterson, e
Perry Barrington, fb

John Stallings, g
T. Southerland, e
Duane Eliason, e
Harry Banville, hb
M. Cammaraso, hb
Robert Kentner, t
Johnny Miles, e
W. C. Allbritten, qb
Ray Graves, qb
Eddy Michalski, hb
Tom Kingery, t
William Smack, t
M. Popavach, trainer
John Voltz, qb
John Resnick, t
James Walsh, g
Bill Thornton, g
Frank Reyna, t
D. Norris, head coach
B. Marshall, ath dir
J. P. Lappin, asst ath dir
D. Watts, bf coach
Larry Tucker, line ch
R. McBride, e coach
Larry Hummel, line ch

EIELSON AFB, ALASKA

1953

Elmendorf AFB 6-24

Team

J. Rudd, rt
R. Guyer, c
Sam Richen, re
Jack Kaminsky, lt
C. Bushick, rt
Clarence Dulek, g
Bob Maimaron, c
Joe Pranzo, qb
Perry Marsh, rhb
Harry Holstein, fb
D. Dunlap, le
E. Davis, rg

H. Karish, le
A. Lorina, lt
V. Verdura, fb
I. Nesbitt, fb
R. Melchionno, rg
A. Anderson, re
C. White, qb
H. Busky, qb
D. Landerman, lhb
C. Dalton, lhb
M. Banks, rhb

ELLINGTON AFB, TEXAS (FLYERS)

1953

Brooks AMC 0-19
Sheppard AFB 13-34
Ft. Hood 7-35
Alexandria AFB 33-0
SMU, "B" Team 2-27
Goodfellow AFB 7-33

Team

J. J. Cunningham, t
Albert Bass, c
Earl Liberty, g
Travis Simpson, coach
Lloyd Singley, hb
Ernie Frady, rhb
D. G. Graham, e
Don McGivney, hb
J. J. Jones, hb
Roger DeRosans, bf
Willie Perkins, fb
L. D. Wilburn, e
Randolph Hall, g
Thomas Nelson, e
Guido Forte, t
Charles Pittman, fb
James Smith, t
Kay Bernson, qb
Wes Abbey, qb

Bob Hileman, e
Joseph Regan, g
Aldo Bredolo, g
L. H. Newhaus, t, g
K. Cullinan, t
Joseph Yanovich, e
Harrison Epperly, g
C. H. Schoneck, e
Ben Dallas, c
Raymond Hendrix, e
Austin Tredway, hb
Mitchel Stefanski, t
Joe Blackwell, g
B. G. Smith, g
Roger Cramer, t
Joe Ciampa, e
Roger Dersoano, hb
Billy Hall, g

Team

J. J. Finneran, e	D. C. Fanuef, c
Eugene P. Jones, e	Peter D. Zivkovic, c
E. J. London, e	R. T. Atchison, b
Anthony Matich, e	Arthur M. Burgess, b
W. L. Sovitch, e	Eugene K. Cherney, b
William R. Sperry, e	E. Deaki, e
Walter J. Zoia, e	Charles W. Goodson, b
Forrest L. Barclift, t	Wayman Hennessey, b
Alfred Boyer, t	T. C. Kessenich, b
Richard A. Cramer, t	C. M. Lloyd, b
L. A. Jackson, t	R. L. Maynard, b
Clifton Norman, t	J. E. Meador, b
S. N. Thomas, t	Franklin D. Reed, b
P. G. Vaughn, t	E. J. Roloff, b
Eugene J. Bastian, g	Alan E. Smith, b
E. F. Dickerson, g	D. R. Tizenor, b
S. W. Etheridge, g	Henry L. Williams, b
L. Guzzi, g	Thomas E. Yinger, b
Joseph G. Loula, g	Roy M. Terry, coach
W. L. Marshall, g	Thomas Braly, coach
William G. Martin, g	Norman Jones, coach
J. H. Suitt, g	C. R. Rainey, mgr
E. W. Walker, g	J. C. Honsinger, mgr
D. J. Arnold, c	"Wink" Banks, mascot

Japan

FEAF (TORNADOES)
1953

Tachikawa AFB 13-12
Misawa AFB 14-6
Iwakuni AFB 25-6
Johnson AFB 19-6
Yokota 7-26
FEAMCOM 0-12

Team

Frank Miyaki, fb,	Don Hildreth
(Northern Conf. All-	Leon Moss, fb
Star team)	Chas. "Ace" Wagoner
Ed Good	Jack Clark
Jerry Bowe	Charlie Ilianakalea
Chuck Weaver, hb	Paul Arthur
Leon Ingraham, hb	Cunningham

FEAMCOM, JAPAN
(MARAUDERS)
1953

Nagoya 6-14
Johnson 0-21
NS, Yokosuka 20-0
Yokota 19-13
Camp Kobe 27-9
Misawa 13-19
FEAF 12-0
Itazuke 12-34

Team

Carlos Gardea, qb	Rocky Campbell, qb
Fred Britton, e	Sam Petrovich, c
Luke Welch, t	Del Flanigan, g
Nick Fernandez, qb	White
Fred Stephan	Spriggs, g
Ted Carson	Bradley, hb
Grady Covington	Wagoner, hb
Gene Giles	Prennitee, hb
Vince Hogan, coach	Coleman, hb

ASHIYA AFB, JAPAN
(MUSTANGS)
1953
9W, 2L.

Misawa AFB 13-0
Sasebo 28-0

Yokota 29-9
Sendai 22-18
Tachikawa 14-0
Clark 44-6
Nagoya 13-39
Brady 24-0
Iwakuni 27-0
Itami 0-9
Itazuke 27-7

Team

James Austin, e	Don Morgan, e
John Burns, g	Red Patton, qb, bf
Billy Cobb, e	coach
Gordon C. Corsaw, t	Charlie Paul, t
Charles Dismukes, hb	Rick Potash, c
Benny Frias, qb	Orbal Ragland, t
Robert Gerth, t	Grady Rooker, e
Joe Gugliotta, hb	Leo Rusinko, fb
Ken Guyton, e	Vito Russo, t
Ray Harrison, g	James Shoaf, t
Wade Hastings,	Walt Spellman, fb
Columbus Hay, e	Bob Swason, hb
Frank Hunt, hb	Harry Vandagriff, t
John Kimmel, fb	Chet Woodall, t
Robert Klemme, fb	Walt Gregg, line coach
Raleigh Lair, e	L. Weiland, end coach
William Lister, c	Monroe Campbell, g
Paul Lumia, qb	

ITAMI AB, JAPAN
1953

Tachikawa 21-0
Itazuke 20-6
Nagoya 7-19
Ashiya 9-0

Team

Don King, t (All-AF,	Chuck Richardson, g
2d team)	Best
Bill Nash, e	Tremont, qb
Ed Jedrezick, e	Anders, fb
Dick Travegline, hb	

ITAZUKE AFB, JAPAN
(GREENWAVE)
1953

Southern District Tournament Champions (1952)

Southern District Tournament: Fourth Place (1953)

Camp Drew 18-0
Yokota 7-14
Clark Field 23-0
Camp Kokura 24-20
Itami 6-20
Nagoya 13-39
Brady 19-18
Iwakuni 20-18
Ashiya 7-27, 17-14
Johnson 7-14
FEAMCOM 34-12

Team

Dale Nycum, hb	Tom Smith
Raleigh Stapleton	Al Edwards
Luke Grizzaffi, fb	Ted Thomas
Chuck Painter	John Woomer
John Brown	Joe Lobb
Myron Nycom, hb	Don Hendel
Wayne Collins, qb	Tom Kelly
Red Johnson, e	Bill Kushmaul
John Hay	Joe Lawrie

Chuck Jones	Fiore Perra
Don Wallace	J. H. Bowman
Don Araujo	Tom McFee
Tom Jenson, e	Bill Anthony
Jim Flowers	Chuck Mease
Irv Stark	L. Brasseaux
Don Champion	Sid Dowling
Quinten Laahs	Bob Milligan
Chuck Andreason	Ed Lovelace
Chuck Smith	Elmer Burney
Don Leppert	Bob Richards

IWAKUNI AB, JAPAN
(INDIANS)
1953

Johnson AFB 7-26
Eta Jima Army 14-7
FEAF 6-25
Ashiya 0-27
Itazuke 18-20
Nagoya 7-21

Team

Hank Googe, qb	Harley Cooper
Billy Edmonson, e	Jim Morris, coach
Dick Hughes, hb	Hesse, e
Gable Gabourel, hb	Sterling, qb

JOHNSON AB, JAPAN
(GUNNERS)
1953

All-Japan AF Tournament Champions (1952)

Tokyo Arsenal 39-0
Yokosuka 13-0
Iwakuni 26-7
Tachikawa 20-6, 19-0
Brady 25-6
FEAMCOM 21-0
FEAF 6-19
Nagoya 13-39
Misawa 6-6
Itazuke 14-7

Team

Clem Mayhis	Bob Warren, b
Ron Morrison, le	Dan Corral
Albert Sump, qb	Richard Stello, lg
Robert Turrentine, re	Ron Morgan
(Northern Conf. All-	J. Truitt
Star Team)	R. J. Rhinehart
L. Zigler	Ken Reynolds
Dick Micham, b	Gene Accola
John Bow, hb	Roy Aguilar
R. Rosemond, b	L. Colline
P. Flanagan, coach	Ken Ott
Bill Calloway	Dick Sump
Grigs Crawford	W. Elliot
John Reese, e	Bob Loomey
Dick Barnes, rg	Rabe Gunter, rt
"Robbe" Robinson	Norman Bertoia, lt
Sam Bailey	Bill Mears
Pat Kelly	Marv Pollard
John Marks	Jack Elliott
Harry Davis	Herb Puddig, coach
Jack Weir, hb	

MISAWA AB, JAPAN
(THUNDERJETS)
1953

Northern Conference Champions
Yokota 25-9
Tachikawa AFB 18-0

FEAF (Tornadoes) 6-14

Johnson AFB 6-6
FEAMCOM 19-13
Camp Sendai 34-0
Nagoya AB 0-7
Ashiya AB 0-13

Team

John Stuart, qb	Roy Hina, t, g, (NC
George Vest, e	All-Star team, Most
Wilbur Pack, qb	Valuable Player)
Frank Cianiallo, qb	Jack Hudson, b
Larry Turner, t, g	Walt Ackerman, b
Art Escude, le	Don Shetter, fb
Bob Heard, g, lt, (NC	J. B. Battista, coach
All-Star team)	(Sports Writers Ja-
Dale Nelson, g	pan, Coach of Year)
Tom Dragna, c	Fred Horton, b

NAGOYA AB, JAPAN
(COMETS)
1953
13W, 1L
Far East AF Champions
Southern District Champions

FEAMCOM 14-6
Yokota 53-6
Johnson 39-13
Misawa 7-0, 9-6
Camp Gifu 28-0
Ashiya 39-12
Iwakuni 21-7
Itazuke 39-13
Brady 41-6
Tachikawa 20-19
Atsugi Navy 25-7
Rice Bowl:
Itami 19-7
Camp Fisher Marines 13-19

Team

Carter Brown, g	Ronald Sislaine, e
Wilber Hatcher, t	Jack Patterson, rhb
Arthur Langerman, b	Jack Kortien, t
James Yokota, b	James Beck, b
Gary Gustafson, g	Theodore Rodrique, qb
Thomas Dyer, b	John Devenero, g
Bob Cunio, g (All-AF	George McGill, g
All-Star team)	Kenneth Hartung, t
William Deshler, c	Eddie White, e
Arnold Allen, b	Odell Moss, e
Joseph McCary, b	Paul Mirowsky, g
James Jenkins, qb	Gilbert Branson, g
Gene Lowe, e	Tony Lemos, b
Daryl Hurdel, hb	Ernest Robichoad, t
Howard Pierson, e	John Gorman, t
(AF All-Star 2d	Menard Hessing, c
Team)	Lewis Mundy, b
James Savada, c	Robert Williams, b
Albert Werneke, b	Lemuel Cummings, e

TACHIKAWA AFB, JAPAN
(RED DEVILS)
1953

Johnson AFB 20-6
Yokota 32-6
Misawa AFB 0-18
FEAF 12-13
Yokohama Eng Depot 22-0
Brady AFB 33-0
Ashiya AFB 0-14
Itami 0-21
Nagoya AFB 19-20

Team

Ted Chine, fb
Ray Besceglia
Cosmo D'Annzio, fb.
  (Northern Conf. All-
  Star Team)
Phil McCollan
Ace Ostreich, fb

Arnold Bridges
Luno
Koch
Nohavitza
McDaniel, fb
Pope, fb

YOKOTA AFB, JAPAN
(RAIDERS)

1953

5W, 5L

FEAMCOM 13-19
Tokyo Area MPs 13-7
Misawa 9-25
Itazuke 14-7
Tachikawa 6-32
Ashiya 9-29
Nagoya 6-53
FEAF 26-7
Brady 13-12
Johnson 15-14

Team

Howard Pierson, coach
Walt Hightower, t
A. J. Teice, b

Connie Carcia, e
Sammy Simms, hb
Al Heffke, t

Orvid Fields, t
Sam Jones, t (North-
  ern Conf. All-Star
  Team)
T. Stuart, qb (North-
  ern Conf. All-Star
  Team)
Bill Boyle, g
Bill Farley, qb
J. J. Burns, qb
Ken Bassett, fb
Francis Jaeger, fb
Rod Ford, fb
Fred Chambers, hb
Bob Hale, g
Sandy Crawley
John Harwood, hb
Arnold Simmons, hb
Claude Hardin, hb
Joe Pascuzzi, hb
  (Northern Conf.
  All-Star Team)
Jack Weber, hb
Bob Fillemore, b
Harold Wood, hb
Don Messerli, head
  coach
Tony Antonio, g
Steve Calascione, t
Dick Hartman, t
Glenn Lamport, c
Don Lawson, c
Tom Birt, t
Bill Stauffer, e

Ted Hobratschk, e
Sherwood Tutweiler, e
Del Wright, e (North-
  ern Conf. All-Star
  Team)
Bob Thraves, g (North-
  ern Conf. All-Star
  Team)
Lee Holt, g
Jack Jackson, g
Jason Chadwick, g
  (Northern Conf. All-
  Star Team)
John Ortega, e
Dave Flemming, t
Clyde Kauffman, t
Charles Wynn, fb
Addison Swindle, e
Gene Browning, e
William Bond, g
Wilson Fitzpatrick, e
  (Northern Conf. All-
  Star Team)
Ken Vaugh, hb, coach
Leroy Thompson, hb
Ray Schaeffer, g
Ed Webber, hb
Clarence Miller, g
Ken Adams, hb
Carlo Shippa, e (North-
  ern Conf. All-Star
  Team)
Red Smith, coach, mgr
Bob Pauley, coach, mgr

395

BASKETBALL

WORLD-WIDE ALL-STAR TEAM
(ARMED FORCES PRESS SERVICE)
1953

First Team:
Paul Arizan, f, USMC, Quantico
Dick Schnittker, f, Army, Ft. Meade (All-American)
Ed Roman, c, Army, Ft. Eustis (All-American)
Paul Unruh, g, Army, Camp Breckinridge (All-American)
Don Sunderlage, g, Air Force, Chanute AFB (All-American)

Second Team:
Zeke Sinicola, f, Army, Camp Breckinridge
Ray Ragelis, f, Army, Ft. Lee
Carl McNulty, c, Navy, Great Lakes (All-American)
Sam Ranzinon, g, Army, MTC, Korea
Leroy Smith, g, USMC, Camp Lejeune

Honorable Mention:
Arnold Galiffa, HSC, Japan
Kermit Weiske, Indiantown Gap
Ted Shiro, Camp Chaffee
Frank Kuzara, Camp Kilmer
Tom O'Keefe, Ft. Myer
Rip Gish, Quantico
George Dempsey, NTC, Bainbridge
Ernie Barrett, Sandia Base
Sal Scalfani, Albrook AFB
Ron MacGilvray, Ft. Dix
Ron Minson, AmpPac
Ken Murray, Camp Drake
Chuck Stevesky, Sampson AFB
Jim Walsh, Quantico
George Yardley, Los Alamitos

1954

First Team:
Paul Arizin, Quantico, f
Johnny O'Brien, Aberdeen Proving Ground, f
Ernie Beck, NTC, Bainbridge, c
Dick Groat, Ft. Belvoir, g
Bobby Watson, Andrews AFB, g

Second Team:
Bill McCullum, Lockbourne AFB, f
Chuck Stevesky, Sampson AFB, f
Carl McNulty, NTC, Great Lakes, c
Larry Hennessey, Ft. Eustis, g
Richie Regan, Quantico, g

Honorable Mention:
LeRoy Smith, Camp Lejeune
Ray Ragelis, Ft. Lee
Stan Albeck, Ft. Ord
Harry Folk, Yokota AB
Don Byrd, Ft. Belvoir
Eddie O'Brien, Aberdeen Proving Ground

Dick Knostman, Andrews AFB
Jack Clark, Scott AFB
Al Roth, Ft. Monmouth
Ron MacGilvray, Ft. Dix

INTER-SERVICE CHAMPIONSHIP TOURNAMENT
1954
Great Lakes, Ill.

CHAMPIONS: Andrews AFB, D. C.
NTC, Great Lakes, Ill.
  Camp Chaffee 90-84
  Andrews AFB 66-91
Andrews AFB, D. C.
  Quantico 81-77
  Great Lakes 91-66
Camp Chaffee, Ark.
  Great Lakes 84-90
  Quantico 80-89
Quantico Marines, Va.
  Andrews AFB 77-81
  Camp Chaffee 89-80

ARMY

ALL-ARMY CHAMPIONSHIP TOURNAMENT
1950
Ft. Belvoir, Va.

CHAMPIONS: Ft. Knox, Ky., Second Army (1949: Bronke AMC)
SECOND PLACE: Ft. Richardson, Alaska
Second Army (Ft. Knox):
  Alaska 57-38, 56-52
  Fourth Army 54-48
  USFA 53-39
  Fifth Army 68-55
First Army (Ft. Monmouth):
  Third Army 60-59
  Alaska 48-59
  Fifth Army 54-58
Third Army (Ft. Jackson):
  First Army 59-60
  USFA 58-36
Sixth Army (Ft. Lewis):
  Pacific 60-68
Pacific (Schofield Barracks):
  MDW 53-69
  Sixth Army 68-60
Fifth Army (Ft. Riley):
  Far East 50-82
  First Army 58-54
  Second Army 55-68
Alaska (Ft. Richardson):
  Second Army 38-57, 52-56
  Fourth Army 60-45
  MDW 68-55

323

6th Sq, SAC 76-71
7805th AU, OAC 75-63
7895th AU, Orleans 76-70
552d Sig Maint Co 93-46

Team

Tony Marinaro	Walt Rohr
Harold Lewis, g	Elidio Francisco
Eugene R. Cain, g, f	George Aceto
John McNiece, coach	Henry Angelini
Hubert O. Morrow, c	Bob Steahle
Donald B. Buckley, f	Don Schoer
Charles T. Hill, g	

BUSSAC
1953-1954

Champions, Western League

La Rochelle 54-38, 64-44, 61-54, 44-57, 73-63, 61-58
Poitiers 59-55, 76-69, 74-37, 72-66, 55-50, 57-51, 50-55
Bordeaux 66-46, 63-49, 38-49, 76-68, 50-58, 59-47, 44-41, 66-57
Verdun 64-91, 78-93

Team

Gary Herey, coach	Bob Burnley
Gary Linstead, c	Charlie Lampley
Ronald Cisco	

NANCY
1953-1954

Metz 80-76, 81-51
Orleans 73-92, 64-66, 79-73, 60-68
Verdun 42-54, 53-52, 70-72
Seine Area Command 69-82, 75-71, 73-74, 85-89

Team

Walter Moore, rf	Waverly Davis, c
Charles Oglesby, rg	Joe Kennard, g
Bill Bauer, g	William T. Jasper, c
Willie Jones, f	Willie Gary, c
Donald Eaton, rf	Maynard Goare, f
Joe Hessling, lg	

ORLEANS-LOIRE (HAWKS)
1953-1954

10W, 11L

Meuse 41-60, 48-68, 52-55, 49-57
Nancy 92-73, 66-64, 73-79, 68-60
Seine Area Cmd 53-54, 59-60, 79-87, 54-70
Metz 73-45, 73-65, 86-50, 94-67
155th Inf Regt 65-75
172d Inf Regt 70-64, 70-79°
102d Inf Regt 81-64
43d Div Arty 62-61
* Exhibition game.

Fontainebleau Invitational Tournament:

Chateauroux AFB 62-60
Fontainebleau AFB 71-66
102d Inf Regt 46-59, 43-53

Team

Jack Elwell, f	Victor Brewer, c
Thomas Cassidy, f	Benjamin Shevchuck, c
James Chadwick, f	Patrick Salerno, g

William Fuller, f	Herbert Hessler, g
Donald Schulte, f	Bobbie Ward, g
Jack Thompson, f	James Bennetti, g
Willie Holmes, f	Herbert Feitelson, g
Ray Smith, f	Samuel Digiosa, g
Jerome Fredericks, c	Carl Hoeninger, coach

VERDUN-MEUSE (CARDINALS)
1953-1954

Eastern League, ComZ Champions

Orleans 55-52, 57-49, 60-41, 68-48
Nancy 54-42, 52-53, 72-70, 73-71
Seine Area Command 45-50, 70-58, 66-60
Bussac 91-64, 93-78
Metz 90-33, 82-42, 113-48
510th Tk Bn 66-65, 98-96
WACom 62-84, 92-73, 83-86

Team

Don Sparks, g	Tom Spencer
Ben Bratter, c	Fred Niemann, c
Faust, f	Tony Windis, f
Mroz, f	Baliga, f
Jim Melmige, f	Hollingsworth, c

FECOM

CENTRAL COMMAND, JAPAN
Conference Standings
1952-1953

Camp Yokohama Sports Conference Area:

40th AAA Brigade 16-0
NAS, Atsugi 11-5
Yokosuka Naval Base 10-6
Yokohama Engineer Depot 8-8
2d ASB, Camp McGill 7-9
Japan Signal Service Bn 6-10
Camp Yokohama 5-11
Naval Radio Facilities 4-12
2d Major Port 4-12

Camp Tokyo Sports Conference Area:

Camp Drake 16-0
43d Engineer 13-3
Tokyo QMD 12-4
Hq and Sv Company 11-5
Camp Omiya 8-8
Camp Drew 5-11
Tokyo Ordnance Depot 4-12
Fuchu Ordnance Depot 2-14
Tokyo Army Hospital 1-15

1953-1954

40th AAA Brig 18-0
Army Security Agency, Pac 15-3
Fuji Marines 12-6
NS, Yokosuka 11-7
Camp Zama 11-7
NAS, Atsugi 9-9
Tokyo QM Depot 6-12

397

Camp Toyko 5-13
McNair Marines 3-15
Yokohama Engr Depot 0-18

All-Star Team

Jim Iverson, 40th AAA Larry Howard, Camp
Wes Herbst, 40th AAA Zama
Tom Range, Yokosuka Bob Morgan, Atsugi
John Theveny, ASA

1ST CAVALRY DIVISION (CAVALIERS)

1949-1950

Team

Franklin McCall   Vincent D. Pacelli
J. Whittington, asst ch Raymond Rogers
Donald T. Coyle   Del Wilson
Delmer B. Hogue   John H. Grady
Jimmy Hughes   Winton D. Cahall
Doton B. Lewis   Jack W. Lewis
Robert J. Phillips   Harold Leitzel
Eddie Garcia   Donald J. Takacs
Jack Downing, coach

1952-1953

5th Cav Regt 99-67
19th Inf Regt 70-57, 70-39, 64-68
Ft. Monmouth 77-70, 71-78
Ft. Sill 53-73
Camp Drake 81-74, 80-79

Team

Alan Tikotsky, coach   Ed Hale, g
Jerry Tabor, f   Don Welty, f
Al Danielson, f   Al Puz, g
Bill Braksick, f   Downing Boucher, g
Ken Anderson, f   Ralph Blohowiak, c
Joe Smyth, c   Jerry Pierce
Bato Govedarica, g   Jim Welch

SPECIAL TROOPS

1952-1953

FECOM Champions
Hokkaido Sports Conference Champions
XVI Corps Champions
Central Command Tournament Champions

All-Far East Command Tournament:
Okinawa All-Stars 75-53
27th Inf Regt 101-66

Team

Bob Govedarica, g   Edward Hale, g
Jerry Tabor, f   William Braksick, f
Allen Danielson, f   Alfred Puz, f
Ken Anderson, g   Donald Welty, c
Joe Smyth, c   Downing Boucher, f
Ralph Blohowiak, c

382D GENERAL HOSPITAL, JAPAN

1952-1953

Osaka Medical U 80-29
Camp Nara 47-55, 72-70, 52-69, 60-74
Camp Gifu 69-40, 64-38, 67-41
Osaka Army Hospital 70-60, 63-57
Camp Otsu 45-78, 51-73, 56-79
279th GH 81-45, 78-47, 68-40, 50-37
Yokosuka Seahawks 59-69

Camp Kobe 55-77, 54-68
USS Sebig 54-61
Kyoto Army Hospital 73-49, 68-60, 67-53
Camp Otsu B 50-54

Team

Elden Cahoon, c   Richard Arnold, g
Oscar Shoemake, f   Thomas Tarwater, f
Donald Redmond, f   Jack Stewart, f
Dewey Tompkins, g   William McNamee, g
William Domning, g

US ARMY HOSPITAL, 8164TH ARMY UNIT

1952-1953

7W, 4L

279th GH 65-37, 31-35
Yokosuka Seahawks 66-83
561st MP 67-46
Camp Gifu 58-41
79th Engr 60-37, 52-57
327th Recon 83-25
8610th AU 58-56
8249th AU 60-49
382d GH 49-73

Team

G. McCrossan, coach   George Reins, c
Kenneth Stapleton, g   James Fort, g
Clifford Tooley, c   Jack Clements, g
Davon Drake, f   Henry Douma, f
Dale McKee, f   Neal Driskell, f
Jerry Lewis, mgr   William Lowe, g
John Norris, mgr   Francis Delgado, g
Ben Waddell, f

CAMP CHICKAMAUGA, JAPAN

187th AIRBORNE RCT

1953-1954

Kyushu Conference: Third Place

13W, 7L

Sasebo 61-48, 79-63, 58-64, 56-72
Eta Jima 49-92, 39-70, 79-74, 61-84
Wood 64-56, 78-33, 73-47, 75-61
Kokura 85-61, 82-63, 75-64, 64-57
Hakata 64-72, 73-56, 84-67, 58-65

CAMP DRAKE (BULLDOGS)

1952-1953

30W, 3L

FEAMCOM 97-83
Army Security Agency 73-50, 76-57
Staff Bn 38-27
71st Sig 64-36
40th AAA 83-74, 68-57, 72-83, 95-72
Camp Omiya Hosp 73-58, 82-51
Camp Drew 77-50, 81-37
TQMD 72-40, 91-52
HSC 78-56, 77-39
43d Engr Constr Bn 65-50, 91-59
TOD 89-41, 69-41
Eta Jima 90-61
Yokosuka 82-70
Fuchu Ord 78-47, 105-47

QUARTERMASTER DEPOT, TOKYO, JAPAN

1951-1952

Team

N. deCoreau, coach
Lawrence Williams, f
John C. Spates, g
Charles Gulley, f
Verdell Jones, f
William Brown, c

Johnny Uhles, g
James Colston, g
John Steer, f
Reggie Coldren, g
Billy Mullins, f

1952-1953

Tokyo Ordnance Depot 70-67
Camp Drake 40-72, 52-91
Nagoya Comets 46-69
Fuchu Ordnance Depot 76-47
Headquarters Service Cmd 56-52

Team

Norbert deCoreau, g
Dre E. Alberts, g
Paul M. Legg, f
Bob L. Holmes, c
Myron D. Pepper, g
S. Schwartz

Lawrence Williams, f
Paul M. Greenblatt, f
Robert G. Murtha, c
George Rodems, Jr., g
D. Scharfenberg, f
A. Weissman, coach

JAPAN MEDICAL DEPOT

1953-1954

Camp Drew League Champions
All-Japan Medical Invitational
Tournament: Third Place
10W, 0L

Team

Lawrence Collins, f
(All-Star Team)
Bernard Warning, c
Lowell Prescott, g
Ernest Nanamkin, g
Robert Schneider, c
Edward F. Watkins, f
Donald Dockerill, g

Louis A. Cesario, f
Ronald A. Newcomer, f
William J. Hooper, f
Robert E. Dyer, g
Marcus Calderilla, g
Charles Nickelson, f
Wilmer M. Britt, coach
George Kennedy, OIC

RYUKUS COMMAND

1950-1951

Interservice Champions

Team

Jimmie P. Scheafer, g
Dennis J. Boyle, g
Carl W. Kinder, f
Jack E. Segar, g
Thomas J. Ulrich, f
Russell J. Moses, c
John M. James, f
Bernard Heinrich, f
Carl Ramsey, f

William L. Scott, f
Henry J. Kremidas, f
Duane D. Earl, g
Raymond Jones, Jr., g
Donald R. Zwolinski, c
Robert C. McCulloh, f
Calvin L. Henderson, c
Gerald L. Hepke, f
Joseph Schneider, coach

1951-1952

Team

Rudy Miner, f
Manuel Perez, g
Eugene Selznick, g

Eddie Noble, c
Robert Weidweld, g
Richard Whetsel, f

Louie Thimes, f
Earnest Moone, c
Sylvester Simms, f
Cyprian Reid, g
Richard Cooke, g

John James, f
Dewitt Driver, f
Robert Biggers, g
Toshie Sano, g
Joseph Schneider, coach

1952-1953

Inter-Service Champions

Team

Robert B. Leibe, g
Elmer R. Mabry, f
Samuel M. Clement, g
Eugene A. Nelson, f
Ray Schwind, g
Milton W. Dow, g
Edward P. Marsh, g
Robert Peters, g

Vincent Ionadi, c
Arthur Morales, f
Richard D. Halpin, f
Carl W. Olsen, f
Sylvester Simms, f
Richard Packer, f
Earnest T. Moone, c
John E. Verby, coach

OKINAWA ALL-STARS

1952-1953

Ryukus Command Champions
Inter-Service Tournament Champions

All-Far East Command Tournament:
27th Inf Regt 75-69, 71-73
Camp Chitose 53-75

Team

Bob Leibe
Bob Peters
Carl Olson

Ray Schwind
Art Morales

Korea

7TH INFANTRY DIVISION

1953-1954

73d TANK BATTALION
Special Troops Tournament Champions

Team

George W. Smith, c
Verdon Lovelace, g
Gilmer L. Greene, g
Donald R. Miller, f
Edwards Andrews, f
Ronald G. Cobleigh, g

W. H. Harris, g
Norman E. Miser, g
Harold R. Moeller, c
Martini Surafian, c
George J. Gachler, f
Owen B. Vice, f

24TH INFANTRY DIVISION

1950-1951

27th INF REGT (WOLFHOUNDS)

Team

Donald Hickman, coach
Len Chaires
Ken Ruddy
Conrad Fishul
Ralph E. Kuhe
Charles Smith
Floyd Cockrell
Clifford Anderson

Douglas Born
William Newman
Albert Cole
Donald Wheeler
Glenn Whitney
Jack Bird
James Walker

399

1952-1953
IX Corps Champions
Eighth Army Champions
All-Korea Tournament Champions
All-Far East Command Tournament:
Okinawa All-Stars 69-75, 73-71
Camp Chitose 66-101

Team

Amburs Horn	Maxie Smith
Marvin Bowlings	Mickey Miller
Terry Simmons	Percy Mack
Sam Clement	Thomas Dee
Milt Highberger	Earl Clark
Ed Wilking	Richard Wojeiechowski
Ross Hughes	

1953-1954
24th Inf Div Champions
Eighth Army Champions
All-Korea Tournament Champions

Team

Sidney Oper, coach	Thomas Dee, g
Terry Simmons, g	Marvin Bowling, f, c
Amburs Horn, c	Milton Highberger, f
Ed Wilking, g	Earl Clark, c
Maxie Smith, g	Ross Hughes, g
Mickey Miller, g	R. Wojeiechowski, f
Percy Mack, f	

31ST INFANTRY REGIMENT
1953-1954
I COMPANY
Regimental Tournament Champions

Team

Virgil L. Moore, g	Donald Sebkowicz, f
Augustus T. Young, g	Steven R. Morse, g
Leo P. Latulipe, g	Ralph L. Snyder, f
Ralph B. Braun, f	Jack R. Steck, f
W. Brannon, c, capt	Lehman Wall, g
Verrel T. Lemen, g	Curtis E. Smith, f

45TH INFANTRY DIVISION
1953-1954
ALL-STAR TEAM

First Team:
Frank Booth, c, 180th Inf Regt
Jerry Robzen, rf, 279th Inf Regt
Marty Donahue, lg, 279th Inf Regt
Johnny Alcorn, lf, 279th Inf Regt
Richie Noonan, rg, 180th Inf Regt

Second Team:
Bob Clarke, c, 175th Inf Regt
Bill Crull, f, Division Artillery
Joe Jackson, f, 179th Inf Regt
Ray Villalobas, g, 279th Inf Regt
Adolph Pugliese, g, 180th Inf Regt

1953-1954
279th INFANTRY REGIMENT
45th Infantry Division Champions

Team

Jerry Robzen, c	Glen Eveland, g
Raymond Villalobas, g	Henry Jonker, f
Robert Newman, c	Robert Doyle, f
James Ray, f	Vernie Reaves, f
Raymond Jones, f	Amos Trapauzano, g
Paul Abrausun, g	

NAVY
ALL-NAVY CHAMPIONSHIP TOURNAMENT
1954
Champions: NTC, Great Lakes, Ill.
NTC, Great Lakes—PhibPac 91-74, 91-84

ATLANTIC FLEET TOURNAMENT
1954
Norfolk, Va.
CHAMPIONS: ServLant, Norfolk, Va.

ServLant:
DesLant 84-93, 78-70
PhibLant 84-78
CinCLant 102-74
AirLant 82-80

DesLant:
ServLant 93-84, 70-78
PhibLant 107-103
AirLant 66-71, 119-76
CinCLant 114-64
FMFLant 99-91

CinCLant:
ServLant 74-102
DesLant 64-114

PhibLant:
FMFLant 102-85
ServLant 78-84
DesLant 103-107
MinLant 73-67
BatCruLant 89-68

MinLant:
PhibLant 67-73
SubLant 69-66
FMFLant 78-111

AirLant:
DesLant 71-66, 76-119
ServLant 80-82

BatCruLant:
SubLant 79-58
PhibLant 68-89
FMFLant 94-110

SubLant:
BatCruLant 58-79
MinLant 66-69

FMFLant:
PhibLant 85-102
MinLant 111-78
BatCruLant 110-94
DesLant 91-99

ATLANTIC SUBMARINE FORCE TOURNAMENT
1953-1954
NEW LONDON, CONN.
CHAMPIONS: New London Ashore
New London Ashore (Raiders):
New London Afloat 63-52, 73-50

400

CONCLUSION

It has been a pleasure and an honor, but sometimes a frustration, attempting to reconstruct events and programs which existed many decades ago. The frustration arises from information gaps, where I would get tantalizingly close to a full picture of the past in some cases, less so in other cases. But complete record retention seems to be more of a modern concept, and many of the primarily paper records of the past have been lost to time, or are simply not reasonably traceable. Every trove of records, from many different locations and sources, generally had only a small percentage of relevant information. But I'm grateful for what I found.

Someone may read this and remember that a relative or friend had a closet full of documents, photos, game programs, memories, and the like – this might merit an updated edition someday - we'll see!

The chronological military memos/communiques and other evidence from contemporaneous documentation of the mid-1950s Far East Service Sports programs is a window on a world in which military men, some plausibly Korean War combat veterans, served with honor and dignity in a faraway place.

We sometimes forget how young these men were when serving; in those days it would not have been unreasonable to imagine that many had never previously been outside of their state of birth, or almost certainly not outside of the Continental United States (CONUS), yet they suddenly found themselves immersed in a foreign land that had, perhaps to them, unusual customs and culture.

Despite challenges, U.S. Military service members seemed to adapt well - thrived, even. Many took skills honed in Korea, Japan and Okinawa back to the United States and applied those skills to college study, college or pro sports, or in fields of business, medicine, or commerce.

This is a story of sports and military intertwined, but at the same time it's a story of courtesy, integrity, perseverance, self-control, and indomitable spirit. These men were, maybe not coincidentally, a continuation of the "Greatest Generation," and for that we are forever grateful.

APPENDIX

PUBLIC LAW 11 DOCUMENTATION

69 STAT.]   PUBLIC LAW 11—MAR. 14, 1955   11

SEC. 4. (a) Section 601 (a) of the Legislative Reorganization Act of 1946, as amended, is amended to read as follows: 60 Stat. 850. 2 USC 31.
"(a) The compensation of Senators, Representatives in Congress, Delegates from the Territories, and the Resident Commissioner from Puerto Rico shall be at the rate of $22,500 per annum each; and the compensation of the Speaker of the House of Representatives shall be at the rate of $35,000 per annum."
(b) Section 601 (b) of the Legislative Reorganization Act of 1946, as amended (relative to expense allowances of Members of Congress), is hereby repealed.   Repeal. 2 USC 31a.
(c) Section 104 of title 3 of the United States Code (relating to the compensation of the Vice President) is amended by striking out "$30,000" and substituting therefor "$35,000".   63 Stat. 4.
SEC. 5. The provisions of this Act shall take effect on March 1, 1955.   Effective date.
Approved March 2, 1955.

Public Law 10   CHAPTER 10
JOINT RESOLUTION   March 11, 1955
To amend the National Housing Act, as amended.   [S. J. Res. 42]

Resolved by the Senate and House of Representatives of the United States of America in Congress assembled, That section 217 of the National Housing Act, as amended, is hereby amended by striking out "$1,500,000,000, except that with the approval of the President such aggregate amount may be increased by not to exceed $500,000,000" and inserting in lieu thereof "$3,500,000,000".   FHA mortgage insurance. 68 Stat. 596. 12 USC 1715h.
Approved March 11, 1955.

Public Law 11   CHAPTER 11
AN ACT   March 14, 1955
To authorize personnel of the Armed Forces to train for, attend, and participate in the Second Pan-American Games, the Seventh Olympic Winter Games, Games of the XVI Olympiad, future Pan-American Games and Olympic Games, and certain other international amateur sports competitions, and for other purposes.   [S. 829]

Be it enacted by the Senate and House of Representatives of the United States of America in Congress assembled, That the Act of July 1, 1947 (Public Law 159, Eightieth Congress; 61 Stat. 243), is hereby amended to read as follows: "That as used in this Act, the term 'Secretary' means the Secretary of Defense, and, with respect to the Coast Guard when it is not operating as a part of the Navy, the Secretary of the Treasury, as the case may be.   Armed Forces. Participation in Olympic Games, etc.
"SEC. 2. (a) The Secretary concerned is authorized (1) to permit personnel of the Armed Forces to train for, attend, and participate in the Second Pan-American Games, the Seventh Olympic Winter Games, the Games of the XVI Olympiad, future Pan-American Games and Olympic Games, and (2) subject to the limitation contained in subsection (b) herein, to permit personnel of the Armed Forces to train for, attend, and participate in other international amateur sports competition not specified in (1) above, if the Secretary of State determines that the interests of the United States will be served by participation therein.
"(b) The Secretary of Defense shall, not later than thirty days prior to the commitment of personnel pursuant to the authority contained in subsection (a) (2) hereof, furnish to the Committees on Armed   Report to Congress.

Services of the Senate and the House of Representatives a report
setting forth the details of the proposed participation by personnel of
the Armed Forces in international amateur sports competition.

Funds and equipment.

"(c) Subject to the limitations contained in section 3 of this Act,
the Secretary concerned may spend such funds and acquire and utilize
such supplies, materiel, and equipment as he determines to be necessary
to provide training of personnel of the Armed Forces for such games,
to provide for their attendance at and participation in such games,
and for training of animals of the Armed Forces for, and their
attendance at and participation in, such games.

"SEC. 3. (a) There may be expended, for the participation of members of the Army, Navy, Air Force, and Marine Corps in the activities
covered by this Act, not more than $800,000 during each four-year
period beginning on the date of enactment of this Act, to be apportioned among the military departments as prescribed by the Secretary
of Defense.

"(b) There may be expended, for the participation of members of
the Coast Guard in the activities covered by this Act, not more than
$100,000 during each four-year period beginning on the date of
enactment of this Act.

"(c) Appropriations available to the Department of Defense and
the Department of the Treasury, as the case may be, may be utilized
to carry out the purposes of this Act.

Allowances.

"SEC. 4. Nothing in this Act shall authorize the payment of allowances at rates in excess of those fixed for participation in other military
or naval activities.

"SEC. 5. Notwithstanding any other provision of law, (a) no member
of the uniformed services shall be entitled to the travel or transportation allowances authorized by section 303 of the Career Compensation

63 Stat. 813.
37 USC 253.

Act of 1949, as amended, for any period during which his expenses for
travel or transportation are being paid by the agency sponsoring his
participation in the games and competitions authorized by this Act,
and (b) no member of the uniformed services without dependents shall
be entitled to receive the basic allowances for subsistence and quarters
authorized by sections 301 and 302 of the Career Compensation Act

37 USC 251, 252.

of 1949, as amended, for any period during which such member is
subsisted and quartered by the agency sponsoring his participation
in the games and competitions as authorized by this Act."
Approved March 14, 1955.

Public Law 12   CHAPTER 12

March 16, 1955
[H. 476]

AN ACT
Relating to the regulation of nets in Alaska waters.

Alaska.
Regulation of
nets.

Be it enacted by the Senate and House of Representatives of the
United States of America in Congress assembled, That the last sentence
of section 3 of the Act entitled "An Act for the protection and regulation of the fisheries of Alaska", approved June 26, 1906, as amended

48 Stat. 595.

(48 U. S. C., sec. 233), is hereby amended to read as follows: "It shall
be unlawful to lay or set any seine or net of any kind within one
hundred yards of any other seine, net, or other fishing appliance which
is being or which has been laid or set in any of the waters of Alaska, or
to drive or to construct any trap or any other fixed fishing appliance,
except a set gill net, stake gill net, or anchored gill net, within six
hundred yards laterally or within one hundred yards endwise of any
other trap or fixed fishing appliance."
Approved March 16, 1955.

SELECT DECLASSIFIED MILITARY MEMO SUPPORT

AFFE/8A SPORTS TOURNAMENTS

HEADQUARTERS
UNITED STATES ARMY FORCES, FAR EAST
and
EIGHTH UNITED STATES ARMY
APO 343

AG 353.8 SS-RX   11 December 1954

SUBJECT: AFFE/8A Sports Tournaments

90 COPIES
REC'D 9
ACTION SS

TO: Commanding General, Eighth U.S. Army Fwd, APO 301
        Commanding General, Korean Communications Zone, APO 234
        Commanding General, IX Corps, APO 14
        Commanding General, Ryukyus Command, APO 331
        Commanding General, 24th Infantry Division, APO 24
        Commanding Officer, Camp Zama, APO 343

        1. References: a. Department of the Army Circular 123, 28 October
1954, subject: "1955 Program of All Army Sports Championships."

        b. Letter, AG 353.8 SS-RX, AFFE, 5 October 1954, subject: "AFFE
Sports Program."

        2. Inclosure 1 hereto lists AFFE/8A Sports Tournaments scheduled for
the calendar year of 1955. Inclosures 2, 3, 4, and 5 establish the policies
and procedures by which the applicable sports events will be conducted
through 31 December 1955.

        BY COMMAND OF GENERAL TAYLOR:

                                        LEO KLEIMAN
5 Incl   Lt Col, AGC
  1. Schedule of Events   Asst AG
  2. Rules and Regulations
  3. Administrative details
  4. Flag Football Rules
  5. Hand Grenade Throw Rules

AFFE/8A SPORTS TOURNAMENTS

Schedule of Events

SPORTS	LOCATION	HOST COMMAND	DATES 1955
Skiing	Cp Crawford	IX Corps	15-20 Feb
Bowling	Cp Yokohama	IX Corps	1-4 Mar
Basketball	Cp Otsu	24th Inf Div	8-12 Mar
Boxing	Cp Yokohama	IX Corps	16-20 Mar
Track & Field & Triathlon	Cp Gifu	24th Inf Div	28-30 May
Golf & Tennis	Cp Zama & Yokohama	IX Corps	6-10 Jul
Swimming & Diving	Cp Nara	24th Inf Div	7-9 Jul
Softball	Cp Drake	IX Corps	10-14 Aug
Baseball	Cp Drake	IX Corps	1-5 Sep
Volleyball	Ft Buckner	Ryukyus Comd	12-16 Oct
Small Games	Cp Zama	IX Corps	19-22 Oct
Flag-Football	Ft Buckner	Ryukyus Comd	7-10 Dec

Incl # 1

AFFE/8A SPORTS TOURNAMENTS

Rules and Regulations

1. General:

a. All rules and procedures stated in paragraph 9, letter, AG 353.8 SS-RX, Hq AFFE, 5 October 1954, subject: "United States Army Forces, Far East, Sports Program," will apply where applicable except that at the discretion of the addressee commands, teams in basketball, baseball, softball, and volleyball may exceed the maximum levels of competition established in paragraph 9d (1) and (2).

b. Personnel of other services, on active duty for periods in excess of 90 days, who are assigned or attached to Army elements may participate as members of Army teams at all levels of competition provided that the parent service of individuals concerned will permit said individuals to compete in All-Army Championships in the CONUS.

c. Addressee commands may enter one team each, with the exception of IX Corps which will be permitted to enter one team from the Northern Honshu Sports Conference and one team from the Tokyo-Yokohama Area Conference, in each of the AFFE/8A Championship Tournaments.

2. Skiing:

a. Teams may consist of any number of skiers not to exceed a total of fifteen men per team, including an officer-in-charge, a coach, and a trainer.

b. The composition of teams may be determined by individual selection or by preliminary competitions, whichever is considered most practicable by commanders concerned.

c. Individual and/or team competition will be conducted in the following events:

    (1) Downhill

    (2) Slalom

    (3) Cross Country

    (4) Jumping

    (5) Military Cross Country

d. In order that commands may qualify for the Team Championship Trophy, a minimum of four contestants must compete and finish in each of the first four events listed above. Each command must also enter and finish one

Military Cross Country Team to qualify for the Team Championship Trophy. Each command may enter a maximum of eight contestants in each of the first four events listed above; however, only the top four contestants in each command will count for the team championship. The Military Cross Country event is a team event; each team will consist of six men and each command may enter a maximum of two teams in this event.

      e. The Commanding General, host command, will appoint a Rules Committee composed of one representative from each team. Chairman of this committee will be from the host command. The Rules Committee will be responsible for:

        (1) Establishing within the limitations of the Official National Ski Association of America Rules, the procedures, regulations and rules for the conduct of the tournament.

        (2) Resolving all protests.

      f. The team championship will be determined by the following scoring for each of the five events: the aggregate sum of the four top contestants' times (or scores for jumping) or team time for Military Cross Country for each team will be determined. The team with the best aggregate time will receive 100 points. Each other team's score will be determined by dividing its aggregate time into the aggregate time of the winning team, thus computing the percentage of points it will receive. The total points received by each team for the five events will be combined to determine the team championship.

      g. Each event will be run on consecutive days, weather permitting, in the following order:

            1st day-Cross Country

            2nd day-Down Hill

            3rd day-Slalom

            4th day-Military Cross Country

            5th day-Jumping

DECLASSIFIED
Authority NND 994029

     h. Ski equipment for both practice and tournament competition will be provided by the command entering a representative team or the individual.

     i. Awards will be presented the championship and runner-up teams. First, second, and third place winners in each of the first four events listed in paragraph 2d above will receive individual awards. Each individual of the first, second, and third place teams will receive awards in the Military Cross Country event.

-2-

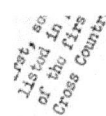

3. Bowling:

    a. Teams will not exceed six men, to include an officer-in-charge, or noncommissioned officer-in-charge. In the event an officer is not a member of the team, an officer can be selected to assume the responsiblities of OIC.

    b. Current American Bowling Congress Rules will govern conduct of the tournament.

    c. Each team will not exceed six men (five-man team with one alternate) all of whom are eligible to compete in all events.

        (1) Team entries (Maximum of one five-man team with one alternate)

        (2) Doubles entries (Maximum of three two-man teams)

        (3) Singles entries (Maximum of six individuals)

    d. The following champions will be determined:

        (1) Five-man team (High score total of nine game total pins)

        (2) Doubles (High score total of three games total pins)

        (3) Singles (High score total of three games total pins)

        (4) Individual All Events (Individual high score of fifteen games)

    e. Trophies will be awarded to the winning and runner-up teams. Individual awards will be presented to the winner and runner-up in each of the four events listed above. Also one trophy will be awarded for the individual high game.

4. Basketball:

    a. The basketball team entered may be a regimental level team or a team selected from a combination of units and organizations with a strength not exceeding 25,000.

    b. Squads will not exceed twelve men to include a coach plus an officer-in-charge. Total thirteen.

    c. The tournament will be a double elimination type.

    d. 1955 Official NCAA Basketball Rules will govern conduct of the tournament.

    e. Trophies will be presented the champion and runner-up teams. Individual awards will be presented to the members of the champion and runner-up teams.

-3-

409

5. Boxing:

a. Squads will not exceed thirteen men, to include one entry in each of ten weight classes, a coach, a trainer, and an officer-in-charge.

b. Participants must meet the qualifications of an amateur as set forth in paragraph 3, AR 680-30. Professional boxers are not eligible to participate in this tournament or preliminary tournaments. All boxers must present a sworn certificate made in the presence of an officer authorized to administer oaths, stating that the participant is an amateur in good standing.

c. Competition will be held in the following weight classes:

(1)	Flyweight	112 lbs
(2)	Bantamweight	119 lbs
(3)	Featherweight	125 lbs
(4)	Lightweight	132 lbs
(5)	Light Welterweight	139 lbs
(6)	Welterweight	147 lbs
(7)	Light Middleweight	156 lbs
(8)	Middleweight	165 lbs
(9)	Light Heavyweight	178 lbs
(10)	Heavyweight	over 178 lbs

DECLASSIFIED
Authority _NND 994029_

d. The championships will be conducted under the 1955 Official Boxing Rules of the Amateur Athletic Union of the United States, except where deviations are stated herein.

(1) Drawings will be made by the tournament committee in the presence of team managers. No contestant will be seeded.

(2) All bouts will be three rounds of three minutes each. At the end of each bout, a winner must be named in accordance with AAU rules.

(3) Each contestant will be examined by a medical officer at the weigh-in on each day when he participates.

-4-

(4) Participating commands will provide boxing trunks, robes, shoes, competitive head guards, foul-proof cup protectors and tooth protectors. All contestants will be required to wear competitive head guards, foul-proof cup protectors, and tooth protectors.

(5) Three judges and one referee will work each bout.

c. The championship and runner-up teams, as well as the individual champion and runner-up. in each weight class, will receive awards.

6. Track and Field:

a. Squads will not exceed nineteen men to include a coach plus an officer-in-charge.

b. 1955 AAU Track and Field Guide Rules will govern conduct of the tournament.

c. Each team competing may enter a maximum of three men in each individual event. Only one relay team may be entered by each team. An individual competitor may enter a total of five events.

d. The order of events will be as follows:

First Day: Event #1 - 10,000 Meter - Finals

"   #2 - Hammer Throw - Finals

Second Day   Event #1 - Shot Put - Trials

"   #2 - High Jump - Finals

"   #3 - Broad Jump - Trials and Finals

"   #4 - 400 meter Hurdles (3ft) - Trials

"   #5 - 100 meter - Trials

"   #6 - 400 meter - Trials

"   #7 - 110 meter High Hurdles - Trials

"   #8 - Broad Jump - Trials and Finals

"   #9 - Discus - Trials

"   #10 - 200 meter - Trials

-5-

Event #11 - 200 meter Low Hurdles - Trials

" #12 - 3000 meter Steeplechase - Finals

" #13 - 800 meter Relay - Finals

Third Day: Event # 1 - 800 meter - Finals

" # 2 - Shot Put - Finals

" # 3 - Pole Vault - Finals

" # 4 - Javelin - Finals

" # 5 - 100 meter - Finals

" # 6 - 400 meter - Finals

" # 7 - 110 meter High Hurdles - Finals

" # 8 - Hop, Step, Jump - Finals

" # 9 - 400 meter Hurdles (3ft) - Finals

" #10 - 1500 meter - Finals

" #11 - Discus - Finals

" #12 - 200 meter - Finals

" #13 - 200 meter Low Hurdles - Finals

" #14 - 5000 meter - Finals

" #15 - 400 meter Relay - Finals

" #16 - 1600 meter Relay - Finals

c. Scoring will be as follows for all events:

Individuals	Relays
(1) 1st place - 5 points	10
(2) 2nd place - 3 points	6
(3) 3rd place - 2 points	4
(4) 4th place - 1 point	2

-6-

412

f. Trophies: The championship and runner-up teams will receive appropriate awards. The individual first, second, and third place winners in each event will receive awards; only the individual members of the relay champions will receive awards.

7. Triathlon:

    a. Teams entered will not exceed three participants.

    b. The order of events will be as follows:

        First Day – Swimming competition

        Second Day (morning) – pistol shooting; (afternoon) – running

    c. Rules to govern Triathlon competitions:

        (1) Swimming.

            (a) Course: 200 meters with free style stroke.

            (b) Rules: 1954 AAU Swimming Rules, except that each swimmer in each heat will be timed. No finals will be held, but places will be determined on a time basis.

            (c) Scoring: The competitor's time will be translated into a numerical score in accordance with paragraph d below.

        (2) Pistol shooting:

            (a) Course of fire:

Range	Type fire	Time each five-shot string	Nr of strings	Targets
25 yards	Timed	40 seconds	4	25 yards standard American

            (b) Weapons: The service pistol, automatic or revolver, caliber .45, with sights and stock as issued.

            (c) Ammunition: Full charge ball cartridge ammunition manufactured by the Government for use in service arms or the commerical equivalent.

            (d) Rules to govern: Paragraph 109, FM 23-35, except that coaching is prohibited and that all devices or equipment which may facilitate shooting and which are not mentioned in these rules and regulations are forbidden. The chief range officer (referee) has the authority to make final rulings on any equipment or device.

(e) Ready position: Competitors will take standing position immediately to the right of their numbered firing point markers and immediately to the rear of the designated firing line. No portion of the shooter's body may rest upon or touch the ground in advance of the firing line. The weapon will be held in one hand, the other hand and arm being used in no way to assist. All portions of the shooter's clothing, body, and weapon must be clear of artificial support. The pistol will be pointed at the ground, with the arm straight and the elbow in contact with the body.

(f) Firing procedure: The chief range officer will direct competitors to their assigned firing point. After a reasonable time has elapsed, he will command "Load" and then inquire of each competitor, "Ready No.____?" etc. When affirmative replies have been received from all occupied firing points, he will command "Ready position." Each competitor assumes the ready position described in (e) above. After a 10-second interval, the command "Commence firing" is given. The competitor then may raise his weapon, fire, and return to the ready position at will—repeating this procedure for each shot of the five-shot string. Forty seconds will be allowed from the command "Commence firing", at which time the commands "Cease firing" and "Unload" will be given. A judge will be assigned to each firing point to determine whether or not the competitor follows the correct procedure. A failure by a competitor to return to the ready position between shots or to fire after the command "Cease firing" will result in the shot in question being scored as a miss in accordance with (g) below. Competitors will fire their four strings of five shots in consecutive order. The chief range officer will institute any additional procedures and all safety measures required by existing conditions.

(g) Scoring: Targets will be scored after each five-shot string. Competitors will remain in their places during marking. The location of all hits will be shown to the competitor by use of a marking indicator. Before scoring targets, the chief scorer will check with the chief range officer to determine if penalties are to be assessed against any competitor for violation of the firing procedure rules. Each violation of the firing procedure will be penalized by scoring that competitor's hit of greatest value as a "miss." The aggregate raw score for the shooting event will be translated into a triathlon score in accordance with paragraph (d) below.

(h) Practice shots: Each competitor will be allowed two practice shots before firing for record. These shots can be taken in accordance with the instructions of the chief range officer after the firing order has reported to the firing line (f) above.

(3) Distance running:

(a) Course: 3000 meters on flat track. It is recommended that a 400 meter track be used.

-8-

414

(b) Rules: 1954-55 AAU Track and Field Rules, except that each runner will be timed.

(c) Scoring: The competitor's time will be translated into a triathlon score for the event in accordance with paragraph (d) below.

d. Scoring of Triathlon: Winners in the Elimination and AFFE/8A Championship competitions will be determined by the order of standing in total points derived from the following scoring system:

(1) Pistol shooting:

(a) For a raw score of 179, award 1,000 points.

(b) For each raw score point more (or less) than 179, add (or deduct) 10 points, and award this score.

(2) Distance running:

(a) For a time of 10 minutes, 15 seconds, award 1,000 points.

(b) For each second more (or less) than 10 minutes, 15 seconds, deduct (or add) 3 points, and award this score.

(3) Swimming:

(a) For a time of 2 minutes, 30 seconds, award 1,000 points.

(b) For each second more (or less) than 2 minutes, 30 seconds, deduct (or add) 5 points, and award this score.

e. Trophies will be awarded to the three individuals who make the highest total score as computed from the table above; no team championship will be determined.

8. Golf:

a. Teams will not exceed eight individuals, including a team captain-manager and officer-in-charge. Teams will consist of not more than four individuals in the men's open division and two individuals each in the senior men's division and women's division.

b. The tournament will be conducted in three divisions, namely, open men's division (team and medalist championship), senior men's division, and women's division medalist championship.

c. Open division, team, and medalist championship will be determined by 72 holes medal play.

-9-

d. Team championship will be determined on the basis of aggregate total score for 72 holes medal play. The four lowest scores of each team will be combined to compute aggregate scores. Team with lowest score wins team championship.

e. Individual medalist and runner-up will be determined by the lowest score made for the 72 holes of medal play.

f. Participants in the senior division must have reached the age of 45 on or before the opening date of the Department of Army tournament. Senior division champion and runner-up will be determined by 54 holes medal play.

g. Women's division champion and runner-up will be determined by 54 holes medal play.

h. Play will be by threesomes in both the open division, the senior division, and women's division.

i. In the event of a tie for first place in the open division team championship, the four lowest scorers of each team involved will play an additional nine holes of medal play. In the event of a tie, the medalist champion will be determined by the additional play of one hole (sudden death).

j. Current United States Golf Association Rules will govern.

k. Trophies will be awarded the team champion and runner-up, and individual awards will be given to the four members of the championship and runner-up teams. Individual medalist champion and runner-up for both open division, senior division, and women's division will also receive trophies.

9. Tennis:

a. Squads will not exceed four men in the open division, two men in the senior division and two in the women's division, plus one officer-in-charge if a member of the squad does not include an officer to assume these duties, (four singles entries and two doubles teams in the open division, two singles and one doubles team in the senior men's and women's divisions).

b. The type of tournament will be single elimination. In the open division the preliminary rounds will be the best two out of three sets; semi-final and final rounds will be the best three out of five sets. The men's senior and women's divisions will be determined by the best two out of three sets for the entire tournament.

c. Current Official United States Lawn Tennis Association Guide Rules will govern conduct of the tournament.

d. Singles and doubles entries will be listed in the order of their ability or rating when rosters are submitted.

-10-

e. One point will be given to the winner of each match. One point will be awarded for a default and one point for a bye if the following match is won.

f. Trophies will be awarded the championship and runner-up teams. Individual members of championship and runner-up teams, and the individual singles and doubles champion and runner-up will also receive awards.

10. Swimming and Diving:

a. Squads will not exceed fifteen men and five women, plus one officer-in-charge if a member of the squad does not include an officer to assume these duties. Total twenty-one.

b. 1954-55 AAU Official Swimming Handbook Rules will govern conduct of the tournament.

c. Swimming Events:

First Day: Event # 1 - 1500 meter Free Style

          "   # 2 - 50 meter Free Style

Second Day   Event # 1 - 200 meters Free Style

          "   # 2 - 100 meters Backstroke

          "   # 3 - 100 meters Backstroke (Women)

          "   # 4 - 100 meters Butterfly Stroke

          "   # 5 - 3 meters Spring Board Dive (Women)

          "   # 6 - 3 meters Spring Board Dive

          "   # 7 - 400 meters Individual Medley Relay

          "   # 8 - 400 meters Individual Medley Relay (Women)

Third Day: Event # 1 - 400 meters Free Style

          "   # 2 - 100 meter Free Style

          "   # 3 - 100 meter Free Style (Women)

          "   # 4 - 200 meters Backstroke

          "   # 5 - 200 meters Breast Stroke

-11-

Third Day: Event # 6 - 200 meters Breast Stroke (Women)

"   # 7 - Dive---Platform

"   # 8 - 800 meters Free Style Relay (4 X 200 meters)

d. Point scoring for team trophies will be in accordance with Rule #X, AAU Official Swimming Handbook 1954-55, Men's Event only. No team scoring for women.

e. Each men's team competing may enter a maximum of three individuals in each swimming event and each diving event. Only one relay team may be entered by each competing team. An individual may compete in a maximum of three swimming events and in the diving in both the men's and women's events.

f. Trophies will be awarded the championship and runner-up men's teams. Individual awards will be made to the first three places in each event except the relays where only first place will receive an award.

11. Softball.

a. The softball team entered may be a company level team or a team selected from a combination of units and organizations with an aggregate strength not exceeding 5,000.

b. Squads will not exceed fifteen men including a coach, a manager, and an officer-in-charge. All members are eligible to play.

c. Type of tournament will be double elimination. All games are to be played as scheduled.

d. 1955 Official Guide of the Amateur Softball Association of America will govern conduct of the tournament.

e. Trophies will be awarded the championship and runner-up teams. Individual awards will be made to each member of the championship and runner-up teams.

12. Baseball:

a. The baseball team entered may be a regimental level team or a team selected from a combination of units and organizations with an aggregate strength not exceeding 25,000.

b. Squads will not exceed eighteen men including a coach and a manager, plus one officer-in-charge, provided that a squad member cannot be utilized in this capacity.

DECLASSIFIED
Authority NND 994029

-12-

418

c. Type of tournament will be double elimination. All games are to be played as scheduled.

d. 1955 Official Baseball Rules will govern conduct of the tournament.

e. Trophies will be awarded the championship and runner-up teams. Individual awards will be made to each member of the championship and runner-up teams.

13. Volleyball:

a. The volleyball team entered may be a company level team or a team selected from a combination of units and organizations with an aggregate strength not exceeding 1,000.

b. Squads will not exceed eight members to include a coach plus an officer-in-charge. Total nine.

c. Type of tournament will be double elimination.

d. 1955 Official Volleyball Guide will govern conduct of the tournament, except that all games will be determined by points and not by time limitations.

14. Small Games: (Badminton, handball, hand grenade throw, horseshoes, and table tennis).

a. Squads will not exceed fifteen men, three men for each sport. No team championship is declared.

b. A maximum of three singles and one doubles team may be entered in badminton, handball, horseshoes and table tennis. A maximum of three entrants from each team may compete in the hand grenade throw.

c. Type of tournament will be double elimination for horseshoes and table tennis and single elimination for badminton and handball.

d. Rules:

(1) Badminton - Current American Badminton Association Rules.

(2) Horseshoes - Current National Amateur Union.

(3) Handball - Current National Amateur Athletic Union.

(4) Table Tennis - Current U.S. Table Tennis Association.

(5) Hand Grenade Throw - Inclosure 5.

-15-

c. Trophies will be awarded the singles and doubles champions and runner-up in badminton, horseshoes, handball, and table tennis, and the first three places in the hand grenade throw.

15. Flag Football:

a. Teams will be representative of company, battery, or comparable-sized units. The grouping of smaller units which have an aggregate strength not exceeding 250 men is authorized.

b. Squad will not exceed fifteen men to include a coach and an officer-in-charge.

c. Type of tournament will be double elimination.

d. Rules are as attached (Inclosure #4).

e. Trophies will be awarded the team champion and runner-up. Individual awards will be made to each member of the championship and runner-up teams.

-14-

AFFE/8A SPORTS TOURNAMENTS

Administrative Details

1. Entries in the AFFE/8A sports tournaments and meets will be as indicated in the rules and regulations for specific sports. When appropriate, a tournament, meet, or play-off series will be conducted between the representative conferences or teams under the supervision of each addressee command to determine the team or individuals to represent that command.

2. The Commanding Generals of commands designated as host commands for AFFE/8A Sports Tournaments as shown in inclosure #1, "Schedule of Events", will be responsible for:

   a. Designating the tournament site and advising participating commands accordingly, 30 days prior to the tournament.

   b. Advising visiting commands as to procedures to be followed in reporting for participation in tournaments and the organization to which personnel will report.

   c. Furnishing playing facilities and tournament balls.

   d. Paying tournament officials.

   e. Arranging for suitable billeting and messing.

   f. Providing competent medical service during all contests.

   g. Arranging for comprehensive publicity.

   h. Submitting results of each day's competition by radio message to commanders concerned, with information copies to Headquarters, AFFE/8A, APO 343, Attention: Special Services Officer. At the conclusion of the tournament a brief historical resume of the activity will be submitted to this headquarters to include the following information (This information is exempt from reports control under provisions of paragraph 17k, Army Regulations 335-15, 12 March 1953.):

      (1) Tournament brackets.

      (2) Results of each contest.

      (3) Two copies of all action photographs.

      (4) Two copies of programs.

Incl #3

1. Maintaining close liaison with Special Services Officer, this headquarters, on matters pertaining to tournaments, meets, or play-offs.

j. Arranging for the presentation of individual and team awards, which will be provided by this headquarters.

k. Appointing tournament committee for each event composed of one representative from each team participating in respective tournaments, with a representative of Headquarters, AFFE/8A, Special Services Section, as advisor of the tournament committee. These committees will meet at least 24 hours in advance of the opening date and will:

(1) Establish local rules and procedures for the conduct of each tournament, based on provisions of official rules for respective sports.

(2) Resolve all protests.

3. Commanders responsible for visiting teams will issue necessary orders placing personnel on temporary duty with the host command as instructed. Orders will specify that personnel are to travel under orders but not on public business, that such travel and temporary duty constitutes duty of a type contemplated by paragraph 6454, Joint Travel Regulations, and that expenses incident to such travel and temporary duty will be borne by locally available nonappropriated funds. Host command will be furnished information below, a minimum of 7 days prior to the tournament, with information copy to this headquarters, Attention: Special Services Officer. (This information is exempt from reports control under provisions of paragraph 17n, AR 335-13, 12 March 1953).

a. Advance notification as to mode of travel and expected time of arrival.

b. Team rosters, including name, grade, service number, home town, designation of military unit to which each member is assigned, and players' positions for team sports.

c. Team and individual photographs, together with personal data, including previous sports experience for publicity purposes. In this connection, the assistance of local Public Information Offices should be solicited.

4. The Commanding General, AFFE/8A, will provide suitable awards from nonappropriated funds for teams and individuals as indicated in inclosure 2, "Rules and Regulations".

5. Officials for AFFE/8A sports tournaments and meets will be selected by Headquarters, AFFE/8A.

2

6. Transportation: Travel of teams by commercial transportation in Japan is chargeable to locally available nonappropriated welfare funds. Addressee commands are authorized to issue orders directing travel by air, using this letter as authority for members of teams and individuals participating in or necessary to the conduct of these contests. Limitations set forth in inclosure 2, "Rules and Regulations", will not be exceeded for inter-island travel. Travel of teams via air within Japan will be on a space available basis. Visiting commands are reminded that teams should not arrive in Japan without sufficient funds to pay commercial transportation costs.

7. It is desired that full promotional effort be utilized in order to sustain a high degree of participation and spectator interest in the 1955 AFFE/8A Sports Program at all levels of command.

-3-

Hand Grenade Throw Rules

The rules of competition for eliminations and AFFE/8A Championship will be as follows:

I. **Target.** The target will consist of three concentric circles drawn on the ground with the center 80 feet from the throwing position. The inner circle will have a diameter of five feet, the middle circle will have a diameter of 10 feet and the outer circle will have a diameter of 15 feet.

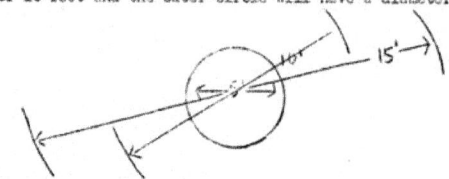

II. **Equipment.** Standard weight practice hand grenade.

III. **Competition.** Each individual entered will throw six grenades from the kneeling position and six grenades from the prone position. Three practice throws to be permitted from both the kneeling and prone positions.

IV. **Scoring.** Scoring will be as follows:

    a. Grenade striking inner circle   5 points

    b. Grenade striking middle circle   3 points

    c. Grenade striking outer circle   1 point

V. The highest aggregate point total for each individual compiled from the 12 throws to determine the champion.

VI. Any other rules not covered herein to be governed by Army Field Manual 23-30.

Incl #5

SPORTS PROGRAM MEMO, 1954

HEADQUARTERS
UNITED STATES ARMY FORCES, FAR EAST
APO 343

AG 353.8 SS-RX   5 October 1954

SUBJECT: United States Army Forces, Far East, Sports Program

TO: Commanding General, Eighth Army, APO 301
        Commanding General, Korean Communications Zone, APO 234
        Commanding General, XVI Corps, APO 14
        Commanding General, 3rd Marine Division, FMF, APO 47
        Commanding General, Ryukyus Command, APO 331
        Commanding General, Central Command, APO 500
        Commanding General, Southwestern Command, APO 9
        Commanding Officer, Camp Zama, APO 343

1. a. Supersessions:

        (1) Letter, AG 353.8 SS-RX, this headquarters, 14 March 1953,
subject: "United States Army Forces, Far East, Sports Program".

        (2) Letter, AG 353.8 SS-RX, this headquarters, 22 December
1953, subject: "Participation in United States Army Forces, Far East
Sports Program".

        (3) Letter, AG 353.8 SS-RX, this headquarters, 12 January
1954, subject: "United States Army Forces, Far East Sports Program".

        (4) Letter, AG 353.8 SS-RX, this headquarters, 7 June 1954,
subject: "General Sports Eligibility Rules".

    b. References:

        (1) Army Regulations 680-20.

        (2) Army Regulations 680-30.

        (3) Army Regulations 210-10.

        (4) Army Regulations 210-50, Air Force Regulations 176-1.

        (5) Training Circular 27, Department of the Army, 1951.

        (6) Training Circular 1, Department of the Army, 1952.

AG 353.8 SS-RX   5 October 1954
SUBJECT: United States Army Forces, Far East, Sports Program

  2. Purpose. This directive establishes a United States Army Forces,
Far East, sports program designed to promote comprehensive sports activities
at all levels of command, through an integrated system of geographical area
conferences under which participation and administration are centralized, and
provides for progression into higher level competitions in certain selected
sports.

  3. Objectives. The objectives of the United States Army Forces, Far
East, sports program are to aid in the mental, physical, and moral development
of Army personnel of the United States Army Forces, Far East, and stimulate
a high degree of esprit-de-corps by:

   a. Encouraging maximum participation in wholesome recreative
sports during free-time hours on a voluntary basis.

   b. Expanding the opportunity for individuals to engage in sports
of their own choice.

   c. Improving sports skills and techniques through the media of
qualified coaching and officiating.

   d. Providing incentives for continually increasing competitive
and spectator interests.

   e. Fostering international good will and understanding by maintaining close relationships with indigenous communities in sports activities
of mutual interest and, where practicable, competing with and against
civilian teams.

  4. Sports Conference Areas. For purposes of sports administration
and competition, the following geographical areas of the United States
Army Forces, Far East, are sub-divided into sports conferences as indicated.

   a. Japan. The Commanding Generals, XVI Corps, Central and
Southwestern Commands are authorized to designate sports conference
areas, within respective command boundaries, which will best serve the
mission and functions of each command. However, titles of sports conferences, so established, will conform to those shown below. Commanders
concerned will advise this headquarters, at the earliest practicable
date, as to the geographic limits of each conference and any changes
which may occur from time to time. Any changes in the composition of
conference areas or the establishment of sports leagues which overlap
into other command areas must have the approval of this headquarters.

    (1) XVI Corps: Hokkaido Sports Conference and Northern
Honshu Sports Conference.

2

426

AG 353.8 SS-RX   5 October 1953
SUBJECT: United States Army Forces, Far East Sports Programs

    (2) Central Command: Tokyo Area Sports Conference and
Yokohama Area Sports Conference.

    (3) Southwestern Command: Southern Honshu Sports Conference
and Kyushu Sports Conference.

  b. Ryukyus Command. The Commanding General, Ryukyus Command, is
authorized to establish such conference areas for Army personnel in the
Ryukyus Command as are considered best adaptable to the policies and
procedures contained herein. The Commanding General, United States Army
Forces, Far East, will be kept advised as to any changes in conference
organizational structure.

  c. Korea. Insofar as practicable, the Commanding Generals,
Korean Communications Zone and Eighth Army, are authorized to establish
conference areas and/or designate tactical organizational sectors as
conference areas, whichever most suitably conforms to the participation
capabilities and mission limitations of respective commands. Any pattern
established, however, will be in keeping with the general provisions of
this directive. The Commanding Generals, Korean Communications Zone and
Eighth Army, will notify the Commanding General, United States Army Forces,
Far East, of any changes in respective conference organizational structures.

  5. Composition. a. Each conference will be composed of all United
States Army Forces units and/or organizations located within conference
boundaries.

  b. Commanding Generals of areas indicated in paragraphs 4a, 4b
and 4c above, may invite individuals, units, and/or organizations of
another service to participate in team and individual sports competitions
at installation and conference levels but not at major command levels
where teams are competing for the right to represent the command in United
States Army Forces, Far East championship events, leading to All-Army
competitions except as indicated in reference 1b (2) above.

  c. No sports tournaments which will conflict with the established
United States Army Forces, Far East, sports program as currently in
operation will be conducted by units or commands.

  6. Definitions: a. Intra-Installation Programs are defined as the
sports programs conducted at each post, camp, and station in which no inter-
installation competitions are scheduled.

  b. Intra-Conference Programs will be those sports competitions
between posts, camps, and stations and/or separate units and organizations
within each conference area. These competitions will be designed so as to
determine conference championships in each sport.

3

AG 353.8 SS-RX   5 October 1954
SUBJECT: United States Army Forces, Far East Sports Program

        c. Inter-Conference Programs will be those competitions between sports conferences in each geographic area covered in paragraph 4, above, to determine a major command championship for entry in AFFE championship events.

        d. United States Army Forces, Far East Championship Events will be those tournaments and meets scheduled by this headquarters for the purpose of ascertaining champions in certain selected sports.

    7. Responsibility. In order to provide continuity and maintain normal command channels, the following responsibilities are announced:

        a. Headquarters, United States Army Forces, Far East, will:

            (1) Exercise command supervision over all phases of the United States Army Forces, Far East, sports program.

            (2) Supervise and govern a United States Army Forces, Far East, Sports Council, sub-divided into committees, as shown below, which will serve as advisory groups on related functions.

                (a) Sports Committee, composed of one representative from each addressee command. This committee will advise concerning all sports covered by this directive.

                (b) Japanese-American Recreation Committee, composed of representatives of this headquarters and addressee commands located in Japan. This committee will be responsible for the promotion and guidance of joint Japanese-American recreational activities designed to encourage wholesome relationships and understanding between the peoples of both nations. Japanese, prominent in the recreational field, will be invited to attend committee meetings and share in committee programs.

                (c) Women's Army Corps Sports Council, composed of one representative from each Women's Army Corps Detachment in AFFE. This committee will recommend and advise on all matters pertaining to the AFFE women's sports program.

            (3) Organize and supervise periodic coaches' and officials' clinics and will assist sports conferences defined in paragraph 4, above, in the conduct of local clinics.

            (4) Organize and supervise sports events conducted for the purpose of determining United States Army Forces, Far East, champions and entries in annual All-Army events sponsored by Department of the Army, as

4

AG 353.8 SS-RX 5 October 1954
SUBJECT: United States Army Forces, Far East Sports Program

well as competitions in connection with the Olympics, Pan-American Games, etc.

(5) Issue such additional directives as necessary in implementing the United States Army Forces, Far East, sports program.

b. Major Subordinate Commands.

(1) Commanders of the following major subordinate commands will be responsible for supervision of sports conferences as shown:

(a) XVI Corps - Hokkaido Sports Conference and Northern Honshu Sports Conference.

(b) Central Command - Tokyo Area Sports Conference, and Yokohama Area Sports Conference.

(c) Southwestern Command - Southern Honshu Sports Conference and Kyushu Sports Conference.

(d) Eighth Army, Korean Communications Zone and Ryukyus Command - Such sports conferences as may be established in accordance with paragraphs 4a and c, above.

(2) Each Commanding General concerned will assign a competent commissioned officer or a qualified civilian sports director, whichever is considered most appropriate, to serve as Conference Director of each sports conference covered by this directive. In Korea, these assignments may be on an additional duty basis or as full time duty performed by personnel assigned to Eighth Army and/or Korean Communications Zone, as determined by the respective Commanding General. Conference Directors will be responsible to the Commanding General concerned for the administration and conduct of conference activities, including the organization and operation of leagues and tournaments and the assignment of officials thereto; promotion of and assisting of intra-installation sports programs; organizing and conducting conference officiating and coaching clinics; coordinating arrangements with WAC Detachment sports representative for WAC sports activities; coordinating arrangements for sports competitions with indigenous teams in civilian communities within conference boundaries; and related conference duties.

(3) Commanding Generals will establish a Sports Council for each sports conference which will be representative of units, organizations, and installations within conference areas. These councils will serve as the commander's advisory groups on all matters pertaining to respective conferences, including joint Japanese-American recreational activities. Meetings will be held as frequently as considered necessary,

5

AG 353.8 SS-RX   5 October 1954
SUBJECT: United States Army Forces, Far East Sports Program

but not less often than once every six months. Conference Directors will
function as chairmen and recorders or these positions may be filled by
majority vote of council members. Minutes will be kept and submitted to
respective major command commanders for approval within ten days following
each meeting. Upon approval, one copy of the minutes will be forwarded to
this headquarters, Attention: Special Services Officer. Councils will be
empowered to settle all disputes and protests connected with intra-conference competitions, suspend, for limited periods of time, players,
coaches, or officials for unsportsmanlike acts; propose rules and regulations, within over-all policies, covering activities of each conference;
assure strict compliance with the provisions of paragraphs 9d (1), (2) and
e, below; and will individually promote and encourage maximum sports
activities and participation within their own units, organizations, and
installations.

        8. Operations. Commanding Generals concerned will organize each
sports conference in order to best accomplish the following:

            a. Intra-Installation Programs. Assure the operation of com-
petitive sports programs at each post, camp, and station, and in separate
units and organizations, with a view toward every military person's
actively engaging in sports of his own choosing. Such activities will be
comprehensive in scope and designed to progress into conference championships.

            b. Intra-Conference Programs.

                (1) Insofar as practicable, operate inter-post, camp, and
station leagues in major sports, to include but not limited to football,
basketball, baseball and boxing, with emphasis being placed on maximum
spectator interest and player participation.

                (2) Conduct tournaments and meets in as many other sports,
such as tennis, track and field, swimming, golf, etc. as practicable.

            c. Coordinate free-time recreational sports with on-duty physical
training programs to accomplish complete cooperation in the development of
physical fitness and to generate interest in improving sports skills.

            d. Conduct a Women's Army Corps sports program for those sports
that WAC personnel may most desirably compete in.

            e. Provide suitable awards for all competitions so as to encourage
maximum participation at all levels. (See paragraph 9h, below).

            f. Conduct training programs and clinics to continually improve
conference coaching and officiating.

6

430

AG 353.8 SS-RX   5 October 1954
SUBJECT: United States Army Forces, Far East Sports Program

    g. Promote close relationships with local indigenous communities in the furtherance of recreational activities of joint interest.

  9. General Policy and Procedures. a. Amateurism.

    (1) Amateurs may compete with and against professionals in all sports except boxing without loss of amateur standing, providing such competition is in connection with the United States Army Forces, Far East, sports program.

    (2) Military teams may compete against civilian professional teams without jeopardizing the amateur standing of competitors, when the contest is staged by a military unit or organization.

    (3) Any member of the Armed Forces who engages in professional games or contests as an individual or as a member of a team other than a service team, shall thereby render himself ineligible to compete as an amateur.

    (4) Prior to permitting them to compete in sports events which are for amateurs only, such as those officially sanctioned by the United States Amateur Athletic Union and the United States Olympics Committee, commanders concerned will ascertain the amateur status of each participant.

    b. The number of officers on teams competing in United States Army Forces, Far East, championship events will not exceed 50% of the total team strength on the playing field or court at any one time.

    c. Unit identity and/or distinctive team names should be preserved at all levels of competition in order to sustain organizational esprit-de-corps. Teams comprised of personnel from two or more units will carry the unit designation of the organization with the predominant number of participants.

    d. Maximum levels of competition.

    (1) Teams entered in inter-conference basketball, baseball, football, and soccer competitions will be from regiment, regimental combat teams and/or units with an aggregate strength not exceeding 5000 men.

    (2) Flag-football, softball, and volleyball teams will be from companies, batteries, or comparable size units. The grouping of smaller units which have an aggregate strength not exceeding 250 men is authorized. Companies and batteries with a strength exceeding 250 men will field two teams.

7

431

AG 353.8 SS-RX   5 October 1954
SUBJECT: United States Army Forces, Far East Sports Program

        (3) Competition levels for all other team sports will be determined by the Sports Council for each conference.

        (4) In individual type sports, the most outstanding athletes will be selected, on an individual basis, as team members at all levels of competition.

    e. Eligibility.

        (1) Personnel will not be transferred, placed on TDY, or otherwise attached to units for the purpose of strengthening sports teams.

        (2) When a team representing its parent unit or organization is entered in the progressive levels of tournament play to determine the United States Army Forces, Far East championship team, the personnel of that team will not be augmented or reinforced at any level of play.

        (3) If a member of a team is transferred, sustains an injury, or for military reasons is unable to continue play, the parent unit or organization may substitute a member of that unit or organization to fill the vacancy. The individual substituted must have been a member of that unit or organization prior to the entry of its team in the progressive tournament play for the United States Army Forces, Far East championship.

        (4) It shall be the responsibility of each Sports Council to establish the dates for submission of rosters for appropriate leagues and tournaments in the lower levels of progressive play.

        (5) An officer authorized by each major commander will certify that his team has not been strengthened through personnel transfers or reinforced by the selection of outstanding individuals from the parent organization as indicated in paragraph e (2) above. This certificate will be submitted to reach the host command headquarters, Attention: Special Services Officer at least 72 hours in advance of the opening date of the United States Army Forces, Far East tournaments. An information copy of this certificate will be forwarded to this headquarters.

    f. Pay of Officials.

        (1) Payment of commissioned officers or warrant officers acting as officials at sports events will be in accordance with paragraph 6c (3) Army Regulations 210-50, 4 November 1953; "Payment from non-appropriated funds to commissioned officers or warrant officers for services rendered is not authorized, except for personal expenses when voluntarily officiating at sports events or in the conduct of educational, religious or entertainment activities. Personal expenses may include

8

relic

AG 353.8 SS-RX   5 October 1954
SUBJECT: United States Army Forces, Far East Sports Program

maintenance of required uniform, necessary travel, subsistence and lodging
incident to participation in such activities.

        (2) The following table shows the maximum rates of pay for
enlisted and civilian sports officials, the levels at which compensation
is authorized, and the maximum number of officials authorized:

Sport	Authorized Level of Compensation	Maximum Rate Per Game	Maximum No of Officials Recommended
Badminton	Tournaments only	$5.00 per day	1 Referee
Baseball	Battalion	$10.00 per game	2 Umpires per game
	Regimental or Intra-Conference	$20.00 per game	3 Umpires per game
Basketball	Company or Battalion	$6.00 per game	2 Officials
	Regimental or Intra-Conference	$20.00 per game	2 Officials
Bowling	Tournaments only	$5.00 per day each	2 Foul judges
Boxing	Regimental or Intra-Conference	$10.00 per day $5.00 per day each	1 Referee 3 Judges
Football(11 Man)	Regimental or Intra-Conference	$80.00 per game	4 Officials
Flag-Football	Company League play	$9.00 per game	3 Officials
Horseshoes	Tournament only	$5.00 per day	1 Referee
Handball	Tournament only	$5.00 per day	1 Referee
Hand Grenade Throw	Tournament only	$5.00 per day	1 Official
Softball	Company	$6.00	2 Umpires
Swimming	Meet only	$7.50 per day each	1 Starter 1 Clerk
Track & Field	Meet only	$7.50 per day each	1 Starter & Clerk

9

AG 353.8 SS-RX   5 October 1954
SUBJECT: United States Army Forces, Far East Sports Program

Sport	Authorized Level of Compensation	Maximum Rates Per Game	Maximum No of Officials Recommended
Table Tennis	Tournament only	$5.00 per day	1 Referee
Tennis	Tournaments only	$2.00 per match	1 Umpire 1 Referee
Volleyball	Tournaments only	$2.00 per match	1 Referee 1 Umpire

(3) Home team installations will be responsible for compensation of all officials who officiate at contests played at such installations. Maximum rates of pay shown in the above table may be exceeded when necessary for AFFE - Level tournament competitions.

g. Supply and Equipment.

(1) Commanders concerned will be responsible for providing supplies and equipment for teams and/or individuals from their commands who compete in inter-conference and United States Army Forces, Far East, championship events.

(2) As protection against eye cuts and ear and head injuries, a light weight headguard will be worn by each participant in boxing matches conducted by any post, camp, and station or separate organization of the United States Army Forces, Far East. These head guards will provide a layer of protective material, at least one-half inch in thickness, covering the ears, eye ridge, temples, and back of head.

h. Trophies and Awards. No cash prizes will be awarded any contestant in any sports event. United States Savings Bonds and similar instruments are considered to be cash prizes. Trophies, medals or awards, (other than cash), may be awarded in connection with sports events within the following maximum costs:

(1) Intra-Installation or Regimental Events. Individual awards $7.50; team awards, $15.00.

(2) Intra-Conference or Major Command Events. Individual awards $10.00; team awards $20.00.

(3) AFFE Championship Events. Individual awards $25.00; team awards $75.00.

i. Rules. Rules of the following organizations will govern conduct of all sports contests conducted as part of the United States Army Forces, Far East, sports program.

10

AG 353.8 SS-RX

3 October 1954

SUBJECT: United States Army Forces, Far East Sports Program

(1) National Collegiate Athletic Association: Football, basketball, lacrosse, soccer, and waterpolo.

(2) National Amateur Athletic Union: Boxing (with exception stated in paragraph 9g (2), gymnastics, handball, horseshoes, ice hockey, long-distance running, swimming, track and field, tug of war, weight-lifting and wrestling.

(3) National Archery Association: Archery.

(4) American Badminton Association: Badminton.

(5) American Bowling Congress: Bowling.

(6) Billard Association of America: Billards and pool.

(7) National Baseball League: Baseball.

(8) Amateur Fencing League of America: Fencing.

(9) United States Golf Association: Golf.

(10) United States Table Tennis Association: Table Tennis.

(11) National Ski Association of America: Skiing.

(12) Amateur Softball Association: Softball.

(13) United States Volleyball Association: Volleyball.

(14) United States Lawn Tennis Association: Tennis.

(15) American Association for Health, Physical Education and Recreation: Women's softball, volleyball, basketball, track and field.

j. Commanders will insure compliance with provisions of Letter, AGAC-C (M) 220.3 (18 May 54) G-1, Department of the Army, 24 May 1954, subject: "Assignment and Utilization of Athletes, Entertainers and other Nationally Known Personnel" and Letter AG 200.3 (22 Dec 52), GA this headquarters, 22 December 1952, subject: "Assignment of Personnel." "Known name athletes" will not receive preferential treatment because of their athletic ability nor will outstanding athletes be retained at processing centers or replacement depots.

11

AG 353.8 SS-RX   5 October 1954
SUBJECT: United States Army Forces, Far East Sports Program

   10. Publicity. It is desired that continuing publicity be given to
the United States Army Forces, Far East, sports program through every
possible source and that each activity be widely publicized in order for
every individual to be completely aware of events being staged and to assure
full and active spectator interest.

          BY COMMAND OF GENERAL HULL:

                                    LEO KLEIMAN
                                    Lt Col, AGC
                                    Asst AG

12

CAPACITY ATTENDANCE AT TORII BOWL, KORAKUEN STADIUM, 1956

	JOINT MESSAGE	SECURITY CLASSIFICATION	
		UNCLASSIFIED	$853,8$

SPACE BELOW RESERVED FOR COMMUNICATION CENTER

PRECEDENCE		TYPE MSG (Check)			ACCOUNTING SYMBOL	ORIG. OR REFERS TO	CLASSIFICATION OF REFERENCE
ACTION	PRIORITY	BOOK	MULTI	SINGLE			
INFO				X	DA		

FROM:

CGAFFE/ARMYEIGHT (REAR) CP ZAMA JAPAN

TO:
DA WASHDC

SPECIAL INSTRUCTIONS

FM 634441   For Taylor. Sgd White.

Know you will be happy to learn that in Torii Bowl Football Game at Korakuen Stadium, Tokyo, this afternoon, Army All-Stars defeated Navy-All Stars thirty-five to zero.

Game played in fine weather before capacity attendance and was in best tradition of interservice contests

AG RECORDS

DECLASSIFIED
Authority NND891514

DATE	TIME
15	06552
MONTH	YEAR
DEC	56

SYMBOL	
SGS /s/ E Wendel Jr	Robert M. DeJung Capt AGC
TYPED NAME AND TITLE (Signature, if required)	TYPED (or stamped) NAME AND TITLE
E WENDELL JR, Lt Col, GS, SGS	for ROY N. WALKER
PHONE 3-2335 PAGE 1 NR. OF PAGES 1	Brigadier General, USA
SECURITY CLASSIFICATION	Adjutant General
UNCLASSIFIED	

DD FORM MAY 58 173   REPLACES DD FORM 173, 1 OCT 48, WHICH IS OBSOLETE FOR ARMY USE.   Army-AG Admin Cen-Japan

BIBLIOGRAPHY

1. **Kim, Jinwung.** *A History of Korea.* 2012.

2. **Army Times** . Big League Scout Praises Army Baseball in Europe. *Army Times newspaper.* January 22, 1955, p. 33. Online archives.

3. **John H. Hoppin, Major, USAF, Chief Special Services Division.** *Far East Air Forces 1957 Sports Clinics.* APO 925 : Headquarters, Far East Air Forces , 6 December 1957.

4. **Army Times.** Eight Army Basketball Aces Get All-Star Team Tryouts. *Army Times newspaper.* December 25, 1954, pp. 24, 25. Online archives.

5. **Scanlon, Tom.** Tom Scanlon column. *Army Times newspaper.* July 31, 1954, p. 24.

6. **Harlan C. Parks, Major General.** United States Air Force. s.l. : United Nations Command side Military Armistice Commission, 18 August 1955. National Archives II archival records.

7. **Hongkun Lee, General, ROK Army.** Seoul, Korea : Headquarters, Joint Chiefs of Staff, Republic of Korea, Office of the Chairman, 27 December 1955.

8. **Chief of Staff.** *Chief of Staff Weekly Conference memo.* U. S. Military. s.l. : U. S. Military, 13 July 1954.

9. **EBSCO Publishing.** *The Status Quo Peace.* August 15, 1955.

10. **Pauline Kollantai, Sebastian Kim, Greg Hoyland.** *Peace and Reconciliation: In Search of Shared Indentity.* s.l. : Ashgate Publishing, 2013.

11. **HQ AFFE Troop Information Division, TI&E Section.** *General Staff News Summary.* Seoul : U.S. Army, HQ AFFE Troop Information Division, TI&E Section, 27 January 1954.

12. **Fairfax, Montgomery.** MacArthur Planned Atom Attack in Korea. *Army Times newspaper.* 23 October 1954, p. M5. Online archives.

13. **Cumings, Bruce.** *Korea's Place in the Sun.* 1997.

14. **Kwon, Hoenik.** *After the Korean War.* s.l. : Cambrodge University Press, 2020.

15. **Headquarters, Eighth Army, APO AP 96271-5236.** *Eighth Army Blue Book.* Headquarters, Eighth Army, APO AP 96271-5236 : Department of the Army, 5 September 2024.

16. **Department of State, Office of the Historian.** Korean War and Japan's Recovery. [Online] [Cited: November 17, 2024.] https://history.state.gov/milestones/1945-1952/korean-war.

17. **Beasley, W. G.** *The Japanese Experience; A Short History of Japan.* Los Angeles, CA : University of California Press, Ltd., London, England, 1999.

18. **Stars and Stripes.** Korea Troops to Stay, U.N. Group Declares. *Stars and Stripes newspaper.* September 12, 1953.

19. **Army Times .** 1st Cav. Move Opens Army Redeployment in Far East. *Army Times newspaper.* July 17, 1954, p. 3. Online archives.

20. **Army Times.** Hood Gets 4th Armored; 'Bayonet' To Stay In Korea. *Army Times newspaper.* February 13, 1954, pp. 1, 8. Online Archives.

21. **Army Times.** It Took a Lot of Muscle To Move the 24th Division. *Army Times newspaper.* December 4, 1954, p. 24. Online archives.

22. **Army Times.** Engineers Helping Korea to Re-Build. *Army Times newspaper.* November 12, 1955, p. 22. Online archives.

23. **HQ AFFE Troop Information Division, TI&E Section.** *General Staff News Summary.* Tokyo : U.S. Army HQ AFFE Troop Information Division, TI&E Section, 29 January 1954.

24. **Hirsch, William P.** Record from National Archives II. Tokyo, Japan : s.n., 28 December 1954.

25. **HQ AFFE/8A Information Division.** *General Staff News Summary.* Seoul : U.S. Army HQ AFFE/8A Information Division, 19 January 1955.

26. **HQ AFFE/8A (Rear).** *General Staff News Summary.* Seoul : U.S. Army AFFE/8A Information Division, 1955.

27. **HQ AFFE/8A.** *News Summary.* Information Division TI&E Office : U.S. Army HQ AFFE/8A, 1956.

28. **Headquarters, United States Army Forces, Far East and Eighth United States Army.** *Community Relations Advisory Council Program.* s.l. : Headquarters, United States Army Forces, Far East and Eighth United States Army, 30 March 1955.

29. **James B. Quill, Brigadier General, General Staff.** *Letter to Honorable Lee, Ik Keung, Governor, Kyonggi-do Province.* Seoul : U.S. Army, 1955.

30. **Adam Smith, Megan Tooker, Chelsea Pogorelac, and Chris Cochran.** *A History of Recreation in the Military Legacy Project #08-388.* Department of Defense. Champaign, Illinois : U.S. Army Engineer Research and Development Center, August 2011.

31. **Army Times.** Big Post Loaded With Gyms, Libraries. *Army Times newspaper.* 27 February 1954, p. 26. Online archives.

32. **Philip G. Whele, Brigadier General.** *Tracer.* s.l. : U.S. Army, 1955.

33. **Broumley, Jim.** A Summary History of the 7th Infantry Division. *The Roving Historian.* [Online] January 25, 2010. [Cited: March 31, 2025.] https://rovinghistorian.blogspot.com/2023/10/a-summary-history-of-7th-infantry.html.

34. **Headquarters 7th Infantry Division.** *Welcome to the Bayonet Division.* APO San Francisco 96207 : Office of the Commanding General, Headquarters 7th Infantry Division, July 1970.

35. **Steve Dolan, Los Angeles Times.** *Military Glory: Service Teams, in Their Heyday, Won Championships, Thrilled the Fans.* San Diego, California, USA : s.n., June 13, 1986.

36. **Stars and Stripes.** Announcements. *Stars and Stripes newspaper.* June 17, 1953.

37. **Stars and Stripes.** American Servicemen in Korea Have World's Highest Morals, Bishop Says. *Stars and Stripes newspaper.* February 16, 1953.

38. **Stars and Stripes.** Ex-Grid Star Frees Fellow Pilot From Burning Fighter. *Stars and Stripes newspaper.* March 13, 1953.

39. **Tony Paul, The Detroit News.** Dick Kempthorn, MVP of 1949 Michigan team and war hero, dies at 92. *Detroit News.* February 14, 2019.

40. **Stars and Stripes.** Grid Coaches End Clinic in Far East. *Stars and Stripes newspaper.* July 25, 1953.

41. **Stars and Stripes.** New AFFE Home Springs to Life. *Stars and Stripes newspaper.* July 25, 1953.

42. **Stars and Stripes.** 27th Reg't Enlarges A&R Section Schedule. *Stars and Stripes newspaper.* September 12, 1953.

43. **Stars and Stripes.** 23d Regiment Constructing Giant Sprts Arena. *Stars and Stripes newspaper.* September 16, 1953.

44. **Stars and Stripes.** Battalion Opens Athletic Center. *Stars and Stripes newspaper.* October 8, 1953.

45. **Gueinzius, PFC John.** British Intensify A&R Activities. *Stars and Stripes newspaper.* October 11, 1953.

46. **Stars and Stripes.** Fisher, Gifu to Vie. *Stars and Stripes newspaper.* November 6, 1953.

47. **Adler, Pfc Jerry.** 10 Years of Entertainment; Special Services Provides the Morale Boost. *Stars and Stripes newspaper.* November 11, 1953.

48. **Stars and Stripes** . Sports Clinic. *Stars and Stripes newspaper.* November 19, 1953.

49. **Stars and Stripes.** Bulldogs, FEAF Prep for Thanksgiving Scrap. *Stars and Stripes newspaper.* November 23, 1953.

50. **Stars and Stripes**. 3rd Div. Builds Four Recreation Morale Centers. *Stars and Stripes newspaper.* 1953.

51. **Stars and Stripes**. Today's Pigskin Descended From Rugby Ball Used in 1800s. *Stars and Stripes newspaper.* November 25, 1953.

52. **Stars and Stripes**. Photo captions. *Stars and Stripes newspaper.* November 28, 1953, p. 20. Online paid arcchives.

53. **Stars and Stripes** . 55th Truck Bn. Cops Rice Bowl Crown. *Stars and Stripes newspaper.* November 28, 1953, p. 20. Online paid archives.

54. **Stars and Stripes.** Middies Win Korea Army-Navy Game. *Stars and Stripes newspaper.* November 28, 1953.

55. **Providence Funeral Home.** taylorprovidencefuneralhome.com. [Online] [Cited: May 23, 2025.] https://www.taylorprovidencefuneralhome.com/obituaries/3740010.

56. **Stars and Stripes.** 187th Drills for Crucial Tokyo Tilt. *Stars and Stripes newspaper.* December 4, 1953.

57. **Flanagan, Edward.** *Rakkasans.* s.l. : Presidio Press, 1997.

58. **Stars and Stripes.** 187th Favored Over Bulldogs in AFFE tilt. December 5, 1953.

59. **Stars and Stripes**. Camp Tokyo Gridsters Crush Rakkasan's 35-0. *Stars and Stripes newspaper.* December 8, 7 December 1953.

60. **Stars and Stripes**. Ashiya Wins Bamboo Bowl. *Stars and Stripes newspaper.* December 8, 1954, p. 20. Online paid archives.

61. **Stars and Stripes**. KBS Champs Get Awards. *Stars and Stripes newspaper.* December 10, 1953.

62. **Legacy.com.** Robert Lovely Obituary. *Legacy.com.* [Online] September 17, 2017. [Cited: April 9, 2025.] https://www.legacy.com/us/obituaries/delmarvanow/name/robert-lovely-obituary?id=22554994.

63. **Stars and Stripes.** AFFE Football Championship. *Stars and Stripes newspaper.* December 18, 1953.

64. **Army Times.** Rycom All-Star Grid Team Dominated by 29th RCT. *Army Times newspaper.* January 2, 1954, p. 25. Online archives.

65. **Stars and Stripes.** Marines Defeat AF in Tokyo Rice Bowl. *Stars and Stripes newspaper.* January 2, 1954.

66. **Army Times.** Ivy League Star. *Army Times newspaper.* January 9, 1954, p. 28. Online archives.

67. **Army Times**. Eighth Army Championships. *Army Times newspaper.* January 23, 1954, p. 29. Online archives.

68. **HQ AFFE/Troop Information Division, TI&E Section.** *General Staff News Summary.* s.l. : U.S. Army HQ AFFE/Troop Information Division, TI&E Section, 28 January 1954.

69. **Army Times.** 'Community Centers' Being Built In Korea. *Army Times newspaper.* February 6, 1954, p. 6. Online archives.

70. **Scanlon, Tom.** Big League Teams Back Plan To Find Prospects. *Army Times newspaper.* February 27, 1954, p. 28. Online archives.

71. **Army Times.** Mays Gets Discharge. *Army Times newspaper.* March 6, 1954, p. 32. Online archives.

72. **Roy B. Maurer, Major, AGC.** *Recreation Facilities.* Headquarters, Korean Communications Zone : U.S. Army, 1954.

73. **Tom Scanlan, Sports Editor.** Is Army Coddling Sports Stars? *Army Times newspaper.* May 8, 1954, pp. 28, 30. Online archives.

74. **Scanlon, Tom, Sports Editor.** Second Guess - Ho-Hum Dept. *Army Times newspaper.* June 5, 1954, p. 24. Online archives.

75. **Stilwell, Blake.** Korean War Veteran Bobby Brown Was Also a Cardiologist and World Series Champion. *Military.com.* [Online] October 6, 2021. [Cited: January 27, 2025.] https://www.military.com/veteran-jobs/korean-war-veteran-bobby-brown-was-also-cardiologist-and-world-series-champion.html.

76. **Army Times.** Army Sports Stars. *Army Times newspaper.* December 12, 1954, p. 26. Onlines archives.

77. **Army Times**. Seoul Post Wins 8th Army Track; McMillen Top Star. *Army Times newspaper.* 3 July 1954. Online archives.

78. **Associated Press/Alamy Stock Photo.** *Alamy.com.* [Online] November 17, 1954. [Cited: January 29, 2025.] A caption reads "Captions are provided by our contributors". https://www.alamy.com/twenty-thousand-koreans-swarmed-into-the-seoul-city-stadium-thursday-nov-18-1954-to-denounce-a-british-canadian-election-plan-for-unifying-north-and-south-korea-the-demonstrators-demanded-united-nations-supervised-election-in-north-k.

79. **Stars and Stripes.** FEC Slates All-Star Tilts. *Stars and Stripes newspaper.* July 20, 1954.

80. **Stars and Stripes**. 105 Coaches Attend Clinic. *Stars and Stripes newspaper.* July 20, 1954.

81. **Army Times.** 100 Coaches Graduate From Clinic. *Army Times newspaper.* July 27, 1954, p. 12. Online archive.

82. **Stars and Stripes.** Marines Call for Players To Fill 7 Football Squads. *Stars and Stripes newspaper.* July 28, 1954, p. 12. Online paid archive.

83. **Army Times.** It's Pigskin Time Again in Korea. *Army Times newspaper.* July 31, 1954, p. 26.

84. **Army Times**. Reveille Is Out at Korea Rest Camp. *Army Times newspaper.* July 31, 1954, p. 10. Online archives.

85. **Stars and Stripes.** Pacific Coast Loop Officials to Conduct AFFE Grid Clinic. *Stars and Stripes newspaper.* August 1, 1954.

86. **Andrew J. Napolitano, Major, AGC.** *Sports Clinic (Basketball Officials).* Headquarters, Korean Communications Zone : U.S. Army, 1954. U.S. National Archives.

87. **New York Times.** *Forrest Twogood, 64, Dies; Basketball Coach for U.S. C.* Los Angeles : New York Times, 1972.

88. **New York Times.** *Howard Hobson; Basketball Pioneer And Coach Was 87.* New York : New York Times, 1991.

89. **Army Times .** Flyweight Chas. Drakeford 115 Pounds of Dynamite. *Army Times newspaper.* August 14, 1954.

90. **Army Times.** 2d Div. Stars Touring Korea. *Army Times newspaper.* August 21, 1954, p. 29. Online archives.

91. **E.J. Enright, 2d Lt, AGC, Asst AG.** *Roster for Basketball Coaches Clinic.* HQ Korean Communications Zone : U.S. Army, 1954.

92. **Army Times.** 2d Div. All-Star. *Stars and Stripes newspaper.* September 11, 1954, pp. 29, 30. Online archives.

93. **Army Times.** Three Major Sports Dropped – Four Inter-Service Tourneys, including Boxing, Next Year. *Army Times newspaper.* September 18, 1954, p. 28. Online archives.

94. **Army Times.** All-Time Grid Great Recalls Early Development of Game. *Army Times newspaper.* October 16, 1954, p. 30. Online archives.

95. **Mahoney, Pat.** Did Ya Know? *Army Times newspaper.* October 9, 1954, p. 30. Online archives.

96. **Army Times.** About to Hit the Dirt. *Army Times newspaper.* October 23, 1954, p. 28. Online archives.

97. **Army Times .** All-Army Schedule Lists 10 Tourneys. *Army Times newspaper.* October 23, 1954, p. 28. Online archives.

98. **Army Times.** Notre Dame Back in Korea. *Army Times newspaper.* October 30, 1954, p. 31. Online archives.

99. **Leo Kleiman, Lt Col, AGC, Asst AG.** *Special AFFE Boxing Tournament.* s.l. : U.S. Army, 1954.

100. **Rosenfeld.** Stops 'Em for Sill. *Army Times newspaper.* November 6, 1954, p. 36. Online archives.

101. **Indiana Football Hall of Fame.** Inductee Matuszak, Marvin H. *Indiana Football Hall of Fame.* [Online] August 15, 1987. [Cited: May 23, 2025.] https://ifca-hof.org/inductee/matuszak-marvin-h/.

102. **Army Times.** All-Star Service Cage Team May Be Organized Soon. *Army Times newspaper.* November 13, 1954, p. 33. Online archives.

103. **Army Times .** Early All-Army Poll Results Indicate Vote Will Be Close. *Army Times newspaper.* November 20, 1954, p. 35.

104. **Army Times.** Great Athlete Departs, Brooke Will Remember Litman. *Army Times newspaper.* November 20, 1954, p. 33. Online archives.

105. **William T. Floyd, Asst Adj Gen.** *Special Army Forces, Far East, Boxing Tournament.* s.l. : U.S. Army, 1954

106. **Army Times .** All-Army 1954 Selection Group. *Army Times newspaper.* December 11, 1954, p. 27. Online archives.

107. **Beyond the Dash.** Longtime Vikings assistant coach John Michels dies at 87. *Beyond the Dash.* [Online] February 15, 2019. [Cited: April 117, 2025.] https://beyondthedash.com/obituary/john-michels-1072217637.

108. **Peters, Craig.** Vikings Send Condolences to Family of Longtime Legendary Assistant John Michels. *Vikings.com.* [Online] January 10, 2019. [Cited: April 17, 2025.] https://www.vikings.com/news/minnesota-vikings-john-michels-longtime-legendary-assistant.

109. **C. G. Maxwell, Lt Col AGC.** *Korean Communications Zone Basketball Tournament.* Headquarters, Korean Communications Zone : U.S. Army, 1954.

110. **Scanlon, Tom.** Army Times Sports - Second Guess. *Army Times newspaper.* December 18, 1954, p. 31. Online archives.

111. **Lilley, Kevin.** Mr. Inside and Mr. Outside: Army Football's Golden Age. *Army Times newspaper.* December 10, 2014. Online archives.

112. **G.C. Maxwell, Lt Col, AGC, Asst AG.** *Korean Communications Zone Boxing Tournament.* Headquarters Korean Communications Zone APO 234 : U.S. Army, 29 December 1954.

113. **Army Times.** Far East Command Stars. *Army Times newspaper.* January 1, 1955, p. 27. Online archives.

114. **Si.com.** Former Iowa Standout Jerry Hilgenberg Passes Away. *Si.com.* [Online] January 16, 2024. [Cited: February 13, 2025.] https://www.si.com/college/iowa/football/former-iowa-standout-jerry-hilgenberg-passes-away.

115. **Iowa History Journal.** iowahistoryjournal.com. *iowahistoryjournal.com.* [Online] undated. [Cited: February 13, 2025.] https://iowahistoryjournal.com/meet-the-hilgenbergs/.

116. **Hall of Very Good.** profootballreasearchers.com. *Pro Football Researchers Association.* [Online] [Cited: February 16, 2025.] https://web.archive.org/web/20170622185257/http://www.profootballresearchers.com/hall-of-very-good-2015.htm.

117. **Tampa Bay Times.** *Tampa Bay Times.* [Online] September 14, 2013. [Cited: February 16, 2025.] https://www.tampabay.com/news/obituaries/tampa-football-legend-rick-casares-dies-starred-for-bears-gators/2141841/.

118. **Stephenson, Beth.** Memories of a Columnist's Dad. *The Oklahoman newspaper.* September 5, 2016.

119. **Army Times .** All-Army Awards. *Army Times newspaper.* January 8, 1955, p. 28. Online archives.

120. **Army Times.** Army Screens Sixty Boxers For Pan-American Trials. *Army Times newspaper.* January 15, 1954, p. 28. Online archives.

121. **www.legacy.com.** C.J. "Pete" Silas obituary. *www.legacy.com.* [Online] December 18, 2014. https://www.legacy.com/us/obituaries/examiner-enterprise/name/c-j-silas-obituary?id=21068296.

122. **Jablonski, David.** UD basketball legend Paxson, Sr. dies at 81. *Dayton Daily News.* October 28, 2014. Online archives.

123. **Army Times .** Stateside Army Sports ... In Brief. *Army Times newspaper.* January 29, 1954, p. 32. Online archives.

124. **Army Times.** Service Stars Top Belvoir. *Army Times newspaper.* January 29, 1954, p. 33. Online archives.

125. **Army Times.** Basketball at Fort Dix. *Army Times newspaper.* 12 February 1955, p. 32. Archived on-line.

126. **Star Ledger.** Kenneth Murray Obituary. *Star Ledger newspaper.* June 17, 2008.

127. **United States Army Forces, Far East, and Eighth United States Army.** *Circular: Special Services Supplies and Equipment.* s.l. : Headquarters, United States Army Forces, Far East, and Eighth United States Army, 4 April 1955.

128. **Army Times.** Far East Athletics. *Army Times newspaper.* May 22, 1954, pp. 29, 31. Online archives.

129. **Schwartz, PFC Larry.** Tatum Among Noted Coaches Coming to Far East Clinics. *Army Times newspaper.* June 4, 1955, p. 33. Online archives.

130. **Stars and Stripes.** AFFE Starts 1955 Grid Coach Clnic. *Stars and Stripes newspaper.* July 12, 1955.

131. **Stars and Stripes**. Football Official's Clinic. *Stars and Stripes newspaper.* August 16, 1955, p. 22.

132. **Seattle Times.** *James Cain Obituary.* Rancho Mirage, California, USA : s.n., September 15-16, 2007.

133. **Army Times.** All-Korea Boxing Tournament. *Army Times newspaper.* September 24, 1955, p. 37. Online archives.

134. **Ziff, Howard M.** 7th Scores Once a Period, Beats SMP 25-0. *Stars and Stripes newspaper.* September 26, 1955, p. 22. Online paid archives.

135. **Stars and Stripes.** AFFE Football Results. *Stars and Stripes newspaper.* October 3, 1955, p. 21. Online paid archives.

136. **Scanlon, Tom.** All-Army Program For '56 Includes Nine Tournaments. *Army Times newspaper.* October 8, 1955, p. 32. Online archives.

137. **Penn University.** Hall of Fame Class IX: Jack L. Shanafelt. *Pennathletics.com.* [Online] June 28, 2016. [Cited: January 7, 2025.] https://pennathletics.com/news/2016/6/28/5772eda0e4b0028e72362ae b_131492766283605713.

138. **Stars and Stripes.** Bulldogs Take 3rd, Humble YED 51-0. *Stars and Stripes newspaper.* October 10, 1954, p. 21. Online paid archives.

139. **Army Times.** New York Yankees In Sendai Oct. 25. *Army Times newspaper.* October 15, 1955, p. 37. Online archives.

140. **Army Times**. Annual All-Army Poll Opens. *Army Times newspaper.* October 22, 1955, p. 32. Online archives.

141. **Stars and Stripes.** 24th Division Looks Like Team to Beat in Far East. *Stars and Stripes newspaper.* October 29, 1955. Online archives.

142. **Army Times.** 24th Division Looks Like Team to Beat in Far East. *Army Times newspaper.* October 29, 1955.

143. **Stars and Stripes.** Bullseyes Spring 19-13 Upset, Crumble 7th Div. Title Hopes. *Stars and Stripes newspaper.* November 13, 1955.

144. **Stars and Stripes.** Marine Mascot Bucking for 3rd Stripe in Bowl. *Stars and Stripes newspaper.* December 9, 1955.

145. **Stars and Stripes**. Passer, 2 Halfbacks Join Army All-Stars. *Stars and Stripes newspaper*. December 9, 1955.

146. **Schwartz, Larry.** Far East All-Stars Gather for Torii Bowl in Tokyo. *Army Times newspaper*. December 10, 1955. Online archives.

147. **Army Times**. Army Stars Wallop Marines Before 25,000 in Far East. *Army Times newspaper*. December 31, 1955. Online archive.

148. **Japan, CG One CavDiv Sendai.** s.l. : U.S. Army, 1956.

149. **Los Angeles Times.** All-American basketball player saw scandal end his career. *Los Angeles Times newspaper*. November 30, 2007. Staff and Wire Reports.

150. **Gould, Ben.** Is The Fix Still On In Basketball? *Police Gazette*. March 1953, Vol. 158, 3, p. 17.

151. **CGAFFE/8A, PIO.** Sendai, Japan : U.S. Army, 1956.

152. **Colonel Roy. N. Walker, ACC Adjutant General.** Camp Zama, Japan : U.S. Army, 1956.

153. **Rubinton, Lt. Colonel S.** *Itinerary for EC Track and Field Coach's Clinic*. HQ, United States Armhy Forces, Far East : U.S,. Army, 1956.

154. **Cantonrep.com | The Repository.** *Stark's Famous: Larry Snyder.* March 15, 2016. CantonRep.com|The Repository.

155. **Garland, PFC Murrell.** Seoul Wins Far East Crown. *Army Times newspaper*. March 3, 1956, p. 43. Online archives.

156. **Roy N. Walker, Colonel.** Camp Zama : U.S. Army, 1956.

157. **Roy N. Walker, Colonel.** Camp Zama : U.S. Army, 1956.

158. **Army Times.** Three Army Players Make Olympic Trials. *Army Times newspaper*. March 31, 1956, p. 47.

159. **Army Times.** 17th Infantry Champs. *Army Times newspaper*. March 10, 1956, p. 43. Online archives.

160. **Lt. Col. Hugh T. Paris, AGC Chief, Sports Branch.** *Track and Field, 1956 Olympic Games.* s.l. : U.S. Army, 1956.

161. **Army Times.** 400 Soldiers Seek Olympic Berths. *Army Times newspaper.* 5 May 1956, p. 54.

162. **Sam C. Russell, Brigadier General.** *Army Participation in the Sports Program.* s.l. : U.S. Army, 1956.

163. **C.J. Koehler, GS-12, Dir, Sports Branch.** *Memo.* Camp Zama : U.S. Army, 1956.

164. **The College Basketball Experience.** Biography "Cliff" W. R. Wells. *The College Basketball Experience.* [Online] [Cited: June 12, 2025.] https://collegebasketballexperience.com/members/w-r-clifford-wells/.

165. **Louis J. Alemann, II, Maj AGC.** *Quarterly Report on Army Recreational Service Activities.* Camp Zama : U.S. Army, 1956.

166. **Robert J Reynolds, Capt. AGC, Asst AG.** *Quarterly Report, Army Recreational Service Activities (Reports Control Symbol AG-224).* APO 343 : Headquarters, United States Army Forces, Far East and Eighth United States Army (Rear), 4 August 1956. National Archives.

167. **Samuel J. Gormley, Colonel.** *Army Participation in Air Force Athletics.* HQ 43d Air Division : U.S. Army, 1956.

168. **James L. Glymph, Lt Colonel, AGC, Exec Officer, SpSerDiv.** *Request for Authority to Participate in the All-Army Track and Field Meet.* San Francisco, CA : U.S. Army, 1956.

169. **Curt S. Riggs, GS-12, NAF Administrator.** *Reimbursement for Expenses Incurred During the Torii and Rice Bowl Football Games.* s.l. : U.S. Army, 1956.

170. **Curtis L. Frisbie, Colonel, USAF.** *Army Participation in Air Force Athletics.* s.l. : U.S. Army, 1956.

171. **Donald G. Lasley, Major, Infantry.** *Application for Olympics.* APO 7 : Headquarters 31st Infantry, 26 June 1956. AG 353.8.

172. **Legacy.com.** Breckingridge Greene Obituary. [Online] 16 November 2007. [Cited: December 18, 2024.] https://www.legacy.com/us/obituaries/recordnet/name/breckinridge-greene-obituary?id=9928270.

173. **Robert J. Reynolds, Capt. AGC, Asst AG.** *Army Participation in Air Force Athletics.* HQ AFFE/8A (REAR) : U.S. Army, 1956.

174. **S. Rubinton, Lt Col, AGC.** *Itinerary for FEC Football Coaches Clinic Instructors (VIP).* APO 343 : Headquarters United States Army Forces, Far East and Eighth United States Army (Rear), 27 June 1956. AG 353.8 & 333.1.

175. **DA WASHDC.** Office of Adjutant General. s.l. : Headquarters United States Army Forces, Far East and Eight United States Army (Rear), 28 June 1956. AG 353.8.

176. **CALIF, CO FT MACARTHUR SPEDRO.** HEADQUARTERS, UNITED STATES ARMY FORCES, FAR EAST and EIGHTH UNITED STATES ARMY (REAR) : Office of the Adjutant General, 3 JULY 1956.

177. **Roy N. Walker, GS-12, Dir, Sports Branch.** Adjutant General. CP ZAMA JAPAN : CGAFFE/ARMYFIGHT (REAR) CP ZAMA JAPAN, 9 July 1956. 353.8.

178. **Stars and Stripes.** Football Clinic Opens. *Stars and Stripes newspaper.* July 11, 1956.

179. **E. H. Koreman, Lt Col, AGC, and T. L. Eastmond, Lt Col, AGC.** *Camp Zama Post Football Team.* s.l. : U.S. Army , 11 July 1956.

180. **Roy N. Walker, Colonel, AGC.** *Camp Zama Post Football Team.* s.l. : U.S. Army, 11 July 1956.

181. **CG AFFE/ARMYEIGHT KOREA.** Headquarters United States Army Forces, Far East and Eighth United States Army (Rear) : CG AFFE/ARMYEIGHT KOREA, 12 July 1956. AG 353.8.

182. **E. H. Koreman, Lt Col, AGC.** *Camp Zama Post Football Team.* s.l. : U.S. Army, 12 July 1956.

183. **Army Times.** 24th Div. To Spend $800,000. *Army Times newspaper.* July 14, 1956, p. 2.

184. **B. R. Watson, Major AGC, Asst AG.** *Camp Zama Post Football Team.* s.l. : U.S. Army, 18 July 1956.

185. **Roy N. Walker, Colonel AGC.** *AFFE/8A Commander's Cup Pt Sys.* CP ZAMA JAPAN : CGAFFE/ARMYEIGHT KOREA, 23 July 1956.

186. **Roy N. Walker, Colonel, AGC.** CP ZAMA JAPAN : CGAFFE/ARMYEIGHT (REAR), 24 July 1956. AG 353.8.

187. **John D. Williams, Major, Artillery, Adjutant.** *Report of Far East Command Coaches Clinic.* Subcamp Drake : Headquarters, Subcamp Drake, 24 July 1956.

188. **M. E. Perry, Captain, AGC.** *1956 Company Level Volleyball League.* Adjutant General. APO 343 : Headquarters Camp Zama, 27 July 1956. AG 353.8.

189. **L. W. Jackson, Colonel, AGC, Chief, Special Services Division.** *Olympic Boxing Trials.* 31 July 1956. AG 353.8.

190. **WASHDC, DA.** *Ref Basketball Coaches Clinic.* Headquarters United States Army Forces, Far East and Eighth United States Army (Rear) : Headquarters United States Army Forces, Far East and Eighth United States Army (Rear), 1 Aug 56.

191. **A B McEowen, Capt AGC, Asst AG.** *AFFE/8th Army Baseball Tournament.* APO 201 : Headquarters 1st Cavalry Division, 2 August 1956.

192. **B. R. Watson, Major, AGC, Asst AG.** *Camp Zama Post Football Team.* APO 343 : Headquarters AFFE/8A (Rear), 3 August and 8 August 1956.

193. **Roy N. Walker, Brigadier General, USA.** CP ZAMA JAPAN : CGAFFE/ARMYEIGHT (REAR) CP ZAMA JAPAN, 8 August 1956. 353.8.

194. **S. A. Hajjar, CSO. USA Asst AG.** *Incidental Expense Money for Sports TDY.* APO 301 : Headquarters, United States Army Forces, Far East and Eighth United States Army, 10 August 1956. AG 353.8 EKSS-R.

195. **DA WASHDC.** *Reference sports officials clinics.* CP ZAMA JAPAN : Headquarters United States Army Forces, Far East and Eighth United States Army (Rear), 13 August 1956. AG 353.8.

196. **V. H. Krulak, Commanding General, 3d Marine Division (Reinf), FMF.** *Recreation for Fuji Camps.* San Francisco, CA : Headquarters, 3D Marine division (Reinf), FMF, 23 August 1956. 353.8.

197. **TH, CGUSARPAC FT SHAFTER.** Office of Adjustant General. s.l. : Headquarters United States Army Forces, Far East and Eighth United States Army (Rear), 25 August 1956. AG 353.8.

198. **Headquarters, Camp Zama.** *Camp Zama Small Games Tournament.* APO 343 : Headquarters, Camp Zama, 6 September 1956. AG 353.8.

199. **John D. Williams, Major, Artillery.** *Report of Far East Command Football Officials Clinic.* APO 613 : Headquarters, Subcam Drake, 6 September 1956. AG 353.8.

200. **M. E. Perry, Captain AGC, Adjutant.** *1956 Camp Zama Post Football Team.* Camp Zama : Headquarters, Camp Zama, 11 September 1956.

201. **Lt Col Carl E Grimsley, MPC, Asst HQ Comdt, 3-2581.** *Reserve Seating, Football Games.* Zama, Japan : U.S. Army, 11 Sept 56.

202. **CGAFFE/ARMYEIGHT KOREA.** Office of Adjutant General. s.l. : Headquarters United States Army Forces, Far East and Eighth United States Army (Rear), 12 September 1956. AG 353.8.

203. **M. E. Perry, Captain, AGC.** *1956 Camp Zama Post Football Team.* Headquarters, Camp Zama APO 343 : United States Army Forces, Far East and Eighth United States Army (Rear), 13 September 1956. AG 353.8.

204. **Charles A. "Rip" Engle, Head Football Coach at The Pennsylvania State College.** State College, Pennsylvania : The Pennsylvania State College, 14 September 1956.

205. **RI, CGRYCOM/NINECOR OKINAWA.** Office of Adjutant General. s.l. : Headquarters United States Army Forces, Far East and Eighth United States Army (Rear), 14 September 1956. AG 353.8.

206. **KOREA, CGAFFE/ARMYEIGHT.** Office of the Adjutant General. s.l. : HEADQUARTERS UNITED STATES ARMY FORCES, FAR EAST and EIGHTH UNITED STATES ARMY (REAR), 20 September 1956. AG 353.8.

207. **Roy N. Walker, Brigadier General, USA, Adjutant General.** CP ZAMA JAPAN : CGAFFE/ARMYEIGHT (REAR) CP ZAMA JAPAN, 21 September 1956. Unclassified.

208. **KOREA, CGAFFE/ARMYEIGHT.** *Results of football games for 2d week of play.* Office of Adjutant General. s.l. : United States Army Forces, Far East and Eighth United States Army (Rear), 24 September 1956. AG 353.8.

209. **Drake, Headquarters Subcamp.** *Far East Command Sports Clinics.* APO 613 : Headquarters Subcamp Drake, 25 September 1956. AG 353.8.

210. **KOREA, CGAFFE/ARMYEIGHT.** Office of the Adjutant General. s.l. : Headquarters United States Army Forces, Far East and Eighth United States Army (Rear), 29 September 1956. AG 353.8.

211. **Robert H. Shell, Colonel, AGC, Acting Adjutant General.** Zama, Japan : CGAFFE/ARMYEIGHT KOREA, 3 October 1956.

212. **T G Schulz, Capt AGC.** s.l. : Headquarters, United States Army Forces, Far East and Eighth United States Army (Rear), 5 October 1956.

213. **Stars and Stripes.** 7th Inf. Div. Holds Cage Carnival. *Stars and Stripes newspaper.* October 9, 1956, p. 21. Online archives.

214. **Stars and Stripes.** AF Gridders Faced Odd Problems in Hong Kong. *Stars and Stripes newspaper.* October 10, 1956, p. 22.

215. **findagrave.com.** *findagrave.com.* [Online] [Cited: March 13, 2025.] https://www.findagrave.com/memorial/266514802/james-marvin-brock.

216. **KOREA, CGAFFE/ARMYEIGHT.** Headquarters, United States Army Forces, Far East : U.S. Army, 11 October 1956.

217. **KOREA, CGAFFE/ARMYEIGHT.** *Results of AFFE/8A football games for week 13-14 Oct.* Headquarters United States Army Forces, Far East : U.S. Army, 16 October 1956.

218. **CGRYCOM/NINECOR OKINAWA RI.** Office of the Adjutant General. s.l. : Headquarters, United States Army Forces, Far East and Eighth United States Army (Rear), 17 October 1956. AG 353.8.

219. **WASH, DA.** Office of the Adjutant General. s.l. : Headquarters United States Army Forces, Far East and Eighth United States Army (Rear), 20 October 1956.

220. **KOREA, CGAFFE/ARMYEIGHT.** Office of Adjutant General. s.l. : Headquarters United States Army Forces, Far East and Eighth United States Army (Rear), 23 October 1956. AG 353.8.

221. **Roy N. Walker, Brigadier General.** Adjutant General. CP ZAMA JAPAN : CGAFFE/ARMYEIGHT KOREA, 25 October 1956. AG 353.8.

222. **James L Glymph, Lt Colonel, ACG.** *Voluntary Services of Southeastern Conference Football Officials Association.* Special Services Division. 25 October 1956. AG 353.8.

223. **KOREA, CGAFFE/ARMYEIGHT.** Office of the Adjutant General. s.l. : Headquarters United States Army Forces, Far East and Eighth United States Army (Rear), 29 October 1956. AG 353.8.

224. **KOREA, CGAFFE/ARMYEIGHT.** *AFFE/8A Football Standings.* Office of the Adjutant General. s.l. : Headquarters United States Army Forces, Far East and Eighth United States Army (Rear), 29 October 1956. AG 353.8.

225. **T. G. Schulz, Capt. AGC.** *Voluntary Services of Southeastern Conference Football Officials Association.* APO 343 : HQ AFFE/8A (REAR), 2 November 1956.

226. **M. E. Perry, Captain, AGC.** Camp Zama : Headquarters Camp Zama, 29 October 1956. AG 3535.8.

227. **Roy A Walker, Brigadier General.** CP ZAMA, JAPAN : CGAFFE/ARMYEIGHT (REAR) CP ZAMA JAPAN, 5 November 1956.

228. **Albert Pierson, Major General, General Staff, Chief of Staff.** *Recreation for Fuji Camps.* s.l. : U. S. Army, 5 November 1956.

229. **M. E. Perry, Captain, AGC.** Camp Zamam Japan : Headquarters, Camp Zama, 5 November 1956.

230. **Lt Colonel James L. Glymph, AGC, Exec Officer, SpServDiv, TAGO.** *1957 USAFFE Sports Clinics.* s.l. : U. S. Army, 8 November 1956.

231. **Roy N. Walker, Brigadier General, USA.** CP ZAMA JAPAN : CGAFFE/ARMYEIGHT (REAR) CP ZAMA JAPAN, 8 November 1956. 353.8.

232. **M. E. Perry, Captain, AGC.** *Camp Zama Basketball Team.* APO 343 : Headquarters, Camp Zama, 19 November 1956. AG 353.8.

233. **Clarence J. Koehler, GS-12, Dir, Sports Branch.** *1956 FEC Football Championship.* Cp Zama, Japan : CGAFFE/ARMYEIGHT (REAR) CP ZAMA JAPAN, 20 November 1956.

234. **Lt Col James Glymph, AGC.** *Conduct of Final in All-Army Basketball and Baseball in Overseas Commands.* APO 343, San Francisco, California : United States Army Forces, Far East, and Eighth U. S. Army (Rear), 20 November 1956. AGMS 353.8.

235. **Roy N. Walker, Brigadier General, USA, Adjutant General.** CP ZAMA ZAMA JAPAN : CGAFFE/ARMYEIGHT (REAR), 24 November 1956. AG 353.8.

236. **M. E. Perry, Captain, AGC.** *Camp Zama Post Basketball Team.* APO 343 : Headquarters, Camp Zama, 5 December 1956.

237. **Topeka Capital Journal.** *OBITUARY: Robert Thomas Godwin.* Topeka, KS : cjonline.com, 13 July 2024.

238. **wusports.com.** *Washburn Basketball Year-by-Year leaders.* s.l. : static.wusports.com.

239. **C.J. Koehler, GS-12, Sports Director, CGAFFE/ARMYEIGHT (REAR) OF ZAMA, JAPAN.** CAMP ZAMA, JAPAN : CGAFFE/ARMYEIGHT (REAR) OF ZAMA, JAPAN, 6 December 1956.

240. **JAPAN, CINCFE TOKYO.** *USAIRA Melbourne message U 465, DTG 050140Z, NOTAL.* Tokyo, Japan : CINCFE TOKYO JAPAN, 7 December 1956.

241. **CG ONE CAVDIV TOKYO JAPAN.** Headquarters United States Army Forces, Far East and Eighth United States Army (Rear) : Headquarters United States Army Forces, Far East and Eighth United States Army (Rear), 11 Dec 1956.

242. **Roy N. Walker, Brigadier General.** CP ZAMA JAPAN : CGAFFE/ARMYEIGHT (REAR) , 15 December 1956.

243. **Army Times.** Various articles in section devoted to All-Army football team selections. *Army Times newspaper.* December 15, 1956, pp. 54-56.

244. **JAPAN, CG ONE CAVDIV TOKYO.** Headquarters United States Army Forces, Far East : Headquarters United States Army Forces, Far East and Eighth United States Army (Rear), 18 December 1956.

245. **WASHDC, DA.** Headquarters United States Army Forces, Far East : Headquarters United States Army Forces, Far East and Eighth United States Army (Rear), 18 December 1956.

246. **Roy N. Walker, Brigadier General.** Tokyo Japan : CGAFFE/ARMYEIGHT CAVDIV, 19 December 1956.

247. **KOREA, CG TWOFOUR INFDIV.** Headquarters, United States Army Forces, Far East and Eighth United States Army (Rear) : CGAFFE/ARMYEIGHT (REAR) CP ZAMA JAPAN, 27 December 1956.

248. **A.B. McEowen, Capt, AGC.** *1st Cavalry Division 1957, All-Japan, Army Wrestling Tournament.* Headquarters 1st Cavalry Division, APO 201 : Headquarters 1st Cavalry Division, 27 December 1956.

249. **RI, CG THREE MARDIV OKINAWA.** Headquarters, United States Army Forces, Far East and Eighth United States Army (Rear) : CGAFFE/ARMYEIGHT (REAR) CP ZAMA JAPAN, 29 December 1956.

250. **U.S. Military Far East Command.** 1956 Rice Bowl. s.l. : U.S. Military Far East Command, 30 December 1956.

251. **U.S. Military Far East Command.** 1956 Sukuiyaki bowl. s.l. : U.S. Military Far East Command, 16 December 1956.

252. **Schmidt, Samantha.** Missing Duluth couple died after turning onto overgrown trail. *Pioneer Press newspaper.* August 8, 2017.

253. **Dougherty Funeral Home.** *Ron and Mary Tarnowski.* s.l. : Dougherty Funeral Home, 29 September 2017.

254. **Roy N Walker, Brigadier General, USA.** Cp Zama, Japan : CG AFFE/ARMYEIGHT (REAR) CP ZAMA JAPAN, 30 December 1956.

255. **Ralph L. Veatch, GS-8.** *Offer of University of Alabama Baseball Team.* Camp Zama : U.S. Army, 13 December 1956.

256. **U.S. Department of Defense.** Armed Forces Sports. *U.S. Department of Defense.* [Online] [Cited: May 26, 2025.] https://armedforcessports.defense.gov/About/History.aspx.

257. **Omar Bradley, Chief of Staff, United States Army.** *Articles of Agreement Covering the Inter-Service Sports Council.* Washington, D.C. : Department of the Army, 13 February 1948. Memorandum No. 80-30-2.

258. **F. M. Cowman, Major, AGC.** *General Sports Eligibility Rules.* s.l. : U.S. Army, 1954.

259. **F. M. Cowman, Major, AGO.** *United States Army Forces, Far East Sports Tournaments.* s.l. : U.S. Arny, 1954.

260. **Roy S. Maurer, Major, AGC, Asst AG.** *Eligibility Rules in Company Level Sports.* s.l. : U.S. Army, 1954.

261. **Lt. Col. Leo Kleiman, AGC.** *News Coverage of Sports Competition.* s.l. : U.S. Army, 1954.

262. **Gerald G. Maxwell, Lt Col, AGC.** *Korean Communications Zone Sports Officials Association.* Headquarters, Korean Communications Zone : U.S. Army, 1954.`

263. **Lt. Col. Leo Kleiman, AGC, Asst AG.** *AFFE/8A Sports Tournaments.* s.l. : U.S. Army, 1954.

264. **Koehler, C.J.** *AFFE/8A Sports Program.* Headquarters United States Army Forces, Far East : United States Army Forces, Far East and Eighth United States Army, 12 July 1956.

265. **Army Times .** New Reg Limits Number of Pros on Post Teams. February 4, 1956, p. 43.

266. **Command, Headquarters Eight Army Support.** *Entertainment Monthly Report.* APO 301 : Headquarters Eight Army Support Command, 20 July 1956. 353.8 AG.

267. **Robert J. Reynolds, Capt AGC.** *Far East Command Inter-Service Sports Council.* APO 343 : Headquarters United States Army Forces, Far East and United States Army (Rear), 18 August 1956. AG 353.8.

268. **C. H. Simcox, Major, AGC.** *AFFE/8A Sports Tournaments.* APO 343 : Headquarters United States Army Forces, Far East and Eighth United States Army (Rear), 20 September 1956. AG 353.8.

269. **M. E. Perry, Captain, AGC, Adjutant.** *Company Level Basketball League.* Camp Zama, Japan : Headquarters, 24 September 1956.

270. **T. L. Gale, Major, AGC, Asst AG.** *1956 Far East Command Football Championship.* APO 343 : Headquarters United States Army Forces, Far East and United States Army (Rear), 18 October 1956.

271. **U.S. Department of Defense.** armedforcessports.defense.gov. [Online] [Cited: June 12, 2025.] https://armedforcessports.defense.gov/Portals/19/Documents/DoDD_13 30.4_1954.09.04.pdf?ver=2017-03-27-154809-233.

272. **84th Congress, 1st Session, 1955.** GovInfo. [Online] [Cited: May 27, 2025.] https://www.govinfo.gov/app/details/STATUTE-69/STATUTE-69-Pg11-2/context.

273. **Nelson, Colonel Herbert.** *Far East Commend Inter-Service Sports Council.* Far East Command APO 500 : U.S. Army, 1956.

274. **U.S. Army AFFE/8A (Rear).** *Special Services Hotels.* HQ United States Army Forces, Far East : U.S. Army Circular, 1956.

275. **James L Glymph, Lt Colonel, AGC, Exec Officer, SpSerDiv.** *Boxing Protective Headgear.* s.l. : U.S. Army, 8 December 1956.

276. **D.H. Callahan, Captain, AGC, Asst Adjutant.** *1957 Sports Program.* Camp Zama APO 343 : Headquarters, Camp Zama APO, 12 December 1956.

277. **Stars and Stripes.** AFFE Clarifies New Far East Duty Tours. *Stars and Stripes newspaper.* August 24, 1953.

278. **U.S. Army.** *Circular 614-2.* s.l. : U.S. Army, 1955.

279. **Army Times.** Korea Tour is Still 16 Months. *Army Times newspaper.* January 2, 1954, p. 1. Online archives.

280. **usarj.army.mil.** *Camp Zama Through the Years … 1950s.* s.l. : www.usarj.army.mil. www.usarj.army.mil.

281. **Im In-tack, Lim Ji-sun, Cho Il-jun, Choi Hyun-june, Steven Borowiec.** *After 10 year delay, USFK starts relocation from Yongsan Garrison.* s.l., Korea : Hankyyoreh English Edition, July 11, 2017. Hankyyoreh English Edition.

282. **Strother, Jason.** The U.S. military's Yongsan Garrison leaves a mixed legacy in Seoul. *USA Today.* December 22, 2017.

283. **Kim, Jinwung.** *A History of Korea.* Taegu : Indiana University Press, 2012. p. 591.

284. **Army Times.** No Saddle Shoes At Yong-San U. *Army Times newspaper.* February 6, 1954, p. 26. Online archives.

285. **Paul A. Disney, Brigadier General.** *Guest Privileges in Women's Quarters - Yongsan Military Reservation.* s.l. : U.S. Arny, 1955.

286. **Army Times.** BB May Approve Rec Facilities. *Army Times newspaper.* March 20, 1954, p. 26. Online archives.

287. **Captain Thomas Simmons, AGC, Asst. Adjutant General.** *Waterproofing Quonset Huts.* s.l. : U.S. Army, 1955.

288. **U.S. Army, Franklin Fisher.** *Stadium Bears Name of War Hero.* Camp Casey : s.n., January 7, 2014.

289. **William R. Hyde, Captain, MC Commanding.** *Report of Army Medical Service activities.* s.l. : U.S. Army, 1955.

290. **Army, Eighth United States.** *Obesity (Overweight).* Headquarters United States Army, Far East : U.S. Army, 1955.

291. **Wilbur McGill, Major, USAF.** *Package Show Report USO show "High Time" at 621-8 AC&W Detachment.* APC 710 : Headquarters Fifth Air Force, 28 July 1956. AG 353.8.

292. **MPC, Eugene A. Ginda.** *Offense or Incident Report.* Hqs UNCMAC APO 72 : 24th Military Police Co. APO 24, 10 October 1956.

293. **Kates, C.O.** *The Armed Forces Sports Almanac.* First Edition. Harrisburg : The Military Service Publishing Company, 1954.

INDEX

D. Goodrich Kingrey lives in the Great State of Alabama with his wife, children, and dog. Mr. Kingrey is thankful for American freedom, as secured by our selfless and noble veterans.

Notes